"In graduate school, when others were selling their textbooks to get money for the next round of required reading, there were some I couldn't part with. I had gleaned so much from them that I knew I would want to refer to them long after I completed my course work. Robert Jones, Kristin Kellen, and Rob Green have provided a resource just like that—a guide that will not only equip students as an introduction to biblical counseling but one that will serve them after years of counseling. Although I've been counseling for over three decades, as I read this great book, I found myself thinking, 'Oh, I need to remember that when I meet with Jane,' or 'This would be helpful when I talk to Lila.' Beginner or veteran, you will appreciate this resource."

—**Amy Baker**, adjunct professor, Faith Bible Seminary and director of ministry resources, Faith Church

"The biblical counseling world has profited greatly from rich resources produced over the past decade. In my opinion, however, none is as comprehensively complete and immediately useful as this introduction to biblical counseling by Jones, Kellen, and Green! The work testifies of the authors' years of personal Bible study, extensive case wisdom, and love for Christ and his gospel. As I read every chapter, I commented often to my wife, 'This is amazing!' The biblical-centeredness and immediate helpfulness of every chapter makes this a must-read and reread for biblical counselors and professors of biblical counseling."

—**Jim Berg**, professor of biblical counseling, Bob Jones University Seminary and founder, Freedom That Lasts®

"If you are looking for a comprehensive introduction to biblical counseling, this is it. If you are looking for a quick reference tool to gain an overview of a particular counseling issue coupled with a prolific, dependable source of resources to explore that issue in greater depth, this is it. *The Gospel for Disordered Lives* should undoubtedly appear on the textbook list of evangelical institutions of higher learning as well as biblical counseling training centers."

—**Howard Eyrich**, director of DMin in biblical counseling, Birmingham Theological Seminary

"While not all biblical counselors will agree with every aspect of this book, it does provide the reader with a thorough survey of biblical counseling issues. One critical matter we learn from these seasoned practitioners is that counseling practice should not be based upon pragmatic reasoning, but flow from theological foundations. Jones, Kellen, and Green have brought their years of counseling ministry to bear in a book that is both thorough and accessible. This is a wonderful introduction to the subject of biblical counseling, but it goes beyond basic material, helping the reader to ask proper questions and to see the breadth of biblical application for the various problems we face in life."

—**T. Dale Johnson Jr.**, associate professor of biblical counseling, Midwestern Baptist Theological Seminary and executive director, Association of Certified Biblical Counselors

"This book fills a long-recognized need for a comprehensive introductory biblical counseling textbook. The authors address counseling theory and methodology and then apply biblical principles to a wide range of important topics. They aspire to be biblical, careful, and balanced. When space does not allow them to deal exhaustively with many of the subjects they raise, they point the reader to specialized resources which address issues in greater depth. This is an important book which will be valuable both in the classroom as a textbook and in the counselor's office as a reference."

—**James R. Newheiser Jr.**, director, Christian counseling program and associate professor of Christian counseling and pastoral theology, Reformed Theological Seminary, Charlotte

"This book is a valuable addition for biblical counseling. It could serve as a primer for those who are new to biblical counseling as well as a reference work to provide initial guidance for common problems, such as anxiety and depression. The authors remind us of the significance of the gospel as they discuss hard issues based on biblical principles with practical applications."

—**Lilly Park**, associate professor of biblical counseling, Southwestern Baptist Theological Seminary

"There is so much trustworthy material here. You can read through it *and* use it as reference. Either way, you will be led in humility and confidence. Humility because we are 'needy' and have faults galore; confidence because 'The Lord is great' and he is pleased to come to the aid of helpers who need him (Psalm 40:16–17)."

—**Edward T. Welch**, counselor and senior faculty, Christian Counseling and Educational Foundation

THE GOSPEL *FOR* DISORDERED LIVES

ROBERT D. JONES, KRISTIN L. KELLEN, ROB GREEN

THE GOSPEL FOR DISORDERED LIVES

AN INTRODUCTION TO CHRIST-CENTERED BIBLICAL COUNSELING

Published by B&H Academic
Brentwood, Tennessee

ISBN: 978-0-8054-4787-3

Dewey Decimal Classification: 158
Subject Heading: COUNSELING / PASTORAL
PSYCHOLOGY / APPLIED PSYCHOLOGY

Cover design by Brian Bobel.

Counselees' names in this book have been changed to protect the privacy of the individuals.

Printed in China
6 7 8 9 10 11 • 29 28 27 26 25

CONTENTS

INTRODUCTION

We wrote this book because *we* need this book. As counseling practitioners working as a writing team, we found that developing forty chapters pushed us to reconsider what we believe and to think more deeply and carefully about a wide array of topics related to our ministries. What does God say about x, y, and z; and how can we wisely, compassionately, and skillfully deliver God's Word to needy people? We are thrilled to share the fruit of our labor with you.

Moreover, as counseling professors actively training men and women, we wanted a one-stop introductory textbook that we could use in our classrooms to give an overview of the principles and methodology of Christ-centered biblical counseling and provide a basic guide to twenty common problems or situations faced by people we counsel.

Our Title and Intended Audience

Our title, *The Gospel for Disordered Lives*, reminds us that the gospel of Jesus Christ—the heartbeat of the Bible—offers life-changing hope and power to real people with real problems. The reference to "disordered" lives alludes to the language of our secular therapeutic culture, as presented in the American Psychiatric Association's *Diagnostic and Statistical Manual of Mental Disorders*, the standard reference resource in the mental health world. Yet we mean something more. Our God is a God of order, and his plan for people involves them living according to his glorious design. Our subtitle, *An Introduction to Christ-Centered Biblical Counseling*, reminds us that Jesus and his Word bring God's life-transforming order to men and women struggling in this fallen, disordered world. We believe that in his Word God speaks more deeply and more powerfully than any mental health professional or other written resource can.

This volume provides an introductory guide to the theory and practice of Christ-centered biblical counseling. We intend this book to serve as a foundational textbook for bachelor- and master's-level students in Christian colleges, universities, seminaries, and graduate schools—although doctoral students will find it useful in the field too. While not aimed at those pursuing state licensing, this book provides a Bible-based perspective that these students can adapt in their broader ministry contexts. Throughout the book we give a positive presentation of biblical counseling and rarely engage opposing views.

Our secondary audience includes all sorts of counseling practitioners—biblical counselors, Christian counselors, pastors, elders, chaplains, men's and women's ministry directors, and small group leaders—all those believers who are actively engaged in helping others handle their personal and relational problems. While this book assumes formal counseling, the principles and steps directly apply to people helping, informal counseling, discipling, and mentoring.

We intend this as an introductory volume, so it has all the strengths and weaknesses that come with trying to be both brief and comprehensive. We realize more could be said within each chapter, yet we resisted the temptation to mention that repeatedly.

Chapter Overview

We begin part 1 (chapters 1–2) with a pair of introductory chapters that define what we mean by Christ-centered biblical counseling and describe who does it and in what setting they do it. It's a ministry of God's Word that is centered on Jesus Christ and is extended to people with various personal and relational problems. It is carried out by a wide range of believers with various roles in diverse settings.

Part 2 (chapters 3–9) grounds Christ-centered biblical counseling in four foundational doctrines—Scripture, the Trinity, anthropology, and sin—and shows their implications for building our model. We believe our distinct approach to counseling emerges from and consistently reflects historic, evangelical orthodoxy in ways other approaches do not. Part 2 also addresses four topics in applied theology that are often involved in counseling people: guilt, repentance, forgiveness, and fighting Satan. We end this section with a chapter on how to think biblically about alternative counseling approaches.

Part 3 (chapters 10–20) moves into methodological matters, the actual practice of biblical counseling. We begin with an overview of how people change, viewed from the perspective of what God calls the counselee to do (chapter 10). We then consider the role a counselor plays in this ministry (chapter 11). After giving practical guidance on how to prepare for and start a case (chapter 12), chapters 13–15 outline our three-step movement in the counseling process: we enter the counselee's world by forming a welcoming relationship, we understand the person's felt needs and biblically defined real needs, and we offer them Jesus Christ and his provisions for those needs.

The next three chapters highlight three specific skills that have been the hallmark of biblical counseling: how to give counselees God-centered hope (chapter 16), how to use growth assignments to follow the present session and prepare the person for the next (chapter 17), and how to wisely conclude the counseling case (chapter 18). The remaining chapters in part 3 discuss counseling non-Christians (chapter 19) and confidentiality (chapter 20).

Part 4 (chapters 21–36), the largest portion of the book, consists of sixteen common counseling matters all counselors will likely encounter over time. Developing these chapters in particular carried a built-in frustration of not having the space to say much more on each topic, but our joy comes from providing a biblically-driven primer to help you wisely and compassionately counsel sinning and suffering people. Each chapter provides suggested resources for further study and counseling homework. And since many of our chapters address various forms of suffering, we included an appendix with further recommended resources.

In part 5 (chapters 37–40), we offer four introductory chapters regarding counseling four age groups: children, teenagers, middle-aged adults, and older adults. We describe common developmental or experiential characteristics of each group and typical life pressures and counseling problems specific to each demographic. We end the book with a conclusion that recommends six ways to grow further as a biblical counselor.

Our Process

Each of us is an evangelical, Bible-believing Christian writing from the perspective of historic orthodox Christianity. We believe sound biblical theology must drive everything we write and do in our ministries. Each of us also loves the local church and actively counsels fellow members within it.

Robert Jones, DTh, DMin, serves as a biblical counseling professor at The Southern Baptist Theological Seminary in Louisville, Kentucky. Before that, Bob served in the same role at Southeastern Baptist Theological Seminary in Wake Forest, North Carolina, for twelve years and as a lead pastor for nineteen years before that. Kristin Kellen, PhD, EdD, serves as a biblical counseling professor at Southeastern Baptist Theological Seminary. As part of that role, she regularly counsels those within the seminary environment and outside of it, primarily serving young people and their families. Rob Green, PhD, serves as the pastor of counseling and seminary ministries at Faith Church in Lafayette, Indiana, and as chair of the Master of Arts in Biblical Counseling at Faith Bible Seminary. While all three of us teach biblical counseling courses, Kristin also teaches classes for students who are seeking state-licensure.

Bob convened our team and provided general guidance and final oversight for our submitted manuscript. For citation purposes, Bob wrote chapters 1–2, 6–8, 10, 12–17, 19, 21, 23, 27, 34–35, and 39–40; Kristin wrote chapters 5, 24–26, 28–30, 32–33, and 36–38; and Rob wrote chapters 3–4, 9, 11, 18, 20, 22, and 31. We then carefully read each other's drafts and provided feedback—often in multiple rounds of edits—to enable us all to make wise revisions. This back-and-forth process challenged, stimulated, and sometimes frustrated us, but brought greater appreciation for each other's insights and passions and produced a superior end product. While individual differences in style, nuance, and emphasis appear throughout, which is the very nature of collaboration, our iron-sharpening-iron interaction led to a more careful, balanced, unified book.

At the recommendation of our publisher, we agreed to use the Christian Standard Bible when quoting God's Word.

With gratitude to our Shepherd, Jesus Christ, and his work in your life and ours,

Robert Jones, Louisville, KY
Kristin Kellen, Wake Forest, NC
Rob Green, Lafayette, IN

PART ONE

AN OVERVIEW OF BIBLICAL COUNSELING

What Is Christ-Centered Biblical Counseling?

It's an exciting time to be a biblical counselor or to train to become one. Begun over fifty years ago,[1] the biblical counseling movement continues to grow in both numbers and maturity. Jesus Christ, through his Spirit, his Word, and his church, is changing lives.

Various Christian counselors use differing terms to describe their particular forms of counseling, including the adjective *biblical*. In this book we present an explicitly Christ-centered, Bible-driven approach to counseling. Our approach syncs with that of groups like the Biblical Counseling Coalition,[2] the biblical counseling contributors to several multi-view books

[1] For a starter study on the history of biblical counseling, see David Powlison, *The Biblical Counseling Movement: History and Context* (Greensboro, NC: New Growth Press, 2010), and Heath Lambert's subsequent work, *The Biblical Counseling Movement After Adams* (Wheaton, IL: Crossway, 2012).

[2] See the Confessional Statement of the Biblical Counseling Coalition, https://www.biblicalcounselingcoalition.org/confessional-statement/, along with their three multi-author volumes: Bob Kellemen and Steve Viars, eds., *Christ-Centered Biblical Counseling: Changing Lives with God's Changeless Truth*, 2nd ed. (Eugene, OR: Harvest House, 2021); Bob Kellemen and Jeff Forrey, eds., *Scripture and Counseling* (Grand Rapids: Zondervan, 2014); and Bob Kellemen and Kevin Carson, eds., *Biblical Counseling and the Church: God's Care through God's People*, (Grand Rapids: Zondervan, 2015).

on psychology[3] and on counseling practice,[4] and our likeminded colleagues who use synonyms like biblical "soul care" or the "care and cure of souls." While we prefer the longer descriptor in our book's title, "Christ-Centered Biblical Counseling," in this chapter and throughout the book we will simply call it biblical counseling.

Let's summarize what we mean by unpacking each term.

Biblical Counseling is Counseling

First, biblical counseling is *counseling*, a personal ministry to help those struggling with personal and relational problems. It helps specific individuals, couples, and families to know Christ better and handle life in God-pleasing ways whatever their situations. Biblical counseling is conversational—interactive and person-specific in ways that go beyond public preaching or teaching. It is personal, the ministry of one person to another person. We might also call it intensive, remedial, or problem-oriented discipleship. More broadly, it is true biblical friendship, wise one-another care, or intentional, helpful conversation.

What do biblical counselors do? They listen (Prov 18:13). They insightfully draw out the purposes of a person's heart (Prov 20:5). They lovingly speak gospel truths to help people grow in Christ (Eph 4:15–16). They wisely instruct and teach (Rom 15:14; Col 3:16). They comfort those who suffer (2 Cor 1:3–4). They restore in gentle, humble ways those overtaken in sin (Gal 6:1–2) and turn back those who are turning away from Christ (Jas 5:19–20).

As a process of personal ministry, biblical counseling shares with secular approaches basic concerns about relational dynamics, interviewing, listening skills, personal warmth and care, empathy, and confidentiality. But it doesn't share their limitations of clinical detachment, dual

---

[3] See David Powlison, "A Biblical Counseling View," in *Psychology and Christianity: Five Views*, 2nd ed., ed. Eric L. Johnson (Downers Grove, IL: InterVarsity Press, 2010), 245–73, along with his responses to the four competing views.

[4] See Stuart W. Scott, "A Biblical Counseling Approach," in *Counseling and Christianity: Five Approaches*, 2nd ed., ed. Stephen P. Greggo and Timothy Sisemore (Downers Grove, IL: InterVarsity Press, 2012), 157–83, along with his responses to the four competing approaches.

relationship avoidance, state-licensure, nonbiblical diagnoses, and other professional trappings (even when biblical counseling is done by specially trained professionals).[5] Nor is biblical counseling the exclusive domain of professional therapists. It's the domain of all believers: pastors, wise parents, spouses, roommates, neighbors, and spiritual brothers and sisters in our churches. It recognizes variables such as training, passions, experience, opportunity, certification, and calling.

Biblical counselors address the same personal problems other counselors address, such as fear, worry, anxiety, rejection, addictions, grief, pornography, sadness, depression, anger, bitterness, trauma, disease and disability, and eating disorders. We handle the typical span of relational problems, including marriage, parenting, singleness, and all sorts of communication and conflict issues in the work world, church world, and school world. We counsel individuals, couples, and families. Biblical counselors help people of all ages: children, teenagers, young adults, middle-aged adults, and older adults. We deal with severe issues like trauma, hallucinations, and psychotic disorders and work with medical professionals as needed. At the same time, we recognize our ongoing need to develop our personal counseling skills and knowledge of and ability to apply God's Word to various crisis situations.

Biblical Counseling is Biblical

Second, biblical counseling is *biblical.* Its truth source is God's inerrant, inspired Word. In this sense, biblical counseling seeks to do nothing more or less than intentionally, consistently apply historic, orthodox, evangelical Christian truth to the realm of personal ministry and human problems. Let's consider five categories of biblical-theological convictions that undergird biblical counseling.

---

[5] For a brief summary of what counseling typically entails in the modern mental health system, see David Powlison, *Speaking Truth in Love: Gospel in Community* (Greensboro, NC: New Growth Press, 2005), 176.

1. The Lord Jesus Christ

Biblical counselors focus on the Bible's central theme: the Lord Jesus Christ and his life-changing, redeeming work for humanity. In that sense, biblical counseling is *Christ-centered*.[6] We present the incarnate, crucified, risen, reigning, and returning Redeemer who through his Word and his Spirit helps people handle their personal and relational problems. Whether the recipients are unbelievers who need to know Christ initially or believers who need to know Christ increasingly, biblical counselors offer Christ to counselees in wise, specific, caring ways.

Jesus alone provides the forgiving mercy (through his saving death and resurrection), practical wisdom (in Scripture), and enabling power (through his Spirit) we need to know and please God in our daily living. Biblical counselors extend to hopeless people our Savior's welcoming words, "Come to me, all of you who are weary and burdened, and I will give you rest" (Matt 11:28). With the apostle Paul, "We proclaim [Christ], warning and teaching everyone with all wisdom, so that we may present everyone mature in Christ" (Col 1:28), recognizing that "in him are hidden all the treasures of wisdom and knowledge" (2:3).

As Heb 4:14–16 assures us, Jesus is our high priest; he was tempted as we are, and he empathizes with us in our weaknesses. Though fully divine, he understands us because he is also fully human. Moreover, because Jesus never succumbed to sin means he can empower us to persevere in the face of our daily pressures. The passage ends with this stirring invitation to "approach the throne of grace with boldness, so that we may receive mercy and find grace to help us in time of need." This is the forgiving grace ("mercy") and the enabling grace ("grace to help us") every counselor and counselee deeply need.

Two crucial counseling implications flow from these gospel guarantees. First, the core identity of those who have trusted in Jesus as their Savior is daughters and sons of the living God (Gal 3:26–29), seated with Christ

[6] Unfortunately, today the adjective *Christian* sometimes connotes counseling approaches not consistently biblical in their understanding of Christ and his Word.

eternally (Col 3:1–4), and recipients of a cascade of spiritual blessings he died and rose to secure for us (Eph 1:3–14). Second, what Christ has done, is doing, and will do—what theologians call the indicatives of the faith—moves believers to be and do what he wants us to be and do—what theologians call the imperatives of the faith. Gratitude for God's grace fuels our obedience. We as counselors help counselees "no longer live for themselves, but for the one who died for them and was raised" (2 Cor 5:15) and to "put on compassion, kindness, humility, gentleness, and patience" as those who are "chosen . . . , holy and dearly loved" (Col 3:12) because of Christ.

2. The Bible

Biblical counselors use the Bible as our God-given, Spirit-inspired tool to diagnose, explain, and solve problems. The Bible alone provides God's true, authoritative, and sufficient wisdom for every person in every life situation. So, our first task is not offering a theological summary but letting Scripture speak for itself. What does the Bible say about what the Bible does?

Psalm 1 compares the person who delights in and meditates on God's Word to "a tree planted beside flowing streams that bears its fruit in its season, and its leaf does not wither. Whatever he does prospers" (v. 3). Scripture makes us constant and fruitful in this life and secure in the final judgment (vv. 5–6).

Psalm 19:7–8 guarantees four benefits of the Bible. It renews people's lives, makes them wise, makes their heart glad, and makes their eyes light up. These verses precisely summarize what every counselee craves and what every caring counselor desires to impart. Biblical counselors believe the Bible alone gives people the renewal, wisdom, joy, and light they seek.

Psalm 119 celebrates the impact of Scripture on the human soul; this impact spans the wide range of human emotion—sadness, grief, despair, shame, distress, anger, indignation, anxiety, and distress, as well as comfort, joy, relief, and peace. In these 176 verses God provides formative perspectives on the common disorders that lead people to seek counseling. In fact, the psalmist tells God:

- "Your decrees are my delight and my counselors." (v. 24)

- "If your instruction had not been my delight, I would have died in my affliction." (v. 92)
- "Trouble and distress have overtaken me, but your commands are my delight." (v. 143)
- "Abundant peace belongs to those who love your instruction; nothing makes them stumble." (v. 165)

The counseling implications burst from these pages.

In 2 Tim 3:14–17, Paul declares the whole Bible is God-breathed and is our unique, explicit, God-given ministry tool for making people wise "for salvation" and "for teaching, rebuking, correcting" and "for training in righteousness." It makes us thoroughly "equipped for every good work"—the ministry of the Word God gave Timothy and by extension God gives us.

Therefore, our counsel depends on God's Word, not on "philosophy and empty deceit based on human tradition" (Col 2:8)—that is, the array of "-ologies, -osophies, and -isms" of the therapeutic world. Scripture remains richly superior to all human wisdom and competing systems of secular and Christian integrationist counseling, while also enabling us to reframe and discerningly use valid observations from other sources. The Confessional Statement of the Biblical Counseling Coalition summarizes it:

> We affirm that numerous sources (such as scientific research, organized observations about human behavior, those we counsel, reflection on our own life experience, literature, film, and history) can contribute to our knowledge of people, and many sources can contribute some relief for the troubles of life. However, none can constitute a comprehensive system of counseling principles and practices. When systems of thought and practice claim to prescribe a cure for the human condition, they compete with Christ (Col 2:1–15).[7]

Unlike those who practice other versions of Christian counseling that merely mention Bible verses or themes, biblical counselors believe the

---

[7] The Confessional Statement of the Biblical Counseling Coalition, https://www.biblicalcounselingcoalition.org/confessional-statement/.

Bible actively *drives* our theory and practice. It's not merely our foundation or standard. It's more than a judicial court that makes no policy, passes no legislation, and executes no events. It's more than a referee who merely reacts to rule violations by blowing a whistle; the Bible is an active player who dominates the field and needs no referee. The Bible is more than a filter that inertly traps unwanted pollutants as air or water actively flows through it. While courts, referees, and filters fulfill a function, such metaphors reduce Scripture to having no more than a passive role in producing our counseling principles and practices.

Instead, we rely on the Bible as alive and active in our counseling: "For the word of God is living and effective and sharper than any double-edged sword, penetrating as far as the separation of soul and spirit, joints and marrow. It is able to judge the thoughts and intentions of the heart" (Heb 4:12). David Powlison explains:

> The living Christ working in his people through his Word is the engine producing depth of insight, accurate theory, and effective practice. The counseling that Christians do must orient to and take its cues from our own source. . . . The Bible's positive message both *is* counseling and *is about* counseling. In content, method, and institutional locus the Bible overflows with counseling instructions and implications.[8]

When done properly, our core concepts and methods don't merely align with or not contradict Scripture; they *emerge from* Scripture as we interpret it accurately and apply it wisely.[9] The Bible does more than guide, inform, or control our counseling model; it proactively forms it. Scripture *generates* our understanding of God, people, and their situations. Biblical counseling is biblically driven counseling. To paraphrase Charles Haddon Spurgeon, we should unleash the lion of Scripture from his cage.[10]

---

[8] David Powlison, "Cure of Souls (and the Modern Psychotherapies)," *Journal of Biblical Counseling* 25, no. 2 (Spring 2007): 11, 14.

[9] This, in turn, demands we hone our exegetical skills, broaden our knowledge of the Bible's books, and deepen our grasp of biblical and systematic theology.

[10] Elliot Ritzema, "Spurgeon's 'Let the Lion out of the Cage' Quote," https://elliotritzema.com/2012/07/31/spurgeons-let-the-lion-out-of-the-cage-quote/.

3. Love, Concern, and Compassion

Biblical counselors reflect the heart of Jesus our Shepherd and his Holy Spirit, our Counselor. Biblical counseling is a caring process of extending Christlike love to struggling sheep. Qualities like compassion, kindness, humility, gentleness, and patience thus mark our ministry (Col 3:12). We seek to follow our Master who, "when he saw the crowds, . . . felt compassion for them, because they were distressed and dejected, like sheep without a shepherd" (Matt 9:36).

In recent years biblical counselors have paid greater attention to human suffering, recognizing more carefully the powerful influence of past and present hardships on people and seeking to provide the same comfort to sufferers we have received from "the Father of mercies and the God of all comfort" (2 Cor 1:3). Biblical counselors recognize those we counsel have experienced the difficult consequences of sin—Adam's sin and the effects of the fall, their own sin and the hardships reaped, and the sins of others that range from neglect and rejection to mistreatment and assault. We live in a groaning creation, longing for our final redemption (Rom 8:17–39; 2 Cor 4:7–18). We look forward to the new heavens and new earth God guarantees (2 Pet 3:13), pointing our suffering counselees to that day when God will "wipe away every tear from their eyes. Death will be no more; grief, crying, and pain will be no more, because the previous things have passed away" (Rev 21:4).

Meanwhile, as we will see in chapters 13 and 14 and throughout this book, we weep with those who weep, we listen with Christlike empathy, and we counsel with Spirit-given compassion.

4. The Heart

Biblical counselors address not only the outward behavioral aspects but also the inward heart aspects of our counseling cases to bring thorough and lasting Christ-centered change.

Biblical counseling is not shallow, superficial, or simplistic. Scripture alone uncovers and solves our heart (beliefs and motives) and behavior (words and actions) struggles. We recognize from Scripture that all behavior flows from the heart—our beliefs and motives; our cognitive, affective, and volitional functions; what we love, treasure, live for, hope in, and depend on.[11] The wisdom writer prioritizes the reader's heart:

> My son, pay attention to my words; listen closely to my sayings.
> Don't lose sight of them; keep them within your heart.
> For they are life to those who find them, and health to one's whole body.
> Guard your heart above all else, for it is the source of life. (Prov 4:20–23)

While the ensuing verses reference our mouths and lips (speech), our eyes and gaze (focus, goal), and our feet (actions, directions), what is more important than anything—"above all else"—is the condition of our hearts. Why? Because the heart is "the source of life," the wellspring from which flows all our activities. What gives the heart its life are God's words.

Jesus underscores the centrality of the heart in Matt 12:33–34, using a good/bad tree and fruit metaphor and then applying it to our speech: "How can you speak good things when you are evil? For the mouth speaks from the overflow of the heart." Our words come from our hearts. Jesus makes the same point about all our behavior in Matt 15:18–19: "But what comes out of the mouth comes from the heart, and this defiles a person. For from the heart come evil thoughts, murders, adulteries, sexual immoralities, thefts, false testimonies, slander."

In Gal 5:13–26, the apostle Paul unpacks these heart dynamics, describing the raging civil war within the hearts of believers. Our flesh (our remaining sin) and the Holy Spirit fight within us against each other. Neither is passive; both are active combatants (v. 17). And each yields its respective fruit: "The works of the flesh are obvious: sexual immorality, moral impurity, promiscuity, idolatry, sorcery, hatreds, strife, jealousy, outbursts of anger, selfish ambitions, dissensions, factions, envy, drunkenness, carousing, and

---

[11] For a comprehensive exegetical-theological study of the heart, see A. Craig Troxel, *With All Your Heart: Orienting Your Mind, Desires, and Will toward Christ* (Wheaton, IL: Crossway, 2020). For the same perspective applied to counseling, see Jeremy Pierre, *The Dynamic Heart in Daily Life: Connecting Christ to Human Experience* (Greensboro, NC: New Growth Press, 2016).

anything similar. . . . But the fruit of the Spirit is love, joy, peace, patience, kindness, goodness, faithfulness, gentleness, and self-control" (vv. 19–23). Both godliness and ungodliness come from the heart.

So, while we as Christ followers have been freed from our old lives and "have crucified the flesh with its passions and desires" (v. 24), the remnants of our sinful natures have not yet been eradicated. They continue to plague us. For this reason, Paul exhorts us to "walk by," be "led by," "live by," and "keep in step with" the Spirit (vv. 16, 18, 25). Biblical counselors depend on God's Spirit to empower their ministries and bring change in their counselees. Biblical counseling is a spiritual endeavor.

The apostle Peter describes the internal struggle in 1 Pet 2:11: "Dear friends, I urge you as strangers and exiles to abstain from sinful desires that wage war against the soul." Biblical counselors recognize the active presence of the flesh-versus-Spirit battle within each Christian we counsel.

We could explore many more passages showing the centrality of the heart in biblical change, including Ps 51:10; Prov 4:4; 23:26; Jer 17:5, 7; Ezek 14:5; and Heb 3:12. Together, they make the same point: the Bible powerfully addresses human motivation. Ultimately, everyone is ruled by God or by someone or something other than God. Biblical counseling targets the heart; God wants our hearts.

Consider Anna, Beth, Christine, and Danielle, four Christians who habitually avoid people. They might be described by those who know them as introverts, people-fearers, shy individuals, or loners; some might theorize they have social anxiety disorder. Whatever the label, deep down these four women know their behavior is wrong, as those closest to them remind them. Each seeks to follow the Lord, and each wrestles with her guilt. Their avoidance behavior takes various forms: declining social invitations, coming late to and leaving Sunday worship early to escape conversation, not volunteering for people-ministry opportunities, ignoring cell calls even from those whose names they recognize, and even choosing or rejecting jobs based on office setting.

While their general antisocial behavior is the same, their four individual hearts are not. What particular heart desires drive each of these people-avoiders?

- Anna fears being judged by others and the rejection she believes will inevitably follow. Since she doesn't measure up to others' standards (at least in her mind), she avoids them. Recalling years of critical words from her mom and one searing comment made by her college roommate doesn't help.
- Beth doesn't make time for others. Reaching her self-driven performance goals consumes her hours and her days. She doesn't dislike people; she simply doesn't need them. People are interruptions.
- Christine obsesses over germs. For her, contact with people equals contact with viruses. The safest way to avoid illness is to stay away from others, so she self-prescribes social distancing.
- Danielle knows her tongue can be sharp. Her critical attitude, combined with shaky social skills and low emotional intelligence, have landed her in hot water many times. She has lost friendships and jobs. For her, it's better to avoid people than upset them.

Each person listed needs specific, tailored help for her specific heart problem. No single Bible passage fits all people-avoiders. Heart sins are idiosyncratic. Those who commit them not only need to change their behavior; they need to change their hearts. Biblical counselors understand this.

5. The Goal of Christlikeness

In contrast to secular approaches that help counselees become self-actualized or use generic terms like personal wholeness, mental health, or inner healing, biblical counseling uses biblical categories to seek the same outcome goals God explicitly seeks. We as biblical counselors strive to help counselees

- love the Lord and their neighbors (Matt 22:37–40; 1 Tim 1:5; 1 Pet 1:22),
- be filled with Christ's joy, peace, and hope, and all of God's fullness (Rom 15:13; John 17:13; Jas 1:2; Eph 3:19),
- be sanctified and built up by God's Word (John 17:17; Acts 20:32),

- be strengthened by God's Spirit, showing his fruit (Rom 15:13; Eph 3:16; Gal 5:22–23),
- please God and live for Christ (2 Cor 5:9, 14),
- obey God, live holy; resist and put to death sin and replace it with godly living (Rom 6:16; Eph 4:22–24; Titus 2:11–12; Heb 12:15; 1 Peter),
- be gracious and loving (1 Cor 13:4–7; Col 3:12–14; 4:5–6),
- actively serve others, being devoted to good works (Eph 2:10; Titus 2:14; 3:1, 8, 14), and
- be mature and complete, overflowing with thankfulness (Col 1:28; Heb 5:14–6:1; Jas 1:2–4; Col 2:7).

Perhaps we can best summarize all these outcome goals with one supreme aim: that our counselees become more and more like Jesus Christ, the perfect human (though divine) who thoroughly embodies every biblical ideal. Amid the hardships our believing counselees face in this fallen world, God is working all things—including those hardships—together to make them like Jesus (Rom 8:28–29). In turn, God calls us to labor and pray for this specific result in those we counsel (Gal 4:19; Eph 3:17).

Conclusion

What is biblical counseling? We close with this simple definition: It is the Christlike, caring, person-to-person ministry of God's Word to people struggling with personal and interpersonal problems to help them know and follow Jesus Christ in heart and behavior amid their struggles.

Who Can and Should Do Biblical Counseling?

In one sense, every human counsels people. We all have opinions and give advice to others—whether that advice is godly or ungodly, solicited or unsolicited, thoughtful or thoughtless. Counseling others is endemic to our humanity.

But there are relatively few who counsel *biblically*. So, what does God say about who can and should counsel? In what settings? Must a person be formally trained; and if so, to what degree? Is some license, certification, or title necessary? Must counseling happen in an office, or can it happen in a coffee shop or at a kitchen table? Let's consider five principles that address these questions.

Principles Supporting Counseling within the Church Family

1. God Calls All Believers in Christ to Counsel People Biblically

As we established in our last chapter, biblical counseling involves caringly ministering God's Word to help people handle their life struggles.

Consider these passages that speak of this general ministry of all Christians to each other.

- Romans 15:14: Believers are "able to instruct one another." The original verb used in this verse involves giving instruction, sometimes with an admonitory edge.
- 2 Corinthians 1:3–4: God's comfort of us in our hardships enables us "to comfort those who are in any kind of affliction, through the comfort we ourselves receive from God." "The Father of mercies and the God of all comfort" calls us to offer to others the same grace and hope he gives us.
- Galatians 6:1–2: Believers living by God's Spirit (5:16–26) should "restore" those who are "overtaken" in some sin and need help. This verb translated *restore* was used in Paul's day to set a broken bone or mend a fishing net. We help struggling brothers and sisters in God's family get back on track in their walk with Christ and back to usefulness within the church.
- Colossians 3:16: Christians filled with Christ's Word should *teach* and *admonish* one another. In the original language in which the text was penned, these are the same two verbs Paul uses in 1:28 to describe his own biblical ministry!
- 1 Thessalonians 5:14: Believers should pay attention to each other's specific spiritual conditions and minister appropriately. We should "warn those who are idle, comfort the discouraged, help the weak," tailoring our specific ministry actions to each recipient's specific need.
- Hebrews 3:12–13: To combat the real danger of apostasy, believers should "encourage each other daily . . . , so that none . . . [are] hardened by sin's deception."
- Hebrews 10:24–25: The church should gather together regularly to encourage and even "provoke" one another to "love and good works." Biblical counselors recognize both the dangers of a hardened heart and the need for practical acts of love.

- James 5:19–20: When another brother or sister in Christ "strays from the truth," we should seek to turn "him back" to "save his soul from death and cover a multitude of sins."
- Jude 22–23: Jude issues a similar directive: "Have mercy on those who waver; save others by snatching them from the fire; have mercy on others." For James and Jude, the stakes are high but the rewards are higher.

We can draw several observations from these passages. First, they assign these ministries to all Christians. Each verse pertains to all believers; none are assigned to pastors, elders, or paid church staff in particular. God calls his people to minister to each other. Second, these ministries involve the personal application of God's truth, explicitly or implicitly. We minister God's Word to help people in various ways. Third, these ministries are embedded in the nature of the body of Christ. Each passage speaks of member-to-member mutual care in the context of the church family. All believers can and should live out these passages in their informal conversations during the week, before or after church gatherings, within their small group meetings, and in training their children. Fourth, Christ commands and authorizes us to counsel each other. We must not and need not leave mutual care only to pastors or counseling professionals. God envisions believers giving biblical counsel to each other.

2. Some Believers Have Specific Counseling and Training Roles within the Church

At the same time, while the passages above speak of all believers ministering to each other in some way, each member of the body of Christ has specific gifts and ministry functions meant to be used to edify the church (Rom 12:3–8; 1 Cor 12:4–31; Eph 4:7–11; 1 Pet 4:8–11). In terms of counseling, a person's specific role depends on many variables: their gifting, calling, skills, time availability, opportunities, training, experience, passions, and assessment and recognition by the church's elders.

What might this look like in a local church committed to biblical counseling? Churches often use a model like the following—though with many variations[1]—that arranges counseling ministries into different categories based on the variables above.

- Category 1: Members provide personal care and basic biblical counsel to one another per the first principle above.
- Category 2: Group leaders and mentors provide formative discipling and spiritual direction and handle simple counseling situations with their group members or with mentees assigned to them.
- Category 3: Designated counselors and trainers provide formal counseling for members needing a higher degree of care. Some can also assist in training others.
- Category 4: Pastors/elders provide formal counseling, train members, and oversee the entire ministry.

Concerning this model, several clarifications are needed. (1) Apart from the specific role of pastors, all these categories are open to both men and women.[2] (2) Within each category, the same variables discussed above can exist. Some members and some small group leaders will have more experience or skill than others in that category. Some category 3 designated counselors might be partially or fully remunerated. A church might call someone to be a dedicated counseling pastor or administrator. New roles can be inserted as a church grows. (3) Each category requires specific qualifications. Some churches might require their category 3 or 4 counselors to pursue certification or make biblical counseling training a requirement when it comes to hiring pastors. (4) Men and women with biblical counseling gifts, training, and passions should consider whether God might want

[1] For example, see Garrett Higbee, "The Practicality of the Bible for Becoming a Church of Biblical Counseling," in Kellemen and Forrey, *Scripture and Counseling*, 226–44 (see chap. 1, n. 2).

[2] Based on varying interpretations and applications of 1 Tim 2:12, varying views exist among biblical counselors on whether God permits women to counsel men or couples. Yet all biblical counselors encourage women to actively minister at least to other women (Titus 2:3–4).

them to serve on a church planting/missionary team. Men should consider the same concerning pastoral ministry.[3]

3. God Calls Pastors and Elders to Counsel, Train, and Oversee

Where do pastors fit into this biblical vision of counseling?[4] In addition to overseeing the entire counseling ministry, Scripture assigns pastors two duties: counseling their members and training them to counsel.

Pastors Counsel Their Members

While the nine passages about believers in point one above include pastors, their specific calling as shepherds involves personally ministering God's Word to individual members of the flock.[5]

We could explore various Old Testament examples in which Israel's leaders—judges, prophets, priests, and kings—were called to shepherd individual Israelites. Some of these leaders were godly (Exod 18:13–26; Num 27:15–23; Judg 4:4–5; 1 Sam 9:6; Ps 78:70–72); some were not (Jer 23:1–6; Ezek 34:1–6).

Turning to the New Testament, we see Jesus showing personal care to individuals throughout his ministry. Based on the Gospel accounts, our Lord seemingly spent more time ministering to individuals than to crowds; he spent more time in private and small group teaching and counseling than in public preaching.[6] We also see this in his personal care for his disciples and the many individuals he counseled. In turn, he called Peter to

---

[3] See Robert D. Jones, "Avoiding Infinite Mischief: Assessing Your Calling to Pastoral Ministry," *Journal of Modern Ministry* 6, no. 3 (Fall 2009): 9–23.

[4] We use *pastors* to include the synonymous terms of pastors, elders, and overseers, whether paid or unpaid, based on texts like Acts 20:17, 28; 1 Tim 3:1; 5:17; and Titus 1:5.

[5] See Jay E. Adams, *Shepherding God's Flock: A Handbook on Pastoral Ministry, Counseling, and Leadership* (Grand Rapids: Zondervan, 1975); Jeremy Pierre and Deepak Reju, *The Pastor and Counseling: The Basics of Shepherding Members in Need* (Wheaton, IL: Crossway, 2015); and Timothy Z. Witmer, *The Shepherd Leader: Achieving Effective Shepherding in Your Church* (Phillipsburg, NJ: P&R, 2010).

[6] See Powlison, *Speaking Truth in Love*, 105–6 (see chap. 1, n. 5); and Peter Adam, *Speaking God's Words: A Practical Theology of Expository Preaching* (Downers Grove, IL: InterVarsity Press, 1996), 59–70.

feed and tend God's flock (John 21:15–17). In Matt 28:18–20, he directed his apostles to win people to him, baptize them, and teach "them to observe everything" he had commanded. Doing so requires giving biblical counsel.[7]

Jesus not only counseled people, he called his followers to do the same. Thankfully, his apostles listened. In Acts 20:20, Paul recalled his three-year ministry teaching the Ephesians "publicly and from house to house." Like Jesus, Paul demonstrated the primacy not of preaching but of ministering God's Word in its dual-delivery system, corporately and privately. In Col 1:28, he summarized his ministry of "warning and teaching everyone with all wisdom, so that we may present everyone mature in Christ." The repetition of "everyone" points to Paul's pastoral care for individuals, a concern he also shows in 1 Thess 2:11–12; Acts 20:31; and 1 Cor 12:25. His words cannot be reduced to merely public ministry.

The apostles consistently urged the church's elders to shepherd their members. Peter understood his shepherding role and exhorted the elders to do likewise (1 Pet 5:2–4). Paul directed the Ephesian elders to shepherd the church, reminding them of his personal, self-sacrificing, tear-filled ministry among them (Acts 20:17–38). Using an assortment of teaching verbs—words certainly not restricted to public preaching—Paul urged Timothy to faithfully minister the God-breathed Scriptures (2 Tim 3:10–4:5). He instructed Titus to appoint godly elders who could bring sound truth and refute erroneous teaching that was destroying whole households—another mark of Paul's pastoral counseling care (Titus 1:5–13). Hebrews 13:7 and 13:17 further underscore the importance of pastoral care and oversight of members, as church leaders teach

[7] Concerning this Great Commission passage, it's not enough to teach *what* Jesus commands. We must teach people *how* to follow his commands. Merely telling a husband in a troubled marriage what Eph 5:25 says and to love his wife based on it is insufficient; we must help a specific husband love his specific wife in their specific marital situation. Biblical counselors bring tangible application to Bible texts. See Robert Jones, "Does the Great Commission Require Biblical Counseling?," Biblical Counseling Coalition, July 17, 2019, https://www.biblicalcounselingcoalition.org/2019/07/17/does-the-great-commission-require-biblical-counseling/.

God's Word, model godliness (v. 7), and keep watch over and lead the members (v. 17).

Based on these passages, pastors who take their role to heart should view themselves and be viewed by others as counselors, called by God to excel in biblical counseling. At the heart of his pastoral task is the personal ministry of God's Word to help those struggling with personal and relational problems.

Pastors Equip Their Members to Counsel

In Eph 4:11–16, Paul wrote of how the ascended, victorious Lord Jesus gave pastors and teachers to equip members for mutual ministry so that the church will grow in unity, maturity, and love. What specific thing should believers do for one another to accomplish that goal? It is "speaking the truth in love" (4:15; cf. Gal 4:16). The "truth" in Ephesians is the gospel message (1:13; 4:21; 6:14); the realm or context is "love." Rather than being some proverbial guideline on how to honestly say hard things in nice ways, this refers to the whole church speaking gospel truths and applications to one another. The Ephesians 4 every-member ministry envisioned is not about everyone serving on a ministry team but everyone talking to each other about Jesus and his Word.

How does this vision develop? Verse 12 calls pastors and teachers to prepare the saints for this kind of ministry. Let's consider six ways pastors can equip their members to counsel biblically:

1. Through public preaching and teaching, they show members how to interpret and apply Scripture to their personal struggles.
2. Through their pastoral prayers and wise song selection for corporate worship, they guide God's people in how to think about and approach God.
3. Through counseling members, especially in the presence of a small group leader or a godly friend of the counselee, they show others how to reproduce measures of their ministry.
4. Through testifying how biblical counseling truths are transforming their lives, they help members do the same.

5. Through recommending and displaying sound biblical counseling resources, they provide timely, life-transforming resources to members for their use and for helping each other.
6. Through providing formal biblical counseling training within their churches as the church is able. Qualified men and women can assist in or lead this training, especially those with advanced biblical counseling training (e.g., a master's degree in biblical counseling). Pastors can also encourage members to pursue other trusted avenues of biblical counseling training at seminaries, Bible colleges, Christian training centers, conferences, on-the-road events, and by watching video curriculum.

4. God Designed the Local Church to Be His Primary Base for Biblical Counseling

According to 1 Timothy, a local church formed by the gospel (1:1–20; 3:16) and ordered properly (2:1–3:13) is "the pillar and foundation" for the ministry of that gospel (3:14–15). When combined with the many one-another passages in point one above and passages summarizing the church's ministry (e.g., Acts 2:42–47), biblical counseling clearly belongs to the church.

Church-based counseling means counseling done by church leaders and members to help other members, regular attenders, and those in the community.[8] For instance, biblical counselors can lead support group ministries for those struggling with divorce, addictions, single parenting, and grief. Depending on the church's size, vision, and overall maturity, a church might situate such ministries in various community locations, including a residential care facility, not just on church property. Regardless, the local church should be a place where people can find all sorts of help for all sorts of personal and relational problems. In that sense, a church should *be* a counseling center, not just have a counseling center.

---

[8] On counseling unbelievers, see chapter 19. For a practical vision of a local church incorporating church-based biblical counseling into its larger outreach, see Stephen Viars, *Loving Your Community: Proven Practices for Community-Based Outreach Ministry* (Grand Rapids: Baker Books, 2020).

What benefits does church-based biblical counseling bring that counseling done in other settings can't replicate? Consider a dozen advantages:

1. The oversight of God-ordained shepherds. Christ has given the church pastors and elders who know their members and can shepherd them in practical and immediate ways.[9] Their position enables them to enter a counselee's world, gain trust, do the counseling (or connect the person to approved counselors), and bring proper God-given elder authority to the situation if needed.[10]
2. Consistency between private counseling and public preaching. The counselor and the counselee know the counsel given in a Tuesday session will align with the Sunday teaching.
3. God-centered, Christ-exalting worship. God uses the songs, prayers, and Bible readings in corporate worship to shift a counselee's focus from himself to God and God's glory, promises, and provisions.
4. Christ's ordinances (or sacraments). As baptized members witness the baptisms of others and partake of the Lord's Supper, they commune afresh with Jesus and fellow believers. For counselees burdened with guilt or fear, the bread and the cup of the new covenant tangibly remind them of the forgiving love and presence of their crucified Redeemer.
5. The fellowship, encouragement, and example of mature fellow believers. We can connect counselees to mature Christians for mentoring and support; members who have successfully navigated similar problems can be excellent mentors.
6. Restorative/redemptive church discipline. Church-based counseling provides the disciplinary care of the church family should a member pull away from the Lord.[11]

---

[9] For advantages pastors have in counseling their church members, see David Powlison, "The Pastor as Counselor," in *For the Fame of God's Name: Essays in Honor of John Piper*, ed. Sam Storms and Justin Taylor (Wheaton, IL: Crossway, 2010), 419–42.

[10] On the elders' authority, see Acts 20:28; 1 Thess 5:12–13; Titus 2:15; Heb 13:7, 17, 24; and 1 Pet 5:3, 5a.

[11] See Robert Cheong and Robert D. Jones, "Biblical Counseling, the Church, and Church Discipline," in Kellemen and Carson, *Biblical Counseling and the Church (see chap. 1, n. 2).*

7. Opportunities to serve others. We can direct counselees to ministry leaders who can deploy them into others-centered forms of service.
8. Resource people. We can link needy counselees to other members who can provide budgeting, medical, legal, or job-hunting advice to supplement our focus. This also allows those members to use their gifts to serve their church and experience the joy of ministry.
9. Benevolence assistance. For counselees needing financial assistance (e.g., help with utility bills and rent) or physical help to relocate out of a difficult housing location, we know who to talk to and how to find help.
10. Access to members' homes for informal counseling, mentoring, discipleship, and small group life. We can encourage involvement with other mature fellow members. Our Lord and his apostles practiced life-on-life ministry.
11. Greater legal protection. We lessen the likelihood of lawsuits by stipulating that our church-based counseling is part of our normal evangelistic and discipleship ministries and do not profess to be state-licensed, professional psychological counselors.
12. We offer all of the above free of charge (with no co-pays or session limits)!

These benefits together make the local church God's ideal setting for offering Christ-centered biblical counseling. As David Powlison observes, "The people of God functioning as the people of God provide the ideal and desirable institution to fix what ails us. That institution can adapt to take on a thousand different problems. . . . 'Counseling' ought to express and come under the church's authority and orthodoxy."[12]

[12] Powlison, *Speaking Truth in Love*, 110. See also Bill Goode, "Biblical Counseling and the Local Church," in *Counseling: How to Counsel Biblically*, ed. John MacArthur (Nashville: Thomas Nelson, 2005), 226.

5. Biblical Counselors Serve in Vocational Counseling and Training Roles beyond the Local Church

While church-based counseling remains the ideal, it's not the only setting God uses to change people. Biblical counselors function in various vocational settings outside the local church and church planting and missions. We'll consider both parachurch settings and those involving state licensure.

Parachurch Biblical Counseling Ministries

Parachurch biblical counselors serve a valuable kingdom function in various settings. They strengthen the overall health of the churches within a community in a number of ways. (1) When local churches are unable or unwilling to counsel people biblically, parachurch biblical counselors provide help for those church members who need it. (2) When a person believes God is calling them to a parachurch ministry position to counsel those who would not normally seek church-based counseling. (3) When the parachurch exists to train church members and leaders, including providing observational training based on its own counseling ministry, that organization sees itself as a servant of the church and works toward the day when local churches will be trained and its job will finish. (4) When the parachurch offers specialized or intensive forms of biblical counseling (e.g., addiction treatment, trauma intervention, residential group homes), it can offer families a level of support that local churches don't normally provide. (5) When regional local churches (e.g., a presbytery or Baptist association) cooperate to create and support a parachurch counseling center, the counselors tend to see their ministries as extensions of those churches.

Specific questions arise about how the parachurch counselors connect and communicate with churches. These should be explored by counselors contemplating a ministry vocation in a parachurch organization and by churches considering partnership with a parachurch.

Settings Involving State Licensure

Beyond church-based or parachurch counseling ministry environments, some biblical counselors serve in settings requiring state licensure.[13] What advantages might a state license bring to a biblical counselor? Proponents mention several categories. First, state licensure can open ministry doors typically closed to nonlicensed counselors. Most people—especially non-Christians—who need counseling seek professional licensed counselors. So, should they have freedom to talk about Christ in their sessions, licensed counselors have evangelistic opportunities. They can even serve in government-related settings, such as hospitals, substance abuse centers, state colleges, and military facilities, and may work on court-appointed cases that might even involve children.

Second, the training and supervision requirements for obtaining state licensure exceed the requirements for biblical counseling certification. This includes explicit training in microskills and interviewing techniques. The knowledge gained about our psychologized culture through all this training enables them to help the church understand clinical diagnoses, to offer informed critiques of the mental health world, and to earn a seat at the table—a kind of union card—to potentially influence other therapists with biblical wisdom.

Third, there are more paid positions available in the mental health field than in churches and parachurches.

At the same time, there are disadvantages to having state licensure. First, biblical counselors seeking a state license can face adversity, restrictions, or censure from the psychotherapeutic community whose values oppose God's Word. Moreover, other biblical counselors might question their biblical commitments and their motives for pursuing licensure.

Second, secular restrictions and ethical requirements can lead to moral dilemmas and temptations that might urge a counselor to compromise his biblical commitments. Placing oneself under the authority of a secular

---

[13] We refer to "state" licensure since a state governing board issues a license and exercises authority over the counselor (e.g., as a licensed professional counselor, licensed marriage and family therapist, or licensed clinical social worker).

licensing board while trying to counsel biblically can create conflicts of allegiance. Areas of concern include

- restrictions in sharing Christian perspectives or recommending Bible study or biblically based resources,
- requirements to use therapeutic language (DSM-5 diagnostic categories and codes) and treatment plans,
- various issues related to unbiblical views of gender, same-sex marriage, and sexual orientation,
- degrees of confidentiality, e.g., not being able to report vital concerns to a counselee's pastor, and
- dual-relationship restrictions, e.g., limits on doing life-on-life with counselees, enjoying small group fellowship, and other forms of Christian community.

In some cases, clear informed-consent agreements might give state-licensed biblical counselors in some states a little flexibility in these areas. The language and strictness of each specific state's professional licensing board's standards also matter.

Third, adding a state license beyond one's biblical counseling training involves significant financial cost and energy.

Fourth, the desire to gain and retain paying clients might tempt professional counselors to bypass the primacy of the local church and inadvertently compete with the counseling ministry the person's church should ideally provide.

So, given these pros and cons, how should we look at biblical counselors seeking state licensure? We suggest viewing it as a wisdom matter—a question of individual conscience and calling. In areas lacking explicit biblical direction, Scripture gives categories that teach us how to view fellow Christians, particularly with respect to those gray areas that Bible scholars refer to as "disputable things" or *adiaphora* (e.g., Rom 14:1–15:7; 1 Cor 7:25–40; 8:1–13; 10:23–11:1). Could it be conscientiously wrong for some people to place themselves under state restrictions but not wrong for others? Could it be that God might lead some to serve him with a state license and others to serve him without one? It seems the answer to both questions is yes.

Conclusion

With whatever training we have received, with whatever credentials or authorization we bear, and in whatever settings and roles we serve, let all of us committed to biblical counseling (as described in chapter 1) wisely, boldly, and compassionately bring to our struggling counselees as much of the gospel and its implications as our situations allow. And however para-church or state-licensed counselors navigate the above waters, let all of us remember and reinforce the priority of the local church. As someone has cleverly put it concerning the uneducated apostles in Acts 4, let us prize above everything a "BWJ"—that is, a "been with Jesus" degree (Acts 4:13).

PART TWO

THEOLOGICAL FOUNDATIONS FOR BIBLICAL COUNSELING

The Bible and Epistemology

In chapter 1 we explained that the Bible comprehensively provides the truths we need to actively build our model of care, a fact distinguishing biblical counseling vis-à-vis other forms of counseling. We used verbs such as *emerge* or *drive* to emphasize the Bible's active role in biblical counseling model building. This chapter expands on that idea and demonstrates its importance for epistemological consistency. We will see how genuine knowledge is possible and how the Bible meets four criteria for epistemological validity and therefore makes it a reliable foundation for our biblical counseling model.

Every system of counseling has a source of authoritative knowledge and a way to add information to that knowledge.[1] There must be a source of truth that is reliable in order to initially build and improve over time a model of care. As a result, knowledge is a crucial component for every form of biblical, Christian, and secular counseling.[2]

---

[1] This chapter focuses on the system, not on a specific practitioner's ability to counsel properly within the system. We believe some so-called biblical counseling has been inconsistent with what is taught in this book. We ourselves, in fact, sometimes fall short of our own standards. For more discussion on the difference between the sufficiency of Scripture and the competency of a counselor, see Bob Kellemen, "10 Common Mistakes Counselors Make, Part 10," RPM Ministries website, March 10, 2020, https://rpmministries.org/2020/03/10-common-mistakes-biblical-counselors-sometimes-make-part-10/.

[2] For example, the authors of *Psychology and Christianity: Five Views*, ed. Eric Johnson, 2nd ed. (Downers Grove: InterVarsity Press, 2010) establish the theological knowledge

For example, let's consider a system that believes the best way to care for people is to help each person live consistently with their values. That belief must come from somewhere—from a body of knowledge or source of truth that *drives* the system. The knowledge might come from experience, a research study, a significant book, or someone's imagination. Regardless, that system of care *emerged from* a set of authoritative truths. Additionally, some Christian counseling systems argue that they take the best knowledge available from the Bible and the best knowledge available from scientific research and integrate them to form their system of care.[3] Biblical counselors argue that the Bible is the source of authoritative knowledge that drives and exhibits active functional control over our model. This means that biblical counseling is a system of care that emerges from the Bible.

Since authoritative knowledge drives every system, one must determine how one can justify or give warrant to the validity of the body of authoritative knowledge used to create and modify the system. Secular counselors use the latest research, Christian counselors normally use some version of "all truth is God's truth," and biblical counselors use their Bibles. How can anyone justify using *their* source of authoritative knowledge? Proverbs 18:17 says, "The first to state his case seems right until another comes and cross-examines him." So, if we advocate for a counseling system, we must be able to defend it in light of various competing approaches.

We have argued that (1) every system of counseling emerges from a body of authoritative knowledge and (2) every system must justify the use of its body of knowledge. Now it is important to consider how a biblical counselor could justify the use of the Bible as the source of authoritative truth that drives, modifies, and controls their model of care. Without such a justification, biblical counseling does not have a reason to exist. In fact, no system has warrant to exist without someone first justifying its source of truth. Let's consider how one could develop a warrant for knowledge.

---

used for each brand of Christian counseling model building. Cognitive Behavioral Therapy proponents also justify their system by explaining the knowledge used to build and improve their model. See David D. Burns, *Feeling Good: The New Mood Therapy*, rev. ed. (New York: HarperCollins, 1999), esp. 7–49.

[3] We could give many examples, but one helpful illustration is Stanton L. Jones, "An Integration View," in Johnson, *Psychology and Christianity*, 101–28.

The Warrant for Knowledge

Epistemology is the study of knowledge. It attempts to answer the question, How can one know anything? This is particularly important because those holding to every system of counseling used a body of knowledge to develop their model. Therefore, we should consider how one might justify knowledge itself and then defend the knowledge used to drive and develop a system of care.

Possibility of Genuine Knowledge

Skeptics of knowledge suggest that knowledge itself is elusive and inaccessible. They claim, ironically, that the only absolute truth is that there is no such thing as absolute truth! In *The Gagging of God*, D. A. Carson thoughtfully engages this idea. He agrees with post-modern thinking that challenges the optimism of modernity because we do not know completely or perfectly, but he also criticizes the skepticism of post-modernity by arguing that knowledge can be gained sufficiently and meaningfully. He concludes by reminding his readers that both modernity's certainty and post-modernity's skepticism are incorrect; there remains a true and genuine knowledge available through a Christian worldview.[4]

Carson is right. While we biblical counselors need to be careful, thoughtful, and concerned about what knowledge we use to build, drive, or develop our system, we also wholeheartedly affirm that knowledge is both accessible and sufficient. Let's consider how we could justify the knowledge we use.

Criteria for Knowledge Claims

In his work *Epistemology: The Justification of Belief*, David Wolfe devises a system to determine whether the foundation of knowledge is justified. He argues there are four Cs that identify the validity of a system of knowledge:

---

[4] D. A. Carson, *The Gagging of God: Christianity Confronts Pluralism* (Grand Rapids: Zondervan, 1996).

consistency, coherence, comprehensiveness, and congruity.[5] Each of these provide a way to test a system of knowledge. Consistency means the system is free from internal contradictions. Coherence refers to how the claims in the system relate to one another. Comprehensiveness addresses how practical the system is to the experience of those in the system. Finally, congruity refers to whether the system of knowledge answers the questions of those who experience challenges.[6]

It is possible to use these four Cs to test a system. For example, in the book *Counseling and Christianity*, five authors explain how they would counsel a fictitious counselee named "Jake." Jake is a young man with many challenges involving suffering and sin. The Levels of Explanation view suggests that Jake needs care at every level of his existence. When it comes to the spiritual level the writer suggests, "Ancient religious models such as Jesus, Buddha, and Mohammad, as well as many of the more contemporary religious and spiritual models such as Gandhi, Mother Teresa, . . . Martin Luther King Jr., and even one's family and friends can act as a template or model for how to live and act in a better way."[7] One may wonder how this statement is *consistent* with what Jesus said in John 14:6 or what Luke wrote in Acts 4:12, and how this sentence could be *coherent* given that Jesus, Buddha, Mohammad, and others did not teach the same things. Apart from the biblical counseling position, it is difficult to find in the other views an explicit, open Bible sharing of the gospel with Jake. We can genuinely ask whether these various approaches to Christian counseling are committed, as a specific and intentional part of their system, to having the gospel at their core. If not, it is hard to understand how these models pass the above four tests for warrant. If an approach claims to take the best of all the resources available to

---

[5] David L. Wolfe, *Epistemology: The Justification of Belief* (Downers Grove: InterVarsity Press, 1982), 50–56. In this helpful resource, Wolfe not only provides a way to evaluate a truth claim, but also discusses some of the wrong ways individuals have justified a belief.

[6] Wolfe, 55.

[7] Thomas Plante, "A Levels-of-Explanation Approach," in Greggo and Sisemore, *Counseling and Christianity*, 79 (see chap. 1, n. 4). The other approaches include integration, Christian counseling, transformational, and biblical counseling.

help people and yet does not bring the gospel, then we wonder if they are taking the best from the Bible.

The Unique Place of the Bible in the Study of Knowledge

We have argued that knowledge is possible and that warrant for that knowledge can be satisfied using a series of characteristics.[8] It is now appropriate to discuss the unique place of the Bible[9] in building the foundation of knowledge we use to build, drive, and improve biblical counseling.[10]

Inspiration: The Bible is Inspired by God

Inspiration, as commonly discussed, involves both the product (the text itself) and the process (the means used to produce the text). In light of 2 Tim 3:16–17, we believe God is the ultimate author of the text we read in the Bible. That is one of the reasons the Bible says that the Word of the Lord stands forever (Matt 5:17–18; Isa 40:8). Since God is the author, the source is reliable. We also believe God used humans in the writing and

[8] Some might object that we are inconsistent since we use something outside the Bible to justify our system of knowledge, which excludes everything from outside the Bible. We respond in two ways: (1) The Bible teaches each of these four Cs. For example, Jesus charged the religious leaders with hypocrisy though that would have little meaning without consistency. The Bible's statement that the Lord has provided all we need for life and godliness is an example of comprehensiveness. (2) As we push deeper into a system, we will realize that faith is one part of the equation. Everyone exercises faith. Even those who prefer evidentialist apologetics will eventually reach the location of faith. Those who favor presuppositional arguments will benefit from Greg L. Bahnsen, *Van Til's Apologetic* (Phillipsburg, NJ: P&R, 1998) or "Does God Exist?," a 1985 debate between atheist Dr. Gordon Stein and Christian Dr. Greg Bahnsen, YouTube video, 2:13:57, https://www.youtube.com/watch?v=anGAazNCfdY. Either way one argues, it is a reasonable faith.

[9] We reject all writings apart from the sixty-six books of the Old and New Testaments called the Bible. See Phillip Comfort, ed., *The Origin of the Bible: A Comprehensive Guide* [. . .] (Carol Stream, IL: Tyndale House, 1992); F. F. Bruce, *The Canon of Scripture* (Wheaton: InterVarsity Press, 1988). For more technical discussions of the New Testament, see Bruce M. Metzger, *The Canon of the New Testament: Its Origin, Development, and Significance* (New York: Oxford University Press, 1987) and E. Earle Ellis, *The Making of the New Testament Documents* (Boston: Bill Academic, 2002).

[10] Chapter 9 will evaluate the role of truth claims outside the Bible, such as those emerging from medical or social science.

assembling of his work (2 Pet 1:20–21). The Holy Spirit's involvement guarantees that human involvement could not corrupt the perfect Word of the Lord. While this short chapter cannot present detailed arguments, we wholeheartedly affirm that God's authorship and intervention in delivering his Word satisfy the criteria for a system of knowledge; namely, consistency, coherence, comprehensiveness, and congruity. There is no other writing that warrants such a title or can make equal claims.

Inerrancy: The Bible Is without Error

If the Bible is God's Word and if it declares clearly that God has not lied (Rom 3:4), then one can conclude the Bible is without error. However, as believers in Christ seeking to determine which system of knowledge we will trust, we can reasonably evaluate the claims of Scripture. While inductively proving inerrancy is not possible, the objections levied against the Scripture do have clear, reasonable, and thoughtful answers. Thus, inerrancy is not only a logical outcome of the inspiration of Scripture, it is also the reasoned conclusion of those who have searched the Scriptures at an individual passage level. The Creator and sustainer of the universe, who is responsible for the content of the Bible, communicated truth.

Sufficiency: The Bible Provides What We Need

The doctrine of the sufficiency of Scripture, dependent on the inspiration and inerrancy of Scripture, means the Bible gives us everything a person needs to understand how to please, glorify, and properly represent God in this present life regardless of circumstances, including (1) how a person can have a right relationship with God through Christ, (2) the truths to believe about God's character, his work in creation, and in the hearts of people, and the way the Lord sees believers, (3) the commands God expects his people to follow, and (4) how to please God in the ways we act and react to our sin, the sin of others, the challenges of living in a sin-cursed world, and how to handle suffering. This means the Bible explains everything needed to live for and honor the Lord.

The doctrine of sufficiency has a long history. The 1647 Westminster Confession of Faith declares, "The whole counsel of God concerning all things necessary for his own glory, man's salvation, faith and life, is either expressly set down in Scripture, or by good and necessary consequence may be deduced from Scripture."[11] The 1689 London Baptist Confession similarly states, "The Holy Scripture is the only sufficient, certain, and infallible rule of all saving knowledge, faith, and obedience. . . . The whole counsel of God concerning all things necessary for His own glory, man's salvation, faith and life, is either expressly set down or necessarily contained in the Holy Scripture."[12] Summarizing this doctrine, Wayne Grudem writes, "[Scripture] now contains everything we need God to tell us for salvation, for trusting Him perfectly, and for obeying Him perfectly. . . . God considers what He has told us in the Bible to be enough for us, and that we should rejoice in the great revelation that He has given us and be content with it."[13] Biblical counselors believe God's Word gives us everything we need for our salvation, faith and life, and for trusting and obeying God perfectly.[14]

Authority of Scripture: The Bible Has the Right to Tell Us How to Think and Act

The characteristics of comprehensiveness and congruity encourage us to question whether the Bible speaks to each aspect of the human experience. Is it true that the Bible relates to the sin issues and the suffering issues that plague human life? Does it speak to those circumstances in a

---

[11] The Confession of Faith, chap. 1, sec. 6, https://www.pcaac.org/wp-content/uploads/2019/11/WCFScriptureProofs.pdf.

[12] The Baptist Confession of Faith of 1689, chap. 1, para. 1 and 6, https://www.1689.com/confession.html. The 1742 Philadelphia Confession uses the same language.

[13] Wayne A. Grudem, *Systematic Theology: An Introduction to Biblical Doctrine* (Grand Rapids: Zondervan, 2004), 127.

[14] See also the BCC Confessional Statement, https://www.biblicalcounselingcoalition.org/confessional-statement/; Jeremy Pierre, "Scripture Is Sufficient, but to Do What?" in Kellemen and Forrey, *Scripture and Counseling*, 94–108 (see chap. 1, n. 2); and Heath Lambert et al., *Sufficiency: Historic Essays on the Sufficiency of Scripture* (Association of Certified Biblical Counselors, 2016).

comprehensive way? Biblical counseling's answer is, "Yes, the Bible speaks to all of the human experience."[15] That is one reason biblical counseling is committed to the authority of the Bible. The Bible doesn't supply a series of suggestions to be evaluated by another system of knowledge. Instead, biblical truth serves as authoritative decrees from God to live as he designed.

These four Bible characteristics set it apart from all other systems of knowledge. The Creator of the universe took personal responsibility to reveal himself to us and provide for us the Bible as the system of knowledge by which human experience can be understood, defined, evaluated, and helped. As a result, a proper understanding of the Bible drives, builds, and determines our system of care. At the same time, we must recognize the inherent limitations offered by truth claims that do not share the Bible's characteristics. Biblical counselors argue that the Bible serves as the source of authoritative truth used to build our model because the knowledge from the Bible is trustworthy, reliable, and sure.

Building Our Counseling Model on the Knowledge Revealed in God's Word

Biblical counselors argue that the Bible serves as the system of knowledge that is worthy to construct our model of care. David Powlison explained competing philosophies using two acronyms, VITEX and COMPIN.[16] The first, VITEX,, says the Bible serves as a filter for various truth claims about how to care for people. "VITEX believes that secular psychologies must make a *VITal EXternal contribution* in the construction of a Christian

[15] See Paul Tautges and Steve Viars, "Sufficient for Life and Godliness," and Pierre, "Scripture Is Sufficient," in Kellemen and Forrey, *Scripture and Counseling*, 47–61, 94–108; Steve Viars and Rob Green, "The Sufficiency of Scripture" in Kellemen and Viars, *Christ-Centered Biblical Counseling*, 89–105 (see chap. 1, n. 2); Heath Lambert, *A Theology of Biblical Counseling* (Grand Rapids: Zondervan, 2016), 37–52; and Heath Lambert et al., *Sufficiency: Historical Essays on the Sufficiency of Scripture* (Association of Certified Biblical Counselors, 2016).

[16] David Powlison, "Cure of Souls (and the Modern Psychotherapies)," *Journal of Biblical Counseling* 25, no. 2 (2007): 5–36. The is one of the most significant articles in the last thirty years on the epistemological issues between biblical counseling, Christian counseling, and secular counseling.

model of personality, change, and counseling."[17] Powlison adds, "The operating premise of VITEX, whether explicit or implicit, is that Christian truths must be 'integrated' with the observations, personality theories, psychotherapies, and professional roles of the mental health world."[18] As long as the Bible does not directly contradict such a truth claim, then it is allowed to become part of the model. In this approach, the Bible is a filter.

The second, COMPIN, emphasizes the fact that our model of counseling emerges from the study of Scripture. Powlison says, "COMPIN believes that the Christian faith contains *COMPrehensive INternal resources* to enable us to construct a Christian model of personality, change, and counseling."[19] He adds, "While the modern psychologies will stimulate and inform, they do not play a constitutive role in building a robust model. . . . The living Christ working in His people through His Word is the engine producing depth of insight, accurate theory, and effective practice."[20] In this approach, the Bible is the driving force. Notice the phrases "constitutive role" and "engine producing." Biblical counselors, as described in this book, are committed to the COMPIN approach because the Bible satisfies the epistemological tests for knowledge and because the Bible provides the needed information to construct our system of care.

Let's consider how this concept functions in practice. During the writing of this work, COVID-19 gripped our nation. Schools closed, businesses were shuttered, churches met online, and the government doled out trillions in relief funding. Scientists sought treatment options and developed vaccines. A Christ-following scientist committed to a COMPIN approach would pray, read his Bible, worship, and seek to honor the Lord throughout his work to fight the virus. This would result in him carefully researching God's fallen creation for patterns, appreciating and utilizing reliable and relevant discoveries, and longing for the final physical healing God promises at the resurrection. He'd know his Bible does not explain how the virus reproduces, what could kill it, or what could help the body

---

[17] Powlison, 11.
[18] Powlison, 11.
[19] Powlison, 11.
[20] Powlison, 11.

fight it; nevertheless, trusting it as truth would teach him to do his job with excellence, to depend on Christ, to use scientific laws God set in place, and to be driven by proper motives. In this case, how he would do his job emerges from the truth of Scripture, and the laws of logic and science he would apply in the lab are consistent with Scripture.

When we address our model of biblical counseling, we are talking about how to care for people made in the image of God, which is a different matter altogether. Scripture proclaims the glory of God and magnifies Christ, but it also presents a biblical approach to people, or as Powlison puts it, "a Christian model of personality, change, and counseling." Biblical counselors are not virologists. They are students of people. The following chapters in this section of the book explain how our understanding of God, people, sin, and repentance all emerge from Scripture. The care of others is not merely consistent with Scripture, it is driven by it. This one fact has a tremendous impact on how we do ministry. Since many people use the term "biblical counseling," we must remember that differences could be superficial, or they could occur at the level of model construction.[21] Biblical counseling develops its model from the Bible. Caring for people is not a series of truth claims to be checked by the Bible filter. Rather, a series of truths emerge from the text of Scripture that explain how the counselor should function and how the counselee should feel, think, love, act, and respond to the various circumstances of his existence.

Conclusion

Every system that cares for people must justify its existence and authority. While our knowledge as biblical counselors is not perfect, it is meaningful

[21] Except for the biblical counseling position, all other positions in the *Psychology and Christianity* and *Counseling and Christianity* books above use a VITEX approach to model building. That is why the gospel is not at their center, the Bible is not clearly presented to the counselees, and the focus is more about how the Bible impacts the counselors than the counselees. In the biblical counseling chapter in *Counseling and Christianity*, Stuart Scott builds his model on COMPIN and the results are striking. Where the counselee would spend eternity, how the counselee would view himself, and how he would deal with his sin and suffering are all based on God's Word.

and sufficient and can be justified by showing how our source of truth satisfies consistency, coherence, comprehensiveness, and congruity. Based on the Bible's inspiration, inerrancy, sufficiency, and authority, it satisfies those criteria. As a result, biblical counseling emerges from biblical knowledge. Instead of merely being a filter to trap error, the Bible is the driving force, the builder, and the engine producer for our system of care. As Isa 40:8 says, "The grass withers, the flowers fade, but the word of our God remains forever."

The Significance of God, Christ, and the Spirit

In the previous chapter we began constructing a proper theological foundation for biblical counseling. We argued that knowledge is indeed possible, and the Bible served as our system of knowledge to build a model of care. However, some might conclude the model of care is based solely on facts, answers to questions, or solutions to problems. Biblical counseling will surely seek to answer questions, provide propositional truth, and discern right from wrong; however, it does not stop there because the Bible does not stop there. As D. A. Carson explains, "Scripture's purpose is not simply to fill our heads with facts, but to bring us to the living God."[1] Since biblical counseling's model of care emerges from the Bible and is not simply consistent with it, successful counseling results in a greater love, passion, and desire for the living God. That brings us to the subject of this chapter: excellent biblical counseling depends on a proper understanding of the triune God and helping a counselee develop a loving relationship with him.[2] This chapter will briefly consider how biblical

[1] Carson, *Gagging of God*, 167 (see chap. 3, n. 4).

[2] See Millard J. Erickson, *Christian Theology* (Grand Rapids: Baker, 1983); and Grudem, *Systematic Theology* (see chap. 3, n. 13). For how these doctrines impact specific counseling situations, see Lambert, *Theology of Biblical Counseling* (see chap. 3, n. 15).

counselors should think about God, Christ, and the Spirit to properly build our model of care.

Understanding God

Biblical counseling directs the heart and mind of the counselee to the Lord. We biblical counselors seek to help our counselees adopt Paul's mindset, not change their circumstances. Even while imprisoned, he wrote, "My goal is to know [Christ] and the power of his resurrection and the fellowship of his sufferings" (Phil 3:10). We seek to connect the counselee's story to the attributes and plan of God.

God's Attributes

An attribute is an irreducible quality of God. One thinks, for example, about God's love or God's mercy as one of his attributes. How do such subjects relate to counseling? Many counselees report deep and painful suffering. They explain that their views of God have been partially formed by the authority figures in their lives that have unjustly wounded and afflicted them. For example, Karen suffered under abuse her entire life. She could not name one positive relationship she'd had with a man. Her father physically assaulted her; her brother created games designed to take advantage of her; her first boyfriend raped her; and the list of abusers grew in length throughout her life. Karen believed that God hated her, did not care about her, and wanted her to suffer. In the language of Ps 34:8, Karen had never tasted or seen that the Lord is good. While it was not difficult to understand where her view of God originated, ministry to her required careful listening, patience, caring for her pain, and eventually a discussion of how to change her understanding of the Lord to align with what is true about him. The counselor needed to patiently and lovingly communicate that God is love (1 John 4:16), God is gracious and compassionate (Exod 34:6), God is a just God who will judge the sins committed against her (Rom 12:19), God is wise and can help her handle her ongoing struggles (Jas

1:5), and God was merciful in providing a way for Karen to be saved and to have a vital relationship with him (Rom 5:8).

Stu, another counselee, was actively engaged in viewing pornography and in masturbation. In a rather twisted approach to logic, he surmised that God chose not to look when he chose to sin. He also told himself God did not care about his "little transgressions" when so many other things in his life were good and right. Even though Stu felt guilt over his sin, he had developed a view of God that allowed the pleasure of sin to outweigh guilt. While some of the same truths shared with Karen were important to share with Stu, the biblical counselor also discussed with him the holiness of God and his ability to forgive (1 John 1:5–2:2). As Stu developed a fuller understanding of God, it both magnified his guilty condition and demonstrated God's power to forgive.

God's Plan

We are often very easily satisfied. All it takes is enjoying a few hours of downtime or of a pleasurable activity, and life seems good. This often leads people to conclude that this world satisfies. But this is such a small and potentially dangerous view of life, especially when counselees' lives are full of pain. Only the pages of the Bible expose humanity to the much bigger plan, purpose, and meaning of life.

It is hard to count the number of counselees who seek help in the midst of feeling hopeless, purposeless, and while questioning the value of their existence. In extreme cases, they might even consider reasons and methods to end their lives. Some see no valid reason to continue living. While safety concerns would be our first priority in addressing such cases of despair, biblical counsel must eventually move counselees to the plan and purposes of the Almighty. God has a master plan for each of us that is far larger than our lives, yet our lives play only parts in his grand plan. As our counselees embrace God's purposes, they will find joy and satisfaction in him. As they properly fear the Lord, they will find wisdom (Prov 1:7; Eccl 12:13). God desires that our believing counselees evangelize others

(Matt 28:19–20), remember that today's sufferings pale in comparison to heaven's glory (Rom 8:18) and that God will remove all death and pain (Rev 21:4), serve the Lord with passion and dependence (1 Pet 4:10; 1 Cor 12:12–27; Eph 4:16), and live worthy of their spiritual calling (Eph 4:1). The better our counselees understand God's plan and their place in it, the more they will live for him with joy and purposefulness.

Our counselees' relationship with God is not comprised merely of understanding God through his attributes and his plan. Understanding his attributes and his plan are not ends to themselves. Instead, they serve the purpose of helping individuals develop an affection for God. As A. W. Tozer rightly said, "I want deliberately to encourage this mighty longing after God. . . . The stiff and wooden quality about our religious lives is a result of our lack of holy desire. . . . Acute desire must be present or there will be no manifestation of Christ to His people. He waits to be wanted."[3]

Emphasizing Christ

As this book's subtitle states, many biblical counselors refer to the ministry they offer as Christ-centered counseling, gospel-centered counseling, or Christ-centered biblical counseling. Indeed, we feel it necessary to explicitly state the importance of Christ and his gospel, sometimes in contrast to broader forms of Christian counseling. True biblical counseling emphasizes at least the following aspects of Jesus Christ.

Christ as Savior

There is no room for compromising the role of Christ as Savior in the counseling room. The Bible says, "There is salvation in no one else, for there is no other name under heaven given to people by which we must be saved" (Acts 4:12). Counselees who do not know Christ may be focused on various problems they are facing. Their largest problem, however, is their lack of relationship with Jesus—being "without Christ" in this life (Eph

---

[3] A. W. Tozer, *The Pursuit of God* (Camp Hill, PA: Christian Publications, 1982), 17.

2:11–13) and thus facing "the penalty of eternal destruction" in the life to come (2 Thess 1:8–9). Biblical counseling, then, is in part an evangelistic ministry. We are seeking to "win" others to Christ (1 Cor 9:24–27). We are pleading with them to confess "Jesus is Lord," and believe in their hearts that God raised him from the dead (Rom 10:9). As churches and individuals make counseling available in their communities, lost people will seek help. Some have a religious connection to the church that is rooted in their childhood; others were drawn to the possibility of free help; and still others attempted other solutions that were not satisfying to them. But whatever their reason for coming, we as biblical counselors proclaim Christ and him crucified to those we counsel (1 Cor 2:2).

Practically speaking, we encourage you as a biblical counselor to speak to the challenges that brought counselees to the point of seeking help. The role requires that you encourage them, care for them, and provide direction in their areas of sin and suffering. But you must always allow those struggles to point counselees to the cross of Jesus Christ.

Christ as Provider

Whether a counselee comes to Christ in the counseling process or whether they have a proven history of faith in him, biblical counseling uses the counselee's relationship with Jesus as the foundation for the advice and care it gives. At conversion, many wonderful things happened to a person. Counselees were placed in union with Christ (Rom 6:5–11; Col 3:1–4), the righteousness of Christ was imputed to them (2 Cor 5:21), they were given security in Jesus (John 10:27–29; Rom 8:31–39), they were adopted as children of the Lord (John 1:12), they were redeemed from their sin (Eph 1:7), and they were declared "not condemned" (Rom 8:1).

We find, however, that many counselees still struggle to experience this new identity, to embrace it as reality, and to respond in love to the One who first loved them. That is, they need Christian growth. That is where we find security in an insecure world.

Let's consider what this might look like in the case of a couple attempting to work past an adulterous relationship. Married couple Scott and Tanya are genuine believers in Jesus, members of a gospel preaching church, and involved in lay ministry. Scott, however, recently committed adultery. In our experience, the first counseling meeting a struggling married couple attends normally occurs shortly after adultery is discovered, when the offender knows he or she has been caught. Scott is embarrassed, a bit angry (if only at himself for getting caught), outwardly remorseful, and wants the ordeal to be behind them as soon as possible. Tanya is grieving, ashamed, embarrassed, angry, and unsure how to move forward.

Each person desperately needs the help of Christ their Savior, albeit for different reasons. This man will need to embrace, remember, and meditate on all that Christ provides his followers because the process of repentance will be challenging. Digging into the depths of his heart will be painful, and only the work of Christ can change him. Since the physical act of adultery flows from a river of sinful lust, desire, deception, and buying into lies, Scott has a long road ahead. Similarly, his wife is almost beside herself. Tanya is in a horrible nightmare that refuses to end. She needs all the same things her husband does, but she needs them for the purpose of having her hope restored and finding encouragement, stability, love, care, and grace. Her road to healing is also long and full of very difficult life-altering questions to answer. For Scott and Tanya, only drawing near to Jesus and knowing he provides and cares for them will give them both a stable position from which to deal with their respective struggles.

Christ as Intercessor

Biblical counseling emphasizes prayer during the session and outside the session. We encourage counselors to pray for their counselees and vice versa because we believe in prayer (Jas 5:16). As wonderful as our prayers are, though, the Bible reminds us that Christ makes intercession for his children (Rom 8:34; Luke 22:31–32; John 17; Heb 7:25). Believers thus have an advocate with the Father, Jesus Christ the righteous. These truths emphasize the personal role of Christ in our lives. Not only has he given us believers a new identity, but he continually intercedes on our behalf. Knowing this is part of the help and encouragement our counselees can rely on as they work through each of their struggles. Those who know Christ can know he intercedes for them; those who do not have a saving relationship with Jesus will note that this is a compelling reason to trust in him.

Christ is central to biblical counseling. Without Christ in the counseling room, we are functionally reduced to a humanistic worldview. Biblical counselors recognize that our sin and our suffering can find ultimate answers in him alone. Jesus gives us a new way to think about doing life in a fallen world. Paul wrote, "More than that, I also consider everything to be a loss in view of the surpassing value of knowing Christ Jesus my Lord. Because of him I have suffered the loss of all things and consider them as dung, so that I may gain Christ" (Phil 3:8).

Biblical counseling not only provides counselees facts about Christ and what he has done. It emphasizes the personal affection and love for the Lord that come from a close relationship with him. The greatest commandment is to love the Lord with everything we are (Matt 22:37–40). Indeed, as J. I. Packer said, "There is . . . great incentive to worship and love God in the thought that, for some unfathomable reason, He wants [us] as His friend, and desires to be [our] friend, and has given His Son to die for [us] in order to realise this purpose."[4]

Relying on the Work of the Holy Spirit

While biblical counselors want to mature in every aspect of counseling, we also know that "unless the LORD builds a house, its builders labor over it in vain" (Ps 127:1). That is, we recognize that the success of our ministry is utterly dependent on God and his Spirit. The third member of the Godhead convicts those who are lost (John 16:7–8) and ministers to

[4] J. I. Packer, *Knowing God* (Downers Grove: InterVarsity Press, 1973), 37. This book is even better if read with insights into Packer's life story. For example, see Justin Taylor, "J. I. Packer's 11th Birthday Present: The Tale of the Bicycle and the Typewriter," Gospel Coalition, May 29, 2012, https://www.thegospelcoalition.org/blogs/justin-taylor/j-i-packers-11th-birthday-present-the-tale-of-the-bicycle-and-the-typewriter/.

believers in many ways. Consider four areas of the Spirit's work and their relationship to counseling.[5]

1. The Spirit's Work of Presence

Our world is full of suffering, pain, emotional hurt, and sin. The more one suffers, the more isolating life can become. Emotionally, it is difficult to watch others enjoy life when every personal moment is full of pain. Physically, it is difficult to engage in the gatherings that others might enjoy. When it comes to spiritual things, it can be humiliating to believe you are dry while others are drinking from flowing waters of spiritual blessings. So, while biblical counselors will encourage gathering, using the strength God provides, and serving others, we should remind sufferers of his constant personal presence with them. Ephesians 1:13–14 tells us believers are sealed in Christ with the Holy Spirit who serves as a pledge of our redemption. The ongoing presence of the Spirit guarantees a believer is never alone.

In a world of sin, the knowledge of the presence of God serves as an ongoing check and accountability system. If a person would not choose to sin in a particular way in the presence of others, then the same should be true when that person considers the ongoing presence of the Lord. Suppose, for example, you are counseling a believing couple. The husband is an angry man who expresses his anger in sinful ways. While there has never been a physical altercation between him and his wife, his harsh words, his hasty departures, and his doling out silent treatments are a normal part of life at their home. The man treats that house as his castle. He is in charge, and there is no accountability above him there. Yet, through the course of listening to the couple's story, you discover that he does not respond in any of these angry fashions at church or with the pastor. Why this discrepancy between home and church? There is something wrong with his theology. His behavior reveals that he is more concerned with what people think about him than what his Lord does.

5 For a more comprehensive discussion of the work of the Holy Spirit, see Erickson, *Christian Theology*, 880–98; Lambert, *Theology of Biblical Counseling*, 158–79.

Part of working with this man will be emphasizing the ongoing presence of the Lord that not only comforts him in pain, loss, and trial, but also constrains him (Prov 15:3). God's presence is comforting in loss and fearsome when we sin. Reminding our counselees of God's presence through his Spirit addresses both realities.

2. The Spirit's Work of Guiding

While we saw in chapter 3 that biblical counseling requires a Bible due to epistemological concerns, there is a second reason we open our Bibles with our counselees: the Holy Spirit guides through the Word of God. The Spirit oversaw the writing of the Bible, enlightens eyes and minds to understand it, and empowers belief in and obedience to it. Peter wrote, "No prophecy of Scripture comes from [one's] own interpretation, because no prophecy ever came by the will of man; instead, men spoke from God as they were carried along by the Holy Spirit" (2 Pet 1:20–21). Consistently throughout Scripture, the Spirit speaks on behalf of the Father and of the Son, not on his own accord (John 14:26; 16:13). There is One who can change the heart and move a conversation from mere words to life change. Biblical counselors open the Word, knowing the Spirit uses the Word to bring about the change needed so that the counselee loves, appreciates, values, and serves the Lord more effectively as a result. This does not alleviate the responsibility of the counselor to be wise, thoughtful, and biblical in his or her care, but it emphasizes that the counselor, rather than being responsible for change, helps the counselee focus on the proper agent of change (Rom 8:13–14; Gal 5:22–23; Eph 4:23; Gal 5:22–23).

3. The Spirit's Work of Assuring

Many Christian counselees struggle with questions regarding assurance of salvation because they feel the weight of their sinful choices. While we would never want to give such counselees false hope regarding the certainty that they are in Christ, we also don't want them to create a functional self-righteousness in a misguided attempt to stay there. The issue of functional self-righteousness is best addressed by helping people remember that assurance is not based on them and their deeds. It is a gift. They are to live faithful and obedient lives, fulfilling all the works God designed for them (Eph 2:10), while still recognizing that salvation is through faith in Christ alone by grace alone. Moreover, Scripture teaches that the Spirit was given as a seal for the day of redemption (Eph 4:30). That is the guarantee and the location of faith and hope.

Believers facing severe hardships can sometimes wonder if God is with them. We praise God for the Spirit's work of gripping believers when they feel they are losing their grip on the Lord.

4. The Spirit's Work of Gifting

The Spirit gives spiritual gifts to believers (1 Cor 12:11). Counselees are designed to serve Christ so that each person is doing his or her part to grow the church (Eph 4:16) with the strength that God supplies (1 Pet 4:11), and in such a way that no one position is either minimized or overvalued (1 Cor 12:12–27). When our counselees fail to serve in those ways, they miss the joy that comes from serving Jesus. In fact, the Spirit's gifting helps counselees understand some of the specifics of their individual purpose and calling.

Conclusion

Biblical counseling is built on a sound trinitarian foundation. The Bible serves as our source of authority and contains news of what we need for life and godliness (2 Pet 1:3). Humanity's greatest need is a reconciled relationship with God through a saving relationship with Jesus Christ. Biblical counseling seeks to build its system of care on a robust understanding of the Bible, of God, Jesus Christ, and the Spirit.

We can't imagine how any counseling approach that doesn't stress the presence and power of the triune God can please him, truly show love to counselees, and bring about his life-changing work in their lives. Our view of God, his Son, and his Spirit definitely influences how we develop a model of care.

Anthropology: How Should We View People?

The Bible says much about who we are as humans, how we were created, who we were intended to be, what went wrong, and our eternal states, including the believer's future restoration. By understanding these realities ourselves, we can more fully grasp our purposes and be better equipped to counsel others.

People as Created Beings

As created beings, we are dependent on and sustained by our Creator. We bear his image; we are relational; nevertheless, we remain individual and unique persons. Each of these qualities has significant implications for a counseling relationship.

Dependent on Our Creator

Because God created and sustains humans, we are dependent on him and he exercises authority over all parts of our being. From Genesis 1 through Revelation 22, the Bible makes clear that people need God for everything: their food, their work, propagation of the species, deliverance from sin and death, and ultimately for re-creation so that we and the planet will function again under the type of goodness and order God originally established. Humans are fully dependent on God for continued life (1 Tim 6:13). In fact, this was true in the garden even prior to the fall. God's first five days of creation week demonstrate that what humans needed to survive, God himself provided in advance. In the garden, God provided food, companionship, opportunities to exercise dominion, and the capacity for humans to bear children and continue the growth of the community. Adam and Eve also needed God's direction. The need for God's word, then, predates the fall. We see this in Gen 2:16–17 but also in Gen 3:8, which seems to suggest that God walked regularly in the garden with the first pair and apparently talked with them too. God gave clear direction to his people because they were—and still are—ultimately dependent on him for everything.

Image Bearers of Our Creator

Genesis 1:26–27 describes the sixth day of creation: "God said, 'Let us make man in our image, according to our likeness. . . .' So God created man in his own image; he created him in the image of God; he created them male and female." These two verses state three times—thus underscoring its importance—that God created humans "in his image."

While there are myriad interpretations as to what the "image of God" means, it indicates that men and women were intentionally created to be like God and mirror him in some capacity. Genesis 1–3 indicates several ways Adam and Eve bore God's image:

- They were given dominion over God's creation (1:26), as is evidenced by Adam naming the animals (2:19).
- They each had a spirit (2:7).
- They had choices to make (2:15–17; 3:6).
- They were created to be in relationship with God and one another (2:18–23; 3:8).
- They initially had no shame because they were holy and sinless before the fall (2:25).

Note that only humans, not animals, bear God's image. We are set apart from the rest of God's creation (Gen 2:20).

Any understanding of people is insufficient if it fails to understand them in light of their Maker. As Anthony Hoekema asserts, "If, as the Bible teaches, the most important thing about man is that he is inescapably related to God, we must judge as deficient any anthropology which denies that relatedness."[1] We cannot separate our understanding of humans from God. Referencing theologian G. C. Berkouwer, Hoekema continues: "For Berkouwer man must always be seen as he stands before the face of the Almighty, bound to God religiously in the totality of his existence. This relatedness to God, moreover, is not something added to man but is constitutive of his being. Whoever tries to see the human person apart from this relatedness to God will always fail to see him as he really is."[2] The most foundational concern counselors should have about counselees is the vitality of their relationship with God.

Relational Beings

As image bearers of God all people were also created to be in relationship. This is primarily a vertical reality, in which we were created in relationship with God, but we also exist in horizontal relationship with others. Humankind's creation in relationship to him and others mirrors the relationship that exists within the Godhead: the triune God has existed for all time in relationship with himself as Father, Son, and Spirit.

The God-human relationship was created from humanity's first day, and therefore should be of utmost importance to both the counselor and the counselee. But closely following were the important relationships of marriage, family, and then community. It was God's declaration in Gen 2:18, not Adam's, that it was not good for Adam to be alone, even though at this point in time Adam already existed in relationship with God. God created Eve so Adam would have a companion in the tasks set before him and could live in relationship with someone "corresponding to him" (2:18, 20).

---

[1] Anthony Hoekema, *Created in God's Image* (Grand Rapids: Eerdmans, 1986), 4.
[2] Hoekema, 58–59.

Unique/Individual

No two people are exactly alike. God is certainly creative in his making of humankind, as he handcrafts each individual in the womb (Ps 139:13–16). Each person has a distinct soul, unique relationships, unique experiences, and is individually responsible before God. Though the Father, Son, and Spirit exist as one (Deut 6:4) within the Trinity, each Person is unique and distinct from the other two. While unified, they are also diverse. Our individuality reflects the triune God's individual personhood.

Both Male and Female

Genesis 1 further teaches that God created his image bearers as gendered people: "he created them male and female" (v. 27). God initially created Adam and then Eve—someone like Adam (a human and an image bearer) but unlike him (a female). The male-female distinction remains significant throughout the Old Testament (Lev 18:22; Deut 22:5). Jesus affirmed this binary reality in Matt 19:4–5 in describing marriage as a lifelong relationship between a male and a female. Paul reinforces the same male-female complementarity in passages like Romans 1; 1 Corinthians 11; and Ephesians 5. While parts of our culture reveal confusion about various matters related to gender, marriage, and sexuality, the Bible plainly describes the Creator's design for two distinct yet complementary genders, male and female, and offers counsel on how they should relate to each other.

Both Physical and Spiritual

Finally, the entire Bible tells us people were created as both bodies and souls, as both material and immaterial. Remarkably, we are physical and spiritual beings (Gen 2:7; Eccl 12:7; 2 Cor 4:16; Matt 10:28). Theologians refer to this anthropological view with various terms: dualism, dichotomy, and people as a duality, a duplex, bipartite, or a psychosomatic unity. In this view, a person consists of two parts, an outer part (the body) and an inner part (variously called the heart, soul, or spirit). While there are competing views, the overwhelming majority of biblical counselors take this dualistic view based on the passages above.[3]

The Physical Nature of Human Life

Passages such as Gen 2:7 and Ps 139:13–16 (as well as many others) teach the physical nature of humans, as does our personal experience as real, physical people living in a tangible, physical world. Apart from death, we are inseparable from our bodies. Through them we express and experience our surroundings. Death, in fact, is viewed by Scripture as unnatural, temporary, and ultimately unacceptable to God, since he promises believers glorious, resurrected bodies (1 Cor 15; 2 Cor 5:1–5; Phil 3:20–21).

Yet Scripture does not give us exhaustive understanding of our bodies. Even the best medical researchers cannot explain many of the body's complex functions. For instance, while science has made great strides, there is much we do not understand about the way the brain works. We have yet to comprehend the way God breathes life into each developing fetus, yet it continues to take place. Ecclesiastes 11:5 reminds us of this continued reality: "As you do not know the way the spirit comes to the bones in the womb of a woman with child, so you do not know the work of God who makes everything" (ESV). Ultimately, while we can affirm the presence of the body, we cannot feign to understand all of its complexities. We are indeed "remarkably and wondrously made" (Ps 139:14).

The Spiritual Nature of Human Life

While people are physical beings, Scripture also teaches we are nonphysical, spiritual beings. While most secular therapists dispute the spiritual aspects

[3] For a thorough theological summary of these two major positions, dichotomy and trichotomy, see Grudem, *Systematic Theology*, 472–82 (see chap. 3, n. 13); and Hoekema, *Created in God's Image*. For counseling implications, see Ed Welch, "The Psychological Does Not Exist," Christian Counseling & Educational Foundation, May 29, 2014, http://www.ccef.org/resources/blog/psychological-does-not-exist/; and Winston Smith, "Dichotomy or Trichotomy? How the Doctrine of Man Shapes the Treatment of Depression," *Journal of Biblical Counseling* 18, no. 3 (Spring 2000): 21–29.

of the person, the Bible uses various words for our nonphysical nature: spirit, soul, heart, and mind. In many ways, these words overlap, functioning essentially as synonyms for the inner person, with occasional nuances in meaning.[4] As we saw in chapter 1, the most common term for the inner person, the heart, alludes comprehensively to a person's beliefs, motives, thoughts, desires, choices, values, or ambitions, including what is worshiped: such is a central concern in biblical counseling.[5] Under all these are concepts such as emotions or feelings, which are whole-person responses that come from our hearts (beliefs, motives, affections) and include physical effects.[6] These terms do not imply separate "parts" of a person, but various facets or functions of our nonphysical nature. The entire inner person—whether called heart, spirit, soul, or mind—thinks, loves, worships, chooses, and desires.

The Relationship between the Body and the Soul

While the above considered a person's physical and nonphysical aspects separately, we should note the relationship between them. The body and soul are inextricably linked. They impact one another: the soul finds its expression through the body and impacts it tremendously; at the same

[4] For these terms, see John Hammett, "Human Nature," in *A Theology for the Church*, rev. ed., ed. Daniel L. Akin (Nashville: B&H Academic, 2014), 285–336. For applications in counseling, see Jay E. Adams, *More Than Redemption: A Theology of Christian Counseling* (Grand Rapids: Baker, 1979), 113–17; Pierre, *Dynamic Heart in Daily Life*, 11–18, 241–242n4 (see chap. 1, n. 11); and standard English Bible dictionaries and Greek and Hebrew lexicons.

[5] On the comprehensive nature of the heart in Scripture, see Troxel, *With All Your Heart*, 15–22 (see chap. 1, n. 11); and Pierre, *Dynamic Heart in Daily Life*, 11–18. Both writers demonstrate how the heart describes how the inner person functions in cognitive, affective, and volitional ways, with all these heart activities interrelating and overlapping with each other.

[6] For a biblical overview on emotions and feelings, see Brian S. Borgman, *Feelings and Faith: Cultivating Godly Emotions in the Christian Life* (Wheaton, IL: Crossway, 2009); Jeff Forrey, "The Biblical Understanding and Treatment of Emotions," in Kellemen and Viars, *Christ-Centered Biblical Counseling* (see chap. 1, n. 2); J. Alasdair Groves and Winston T. Smith, *Untangling Emotions* (Wheaton, IL: Crossway, 2019); and Sam Williams, "Toward a Theology of Emotion," *Southern Baptist Journal of Theology* 7, no. 4 (2003): 58–73.

time, bodily issues can impact the inner person. For instance, anxiety presents itself in the heart/mind (desires/fears/thoughts) and the body (physical responses). One is not anxious solely physiologically or solely spiritually.

Ed Welch summarizes how both parts of the heart-body duality can influence each other in the realm of counseling: (1) the heart can affect the body (with psychosomatic consequences), (2) the body can affect the heart (by limiting its expression), (3) the heart does not obviously affect the body (ungodly people can enjoy good health; godly people can suffer poor health), and (4) the body does not obviously affect the heart (it can't deprive the heart of moral responsibility or spiritual vitality).[7] Ultimately, the relationships between the inner and outer person are extremely complex; we cannot oversimplify causation or neglect their interrelationship.

The Whole Person Impacted by Sin Yet Redeemable in Christ

Having explored the dual dimensions of each person—our outer person and inner person—we must remember that the whole person is fallen and impacted by sin. God created man and woman as bodies and souls; therefore, the tragic events in Genesis 3 impacted them as whole beings. More specifically, much of the curse on man and woman was explicitly physical—they would surely die and in the meantime struggle against God's fallen creation (e.g., working the cursed ground, suffering pain in childbirth). Yet their separation from God included a spiritual component: they were cast out of the physical presence of God and, as Rom 5:12 reminds us, that separation from God and the curse of death would spread to all people through them. Romans 5:16 goes on to tell us that the sin of Adam brought judgment and condemnation to us all. All humans, from almost

[7] Edward T. Welch, *The Counselor's Guide to the Brain and Its Disorders: Knowing the Difference between Disease and Sin*, rev. ed. (Glenside, PA: Christian Counseling and Educational Foundation, 2015), 29–36; and his earlier lay-level work, *Blame It on the Brain? Distinguishing Chemical Imbalances, Brain Disorders, and Disobedience* (Phillipsburg, NJ: P&R, 1998). Both books address the heart-body relationship in the context of counseling.

our beginning, have stood under that judgment and condemnation because of our first parents.

Furthermore, humans are totally depraved. Sin pervasively touches all parts of us, including the inner and outer persons, our relationships with God and others, and our capacities to carry out what God has designed us to do. We humans no longer naturally live in right relationship with God and others, and our bodies groan under the curse of the fall as surely as the rest of creation does (Rom 8:18–39). Apart from Christ, all people are enslaved to sin; even in Christ, believers are still in the process of being redeemed from it. But that redemption only comes by the power of his Spirit, not by any ability of our own. Alone, we have complete inability to know, love, obey, or honor God: the fallenness of the human soul and our tendency toward sin remains. We will explore this problem more in the next chapter.

Yet the example of Jesus, the perfect human, remains. Jesus Christ is the divine Son of God and the glorious, flawless image of God (John 1:1–18; 14:8–11; Col 1:15; Heb 1:3); becoming like him is God's goal for us and for those we counsel (1 John 2:6). In the chapters to come, we'll discuss how this plays out for various life struggles. But Jesus, as the last Adam, perfectly loved God his Father, loved his fellow humans, and ruled over creation, perfectly imaging God in the way God intended the first Adam and every subsequent human to do. Despite our failure, he has redeemed those who trust in Christ's death and resurrection on their behalf, and he is progressively conforming believers into his image until the day we will see him and be made like him (1 John 3:2). On that day each will have a sinless heart embodied in a glorious, eternal, resurrected body.

The most fundamental reality for humans is their need for this Savior. They need a restored relationship with their Creator. Since people are totally depraved and completely unable to come before God without his direct intervention, this reality overshadows any life struggle that is presented to counselors. Where humans are steeped in sin, the need for grace abounds. And that grace only comes through the saving work of Jesus and the power of his Spirit. This is what brings about lasting change and growth.

Implications for Counselors

As we saw in the previous section, humans are complex, so counselors must understand their struggles in light of this complexity. We should view people comprehensively rather than reducing them to only one facet (body versus soul or relational versus functional versus emotional). Disorder is inextricably tied to sin in all its presentations: volitional sin, the (wholistic) sinful condition, the impact of the sin of others, and a person's familial and societal context. To simplify disorders to only one of these fails to understand the complexity of a counselee's struggle and the path toward growth and change. Doing so impairs their growth and fails to love them well.

Further, because each aspect of human beings is fallen, humans in their totality need redemption. An individual's greatest need is not a body that is physically healthy, socially strong, or emotionally stable. He or she most needs the Savior. As biblical counselors, we must share the gospel with those who come to us for help, model the Savior to them, and point them to God's Word. We must care for each person's soul as it relates to God, as all of their life is lived before him and they are fully dependent on him.

As counselors, we also must remember the role of the body and help our counselees view and care for their own bodies properly. First Corinthians 6:19–20 reminds believers, "Your body is a temple of the Holy Spirit who is in you, whom you have from God[.] You are not your own, for you were bought at a price. So glorify God with your body." Our bodies and what we do with them matter, so we must use our bodies to express desires, thoughts, or emotions as instruments for righteousness, brought into submission to the Lord in all things (1 Cor 9:27). Biblical counselors understand that treating the body is the primary role of a medical professional; we must not step outside our role of caring primarily for the soul. Nevertheless, we should show concern for a counselee's wholistic health and help them foster an appropriate awareness and concern about their body. Indeed, we should be concerned for their eternal souls (encouraging obedience, Christlikeness, relationship with God and others), but also their bodies (encouraging proper diet, sleep, exercise, and medical evaluation and treatment as needed). While the balance between sin and sickness is not always clear, counselors must not ignore possible physical factors at work in a counselee's life.[8] A wise counselor seeks to understand these complex dynamics and care for the counselee accordingly.

Given the uniqueness of each person we encounter, counselors should see and treat each individual with dignity, honor, and respect (Gen 9:6; Jas 3:9). We must resist the temptation to think solely in terms of common life struggles or situations. For instance, after seeing twenty depressed counselees, some counselors might wrongly assume they are all basically the same. While there are commonalities among them, each person and their struggles are distinct. We must never assume we know a person simply based on what they are experiencing; rather, we should intentionally get to know each counselee as an individual, unique image bearer of God.

God created us as relational beings to express love within both our vertical and our horizontal relationships. Primarily, we must love him, but we must also love our neighbors—doing so fulfills the two greatest commandments (Matt 22:35–40). Not only should we exist in relationships, we should act in particular ways within those relationships. Counselors must understand the importance of a counselee's relationships with others. No man is an island; relationships impact those we counsel. We must understand the relational context of the person, primarily in terms of where they are with God but also how they interact with others (marriage, family, community, etc.).

Finally, we should pay attention to our relationships with our counselees inside the counseling room. How we relate to them and how they relate to us are vital dynamics in the counseling process. Similarly, to love the counselee well we must know them as individually and completely as possible. We must seek to know their unique struggles since each counselee is a unique and complex being created by God. To fail to know your counselee well is to fail to love them well.

---

[8] For more on discerning the role of sin versus sickness in understanding disorders, see chapter 36, as well as Ed Welch's *Blame It on the Brain?* and his *Counselor's Guide to the Brain and Its Disorders* mentioned above.

Conclusion

People are complex. Each person we counsel is a created, eternal, and unique image bearer of God, yet he or she is also fallen. Thankfully, God's Word speaks at length about the human condition and the solution to our fallen condition. Though fallen, we as believers are being redeemed. Though we are sinful, God offers wisdom and instruction. And though sin reigns in the present world, the Savior one day will destroy sin and death, and followers of Christ will live eternally in the presence of God. There we will be restored fully and yet even more gloriously than if the fall had never happened. It is this hope that allows us to walk alongside broken, sinning, hurting persons and lead them toward change.

Disorders: Sin as the Ultimate Problem*

In any helping field, accurate treatment requires accurate diagnosis, and accurate diagnosis requires knowing what to look for and why. Physicians know what tests to order for their patients because they understand how the body malfunctions and deteriorates. Similarly, counselors must understand the nature and origin of human problems if they are to know what questions to ask, what answers to listen for, and what remedies to apply. This issue lies at the foundation of every question a counselor must answer.

Competing theories abound. Some root counseling disorders in a person's nature—their inborn biological factors—while others see a person's nurture—their social environment—as the cause. Still others stress a complex combination of both.

Biblical counselors provide a more profound explanation. As we saw in chapter 5, people are embodied souls, created in God's image and inescapably related to him. Yet we also saw how sin corrupted our humanity. While both biological and social factors can influence human behavior, assigning causation to nature and/or nurture excludes this essential, deeper,

---

*This chapter is revised, with permission, from Robert D. Jones and Brad Hambrick, "The Problem of Sin," in Kellemen and Viars, *Christ-Centered Biblical Counseling*, 137–50 (see chap. 1, n. 2).

Godward factor—the soul in relationship to God. We must never look at people apart from their connection to God.

Sin as the Ultimate Problem

Accurately understanding people and their problems begins with assessing them through the lens of God's Word. The Bible's answer to what causes humanity's ills is simple yet profound: the root cause is sin. We were created in God's image but have fallen into sin (Gen 6:5; Eccl 7:20; Matt 15:17–20; Rom 3:23). Adam and Eve's disobedience in Genesis 3 set in motion a deadly dynamic that has produced immeasurable personal, social, and natural devastation. Apart from God's saving grace, we humans share a bad record, a bad heart, a bad master, and a bad destiny.

What do we mean by *sin*? Perhaps the 1674 Westminster Shorter Catechism supplies the most famous historical definition: "Sin is any want [that is, lack] of conformity unto, or transgression of, the law of God."[1] Evangelical theologians concur. "Sin," writes Millard Erickson, "is any lack of conformity, active or passive, to the moral law of God. This may be a matter of act, of thought, or of inner disposition or state."[2] In all its varied forms, sin is a failure to measure up to God's character revealed in God's law.

Biblical counselors seek to apply this historic, biblical understanding of sin to counseling. David Powlison summarizes: "Sin, in all its dimensions (for example, both motive and behavior; both the sins we do and the sins done against us; both the consequences of personal sin and the consequences of Adam's sin), is the primary problem counselors must deal with."[3] Ed Welch concurs: "The problem with sin is deeper than the problem with suffering. . . . A model of counseling that rises out of Scripture makes sin

---

[1] Question 14 in the 1674 Westminster Shorter Catechism, https://www.westminsterconfession.org/resources/confessional-standards/the-westminster-shorter-catechism/.

[2] Millard J. Erickson, *Christian Theology*, 2nd ed. (Grand Rapids: Baker, 1998), 596. See also Grudem, *Systematic Theology*, 1254 (see chap. 3, n. 13).

[3] David Powlison, "Biblical Counseling in Recent Times," in MacArthur, *How to Counsel Biblically*, 28 (see chap. 2, n. 12).

the critical human problem."[4] At the same time, Welch acknowledges, "Yet any Christian can recount times when someone spoke about sin in a way that treated people harshly and without love. In response, rather than shy away from sin, this challenges us to speak of sin with humility, patience, and kindness."[5] Sadly, biblical counselors don't always address sin wisely and graciously.

If sin against God is the core human problem, how should we apply this truth to the countless personal and interpersonal issues our counselees face? How does a robust biblical understanding of sin's presence, influence, and corrosive effects help us as counselors? And how do these wide-ranging descriptions of sin point us to Christ as our ultimate source of hope? To grasp the full breadth of life's struggles, we need a deep view of sin. Let's consider ten functional distinctions about sin that can help us minister to people wisely.

Thinking Carefully about Sin: Ten Functional Distinctions

1. The Personal Sin We Commit and the Suffering We Experience Due to Sin

We don't just sin; we suffer its consequences. Adam and Eve's sin brought God's judgment on them, their descendants, and the entire creation, resulting in suffering (Rom 8:18–27). In fact, it is our fallen, groaning, cursed creation that brings on natural disasters and physiological problems. While these do not cause us to sin, they can make having faith and living in obedience more difficult. In cases involving these factors, wise biblical counselors work with wise physicians and other professionals with expertise in alleviating suffering.

We humans are also sinned against. Much of counseling involves helping people handle past and present mistreatment. This category of suffering

[4] Edward T. Welch, "Are You Feeling Inadequate? A Letter to Biblical Counselors," in *On Redeeming Psychology*, Must Reads from the *Journal of Biblical Counseling* (Glenside, PA: Christian Counseling and Educational Foundation, 2013), 86–87.

[5] Welch, 87.

includes the fallout from trusting in false teachings within secular psychologies and unbiblical "common sense" advice, as well as what comes of pastoral neglect, various types of abuse, sinful family-of-origin influences, and societal and corporate sins, which vary by culture and time period.

Furthermore, we reap the consequences of our own sin. For instance, a man faces undesired singleness after sinfully divorcing his spouse, an alcoholic's drinking leads to his job loss, a woman is lonely because her abrasive tongue has driven away friends. The prolonged effects of personal sin should be viewed as a form of suffering, even when self-generated.

When we categorize suffering under the effects of sin, we confirm our thesis: *the* central problem *every* counselee faces is sin. Counseling thus involves both calling people to repent of specific sins and helping them handle their suffering brought on by sin, especially when the suffering is intense. At the same time, we help them learn to long for Christ's return and the renewed earth he will bring, where there will be no more sin, sickness, pain, or tears (2 Pet 3:13; Rev 21–22). Unlike our secular counterparts, biblical counselors hold out profound, eternal answers; we know and share that ultimately only King Jesus's return will make all things right.

2. Sin as Our Inborn Condition and Sin as Our Behavior

In viewing sin as the root human problem, we must not assume all sin results from deliberate personal choices. A fuller understanding of our fallen nature recognizes sin as an inner disposition or state, not just acts or thoughts. The apostle John seemingly draws this distinction between condition and behavior: "If we say, 'We *have no sin* [condition],' we are deceiving ourselves, and the truth is not in us. . . . If we say, 'We *have not sinned* [behavior],' we make him a liar, and his word is not in us" (1 John 1:8, 10, emphasis added).[6] In Ps 51:3–5, David self-describes both his actual sinful behavior and his sinful congenital depravity.

[6] See Phillip W. Comfort and Wendell C. Hawley, *1–3 John*, in Cornerstone Biblical Commentary, vol. 13, ed. Philip W. Comfort (Carol Stream, IL: Tyndale House, 2007), 333; and Tom Thatcher, "1 John," in *Hebrews–Revelation*, The Expositor's Bible Commentary, vol. 13, rev. ed., ed. Tremper Longman III and David E. Garland (Grand Rapids: Zondervan, 2006), 433.

Theologians call this inborn condition "original sin," referring to every human's natural sinful bent. This truth counters counseling theories built on the premise that people are inherently good and only do bad things because of outside influences. When people rightly see sin as more than bad behaviors, "they become conscious of the fact that they have been merely fighting the symptoms of *some deep-seated malady* . . . , an evil *that is inherent in human nature*."[7]

How do sin-as-condition and sin-as-choice affect our counseling? Counselors who minimize sin-as-choice risk ignoring the countless biblical commands to put off sinful behavior and put on godly words and actions. Counselors who minimize sin-as-condition might become unduly harsh or impatient with counselees who continue in sin. Because biblical counseling understands our fallen nature, we who practice it minister with compassion and humility as we lead people to choose biblical patterns. And we recognize that our ultimate hope is not in a superior theory and practice of counseling but in Jesus the Redeemer.

3. Sin as Unbelief and Sin as Rebellion

Theologians have long discussed whether Adam and Eve's sin was chiefly unbelief or rebellion: did they eat the forbidden fruit because they questioned God's goodness and doubted God's promises or because they rejected God's rule over their lives and wanted to do their own thing despite God's clear words?

As counselors, we must be careful not to classify sins but to get to know sinners. We might generically assume, for example, that anxiety and fear arise from unbelief, whereas adultery indicates rebellion. Yet while an anxious man might worry because he doubts God's ability to protect and provide for him, his anxiety might also arise from a rebellious heart that demands control of situations and refuses to trust God's guidance. Similarly, an adulterous wife might pursue an immoral relationship because she rebelliously wants to do what she wants, despite God's command for moral

[7] Louis Berkhof, *Systematic Theology* (Grand Rapids: Eerdmans, 1996), 227. See also Erickson, *Christian Theology*, 2nd ed., 518.

purity and marital fidelity. But she also might wrongly believe her marriage should have provided a kind of ultimate fulfillment, and since it has not, she is looking for another relationship, failing to believe the gospel promise that true fulfillment only comes in relationship to God.

We see the kind of discriminating wisdom biblical counselors need referenced in 1 Thess 5:14: "We exhort you, brothers and sisters: warn those who are idle, comfort the discouraged, help the weak, be patient with everyone." Consider the father who fails to lead his family in Bible reading and prayer. Why does he fail? Perhaps he is idle and needs to be admonished and called to repent. But perhaps he fears that his inaccurate understanding of the Bible will mislead his family, that his wife might correct him in front of their children, or that he might start such a practice only to stop again (like the smoker who says, "It's easy to quit smoking; I've done it thirty-seven times"). So, the question becomes, How should we counsel various people who struggle with the same sin but from different motives or attitudes? Wise counselors get to know each counselee.

4. Sin as Desiring Forbidden Objects and Sin as Desiring Good Things Too Much

There are forbidden items in God's law. God does not allow us to take someone else's property, sleep with someone to whom we are not married, or rob a bank. But most counseling doesn't involve addressing forbidden things. There is a difference between a wife wanting her husband to rob a bank and a wife wanting her husband to listen to her. The first act is forbidden; her desire is wrong because it's aimed at an immoral action. The second act, though, can begin as a good desire but can swiftly become a controlling one that crowds out more important things or replaces God as the basis of security. We must put to death both desires for forbidden things and submit to God our ruling desires for good things.

We see this second dynamic referenced in Jas 4:1–2: "What is the source of wars and fights among you? Don't they come from your passions that wage war within you? You desire and do not have. You murder and covet and cannot obtain. You fight and wage war." While James does not tell us what his readers wanted, he implies, by holding out the possibility God might give them their desired items, that they were not inherently evil. They were good things that had become inordinate, controlling desires—desires that became demands. In our experience, most counseling cases involve overgrown or steroidal desires for good things. In these cases, the most relevant passages of Scripture to share may not be those that rebut particular manifestations of sin, but those that remind us to love God with all our hearts. Our inordinate desires are modern synonyms for idolatry. Our aim in counseling is to encourage right worship more than just to eliminate bad behavior.

5. Sin as Internal (Concealed) and Sin as External (Revealed)

A person's outward behavior may appear godly, but inwardly he may be seething with sin. Jesus, after all, distinguishes between the outward sins of murder and adultery and the inward sins of anger and lustful perusal (Matt 5:22, 27–28). We also recall Jesus's stinging rebukes to the religious leaders of his day: "You clean the outside of the cup and dish, but inside they are full of greed and self-indulgence. . . . On the outside you seem righteous to people, but inside you are full of hypocrisy and lawlessness" (Matt 23:25–28).

This means biblical counselors should not settle for mere outward behavioral change from those they counsel. We will assess attitudes and intentions consistent with behavioral changes. For instance, resisting revenge should be accompanied by a willingness to pray for an enemy's ultimate good. Furthermore, we will distinguish the different types of replacement steps needed for internal and external sins. Putting off internal sins calls us to put on *Christ-centered attitudes* by repenting in private prayer. Putting off external sins calls us to put on *Christ-centered actions* by also confessing to those we sinned against.

6. Sin as Commission and Sin as Omission

Sins of commission involve words or actions which *should not* have been said or done. Sins of omission involve words or actions which *should* have been said or done but were not. First John 3:4 describes the first: "Everyone who commits sin practices lawlessness; and sin is lawlessness." James 4:17 warns against the second: "It is sin to know the good and yet not do it." Whether we transgress God's law or fail to conform to God's law, we sin. As we saw above, the Westminster Shorter Catechism captured this dynamic by defining sin as "any want [i.e., lack] of conformity unto [i.e., omission], or transgression of [i.e., commission], the law of God."[8] The well-worn Prayer of Confession from the Anglican Book of Common Prayer suggests this same idea:

> Almighty and most merciful Father, we have wandered and strayed from your ways like lost sheep. We have followed too much the devices and desires of our own hearts. We have offended against your holy laws. We have left undone those things which we ought to have done; and we have done those things that we ought not to have done; and there is no health in us.[9]

7. Sin as Rational and Sin as Irrational

Counselees understandably want to grasp the why behind their wrong behavior. Sometimes rational explanations make sense: people often do what they want for reasons understandable to them and to us who counsel them. Yet, on a deeper level, a robust view of sin reminds us, "All sin is ultimately irrational. . . . Sin ultimately just does not make sense."[10] Theologians call this "the noetic effect of sin," that aspect of total depravity involving the moral corruption of our thinking. Sin, in that sense, is insane. Ecclesiastes 9:3 observes, "the hearts of people are full of evil, and madness is in [them]." Therefore, it's no wonder Jesus described the prodigal son's repentance as coming to his senses (Luke 15:17).

---

[8] Question 14 in the 1674 Westminster Shorter Catechism.

[9] "The Prayer of Confession" from the Book of Common Prayer of the Church of England, https://www.churchofengland.org/prayer-and-worship/worship-texts-and-resources/common-worship/daily-prayer/forms-penitence.

[10] Grudem, *Systematic Theology*, 493.

Recognizing sin's irrational nature protects the counselor from the obligation or temptation to explain all behavior. To explain some sins in rational terms can easily lead to excuse-making or blame-shifting. Rational explanations can't always capture human struggles. To paraphrase philosopher Blaise Pascal, the heart has reasons that reason cannot reason. People want what they want when they want it.

Seeing sin as both rational—there are reasons for it—and irrational—there might be deeper, unknowable desires undergirding it—reminds us that change requires more than having accurate information, even divinely inspired biblical information. Problems don't come from raw cognitions; real change won't come from mere cognitive therapy. That requires the Spirit's work to transform a heart—not only its thinking but also its desires, motives, affections, and attitudes (2 Cor 3:18; Eph 4:17–19; Heb 4:12; 1 Pet 2:11). Counselees not only need God's Word; they need to commune directly with a Person (Jesus) in conversation (prayer) about that Word. Furthermore, they need God's Spirit to turn them inwardly and progressively from sin toward God.

8. Sin as Degenerative and Sin as Self-Contained

Too often we think of sin as self-contained, point-in-time bad choices lacking interconnection or momentum. Sometimes this is true. A person might sin in some one-time way and not repeat that particular sin. But sin is a predator with a progressive strategy for destruction. Galatians 5:13–26 reminds us the Christian's internal civil war is active and bilateral: while the Holy Spirit battles against our flesh, our flesh vigorously fights back. Ephesians 4:19 describes the hardness of heart within unbelievers who "became callous and gave themselves over to promiscuity for the practice of every kind of impurity with a desire for more and more." Sin is active: it "crouch[es] at the door," desiring to consume us (Gen 4:7). It can "harden" our hearts in deceitful, incremental ways (Heb 3:12–15).

This understanding of sin can help our counselees see that the whole impact of their sin is greater than the sum of its parts. Without it, a neglectful parent may look at each choice that put self before family and not think it adds up to a lifelong estranged relationship. The addict is often surprised at the subtle entrapment of substance abuse. Biblical counseling must warn people that their sin does not remain a contented servant; it seeks to seize and master. Passivity on the part of the counselor or the counselee will produce further degeneration. Sin must be killed, not merely kept in check.

9. Sin as Intentional and Sin as Unintentional

Leviticus 4–5 provides awareness of the sometimes-overlooked sin category of unintentional sin. Leviticus 5:17 explains it: "If someone sins and without knowing it violates any of the LORD's commands concerning anything prohibited, he is guilty, and he will bear his iniquity." In such a case, the sinning person of old covenant times was to bring an animal sacrifice "for the error . . . committed unintentionally, and he [would] be forgiven" (5:18; cf. 4:2, 20, 26, 31, 35; Exod 14:8; Num 15:22–31). While God views inadvertent sins as less severe than defiant ones, they too violate God's law, incur guilt before him, and require atonement.

As engaging God's Word brings increased light to our counselees (Ps 119:105) and they look more carefully at it (Jas 1:22–25), they will see new aspects of unintentional sin, including any tendencies to defend themselves, and they will draw near to Jesus for fresh forgiveness and help. As counselors, we should not assume every counselee's sin was defiant but should discuss sins with grace and charity. Thankfully, the Lord guarantees forgiveness and cleansing for all who sin—intentionally or otherwise—when they turn to him by faith.

10. Sin as Violating God's Explicit Law (Clear Guilt) and Sin as Violating One's Conscience (Confused Guilt)

While the Bible doesn't use the phrases "clear guilt" and "confused guilt," these terms can help us capture distinctions the Bible makes.[11] Clear guilt

[11] For a previous discussion of this distinction, see Robert D. Jones, "Distinguishing Between Guilt and Guilt, Biblical Counseling Coalition, https://www.biblicalcounselingcoalition.org/2017/07/18/distinguishing-between-guilt-and-guilt/.

comes when we violate God's explicit law stated in the Bible, whether we do so intentionally or not. Confused guilt comes when we allow some standard other than God's law to rule our consciences. The standard could be a misinterpreted or misapplied Bible passage (e.g., some Levitical law now fulfilled in Christ) or a human-made "law" (e.g., Christians must not go to movies). When we violate our own law, we are objectively guilty before God, not because we violated a clear command but because we allowed our consciences to submit to a standard *other than* God's law and then selfishly violated what we thought God wanted.

Passages such as Romans 14 and 1 Corinthians 8 and 10 describe Christians with weak consciences—people ruled by laws that are not God's.[12] Paul puts their dilemma this way: "to someone who considers a thing to be unclean, to that one it is unclean" and "whoever doubts [that a food is clean] stands condemned if he eats, because his eating is not from faith, and everything that is not from faith is sin" (Rom 14:14, 23).

If a woman who has sought to follow Christ in her marriage is sinfully abandoned by her husband, she *is not* guilty and *should not feel* guilty. But if she wrongly believes she is responsible for his sinful decision, then she will carry confused guilt. Why? Because she placed herself under a law (e.g., "I must keep my husband faithful; I must make him love and never leave me") that is not God's law. God did not hold her responsible to keep him from leaving; she couldn't prevent that. But she is guilty of imbibing an unbiblical law.

Conclusion

These ten distinctions show our need for a careful, practical biblical understanding of sin and for a Redeemer—Jesus—to save us from our sin (Matt 1:21). They evidence our belief that "sin is the deepest explanation,

---

[12] For a biblical approach to this topic and these passages, see Andrew David Naselli and J. D. Crowley, *Conscience: What It Is, How to Train It, and Loving Those Who Differ* (Wheaton, IL: Crossway, 2016).

not just one more problem begging for different and 'deeper' reasons."[13] No counseling diagnosis runs deeper than a detailed grasp of sin.

We can draw at least three implications from our study. First, our view of human problems determines who is qualified to speak to them. If sin is the primary human problem, then those with theological and practical expertise in dealing with sin—in its varied and complex forms—should lead the way in the field of people helping. The best counselors to offer Jesus's help to struggling people are skilled, theologically trained ones.

Second, our expansive view of sin requires expansive methods of ministry. Wise people helping involves flexibility in diagnosis and in treatment. As Powlison notes, "Differing diagnoses of the human condition inevitably demand different 'words' of cure, contain different implications, and construct different responses."[14] A biblical grasp of sin requires counseling dexterity.

Third, the biblical approach to sin allows us to relate more compassionately to those we counsel. We wrestle against the same tenfold sin problems our counselees face to greater or lesser degrees. All share a common struggle against sin. And because biblical counselors personally experience the same dynamics of sin, we can testify about and lead counselees to the same Redeemer for help and hope.

In our next chapter we will see how Christ calls our counselees to repent and how he provides his forgiveness for them—and us.

---

[13] David Powlison, *Seeing with New Eyes: Counseling and the Human Condition Through the Lens of Scripture* (Phillipsburg, NJ: P&R, 2003), 206.

[14] David Powlison, "Affirmations & Denials: A Proposed Definition of Biblical Counseling," *Journal of Biblical Counseling* 19, no. 1 (Fall 2000): 24.

Understanding Guilt, Repentance, and Forgiveness

As we saw in chapter 6, the ultimate problem all counseling addresses is sin and the curse and consequences resulting from them, even if the counselee doesn't acknowledge God's diagnosis or accept biblical terminology. This does not mean every counseling problem results from an individual's wrong choices. The person might be suffering from the sins of others, the consequences of Adam's sin, or a mixture of all the above.

In this chapter we want to prepare counselors to help people understand their guilt, repent, and receive God's forgiveness in Christ. Biblical counseling calls people to change, and true and lasting change requires repentance and living in light of God's forgiveness. Biblical counselors delight in helping counselees resolve their guilt and enjoy the freedom that comes from a restored relationship with the Lord. God the Father, after all, wants to hear a counselee's confession and forgive.

Helping Counselees Understand Guilt

Based on the biblical distinctions we saw between intentional and unintentional sin and between clear and confused guilt in chapter 6, let's consider four scenarios, each involving a recently married Christian woman.

Scenario 1: Angela knew believers should marry only believers (1 Cor 7:39; 2 Cor 6:14). She married a Christian man. She was neither guilty of sin nor feeling guilt.

Scenario 2: Beth also knew the Bible's teaching but despite the objections of her Christian friends, she married a non-Christian man. She was guilty of intentional sin and felt guilty.

Scenario 3: Crystal also married a non-Christian man, but she was unaware of the Bible's prohibition against it. Though guilty of violating God's commands, she felt no guilt, nor would we expect her to. Her sin was unintentional.

Both Beth's willful sin and Crystal's unintentional sin incurred true, objective guilt before God. Any thought, word, action, or desire that violates God's law, intentionally or not, is sinful. Yet the women's experiences differed in terms of guilt feelings. Guilt feelings are a function of the conscience. A healthy conscience is biblically instructed; it aligns with God's Word. Beth's conscience functioned properly. We rightly feel guilty when we violate Scripture. In this sense, guilt feelings are friends. They alert us to inspect ways we might have sinned. Sin is bad, but guilt—if dealt with properly—is good. Crystal's conscience was not biblically trained; therefore, unfortunately, she felt no guilt.

Now, let's consider *scenario 4*. Like Angela, Danika married a Christian man, in keeping with God's standards. Yet, unlike Angela, she felt guilty about her decision. Why? Because she believed she had sinned. How so?

Danika came from a wealthy home with successful, career-driven parents who insisted she marry a professional. Instead, she dated a godly man with a low-paying job and little prospect of upward mobility. She married him but believed deep down she had done something wrong by not obeying her parents. When she violated her conscience—her weak, biblically ill-informed conscience—she (properly) felt guilty. We not only *will* feel guilty when we violate pseudo-laws, we *should* feel guilty

(Rom 14:14, 23). Change will require Danika placing herself under God's law, not her own.

Four Scenarios of Objective Guilt and Subjective Guilt Feelings

	Guilty Before God?	Guilt Feelings?	Remedy?
1 Angela	No. She obeyed God's command.	No, nor should she	None needed
2 Beth	Yes. She intentionally sinned.	Yes, and she should	Repentance and renewed faith in Christ
3 Crystal	Yes. She unintentionally sinned.	No, her conscience was ignorant.	Conviction of sin, then repentance and renewed faith in Christ
4 Danika	Yes. She placed herself under an unbiblical law and did what she thought was wrong, violating her conscience.	Yes, but a confused form of guilt	Biblical instruction, then conviction of sin, repentance, and renewed faith in Christ.

In addressing this situation, some secular (nonbiblical) counselors or well-meaning friends might call Danika's guilt "false guilt" and plead, "Danika, stop feeling guilty. You did nothing wrong. That's false guilt you're feeling." After all, unlike Beth and Crystal, Danika did not disobey a clear command: the Bible does not require a twenty-four-year-old to obey her parents. But calling this "false guilt" can convey to Danika we are minimizing her feelings, denying her internal struggles, or issuing a moralistic "stop it, grow up, that's stupid" message. Guilt feelings can't be switched off or willed away. We must not dismiss her emotions, however confused they are. Moreover, labeling it "false guilt" misses the element of objective guilt that is present. Danika did indeed do something wrong—she wrongly placed herself under a law that wasn't God's law, then violated her conscience and felt guilty. Loving Danika means helping her understand and liberating her from her confused guilt.

Beth, Crystal, and Danika each need biblical counsel to deal with their actions before God and their consciences' interpretations and responses. The counseling task involves helping them sort out any confused guilt, feel appropriate guilt, confess and repent of actual sin, and receive God's forgiveness in Christ. Thankfully, whether their guilt and guilt feelings are intentional or unintentional, or clear or confused, this one answer gloriously soars before these struggling brides: the cross of Jesus Christ, the Savior who "is faithful and righteous to forgive us our sins and to cleanse us from all unrighteousness" (1 John 1:9).

So, how should we lead our counselees into true repentance and the joyful, liberating reality of forgiveness?

Helping Counselees Repent

Mindful of the discussed distinctions, we should help counselees see and own whatever sin is present. We do so in two ways. First, we help them see their sin in light of God's Word as it's rightly interpreted and applied. Paul tells Timothy that God's inspired Word "is profitable for teaching, for rebuking, for correcting, for training in righteousness" (2 Tim 3:16). We measure ourselves by the Bible as our standard. Hebrews 4:12–13 describes God's Word as a sword that cuts into the core of our souls and exposes the depths of our sin. James likens the Bible to a mirror by which we can truly see what we really are (Jas 1:22–25).

Secondly, given the Bible as our standard, sword, and mirror, we encourage people to ask God to search them for any sin, including hidden sin. Consider Ps 139:23–24 as a model prayer: "Search me, God, and know my heart; test me and know my concerns. See if there is any offensive way in me; lead me in the everlasting way." Our goals should reflect Paul's heart: "I always strive to have a clear conscience toward God and men" (Acts 24:16), and Paul's gospel-driven exhortation: "So then, dear friends, since we have these promises, let us cleanse ourselves from every impurity of the flesh and spirit, bringing holiness to completion in the fear of God" (2 Cor 7:1). As we saw in chapter 4, change occurs as God's Spirit convicts us of sin and leads us toward godliness in light of Christ's work.

As we lead people to see their sin, we should lead them to repentance. Consider weaving these eight vital marks of true repentance into your counseling as appropriate.

1. Realize You Have Sinned Primarily against God, and against His Law and Grace

After Adam and Eve sinned, they covered themselves with fig leaves and "hid from the LORD God among the trees" (Gen 3:6–8). In other words, they sought their own way to deal with their internal shame and avoided God. Thankfully, God pursued them and showed grace, promising a Redeemer and covering their sin (3:9–21).

In Scripture we find moving examples of God-centered repentance. In his confessions David was explicitly conscious of God:

- Psalm 32:5: Then I acknowledged my sin to you and did not conceal my iniquity. I said, "I will confess my transgressions to the LORD," and you forgave the guilt of my sin.
- Psalm 41:4: I said, "LORD, be gracious to me; heal me, for I have sinned against you."
- Psalm 51:3–4: For I am conscious of my rebellion, and my sin is always before me. Against you—you alone—I have sinned and done this evil in your sight.

We might also consider the God-focused prayers of confession embedded in Ezra 9; Nehemiah 9; and Daniel 9.[1] Asking counselees to study these passages and the above psalms will increase their God-focused confessions.

Moreover, in true repentance we acknowledge that we have sinned not only against God the lawgiver but also against God the Redeemer, the God

---

[1] Consider using the acronym END9 as a memory aid on where to find these helpful passages.

who graciously sent his Son to pay for our sins. We've spurned both his law and his grace.

2. Recognize the Severity of Your Sin

Many counselees don't grasp the depth of their sin. They minimize or excuse it. When questioned, they might reply, "Yes, but after all, I'm only human." This attitude ignores the fact that Jesus was (and is) fully human (as well as divine) yet resisted sin (Phil 2:5–8; Heb 12:3–4). True, we are fallen humans, awaiting the perfecting Christlike humanity God will bring about for his people (Eph 4:24; Col 3:10; 1 John 3:2). But even now we Christians are not merely human; we are regenerate, having new hearts. The same Spirit that raised Jesus from the dead lives in us (Rom 8:11)! We can offer these helpful insights to those who downplay their sin by saying, "That's just the way I am" or "I guess my flesh just got the best of me." Flippancy betrays an underestimation of the sinfulness of sin.

Moreover, when we believers minimize our sin, we fail to see how our sin led to Jesus's horrible death on the cross (1 Pet 2:24) and how it grieves his Holy Spirit (Eph 4:30). Freshly reading the crucifixion narratives that end each of the four Gospels can sober souls dealing with sin.

3. Own Full Responsibility for Your Sin

We cannot blame anything or anyone else for our sin. It does not result from our physiology, economic situation, in-laws, or ungodly culture. Satan tempts, but we succumb. While we might be victimized, we don't sin because we are victims. We can't explain our sin away by various notions of a "wounded inner child," an "empty love cup/tank/bank," or any similar deficit or psychological-need theory. No one sins because he is a 2 on an Enneagram test or a high "D" on a personality profile. Each person sins because each is a sinner.

This unpleasant reality is why we must help counselees in, say, a conflicted relationship give primary focus to any and all ways they have sinfully contributed to the relational breakdown. Jesus highlighted this in several ways:[2]

- In Matt 7:3–5, Jesus called us to focus on and deal with our own sin before addressing anyone else's, calling us hypocrites if we fail to do so. He urges viewing personal sin as worse than the other person's sin.
- In Luke 18:9–14, Jesus declared that self-righteousness breeds judgmentalism and that the only thing worse than being "greedy, unrighteous, adulterers" is being proud that you're not one.
- In Matt 18:21–35, Jesus showed how God's merciful forgiveness of our massive sin debt against him should move us to show mercy to those who have sinned against us in far lesser ways.

4. Deal with Your Sin on the Heart and Behavioral Levels

As we saw in previous chapters, the human heart is the center of all internal functioning—beliefs, motives, attitudes, will, thoughts, emotions, affections, desires, and volition. It's the seat or control center of the inner person—what rules us, drives us, and controls us—and is the source of all our behavior. True repentance not only addresses behavior, then; it cuts to the very heart of the person.

5. Acknowledge Your Sins of Commission and Omission

As we saw in chapter 6, sins of commission involve what we said, did, believed, and wanted that we should not have said, done, believed, and wanted (1 John 3:4). Sins of omission involve what we did not say, do, believe, or want that we should have (Jas 4:17).

Counselees sometimes unwisely focus on commission sins and forget omission sins, which are often the ones that wound more deeply. For example, while most married couples don't punch each other (commission),

[2] For further discussion of these themes, see Robert D. Jones, *Pursuing Peace: A Christian Guide to Handling Conflict* (Wheaton, IL: Crossway, 2012), 79–82, 139–42.

they often offend each other by omission sins: "He doesn't spend time with me"; "she doesn't respect me." This distinction helps guide our ministry agenda: it's one thing to help counselees curb their or her cussing tongue; it's another thing to help them replace ugly words with gracious ones. Wise biblical counselors urge counselees to identify, confess, and change their sins of both commission and omission.

One practical growth assignment that can aid in this goal involves a counselee completing a four-quadrant analysis (see sample below) and prayerfully considering both columns.[3]

	Sins of Commission	Sins of Omission	
Words	I yell at you.	I fail to ask how you are.	Words
Acts	I hit you.	I fail to do an errand I promised to do.	Acts

6. *Admit Your Specific Sins*

Some counselees settle for making generic confessions, attributing their sin to abstract categories, such as "flesh," "pride," or "self." Or they use summary terms without specific examples. We should labor to specify the form of flesh, pride, or self-centeredness the counselee manifests rather than accepting fuzzy language. After all, a confession such as "I'm sorry I was angry" is a good start, but it is insufficient for helping a warring couple resolve marriage conflicts. Better would be, "I'm sorry I spoke harshly to you. It was inappropriate and unkind. Please forgive me."

[3] Jones, 76–79.

7. Grieve over Your Sin

True repentance expresses sincere, godly emotions, including hatred, grief, and sorrow over our sin. James 4:8–10 urges, "Draw near to God, and he will draw near to you. Cleanse your hands, sinners, and purify your hearts, you double-minded. Be miserable and mourn and weep. Let your laughter be turned to mourning and your joy to gloom. Humble yourselves before the Lord, and he will exalt you." Of course, there is no defining or legislating how deep or how long someone's sorrow over their sin should be. A person's temperament, culture, or family background can influence how they expressed sorrow. Regardless, we certainly must not confuse worldly grief—that which lacks the marks of repentance in this chapter—with godly grief (2 Cor 7:10).

8. Desire to Change

True repentance carries a desire to forsake our sin and change, whether or not our circumstances change. In fact, one evidence of genuine repentance is a commitment to change even if the situation that occasioned the counselee to seek counseling improves. As Prov 28:13 announces, "The one who conceals his sins will not prosper, but whoever confesses and renounces them will find mercy." In its chapter on repentance, the Westminster Confession of Faith concisely combines the emotions of hatred and grief with this desire to change:

> By it, a sinner, out of the sight and sense not only of the danger, but also of the filthiness and odiousness of his sins, as contrary to the holy nature, and righteous law of God; and upon the apprehension of his mercy in Christ to such as are penitent, so grieves for, and hates his sins, as to turn from them all unto God, purposing and endeavoring to walk with him in all the ways of his commandments.[4]

[4] The Westminster Assembly Confession of Faith, 15:2, https://www.opc.org/documents/CFLayout.pdf.

Based on God's grace in Christ and dependent on his Spirit to help us, we commit to the practical steps of putting off sin and putting on righteousness (Col 3:8–10). In light of God's compassion and grace we can and should return to him.

We see a stunning call to grace-propelled repentance and change in Joel 2:12–13. Amid the Lord chastening his sinning people through a locust invasion, he offers through those dark clouds a bright shaft of hope: "Even now . . . turn to me with all your heart, with fasting, weeping, and mourning. Tear your hearts, not just your clothes, and return to the Lord your God." What is the basis for the call to return? God's preceding grace: "*For* [an explanatory conjunction] he *is* [not just will be] gracious and compassionate, slow to anger, abounding in faithful love, and he relents from sending disaster." (italics added) God's people need to grasp his grace, turn to him, and tear their hearts in true repentance. God's grace does not merely come in response to repentance; it precedes and motivates it. His grace makes our return to him both possible and desirous.

Helping Counselees Freshly Receive God's Forgiving Grace

To rightly conclude a chapter or a counseling session about guilt and repentance, we must rehearse the gospel. Stopping with the topic of repentance can lead to despair. We must not leave counselees depressed about their sin. Wallowing in guilt and living in endless remorse won't produce Christian growth. When counselees repent, we want them to grip and be gripped by God's forgiveness.

What do we mean by God's forgiveness? We might define it as God's decision, promise, and declaration not to hold our sins against us, because of our faith in what Jesus Christ did for us on the cross. Before the foundation of the world God designed a salvation plan (Eph 1:3–14) that includes "redemption through his blood, the forgiveness of our trespasses, according to the riches of his grace" (1:7). In that plan he decided to forgive all who repent and believe in his Son Jesus.

Furthermore, God declares his forgiveness to those who turn to Jesus. The gospel is God's announcement to guilty sinners that he will not hold their sins against them:

- Nathan said to David, "The LORD has taken away your sin; you will not die" (2 Sam 12:13).
- Jesus said to the paralytic man, "Son, your sins are forgiven" (Mark 2:5).
- Jesus said to the sinful woman, "Your sins are forgiven" (Luke 7:48). Note how Jesus not only told Simon that he forgave her; Jesus also told her directly.
- Peter said to the Jewish hearers at Pentecost, "Repent and be baptized, each of you, in the name of Jesus Christ for the forgiveness of your sins, and you will receive the gift of the Holy Spirit" (Acts 2:38).
- Paul said to the Jewish and Gentile proselytes, "Therefore, let it be known to you, brothers and sisters, that through [Christ] forgiveness of sins is being proclaimed to you" (Acts 13:38).

How should we minister God's forgiveness to our repentant counselees? We should call the nonbelievers among them to repent and believe in Jesus Christ to find God's initial forgiveness (see chapter 19). We should remind our Christian counselees first of the forgiveness God has already given them in Christ through his death and resurrection. Then, along with the passages above, we can assign these passages for study and reflection:

- Psalms 103:11–12; 130:3–4; Isa 1:18; 38:17; 44:22; Jer 50:20; and Mic 7:19 picture God's forgiveness of his people by supplying moving metaphors.
- Colossians 1:13–14; 2:13–14; 3:13–14 can bring direct gospel hope to guilty counselees. These passages address various common individual and relational problems.[5]

[5] We might also assign David's penitential psalms (Pss 32:5; 41:4; 51:4–5) and the prayers of confession in Ezra 9, Nehemiah 9, and Daniel 9. Both Neh 9:16–19 and Dan 9:14–19 provide striking displays of God's grace, compassion, and love toward repentant people.

Second, we should remind our Christian counselees of the fresh, daily, ongoing, Fatherly forgiveness God gives believers when they turn back to the Lord. In 1 John 1:5–2:2, the apostle reminds us that believers do indeed frequently sin, that regular confession is the normal rhythm of the Christian, and that Christ's atoning sacrifice pays for our sins. The promise of verse 1:9 should bring constant assurance to every believer: "If we confess our sins, he is faithful and righteous to forgive us our sins and to cleanse us from all unrighteousness."

A biblical counselor can reinforce the declaratory nature of God's forgiveness by functioning as a believer-priest (1 Pet 2:9) and orally pronouncing to repentant counselees words from a gospel passage that assure them of that forgiveness.

Conclusion

We close this chapter with the moving words of Charles Spurgeon that pull together the severity of sin and the glories of Christ with this image of a person about to be executed for his capital crime: "Too many think lightly of sin, and therefore think lightly of the Savior. He who has stood before his God, convicted and condemned . . ., is the man to weep for joy when he is pardoned, to hate the evil which has been forgiven him, and to live to the honor of the Redeemer by whose blood he has been cleansed."[6] We praise Jesus Christ for taking that death penalty we and our counselees deserved and freeing us from sin's curse.

---

[6] Charles Haddon Spurgeon, *The Autobiography of Charles H. Spurgeon, Compiled from His Diary, Letters, and Records by His Wife and His Private Secretary,* vol. 1, *1834–1854* (New York: Fleming H. Revell, 1898), 76.

Battling Satan and His Demons

Biblical counseling involves spiritual warfare against forces of evil stronger than you that hate you and those you counsel. Thankfully, they are not stronger than God the Father, Son, and Holy Spirit.

Bible scholars rightly view the Christian's enemies as threefold—the world, the devil, and the flesh. The first two are external to our souls and can merely (albeit severely) tempt us to sin but cannot cause us to sin. In that sense, we war against the temptations that the world and the devil bring against us. "The flesh" refers to that lingering sinful impulse or principle of sin that remains within the believer until death. While the believer has a new, regenerate heart, it remains a not-yet-glorified heart, leaving every true Christian longing for Christ's final work of perfecting us (1 John 3:1–3). Contrary to some misconceptions of Christian living, the primary form of spiritual warfare the Bible stresses is not warfare against Satan but the *internal* civil war of the flesh versus the Spirit (Rom 6–8; Gal 5:16–18; Col 3:1–17; 1 Pet 2:11). Our own remaining sin is our biggest enemy in walking with Christ.

While Scripture identifies all three enemies mentioned above, it presents a more complex picture than simply parsing which enemy is active when. The apostle Paul intertwines all three at work in the lives of unbelievers in Eph 2:1–3, while the apostle James intertwines them in Jas 3:13–4:10 in guiding Christians. At times, the Bible makes one enemy seem more prominent than the others. The world, for example, looms large in some passages (Rom 12:2; 2 Cor 10:1–5; Col 2:16–23; 1 John 2:15–17), yet in their broader context the devil and the flesh are never far away.

This chapter focuses on one of these enemies, Satan and his demons.[1] In one sense they are continually operating in the background—like a computer's operating system—"for our struggle is not against flesh and blood, but against the rulers, against the authorities, against the cosmic powers of this darkness, against evil, spiritual forces in the heavens" (Eph 6:12). Satan is the subtext of all Christian living passages, constantly opposing God and his people in both subtle and overt ways. Yet at times a Bible writer pulls back the curtain to explicitly show us the devil's direct working and to specifically tell us how to fight against him and his demons.

Why a separate chapter on Satan? Because biblical counselors sometimes forget the formidable role he and his demons play in opposing God's agenda and seeking to devour his people (1 Pet 5:8). We don't talk about demonic matters. Moreover, our counselees sometimes come with imbalanced views about Satan, either overemphasizing or underemphasizing the demonic. This can happen not only on the individual level but also on church and societal levels. As C. S. Lewis wisely warned, "There are two equal and opposite errors into which our race can fall about the devils. One is to disbelieve in their existence. The other is to believe, and to feel an excessive and unhealthy interest in them. They themselves are equally pleased by both errors and hail a materialist or a magician with the same delight."[2] While we must not underestimate Satan by ignoring him or forgetting his schemes, we must not overestimate him by saying more about him than the Bible says.[3]

---

[1] Since Satan is not omnipresent, we recognize he also works through demons. At the same time, Scripture routinely refers to him in the singular as our enemy. Our chapter will reflect both perspectives interchangeably.

[2] C. S. Lewis, *The Screwtape Letters* (New York: Macmillan, 1961), 4.

[3] For example, Satan disappears from the book of Job after Job 2:7. The rest of the narrative doesn't mention him. Similarly, there is no evidence in John 10:10 or its context that the "thief" who comes to steal, kill, and destroy is Satan. Exegetically, we need no earthly referent for Jesus's illustration to make sense. But if we do, the thief more likely refers to false Jewish leaders, shepherds, or so-called "messiahs" (10:8), although Satan's background operations appear in the broader context (8:42–47; 12:31).

Satan's Strategies

We have a real spiritual enemy named Satan who tempts us in many ways.[4] His methods involve persecuting believers (1 Thess 2:18), physically afflicting people (see the Gospel records), lying and deceiving (Gen 3:1–6; 1 Tim 2:14; 2 Cor 4:4; 11:1–4, 13–15), and accusing God's people before God (Rev 12:10; Job 1–2).[5] His temptation of Eve is particularly instructive as he appeals to desirable things: "[She] saw that the tree was good for food and delightful to look at, and that it was desirable for obtaining wisdom" (Gen 3:6). The apostles note direct Satanic connections to sexual temptation (1 Cor 7:5), unforgiveness and excessive guilt (2 Cor 2:10–11), and unresolved anger (Eph 4:26–27), although the nature of each connection requires further study in light of the interplay with the flesh and the world. His purpose is to conform us into his moral likeness, to make us like himself (John 8:31–47; 1 John 3:7–15).

Satan cannot make believers sin or prevent us from faith and obedience; the choice of sinful versus righteous behavior comes from the heart (Gen 3:6; Jas 1:13–15; 3:13–4:12; Prov 4:23; Matt 12:33–35; 15:17–20). The devil never made us do anything; we must not blame Satan for our sin.

Fighting against Satan

How should believers engage in battling against Satan and his demons?[6] Consider three warfare strategies.

---

[4] See Gen 3:1–6; Job 1:6–2:10; 1 Sam 16:14–23; 28; 1 Kgs 22:1–23; 1 Chr 21:1 (cf. 2 Sam 24:1); Zech 3:1–3; 1 Cor 12:7–10; 2 Cor 2:10–11; 4:4; Eph 6:16; 1 Thess 2:18; 1 Pet 5:8; Rev 2–3; 12:10.

[5] In Rev 12:10, Satan makes accusations *to* God *about* believers, not *to* believers. This text doesn't address whether Satan accuses Christians directly (e.g., seeks to make us feel guilty).

[6] For a brief treatment of this dimension of spiritual warfare, see David Powlison, *Safe and Sound: Standing Firm in Spiritual Battles* (Greensboro, NC: New Growth Press, 2019). For a more thorough treatment, see Powlison "The Classical Model," in *Understanding Spiritual Warfare: Four Views*, ed. James K. Beilby and Paul Rhodes Eddy (Grand Rapids: Baker, 2012). Other likeminded approaches include John Bunyan's classic, *Pilgrim's Progress*; Thomas Brooks, *Precious Remedies against Satan's Devices* (Carlisle, PA: Banner of Truth, 1980); William Gurnall, *The Christian in Complete Armour* (Carlisle, PA: Banner of Truth, 1964); John MacArthur Jr., *Standing Strong: How to Resist the*

1. Trust in Jesus Christ and His Certain Victory over Satan and Demons

Let's consider this victory through an already/not yet redemptive-historical lens:

Christ's Victory Was Prophesied at the Fall

Amid his judicial sentence against the serpent in Genesis 3, God issued the first gospel promise, what scholars call the *protoevangelium*: "I will put hostility between you and the woman, and between your offspring and her offspring. He will strike your head, and you will strike his heel" (Gen 3:15; cf. Rom 16:20).

Christ Began His Victory in His Earthly Life When He Withstood Satanic Attacks against Himself and Protected and Empowered His Disciples

We read about his successful resistance of the devil in his threefold desert temptation (Matt 4:1–11; Mark 1:12–13; Luke 4:1–13). By his intercession Christ protected his followers from Satan's attempt to destroy their faith (Luke 22:31; John 17:15), an intercession he continues to make even today (Rom 8:34; Heb 7:25; cf. 1 John 5:18). Moreover, he empowered his disciples to exercise authority over Satan's kingdom—"Look, I have given you the authority . . . over all the power of the enemy" (Luke 10:19).

Christ Secured His Victory with His Deathblow against Satan at the Cross and His Ascension to God's Right Hand of Authority over All Demonic Powers

Just before his cross, Jesus declared, "Now is the judgment of this world. Now the ruler of this world will be cast out" (John 12:31; cf. 14:30; 16:11).

Enemy of Your Soul (Elgin, IL: David Cook, 2012); and William F. Cook III and Chuck Lawless, *Spiritual Warfare in the Storyline of Scripture* (Nashville: B&H Academic, 2019).

The apostles explain this climactic cross-resurrection-ascension-session victory in several ways:

- "[Christ] disarmed the rulers and authorities and disgraced them publicly; he triumphed over them." (Col 2:15).
- "[God] exercised this power in Christ by raising him from the dead and seating him at his right hand in the heavens—far above every ruler and authority, power and dominion, and every title given, not only in this age but also in the one to come" (Eph 1:20–21).
- "Now since the children have flesh and blood in common, Jesus also shared in these, so that through his death he might destroy the one holding the power of death—that is, the devil" (Heb 2:14).

Christ Will Complete His Victory When He Returns and Brings Satan's Final Banishment and Eternal Punishment

The apostle John's vision heralds the final victory the returning Lord Jesus will bring: "The salvation and the power and the kingdom of our God and the authority of his Christ have now come, because the accuser of our brothers and sisters, who accuses them before our God day and night, has been thrown down" (Rev 12:10; cf. 20:10).

2. Rest in and Rely on Your New Birth and the Holy Spirit within You as Your Security and Source of Power against Satan

While Satan is stronger than we are, the Holy Spirit who lives in believers is stronger than Satan. Referring to the Spirit, 1 John 4:4 assures us that "the one who is in [us] is greater than the one who is in the world." For this reason most evangelical theologians rightly teach that believers—indwelt by the Spirit—cannot be demon-possessed. In our fighting against demonic temptations, the Lord invites us and the believers we counsel to cultivate a conscious, growing sense of the Spirit's constant presence within us and a confident trust in his protective power against Satan on our behalf (1 John 3:7–10; 4:1–4; 5:18–19; Eph 2:1–10).

3. Resist Satan through Gospel-Based Prayer, Faith, Repentance, and Obedience

What mode of warfare does the New Testament call believers to employ as we fight against the devil? While Jesus and those he sent out in Luke 10 cast out demons, it's doubtful whether other average followers of Jesus did so or were commanded to do so in the Gospels or Acts.[7] Instead, our Lord instructed us to pray, "And do not bring us into temptation, but deliver us from the evil one" (Matt 6:13). The same Jesus who resisted and overcame Satan's attacks in Matthew 4 directs his followers to cry out to God for help. Christ's intercession for us reminds us of both Christ's power over Satan and our deep need to seek that help.

Nowhere in their letters to the churches do Christ's apostles describe or prescribe exorcistic ministries. Instead, the key word for fighting against Satan and his demons—repeated by the apostles Paul, James, and Peter, in Eph 6:13; Jas 4:7; and 1 Pet 5:9 respectively—is the Greek verb *anthistēmi* (and its variants), usually translated as "resist" or "stand against."[8]

- "Therefore, submit to God. Resist the devil, and he will flee from you" (Jas 4:7).
- "Resist him, firm in the faith, knowing that the same kind of sufferings are being experienced by your fellow believers throughout the world" (1 Pet 5:9).
- "For this reason take up the full armor of God, so that you may be able to resist in the evil day, and having prepared everything, to take your stand" (Eph 6:13).

---

[7] One possible exception appears in Mark 16:17, but only if we assume it refers to all believers (who will also safely handle snakes and drink poison) and if we accept Mark 16:9–20 as original, though it is absent from the earliest known ancient manuscripts of Mark. Unlike unbelieving Jews in Acts 19:11–16, believers who did exorcistic ministries seemed to carry special authority: like the seventy-two Jesus sent in Luke 10:17–20 and Philip the evangelist, one of the Seven (Acts 6:5; 21:8), in Acts 8:5–13.

[8] The Greek verb appears twelve times in the New Testament: Matt 5:39; Luke 21:15; Acts 6:10; 13:8; Rom 9:19; 13:2; Gal 2:11; Eph 6:13; 2 Tim 3:8; 4:15; Jas 4:7; 1 Pet 5:9.

Based on these verses and their surrounding contexts (Jas 3:13–4:12; 1 Pet 5:5–11; Eph 6:10–20), resisting Satan involves submitting to God, being self-controlled and alert, standing firm in faith, and putting on the whole array of spiritual armor God provides. Assigning counselees to study, pray over, and apply these passages will give them abundant biblical counsel to fight against the evil one. The Ephesians 6 passage especially highlights the place of God's Word (v. 14, "Stand, therefore, with truth like a belt around your waist"; v. 17, "Take the helmet of salvation and the sword of the Spirit—which is the word of God") and prayer (v. 18, "Pray at all times in the Spirit"). In other words, rather than being mystical or eerie, resisting the devil involves diligently pursuing the basic disciplines of gospel-based Christian growth seen throughout these letters. The apostle Peter called Simon the Sorcerer to repent and pray (Acts 8:9–25; cf. 19:18–20), confronting Simon directly and not Satan. Consider also Eph 2:1–3; 4:26–27; 1 John 2:12–14; 3:8–12; Matt 6:13; 4:4, 7, 10; Jude 9; and Rev 12:10–12, where similar themes of resisting the devil through faith, repentance, Scripture, prayer, and obedience appear.

Distinguishing Demonic Attacks from Remaining Sin

Let's consider another question we might face as biblical counselors: Can we distinguish between temptations that might arise primarily from our hearts and primarily as direct temptations from Satan? If so, how? Our general answer is that we cannot. Our triad of enemies—the world, the flesh, and the devil—typically function together against us.

Yet there seem to be occasions when one of these enemies—in this case Satan and his demons—might seem more prominent than the other two. The seventeenth-century English Puritan pastor, Thomas Watson, recognizes the difficulty in making such distinctions. Yet he suggests three guidelines to discern when a temptation—a "motion" to sin—might come primarily from the flesh versus the devil:

1. "Motions to evil that come from our hearts spring up more leisurely and by degrees; motions from Satan arise more suddenly."

Watson cites David taking a census of Israel in 1 Chr 21:1 and the flaming arrows of the evil one in Eph 6:16.

2. "Motions to evil that come from our hearts are not so terrible; motions from Satan are more ghastly and frightful." Watson includes motions such as blasphemy and self-murder. He again cites Eph 6:16, noting that the fiery darts are flashes of fire that startle and frighten the soul.
3. "Motions to evil that come from our hearts are less loathsome; motions from Satan are loathsome to us and we strive against them and flee more quickly from them." Watson cites Moses fleeing from the serpent in Exod 4:3 and Joab's deceitfulness in 2 Samuel 14.[9]

Watson's three criteria helped me (Bob) with two counseling cases. Gail was a mature Christian wife and mother who struggled with common forms of anxiety and perfectionism. She was serious about her faith and was making good progress through our sessions. Yet on one Saturday morning she had a rage episode unlike anything she had experienced before. "I let loose," she mourned, "screaming at my kids, getting in their faces, shouting profanity." After explaining this three-minute tirade, she calmed down and then cried. Gail was angry at God, feeling betrayed by him after her several weeks of previous progress. *Where did that come from?* she wondered. *I've never blown up like that.* Up to that morning, her relationship with the Lord had been growing, she had been feeling less fearful, and she was more aware of her sin and God's grace. Her children were no more disobedient than usual and her hormonal struggles that often tempted her toward impatience were not factors that day. She had even attended a church mother-daughter banquet the night before and was especially encouraged by the speaker.

So, where did Gail's fury come from? I led her to Eph 6:10–20 and Watson's list. While she bore responsibility for her anger, we both agreed that it likely was a fiery dart from the evil one. Gail's intense tirade met Watson's three criteria: it was sudden and certainly not part of her normal

[9] Thomas Watson, *The Lord's Prayer* (London: Banner of Truth, 1965), 261.

sin pattern, it frightened her, and it was loathsome to her. We therefore addressed it according to the perspective of Ephesians 6 and helped her implement the biblical counsel above.

Richard was an international church planter who had just come back from a successful six-month home assignment to raise funds, see extended family, and get recharged. His marriage was fine, his family was healthy, and his church plant was progressing. In other words, his life was sailing smoothly with no significant circumstantial problems. Yet one time Richard awoke in the middle of the night with a panic attack and with a deep, dark sense of his failure as a minister. This disturbing experience, having no logical explanation, haunted him a few days. Richard contacted me. "Am I going crazy?" he asked. "Am I having a mental breakdown or some neurological event?" Like Gail, Richard found Watson's perspective helpful. He too asked God to deliver him from the evil one (Matt 6:13) and to help him follow the counsel of this chapter to battle not only against the world and his remaining flesh but also against Satan.

How can we distinguish what's primarily flesh-incited and primarily demon-incited? Humbly and tentatively. Reflecting approvingly on Watson's three criteria, Sinclair Ferguson wisely concludes, "At no point of our experience do we come to the place where we can rely on a foolproof system. . . . As we grow in grace and in the knowledge of God's Word and his ways, we will naturally become more sensitive to the distinctions between the imaginations of our own minds, the temptations of our own hearts, the workings of Satan, and the clear voice of Christ."[10]

Conclusion

As biblical counselors we should cry out to God for increasing wisdom to discern and follow the voice of our Shepherd-King. While there is not a demon behind every bush causing our sin, Satan's demons are active, along with the world and our own flesh, in tempting us to sin. Therefore,

[10] Sinclair B. Ferguson, *The Christian Life: A Doctrinal Introduction* (Carlisle, PA: Banner of Truth, 1981), 142–44.

trust in and lead those you counsel to trust in Jesus's victory over the world, the flesh, and the devil; rest in and rely on your new birth and the Holy Spirit within you; and resist Satan through gospel-based prayer, faith, repentance, and obedience. In that sense, we concurrently fight the world, the flesh, and the devil on the multiple spiritual-warfare fronts described earlier.

Interacting with Alternative Counseling Models

We believe the best form of counseling is Christ-centered biblical counseling. We do not believe we need to whisper that commitment under our breath, conceal it, or feel shame for believing it (Rom 1:16). We believe it is superior to all other forms of counseling. No true Christian, after all, will advertise "unbiblical counseling" or "non-Christ-centered" counseling.

Part 2 of this work explained what we mean by Christ-centered biblical counseling. Chapters 3–8 provided the theological foundation for those genuinely committed to biblical counseling as defined in this book. For example, biblical counselors are committed to using their Bibles not only to inform how the counselor behaves or conducts the session, but also to share the gospel with those who do not have a saving relationship with Christ and to discuss the beauty and implications of the gospel with those who do.[1] Those who follow this route seek to understand how the counselee's relationship with the Lord impacts their loves, wants, thoughts, and behaviors.

[1] While one book cannot summarize everything a given position advocates, it can reveal in interesting ways how different approaches counsel. For this, see Greggo and Sisemore, *Counseling and Christianity* (see chap. 1, n. 4), along with the review by John Henderson, on the website of Gospel Coalition, October 3, 2012, https://www.thegospelcoalition.org/reviews/counseling-christianity/.

For those committed to this approach, this raises a vital question: "How does a Christ-centered biblical counselor interact with different counseling models and methods?"

Acknowledge the Differences and Refuse to Compromise

Those committed to sharing the gospel along with all its implications with counselees will inevitably find themselves at odds with those who hold to a different position. Some systems of counseling, whether secular or Christian, will not believe that presenting the gospel or sharing gospel-centered truths is necessary. We disagree.

As Christ followers, we believe we are ambassadors for Christ. When confronted with psychologized counselees, other counseling models and applications of their models, or truth claims vying for a place in our approach to counseling, we must exercise zeal and courage for the name of Christ.[2]

We thus encourage you to adopt the practical model explained in the forthcoming chapters (esp. 10 and 13–15) because how you develop and use your model in counseling practice will determine what kind of counselor you will be. As you continue to learn, study, and practice counseling you will improve your model and your use of it. How that model grows will depend on the kinds of information you incorporate. If the growth or application of your model results in giving up the primary place for Jesus and his gospel, then you are no longer functioning as a Christ-centered biblical counselor.

Give Thanks for Other Forms of Available Counseling

Imagine a counselee attending a first session and deciding that biblical counseling is not his desire. For reasons known only to him, he decides

---

[2] Consider, for example, the blessing that came of Phinehas's zeal in Numbers 25 (see Ps 106:29–31) or what happened as a result of the apostles choosing to obey God rather than men (Acts 5:29). Without their faithfulness, we would not know the good news of Christ today.

that he does not want to talk about Jesus or the Bible. You know that a "God-sized" hole nevertheless exists in him. However, you also know that he desperately needs to speak with a person who cares about him, who wants to help him, and who will give him strategies and suggestions that might stabilize his thinking. It is even possible the Lord will use another form of counseling to help your counselee be in the best possible position to hear, listen, and obey the gospel of Jesus Christ in the future. For this, you can give thanks.

Moreover, giving thanks for and respect to other service providers helps a biblical counselor establish a meaningful place as a community service provider. In our experience, the secular world can be tolerant and even thankful for our ministry. I (Rob) have personally been involved, as have many of our other counselors, in court-ordered counseling. They have accepted our counsel at both the adult and juvenile levels. Their acceptance came from us being a valuable part of the community rather than adversaries. When biblical counselors are respectful and thankful for the work done by others in the mental health community, it shows our interest in loving our neighbors and contributing to the community. It is helpful, in fact, to ask for one seat at the table to address community needs rather than trying to take over the table. As we serve alongside other mental health service providers, we will find many more opportunities to share Christ and to be thankful for what other groups provide.[3]

Learn from Other Experts

Many counselors tend to serve those who present with certain kinds of challenges. For example, one counselor may normally help those in sexual sin, another serves marriages in trouble, and a different counselor works with pastors struggling in ministry. While ministries often attempt to put counselees with counselors who have specific experience or expertise, sometimes we have to compromise. For example, a pastor or counselor

---

[3] For a fuller explanation of how a church can be a valuable and thankful part of the community, see Stephen Viars, *Loving Your Community: Proven Practices for Community-Based Outreach Ministry* (Grand Rapids: Baker, 2019).

who normally works with marriages might get a case involving significant childhood sexual abuse or a certain psychiatric diagnosis. How the biblical model is applied could change significantly with this new case. There may be things that he needs to keep in mind, specific questions to ask, or pitfalls to avoid. Thus, in reading material—secular or Christian—he might learn from his new counseling experience. This does not take the place of learning from the actual counselee (see esp. chapter 13); rather, it is an opportunity for him to glean from those who have worked repeatedly with those kinds of situations for many years.

Consider the example of suicidal threats or ideation. Decades ago, clinicians developed a triage system to judge the likelihood that a person would attempt to take their life. Now, after decades of analysis, we have learned that the triage system was not as accurate as hoped. One practical implication is that counseling ministries now must evaluate whether one discussion of suicidal threats should result in an additional consent form, a behavioral contract, or even a revision of the confidentiality agreements.

Counsel long enough, and you will experience new cases and various kinds of challenges. When that occurs, you need to read. Thankfully, there are many more biblical counseling, Christian counseling, and secular resources available to us now than even twenty years ago. Sometimes people with diverse views have an area of expertise that can helpfully describe the typical characteristics of the situation. For example, how might we counsel a Christian diagnosed with schizophrenia? While most biblical counselors haven't worked regularly with those having this diagnosis, some secular counselors who work with these individuals daily can give us important insights that we can actively process through our biblical model.

There is another reason to read. Depending on the context for your future counseling, you might have many counselees who are heavily psychologized. Even pastors, who normally devote most of their attention to those within their local churches, inevitably serve those who have been heavily influenced by a counseling model different from their own. Counselors in these situations may have to navigate some tricky issues. Learning about the approach and philosophy of these alternative approaches can help.[4]

Interact with Other Approaches to Improve Your Counseling

We have suggested to this point that we should not wane in our commitment to Christ-centered biblical counseling, that we should give thanks for the alternative approaches that serve those who want them, and that we should be willing to learn from them. Now, we must address the most challenging question: How should a person committed to Christ-centered biblical counseling interact with a counselee who holds a different view? Or how would a counselor continue to improve their model or use of their model based on what they read or hear from those who advocate a different position?

Counseling models, ministry purposes, and caring for people do not always get better with time. We do not automatically become more faithful, more biblical, or wiser with age and experience. We might have twenty years of improved experience or have one year of experience we repeat twenty times. It's even possible to get worse at counseling, especially when we allow sin in our own lives to cloud our judgment.

How do we grow, mature, and interact with alternative models so that our model improves? How do we speak to a heavily psychologized counselee? We need a careful process.

Step 1: Master What the Bible Says about the Subject Matter Addressed

This statement contains several significant components. First, it means we must start with our Bibles. We want to know what the Bible says about a topic, to the degree that we can study it, so that is our starting point.

---

[4] David Powlison, "How Do You Help a 'Psychologized' Counselee?" *Journal of Biblical Counseling* 15, no. 1 (1996): 2–7.

Second, it means we must apply thoughtful and critical thinking to our Bible study.[5] As biblical counselors, we have exegetical observations to make, but we also have biblical and systematic theology considerations. Your exposure to the Bible, whether through exegesis and theology courses, your own faithful reading, or the usual preaching and teaching ministries, equips you with needed skills to understand what the Bible teaches and how to wisely apply it. To the degree possible, you should enter evaluations with an initial understanding of what Scripture teaches on a particular subject.[6] Many of our psychologized counselees have become "experts" through Internet searches. Whether clinically diagnosed or self-diagnosed, our counselees are quick to explain various aspects of their conditions and the reasons for them. At the same time, these counselees tend to be ignorant of what the Bible teaches about their behaviors, their heart attitudes, and the concerns for the immaterial part of their being.

Whether we are speaking to a counselee or considering incorporating ideas or techniques into our counseling approach, we begin by mastering what God says about the subject matter at hand.

Step 2: Understand Accurately and Charitably What the Other Approach Teaches

The Bible warns against making assumptions (Prov 18:13). This applies to how we relate to our counselees and also how we relate the material of others. Other counseling systems and psychologized counselees often refer to the material in the *Diagnostic and Statistical Manual* (*DSM-5*), the authoritative resource on mental health disorders used by practitioners and insurance companies to provide diagnosis and recommended

[5] See the chapters on using biblical narrative (John Henderson), Wisdom literature (Deepak Reju), the Gospels (Rob Green), and the epistles (Heath Lambert) in Kellemen and Forrey, *Scripture and Counseling*, 318–79 (see chap. 1, n. 2).

[6] To gather some key Bible passages, consider your biblical counseling training course materials, biblical counseling books and minibooks on the specific topic, the resource section of the Biblical Counseling Coalition's website, and the twenty chapters that compose Parts 4 and 5 of this book.

treatments.[7] Some may find it easy to minimize what the *DSM*-5 says for several reasons: (1) A counselor does not determine a diagnosis through medical testing such as a blood test or a scan (e.g., CT, PET, or MRI). The definition, diagnosis, and description of mental disorders emphasize the porous nature of the categories, the wealth of environmental factors that affect mental health, the definition of what is "normal" in a given time and culture, and the importance of clinical wisdom even when a client satisfies the criteria for a disorder.[8] (2) This is the seventh version since the initial publication in 1952 [*DSM-I, II, III, III-R, IV, IV-TR*, and *5*]. The versions have changed in such substantive ways that the editors of early additions have criticized the later ones.[9] (3) Some categories in the *DSM-5* seem dubious and much more behavioral than medical.[10] (4) Contrary to a biblical anthropology, it fundamentally assumes people are physical bodies without spirits.

Nevertheless, we find at least four valuable uses for the *DSM*: (1) When speaking with a psychologized counselee who has been given a *DSM* diagnosis, the counselor can read about the diagnosis and discover some of the questions to ask their counselee. (2) When a counselee exhibits many of the characteristics associated with a particular diagnosis, it can help us consider other potential risk factors and formulate additional questions. (3) As we continue to grow, understand, and apply our biblical counseling model, we can gain insights from what others with counseling experience have to say. (4) For those who practice as state-licensed counselors, *DSM* diagnostic codes are typically required for insurance reimbursement.

I (Rob) supervised a master's thesis on the issue of domestic violence. Our student had been working in the legal system for years. He

---

[7] American Psychiatric Association, *Diagnostic and Statistical Manual of Mental Disorders*, 5th ed. (Arlington, VA: American Psychiatric Association, 2013) (hereafter cited as DSM-5).

[8] See *DSM-5*, 1–23.

[9] For an interesting perspective on the history and trajectory of the *DSM*, see Roger K. Blashfield et al., "The Cycle of Classification: *DSM-I* through *DSM-5*," *Annual Review of Clinical Psychology* 10 (2014): 25–51.

[10] E.g., new diagnoses include hoarding disorder, caffeine withdrawal disorder, and binge eating disorder.

wanted to help the church grasp a very simple point: when dealing with an abuser, you cannot do marriage counseling before you do individual violence counseling with the abuser and bring separate care for the victim.[11] His exposure to abusers in the court system and the class that he conducted for hundreds of offenders gave him insight into the mind of an abuser and to some extent into the mind of the abused. What he learned from the experience of working in a secular environment, when processed through Scripture and applied to counseling, has changed the way he and others counsel parties in physically abusive situations. Whether speaking to a counselee or reading to improve our knowledge of counseling, we should honestly evaluate what others are saying so that we can properly critique it as needed.

Step 3: Evaluate What You Learned Using Your Bible.

Doing this properly might require several layers of evaluation. First, we often must do some additional Bible study. Since our initial study of Scripture occurred before we had all the questions and potential insights from others to use as reference, we may have new questions to pose to the Bible. Before we move to the evaluation process, we may need to take what we learned and go back to be sure we have captured all the biblical teaching pertaining to the relevant subject.

Second, in chapters 3–8 we argued that there is theological and exegetical foundation for biblical counseling. The things discussed in those chapters also serve to evaluate the truth claims of other systems. Consider these questions:

- What is the source of truth and the role of the Bible?[12] Some approaches may claim their insights are from the Bible, others may claim they are consistent with the Bible, and still others may suggest they are outside the Bible.

---

[11] See Chris Moles, *The Heart of Domestic Violence: Gospel Solutions for Men Who Use Control and Violence in the Home* (Bemidji, MN: Shepherd Press, 2010).

[12] See David Powlison, "Modern Therapies and the Church's Faith," *Journal of Biblical Counseling* 15, no. 1 (Fall 1996).

- What is the role of God or the Godhead in the system? Any system without the Trinity, without allegiance to Jesus, and without the gospel is not Christian.[13]
- How does the system understand people? What does it say about our spiritual and physical components?
- What problem(s) is the system trying to solve? (See chapter 6.) Some may seek to help a person function in society, other systems incorporate a number of problems together.
- What motivates people?[14] What should?
- What should be the end result, the outcome goal of counseling? How should a healthy person act or think?[15]
- How does change work in actual practice?[16]
- What role do other people, for example, the church and its pastors, play in the life of a counselee?

How a system thinks about such matters shapes how its practitioners intend to help others. One piece of advice is more than a piece of advice; it is part of an overall worldview or system of thought.

Sometimes counselees do not understand that some of what they thought they "knew" is built on a worldview not large enough to actually explain their world. They may have adopted contradictory elements into their worldview (see chapter 3). Counselors can make the same mistake. They adopt, without proper thought and evaluation, truth claims into their model or applications of their model that contradict the Bible. Rather than improving their ability to minister, this degrades it.

However, since it is possible for some worldviews to overlap, this allows us to finish our analysis with the final step.

---

[13] For more on the role of Jesus Christ as the crucified sin bearer, risen empowerer, and returning King, see Robert D. Jones, "The Christ-Centeredness of Biblical Counseling," in Kellemen and Forrey, *Scripture and Counseling*, 109–25.

[14] For an interesting discussion about the common ground some secular psychologists share with biblical counselors, see Jeremy Lelek, *Biblical Counseling Basics: Roots, Beliefs, and Future* (Greensboro, NC: New Growth Press, 2018), 242–45.

[15] Jay E. Adams, "Change Them? . . . into What?" *Journal of Biblical Counseling* 13, no. 2 (Winter 1995): 13–17.

[16] See David Powlison, *How Does Sanctification Work?* (Wheaton, IL: Crossway, 2017).

Step 4: Explain the Other Approach in Light of Scripture to Win Those Who Hold That Approach and to Improve Your Own Biblical Counseling

Let's consider a book that many of our counselees believe to be true, *The Five Love Languages* by Gary Chapman. No biblical texts argue for these love languages and when we consider the exegetical basis for such a book, the results are disappointing. However, not every insight the book offers is wrong. In his critique, David Powlison sets an example for us to follow by showing that valid insights from others, when properly considered and taught, can be powerfully helpful.[17] Other writers may encourage us to see in the Bible what we missed previously.

Counselors follow these steps to continually improve. Their motivation may have been a new case, a desire to minister better in future situations, or a longing to learn. As we follow these steps, we should incorporate our biblical reframed insights into our model. For instance, earlier we discussed how understanding physical abuse from the perspective of the abuser helped us remember that violence counseling must precede any marriage counseling. Yet that thought only improves the model if the counselor changes the way the counseling proceeds the next time. God willing, the more one studies, ministers, and evaluates, the more consistent the model is with the approach that most glorifies the Lord. In the end, the insights from other approaches can help us dig deeper and more wisely in the Scriptures than we would have otherwise.

---

[17] See David Powlison, "Love Speaks Many Languages Fluently," chap. 14 in his *Seeing with New Eyes* (see chap. 6, n. 14), along with his other chapters in this book that exemplify this reframing method of interaction with other approaches, including "What If Your Father Didn't Love You?" and "Human Defensiveness: The Third Way."

Conclusion

As we move to the section on methods and practice, it is important to be sure your foundation is secure. You may, therefore, find it helpful to reread part 2 before proceeding. Over the years, counselors in training have sometimes wrongly separated the process elements of counseling from the foundation on which it is built. We encourage you to carefully articulate, in your own mind at least, the definition of and foundation for Christ-centered biblical counseling.

PART THREE

THE PROCESS AND METHODS OF BIBLICAL COUNSELING

10

An Overview of the Change Process

Here we begin a series of chapters addressing the role of biblical counselors and giving recommended methods and techniques to help people change in the context of Christ-centered counseling. As we saw in chapter 1, our counseling goal is this: that our counselees will "grow in the grace and knowledge of our Lord and Savior Jesus Christ" (2 Pet 3:18).

How will such growth happen? This chapter presents a comprehensive overview of the change process, beginning with foundational theological principles, followed by a conceptual model and three key movements.

Foundational Principles of Christ-Centered Change

Let's consider five theological truths that undergird this process of change.

1. Godly Change Is God's Work (Rom 8:28–39; Phil 1:6)

The entire Trinity actively works to change us. No secular counseling can fathom the depths of the heart and transform people into Christ's image. Biblical counselors rely on the triune God; apart from the Father (Ps 127:1), Son (John 15:1–5), and Spirit (2 Cor 3:18), we can do nothing. The Christian life is the Spiritual life, the life of the Spirit within us.

While we will consider some key elements God uses, we must recognize God's sovereignty in how he changes people.[1] Biblical change isn't formulaic; it's the work of his Spirit who produces change in his own timing and ways. Even the most skilled and seasoned biblical counselor knows change depends on the Lord, not the counselor.

2. Godly Change Is Motivated by God's Grace and Promises

Biblical counselors stress the gospel indicatives as the impulse for change. We call for necessary behavioral change based on the grace of God. Christ's love for us compels us to live for him who died and rose for us (2 Cor 5:14–15). When pointing counselees to Scripture passages requiring change, grace-infused counseling spots and highlights the work of God that underlies God's command.

3. Godly Change Involves the Believer Actively Responding in Faith and Obedience to God's Work (Phil 1:6; 2:12–13)

We don't just "let go and let God," as the saying goes; rather, his grace enables us to actively follow him. Biblical counselors call their counselees to specific actions of faith and obedience. Gospel indicatives lead to gospel imperatives.

4. Godly Change Is a Process of Maturation, of What Theologians Call Progressive Sanctification (2 Pet 1:3–11)

Biblical counselors offer no quick fixes. Spiritual growth takes time; thankfully, it can start in the first counseling session.

---

[1] See Powlison, *How Does Sanctification Work?* (see chap. 9, n. 16).

5. Godly Change Occurs in the Context of God's Church, That Is, within the Body of Believers (Acts 2:42–47; Eph 4:11–16; Heb 10:24–25)

Even when helping those outside our church family, biblical counselors stress active, meaningful church participation as a vital complement to the counseling process. The church is God's designed community for maximal change.

A Conceptual Model for How Change Occurs in Counselees

Based on this theological foundation, let's consider a conceptual model that explains how counselees change. Many biblical counselors use a version of an illustration called the three-tree model, developed by David Powlison.[2] He derived the visual model from Jeremiah 17, a desert scene in which Israel faces the heat of divine judgment (vv. 1–4). In that chapter we see two kinds of people, metaphorically pictured as a thorny bush (the CSB says "juniper") and as a fruitful tree. The former is the ungodly person who trusts in self (17:5–6); the latter is the godly person who trusts in the Lord (17:7–8). Both face the same heat but respond in two distinct ways and bear two diverse kinds of fruit, depending on heart conditions (that is, trusting in self versus in the Lord).

Rather than unpacking the three-tree model here, the diagram below presents my (Bob's) modified version of Powlison's six-box model. Like virtually any Christian counseling model, this particular biblical counseling model helps us understand the person's life situation (box 1), any current wrong responses to it (boxes 2 and 3), how God wants them to respond (boxes 5 and 6), and God's provisions in Christ to help them (box 4).

[2] As a faculty member, counselor, and later the executive director of the Christian Counseling and Educational Foundation, Powlison taught this model for decades in his course, "The Dynamics of Biblical Change." I (Bob) learned it as his DMin student at Westminster Theological Seminary in August 1993.

THE
Six-Box
MODEL

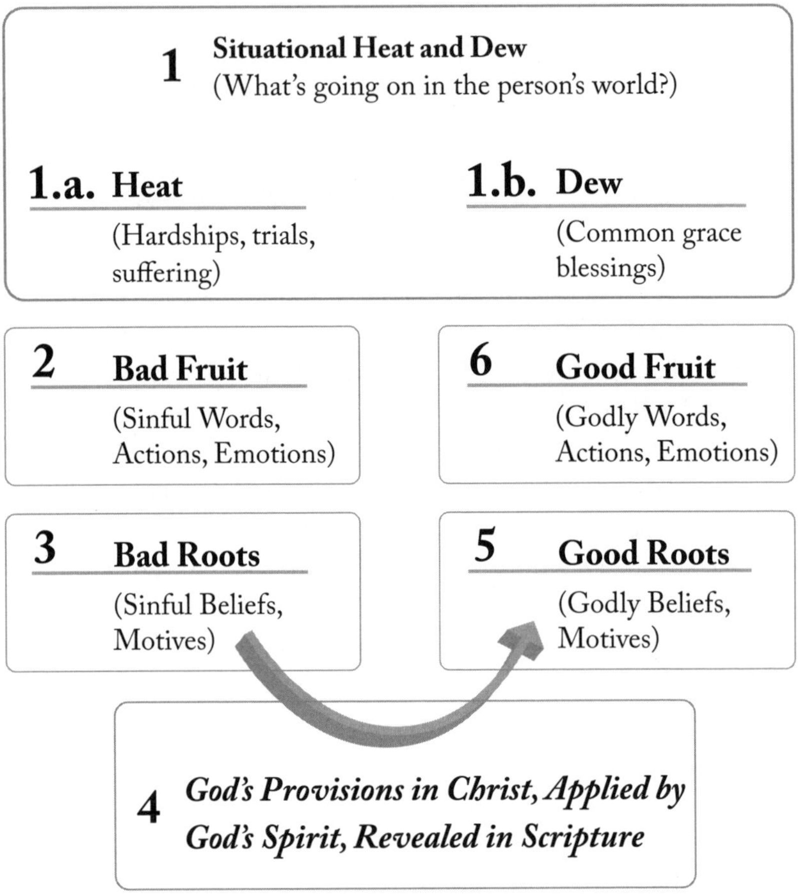

1 **Situational Heat and Dew**
(What's going on in the person's world?)

1.a. Heat
(Hardships, trials, suffering)

1.b. Dew
(Common grace blessings)

2 **Bad Fruit**
(Sinful Words, Actions, Emotions)

6 **Good Fruit**
(Godly Words, Actions, Emotions)

3 **Bad Roots**
(Sinful Beliefs, Motives)

5 **Good Roots**
(Godly Beliefs, Motives)

4 ***God's Provisions in Christ, Applied by God's Spirit, Revealed in Scripture***

Box 1 summarizes the person's situation, including both the hardships God permits (heat, 1.a.) and the common grace blessings God bestows (dew, 1.b.).[3] Both the heat and the dew can include past and present fac-

[3] Biblical theologians understood common grace—or perhaps more accurately called common goodness—include a wide range of God's undeserved blessings poured out on all people—believers and unbelievers alike (e.g., Ps 145:9; Matt 5:44–45).

tors. Past factors include family of origin, influential events, formative relationships, and significant experiences, among others. Present factors include current trials and blessings, significant relationships, life context, and health concerns. Here we can also include specific events the person believes might happen (e.g., his company downsizing) that exert current pressure.

While the types of hardship that bring someone to counseling vary, common categories include these:

- general life hardships (e.g., bereavement, natural disasters, economic downturns),
- being sinned against (e.g., rejection, abuse, assault, gossip),
- bodily problems (chronic or acute; minor or severe; including brain injuries/disorders),
- demonic attacks, and
- ungodly counsel, false teaching, and worldly cultural influences.

Box 2 summarizes any bad fruit behavior that might be present—such as the counselee's sinful words, actions, and emotions that flow consciously or subconsciously from their heart in response to their box 1 situation. This includes both sins of commission and omission—what the person is doing or not doing, saying or not saying, and feeling or not feeling that doesn't align with what God wants. Box 2 also includes passing thoughts, something distinct from and more transient than their box 3 core beliefs and motives. In this sense, words are spoken thoughts and thoughts are unspoken words; both emerge from the heart.

Box 3 summarizes any bad root beliefs and motives that might be present—sinful heart responses that come *in response to* box 1 and *produce* box 2 behavior. In box 3 we consider how counselees wrongly organize, interpret, and explain themselves, God, and their world. What do they desire, want, value, cherish, idolize, treasure, hope in, worship, live for, love, hallow, and rest in? The nature of heart sin means our hearts can focus us on someone or something other than God. As we saw in chapter 6, such sins might not be volitional choices and can include precognitive, pre-experiential aspects. For example, no one chooses to worry (box 2); it arises from remnant strains of unbelief in our hearts (box 3). Biblical counselors help people learn progressively to replace remnant unbelief with growing, mature faith. Or in cases of suffering—(in box 1)—biblical counselors help people respond in godly ways (boxes 5 and 6).

This visual captures a critical biblical dynamic: our circumstances are important, influential, and significant, but not causative, determinative, or ultimate. Box 1 is the occasion, provocation, or soil for our behavior—not the cause. As we saw in chapter 1, causation for outward human behavior (boxes 2 or 6) comes from an ungodly or godly heart (boxes 3 or 5), not from our situations, whether the circumstances are bad (box 1.a), good (box 1.b), or a combination of both (which is usual).[4] Counseling approaches that deny or downplay this connection contradict Christ and his Word. Assigning behavior causation to box 1 factors dehumanizes people, making them automatons and removing their inherent human responsibility and response-ability as divine image bearers. Such approaches bypass or neutralize the active, dynamic human heart. This includes medical models that reject biblical heart/body dualism and assign causation to body factors, or victimization models that attribute sinful behavior to past or present events or deficits. While people can victimize us, they can't make us capital-V Victims. Being rejected is an experience, not an identity. By God's grace, a Christ follower has a new core identity. As his sons and daughters, we can handle victimization his way.

In counseling situations involving suffering (e.g., grief or assault), you might not detect and your counselee might not report any box 2 or 3 sinful components. We certainly must not presume or create such. In such cases we should affirm from God's Word (box 4) their godly box 5 and 6 responses. At the same time, we should alert counselees to the danger of box 2 and 3 responses (1 Cor 10:11–14); we also should evaluate their ongoing responses in case such components later emerge. God sometimes uses the heat of suffering to expose box 3 themes not initially evident (Deut 8:1–5; Job).

---

[4] For example, see Prov 4:23; Jer 17:5–8; Matt 12:34–37; 15:18–20; Gal 5:19–23; and 1 Pet 2:11.

Box 4 summarizes God's provisions in Christ that the Holy Spirit uses to enable his people to respond God's way, to move from their bad fruit/roots (boxes 2/3) to good roots/fruit (boxes 5/6). These chiefly involve specific truths from God's Word. The Spirit wrote the Bible, illumines our minds to understand the Bible, and empowers us to believe and obey the Bible. One principal God-given purpose for the Bible is to change us (Deut 29:29; Matt 4:4; John 17:17; Acts 20:32; 1 Thess 4:1–2; 2 Tim 3:14–17; and Heb 13:22).

In addition, box 4 includes God's people—the church—those (like you, the biblical counselor) the Lord uses to help people change. By our words, examples, deeds, prayers, and presence, we minister to each other. We also include here the increasing number of scripturally-based resources biblical counselors produce.

The Agent of change, that is, the One who makes the box 4 provisions effective in moving a person from boxes 2 and 3 to boxes 5 and 6, is God's Spirit. Our big arrow in the visual model shows that desired Spirit-generated movement.

Box 5 summarizes the godly root beliefs and motives we envision God's Spirit forming in our counselees, the opposite of the bad roots in box 3. The change process involves the person repenting of any box 2 bad fruit and box 3 bad roots, embracing the box 4 biblical truths, and applying those truths to their hearts. Such a heart growingly grasps the believer's identity as God's son or daughter and increasingly knows, loves, trusts, worships, pleases, and obeys the Lord more than or instead of the box 3 heart substitutes. The difference between box 4 and box 5 is simple: box 4 contains objective gospel truths; box 5 involves the subjective implanting of them in our heart. For example, box 4 involves God's love for us and adoption of us; box 5 involves embracing that identity that leads to new box 6 behavior.

Box 6 summarizes the desired good fruit behavior we envision God's Spirit forming in our counselees; this flows from a renewed and renewing box 5 heart. It's the opposite of the box 2 bad fruit. In contrast to the works of the flesh in Gal 5:19–21, 5:22–23 lists a catalog of Christlike graces that flow from God's Spirit working in the heart of the believer. The categories of commission and omission in box 2 are reversed: we must put off (omit) sinful behavior and put on (commit) godly replacements. Where the counselee already demonstrates box 5 and 6 godly responses, we affirm those aspects and consider what more needs to happen.

Let's recap the movement of the model from our perspective as counselors, allowing the arrows in the diagram to guide us progressively from box to box.

1. Box 1: We listen to our counselees and learn about their situations, especially their "heat."
2. Box 2: As we listen, we learn about any disordered behavior that needs to be changed.
3. Box 3: As we listen, we learn about the sinful heart beliefs and motives producing that behavior. (We must not seek behavioral change by moving from box 2 to box 6, bypassing the heart.)
4. Box 4: We then discern what biblical truth(s) God wants to use to help our counselees change. (We must not move from box 3 to box 5 apart from box 4, thus bypassing God's provisions.)
5. Box 5: Based on God's Word, we envision the godly heart beliefs and motives God wants to cultivate in our counselees; we affirm those godly heart responses that are present.
6. Box 6: We note what godly behaviors should flow or are flowing from the counselee's heart.

Key Movements in Godly Change

Considering this six-box model, what steps must counselees take to move from boxes 2/3 to boxes 5/6? (In chapter 14 we will revisit these boxes to consider how we as counselors can use them to give direction to our sessions.) Let's examine three key movements in the change process—the actions of believing, repenting, and obeying.

Believing

Believing means clinging to God and embracing his presence, his provisions, and his promises of forgiveness, wisdom, and power in our individual situations. While belief and repentance are inextricably linked—essentially two sides of the same coin—our repentance typically flows from our confidence in God's gracious posture toward us and promises for us. Consider three categories—past, present, and future—that we want our counselees to dwell on:

1) Past Provisions

Help your believing counselees recognize and rejoice in God's election, redemption, forgiveness, justification, adoption, and initial sanctification work of setting them apart as his possession. Central passages include Rom 8:28–39; Eph 1:3–14; and 1 John 4:7–16.

2) Present Provisions

Help your counselees grasp God's continual forgiveness, love, and mercy toward them (1 John 1:7, 9; 2:1–2; Psalm 51; Heb 7:25) and his continual wisdom and strength for them (Luke 11:13; Eph 6:10; 2 Tim 4:17; Phil 2:12–13; 4:13; and 2 Pet 1:3–4). Passages like Heb 4:16 sweetly pull these together: "Therefore, let us approach the throne of grace with boldness, so that we may receive mercy and find grace to help us in time of need." God guarantees believers both his forgiving grace ("mercy") and his enabling, empowering, sustaining grace ("grace to help us in time of need").

3) Future Promises

Help your counselees believe and long for four provisions Christ will bring. The first of these is a perfect heart, the end of the civil war between the Spirit and the flesh. First John 3:2 promises, "We know that when he appears, we will be like him because we will see him as he is." Second, each perfected heart will reside within a perfect body. Philippians 3:20–21 declares that when our Savior returns, "He will transform the body of our humble condition into the likeness of his glorious body, by the power that enables him to subject everything to himself." First Corinthians 15:50–58 unpacks the details of those glorious bodies to come. Third, our perfected souls and bodies will flourish forever in a perfect place, the "new earth, where righteousness dwells" (2 Pet 3:13). Revelation 21:3–5 foresees that new eternal reality:

> I heard a loud voice from the throne saying, "Look! God's dwelling place is now among the people, and he will dwell with them. They will be his people, and God himself will be with them and be their God. 'He will wipe every tear from their eyes. There will be no more death' or mourning or crying or pain, for the old order of things has passed away." He who was seated on the throne said, "I am making everything new!" (NIV)

Fourth, we will see our Lord face-to-face, the object of our faith and desires (John 17:24; 1 John 3:2; Rev 22:4) and dwell with him forever. Our Christ-following counselees need to know that on that soon-coming day God will remove all their box 1 hardships. All their box 2 and box 3 sin problems will end. And because of God's box 4 salvation work, they will enjoy perfect box 5 hearts, issuing in perfect box 6 love and righteousness toward God and others, fulfilling each counselee's eternal destiny.

As a sample passage, consider the powerful box 4 promises in Isa 41:8–10. Amid their fears, the Lord first reminds his people of their redeemed identity (vv. 8–9):

- He directly connects them to their covenantal relationship with him: "But you, Israel, my servant, Jacob, whom I have chosen, descendant of Abraham, my friend."
- He then recalls his redemption of them: "I brought you from the ends of the earth and called you from its farthest corners."
- He then assures them of his acceptance: "You are my servant; I have chosen you; I haven't rejected you."

Based on these redemption realities, he urges them in verse 10, "do not fear and do not be afraid," and he reinforces his command with even more promises:

- He guarantees his presence with them: "for I am with you," "I am your God."

- He promises to strengthen and secure them: "I will strengthen you; I will help you; I will hold on to you with my righteous right hand."

Our work as biblical counselors involves helping our counselees—in this case, anxious ones—to understand and flesh out these truths in their specific situations.

Repenting

As we saw in chapter 6, repenting means turning from and forsaking both our behavioral sins (box 2) and heart sins (box 3). James 3:13–4:12 pictures the components of our six-box model. The wider context in James involves box 1 heat and hardships (1:2, 12; 5:1–6, 12–14). We see a general description of ungodly behavior in 3:16 and specific examples in 4:1–2, 11–12. That box 2 bad fruit emerges from box 3 bad roots which the apostle describes in various, synonymous ways: bitter envy and selfish ambition (3:14, 16); encamped desires, ruling wants, cravings, warring desires (4:1–3); spiritual adultery and friendship with the world (clinging to some thing or person other than God) (4:4); pride (4:6), devil ruling, which is paralleled with the flesh in 3:15 (4:7); double-mindedness, understood as professing allegiance to Christ, yet loving self and pleasure (4:8); and judgmentalism, God-playing, exalting self (4:12). No secular diagnosis can plumb these depths nor bring thorough answers.

In Jas 4:6, we see a concise summary of God's box 4 provisions for change: "He gives us more grace. That is why Scripture says: 'God opposes the proud, but shows favor to the humble'" (cf. 3:17 NIV; 4:10). And we see detailed descriptions of needed box 5 and 6 change in James's multiple calls in 3:17–18 and 4:4–12 to humility and the pursuit of godly fruit.

Obeying

Obeying means loving God and others by putting off sin and putting on righteousness because of his grace. As we have seen above and throughout this book, the obedience we aim for is grace-motivated obedience—being grateful for God's forgiving grace and dependent on God's enabling grace.

Ephesians 4:17–32 provides an explicit summary of this put-on/put-off dynamic. As with any passage, we must set it in its larger context to read it rightly. In Ephesians 1–3, Paul masterfully reminds his readers of God's saving grace. In 4:1–6, he pivots from what God has done for us to how we should live out the salvation we received. His initial focus is relational—humility, gentleness, patience, forbearance, love, and unity based on the unity God has already created. In 4:7–16, he addresses what Christ the head of the church has done and is doing to produce unity and maturity within his church.

In 4:17–19, Paul describes their former godless living and calls them to turn away from it. The ungodliness was rooted in their hearts—that is, in their beliefs and desires—and issued forth in ungodly behavior. (This illustrates how box 3 heart problems produce box 2 behavior problems in our six-box model). In 4:20–24, he reminds them of the new life Christ has given them (box 4) and the threefold call to put off their former way of life, to be renewed in their minds, and to put on the new Godlike self (boxes 5 and 6). God's redemptive purpose is nothing short of a whole-person makeover. Paul continues in 4:25–32 to stress this put-off/put-on dynamic with five specific behavioral changes.

The Put-Off and Put-On Dynamic in Ephesians 4:17–32

Put-off (general, box 3)	*Put-on (general, box 5)*	*How? (box 4)*
Former godless life, 17–19, 22	The new self, 24. You now know Christ, 20–21, and you should continue to renew your mind, 23.	Prayerfully reflect on the box 4 truths in Ephesians 1–6, including heart repentance/belief.
Put-off specific bad fruit from that old life (box 2)	*Put-on specific good fruit from this new life (box 6)*	*How? Specific Actions*
Lying, 25	Truth (honesty), 25	

Anger, 26–27	Resolve anger immediately, 26	
Stealing, 28	Work and generosity, 28	
Ungodly speech, 29	Edifying words, 29	
Bitterness, anger, etc., 31	Kindness, compassion, forgiveness, 31–32	

The chart is a tool for conceptualizing and visualizing this put-off/put-on dynamic, even if the counseling problem does not involve one of the five specific sins. You can even draw it for your counselee. We could use it to do a similar analysis of Col 3:1–17 and apply it to its list of behavioral sins (e.g., sexual sin, v. 5; anger, v. 8; relational conflict, vv. 12–15). Notice the chart includes a third "How?" column for specific put-off/put-on action steps a counselee can take. The counselor and counselee can select several during the session, or it can become part of a homework assignment. Either way, biblical change calls for concrete actions of grace-propelled obedience.

Conclusion

While no single passage or ministry model furnishes an exhaustive summary of the Bible's sixty-six books, our five foundational principles, our six-box model, and the three key movements (belief, repentance, and obedience) provide a roadmap to guide counselees to grow in Christlikeness and handle their personal and relational problems his way.

The Role of the Counselor

Counseling can be a very effective ministry to believers needing help and to unbelievers needing Christ as Savior. So, in addition to thinking about process, tools, and structure, it is also important to discuss the role of the counselor. This discussion is not simple or straightforward because biblical counselors hold different views regarding the role and qualifications of a biblical counselor. The tension exists for at least three good reasons.

First, biblical counselors have different understandings of the importance of their role in the change process. We all believe in the significant role of the Holy Spirit. God gave believers his Spirit to guide them through the Word and to extend grace for both salvation and sanctification. These convictions might lead some counselors to believe that the way they do ministry is not important since God will do the work anyway. Unfortunately, this can lead to counselors being unwise in certain conversations or even careless. Sometimes the Lord works despite a servant's goals and motives, but that can hardly be viewed as a free pass.

Second, there is also a healthy concern for the kind and amount of training biblical counselors receive. Certifications from various groups (e.g., ACBC, ABC, IABC) can be earned with a relatively small amount of training and counseling experience when compared to secular licensure.[1] Some believe the lack of training and experience of some biblical counselors has led to poor ministry or even spiritual abuse, and that counselors need stricter requirements and a more robust supervision process.[2]

Third, biblical counseling is concerned about the character of the person doing the counseling. Biblical counselors should expect to be held to higher standards of character and conduct than those with secular licenses and certifications who focus mostly on the educational and experiential training. Even the accountability structures differ. Biblical counseling ministries in the church typically have a group of overseeing elders who provide guidance, care, and aid to the overall counseling process. Those in independent centers may not share equal advantages of elder oversight, but will still have a system to provide coaching, care, and accountability for the counselors.

While the issues surrounding the role of the counselor are complex, this chapter will focus on three common commitments regarding the role of a biblical counselor.

A Commitment to Humble and Effective Self-Counsel

Galatians 6:1 says, "Brothers and sisters, if someone is overtaken in any wrongdoing, you who are spiritual, restore such a person with a gentle spirit, watching out for yourselves so that you also won't be tempted."

The counseling enterprise is a series of conversations about difficult subjects. The underlying problem might be the sin of the counselee, the sin of a person who harmed the counselee, or the challenge of living in a sin-cursed world. All those who have spent time in the counseling room understand the potential for temptation. But to what temptation does Paul

[1] The secular license system requires far more training, observation, and therapeutic practice. A Licensed Marriage Family Therapist (LFMT) in Indiana, for example, must have a master's degree from an accredited program, including a practicum of 1,000 supervised hours and completion of the AMFTRB exam. Indiana Professional Licensing Agency, https://www.in.gov/pla/files/LMFT_FAQs_2015.pdf.

[2] Rob Green, "Bullying with the Bible and Biblical Leadership," *Faith Biblical Counseling Blog*, October 14, 2014, https://blogs.faithlafayette.org/counseling/2014/10/bullying-with-the-bible-and-biblical-leadership/.

refer? Without further clarification it seems reasonable to conclude that any temptation associated with the restoration process is in view.[3] That allows the interpreter to provide a rather substantive list of possible temptations:

- The counselor might believe he is the answer to the counselee's problem.
- The counselor might develop an ungodly emotional or physical relationship with the counselee.
- The counselee's confessions of wrongdoing might spark areas of sin or struggle that are already present in the counselors' life.
- The counselee could introduce new ways of sinning to the counselor.
- The counselor could sin in the way he responds to the counselee.

I (Rob) once participated on a panel discussion at a secular university; it was for advanced undergraduate students pursuing degrees in marriage and family therapy. When asked how a counselor handles it when the counselee is sexually attracted to him or her, I initially responded, "When you look like I do, you do not have that problem." The audience roared with laughter at that, but the question was a serious one and needed a serious answer. The student's concern had to do with a counselor's spiritual life. In biblical counseling, the counselor must cultivate their own relationship with the Lord through prayer, study of Scripture, and regularly reminding themselves of his truth. For example, the more the counselor appreciates the death, burial, and resurrection of Christ, the less likely they will be to give in to temptation. The more thankful they are for the sustaining and ongoing grace they receive to serve the Lord in sensitive ministry situations, the more likely they will be to let Jesus motivate their

[3] While a counselor might be tempted to commit the same sin as the counselee, it is more important to recognize that we have to be diligent because we are susceptible to various sins. Commenting on the exhortation "looking to yourself," John MacArthur notes, "Paul uses a strong word (*skopeō*, to observe or consider) in the present tense, which emphasized a continual, diligent attentiveness to their own purity." John MacArthur, "Galatians" in *The MacArthur New Testament Commentary* (Chicago: Moody Press, 1983), 179. See also F. F. Bruce, *The Epistle to the Galatians: A Commentary on the Greek Text,* New International Greek Testament Commentary (Grand Rapids: Eerdmans, 1982), 260.

thoughts and actions. The more we believers run to gospel truths, the less likely any temptation will produce sin. We would add that appropriate precautions such as having a counseling advocate or friend in the room, communicating the counseling schedule to spouses, and staying focused on the counseling task and not the long-term discipleship task are helpful safeguards. In addition, the more encouragement, accountability, and care provided by the counselor's elders or supervisors, the less likely he or she will fall into sin.

Another aspect of watching out for temptation requires the counselor to remain aware of the potential to sin in the counseling process itself. Many biblical counselors have been in a room with a defiant counselee or in a conversation with a mean, spiteful, and angry person who spewed venom at whoever would listen. Biblical counselors willingly place themselves in these contexts. We willingly agree to speak to angry, hurt, frustrated, and bitter people. And that can stir up similar emotions in us.

In fact, I have been tempted to be sinfully angry.[4] When I hear a man minimize his sin despite the chaos he created, I am angry. I have heard a man say he deeply loves his wife. Yet as he participated in sexual adultery for the last five years, he deceived her and others. Children from his home and the home of the adulteress are now processing their respective parents' divorces and the consequences for their lives. Their churches are enacting church discipline. The pain, hurt, and betrayal he caused is everywhere and the adulterer does not see it. In fact, he acts as if it is his wife's fault. Such a situation can make me very angry. But while I believe one should be angry as God is over sin and destruction, it is not an excuse to sin. In this case, it would be a failure on my part to blow up at him and expose his folly. That is why Matt 7:3–5 is not just an important passage to share with counselees. It is an important passage for the counselor.

> Why do you look at the speck that is in your brother's eye, but *do not notice the log that is in your own eye?* Or how can you say to your brother, 'Let me take the speck out of your eye,' and look, the log

[4] Hendrickson emphasizes that entering into the life of one caught in a trespass brings with it the potential to be rude and boastful. William Hendriksen, *Exposition of Galatians,* Baker New Testament Commentary (Grand Rapids: Baker, 1968), 232.

> is in your own eye? You hypocrite, first take the log out of your own eye, and *then you will see clearly* to take the speck out of your brother's eye! (NASB, emphasis mine)

Without removing the logs in their own eyes, counselors will be qualitatively hypocritical, much like the counselee I described. In addition, they will suffer from the same spiritual problem as those they are trying to help—they will not be able to see clearly. Sinful responses may even blind the counselor to the genuine issues involved in the counselee's situation. This will not result in gospel-centered conversations that bring glory to Jesus or put the counselee in the best position for change.

One final aspect of this point is the counselor's need for humility. The first reason is that God will not share his glory. Second, as James 4:6 reminds us, "God resists the proud, but gives grace to the humble." Galatians 6:3–5 emphasizes the need for humility, too. The counselor will either learn humility or face the difficulty of humiliation. Counselors, even experienced ones, need continual reminders to exercise humility, for that is the path of God's grace.

As I started counseling, I was very focused on getting over the initial anxiety of meeting people in difficult circumstances, having meaningful responses that encourage their relationship with Christ, asking probing questions to discern heart issues, and providing a wise structure to facilitate practical change. Soon I felt I was getting it, and what started as humble dependence on God's help for every session gave way to experienced complacency. It was just about then that the Lord gave me several cases that practically blew up in my face. That was a painful season for the counselees and me. Through it, the Lord taught me that in my pride I had gotten too comfortable and forgotten I need God's grace for every case and every session.

In summary, the person who humbly and effectively self-counsels will also be the one who qualifies as "spiritual" in relation to Gal 6:1 and will exhibit the fruit of the Spirit.[5]

---

[5] In the preceding contextual flow of Gal 5:13–26, the "spiritual" ones in 6:1 are those who walk by the Spirit and bear his fruit.

A Willingness to Exhibit Biblical Servanthood in Formal Settings

Every Christian has the responsibility and capability to live out the one-another passages of Scripture.[6] One-another opportunities occur in the normal course of life and in formal counseling settings. Whether serving as a counselor in a church or in a private practice, you must take care that your attitudes and actions are consistent with the one-another truths found in Scripture. This will be important when you are seeking to fulfill the Great Commission ministries of winning people to Christ and helping believers grow.[7] In addition to the one-another truths, Gal 6:1–5 identifies several other concepts that are important for counseling sessions.

Restoration (v. 1)

Restoration terminology refers to returning something to proper function. Thus, counselors are dedicated to helping counselees return to proper functioning. A counselee caught in suffering, sinning in response to suffering, or acting in high-handed rebellion is no longer capable of fulfilling their role in the church body. First Corinthians 12 teaches that every part of the body is important; no part can either minimize its own role nor minimize the role of another part of the body. Thus, the counselee's lack of

---

[6] Many passages emphasize one-another ministry among believers. Toward our fellow Christians, we each should be loving (Rom 13:8; 1 Thess 3:12; 4:9; 2 Thess 1:3; Heb 10:24; 1 Pet 1:22; 1 John 3:11, 23; 4:7, 11–12; 2 John 5), edifying (Rom 14:19), accepting (Rom 15:7), instructive (Rom 15:14), welcoming (Rom 16:16; 1 Cor 16:20; 2 Cor 13:12; 1 Thess 5:26; 1 Pet 5:14), forgiving (Col 3:13), kind (Eph 4:32), accommodating (Eph 5:21; 1 Pet 5:5), and encouraging (1 Thess 4:18; 5:11, 14). We are also to confess to and pray for one another (Jas 5:16) and fellowship together (1 John 1:7).

[7] See, for example, John Piper, "Biblical Counseling for the Great Commission," October 21, 2014, https://www.desiringgod.org/articles/biblical-counseling-for-the-great-commission; David Powlison, "The Great Commission is a Great Place to Begin to Understand Biblical Counseling," March 4, 2013, https://www.ccef.org/great-commission-great-place-begin-understand-biblical-counseling/; Robert Jones, "Does the Great Commission Require Biblical Counseling?," July 17, 2019, https://biblicalcounselingcoalition.org/2019/07/17/does-the-great-commission-require-biblical-counseling/; Paul David Tripp, "The Great Commission: A Paradigm for Ministry in the Local Church," *Journal of Biblical Counseling*, Vol 16, no. 3 (1998): 2–4.

proper functioning hurts the entire church body. Its ability to build itself up in love (Eph 4:16) is weakened when believing counselees are struggling. Counselors view themselves as instruments in the Redeemer's hands, as tools that help restore counselees.[8]

The biblical counselor grasps that each counselee has a vital role to play in the overall mission of both the global and local church. We desire to lead them to find security, hope, and help in Christ. This allows a counselee to follow the example of Christ in suffering (1 Pet 2:21), to respond properly to suffering (1 Pet 2:22–25), and to submit to the commandments and teachings of Christ. Every counselee restored to proper functioning will be in the best position to contribute to the body, whatever God designed them to do.

Gentleness (v. 1)

In some counseling situations it is easy to be gentle. For instance, some counselees will highly value us, speak well of us, listen carefully to what we say, and try to change. Others will share common experiences with us, and we will find them fun to be with. And when counseling succeeds, we enjoy our front seat to see God's work in the person we are helping.

However, in other situations extending gentleness is difficult. For example, some counselees do not listen; at other times, they disagree with us; at still other times they accuse us of being unloving or uncaring. And sometimes they just want to speak with someone else. The Lord does not say to be gentle only with those who respond well. Rather, the Lord said that his servant must not be quarrelsome but must gently correct those who do not want to listen (2 Tim 2:24–26).

Showing gentleness in the face of hardship is one way to properly love and care for our counselees. When a counselee may be significantly older than you, scripture encourages you to be an example of godliness

---

[8] This terminology comes from Paul David Tripp's helpful work, *Instruments in the Redeemer's Hands: People in Need of Change Helping People in Need of Change* (Phillipsburg, NJ: P&R, 2002).

(1 Tim 4:12) and to be careful with our rebuke (1 Tim 5:1–2). And while it can be hard to be gentle when you have said the same thing repeatedly or when you believe your counselee should know better than to do this or that, counselors must remember that what might be common knowledge to them may be new to their counselees. Following the exhortation of the Lord to exhort older men like fathers, younger men like brothers, older women like mothers, and young women as sisters will go a long way toward helping us exercise godly gentleness.

Accepting an Additional Load (v. 2)

Galatians 6:2 says, "carry one another's burdens." It is emotionally costly to be a biblical counselor. Counselees provide us significant access to information that may be known by very few; we are granted access to intimate knowledge about them. Our prayer lives thus change because we know their struggles. The way we read the Bible changes because we look for new passages or truths to present to them even as we commune with the Lord. Ours thoughts change because we live each day with the additional weight of wondering whether a counselee is making godly choices or refusing the grace of Christ.

Yet great joy comes with bearing others' burdens. Watching a counselee return to a place of godly function, for example, is a joyful privilege. Ten years ago, our family vacationed at a place with a long and isolated hiking trail. We heard it was beautiful, unlike anything we had ever seen. We then learned that the hike was thirteen miles long. Back then, our children were thirteen, nine, and four. It seemed a bit outside our ability to do unless some were willing to take heavier loads. So, that day I carried our four-year-old daughter ten of the thirteen miles. The hike was glorious; my family still talks about it. At the end of that day, though, my shoulders were screaming. I could barely touch the top of my head. Yet seeing with my family the majesty of God's creation, much of which was accessible only through pain and hard work on my part, was more than worth it. Similarly, counseling will bring pain, but it will also lead to joy—if you are willing to carry an extra load.

A Desire to Thrive in Ministry

Counseling has a cost. If not careful, counselors can experience the discouragement and tiredness we often call burnout. This condition is not an indicator of how busy we are, but of how poorly we care for our own souls. Let's consider several practical ways a counselor can care for their soul that will make a difference over the long haul.

Be an Excellent Student of the Word.

Jay Adams says the best training for a biblical counselor is a seminary education.[9] He doesn't mean everyone has to get a seminary education but that the more Scripture we know, the more likely we will be able to share meaningful passages with our counselees according to their needs. Those who want to serve in biblical counseling should regularly increase their skills in biblical interpretation. After all, Jesus said in Matt 4:4 that "Man must not live on bread alone but on every word that comes from the mouth of God." Scripture is a source of nourishment.

Develop a Passion for Continual Training.

If we believe in the continual need for personal Christian growth (Col 3:5–17)—what theologians call progressive sanctification—and growth in counselor competence (1 Tim 4:12–16), then we should embrace continual training. This can include reading, attending conferences, going through a certification process, asking a person to join you for a case to evaluate you, or organizing a continuing education program for counselors. Part of the call to stewardship and sanctification is a willingness to keep learning. This includes the Scriptures, but also researching cases in which you have little experience, learning about our culture and how

[9] Jay Adams, *The Christian Counselor's Manual: The Practice of Nouthetic Counseling* (Grand Rapids: Zondervan, 1973), 12. See also David Powlison, "Why I Chose Seminary for Counseling Training," in *Speaking the Truth in Love: Counsel in Community* (Greensboro, NC: New Growth Press, 2005), 153–65.

cultural influences impact thought processes, learning about different ways to address problems, and growing in your ability to listen to others. Such training will ensure counseling skills do not become stagnant.

Training is not limited to gaining knowledge about cases or particular counseling struggles, though. There is also value in learning how to equip others in counseling, how to serve as an elder in a church, how to evaluate your own heart motivations as you counsel, and how to grow in relational skills.

Maintain the Spiritual Disciplines.

All believers battle the flesh, the worldly philosophies that war against God, and Satan and his host. Sometimes it is not easy to tell which you are fighting. Yet how you fight all three involves your daily walk with Christ, which includes putting on the armor of God (Eph 6:10–17), dealing with your own idolatry (Jas 4:1–2), and recognizing worldly philosophies for what they are (1 John 2:16). Put simply, cultivating a meaningful prayer life, Bible study time, evaluation of your spiritual life, and faithful commitments to your local church and your Christian community will be vital to you having a thriving ministry (1 Tim 4:12–16). Finding rest in the person and promises of Jesus will continually provide the help a weary soul needs.

Know Your Limits.

Not everyone can handle the same amount of responsibility and load. According to Gal 6:5, we are to each bear our own load. In the parable of the talents, the master did not expect the one with five talents to make ten nor for the one with one talent to make twenty (Matt 25:14–30). Rather, the Lord evaluated the stewardship of each individual based on what they were given. Humble counselors recognize their limits. They joyfully serve within the bounds of those God-given limits without using them as a tool to be lazy or to poorly steward their gifts through overextension. When you find yourself struggling with your attitude, responding in anger, bitterness, and frustration, it may signal overload.

Conclusion

Counselors have the privilege of participating in valuable ways in Great Commission ministry. While this chapter is only a starting place, the three ideas of committing to humble and effective self-counsel, exhibiting biblical servanthood in the counseling room, and seeking to thrive in ministry will help you as you seek to steward all God has given you in his service for a long-term ministry.[10]

[10] Additional resources on the role of the counselor include: Lelek, *Biblical Counseling Basics* (see chap. 9, n. 14); Robert Smith, "Spiritual Discipline in the Biblical Counselor," in *Introduction to Biblical Counseling*, ed. John MacArthur et al. (Nashville: Thomas Nelson, 1994), 142–53; Stuart Scott, "Pursue the Servant's Mindset," *Journal of Biblical Counseling* 17, no. 3 (1999): 9–15; David Powlison, "To Take the Soul to Task," *Journal of Biblical Counseling* 12, no. 3 (1994): 2–3; Jay Adams, "Handling Failure," *Journal of Pastoral Practice* 6, no. 3 (1985): 3–5; and Andrew Boswell, "The Counselor and Pride," *Journal of Pastoral Practice* 4, no. 1 (1980): 11–15.

12

Preparing to Counsel and Leading a First Session

Students in biblical counseling courses repeatedly tell us professors how the course materials have changed their own lives, so much so that they are excited to help others—until the time comes when they actually have to sit down with someone. Then their hearts pound, their blood pressure spikes, and their palms sweat.

One way for a counselor to lessen nervousness in the first session is to prepare well and have a wise plan to follow. In our previous chapter we considered key qualities you as a counselor should possess. This chapter provides practical guidance on how I (Bob) prepare for and lead a counselee through a first session. Of course, there is no one right way to do this; biblical counselors vary in their methods.[1]

Pre-Session Preparation

Making the time to properly prepare for a session, especially a first session, will give you greater confidence and control of the session and help assure your counselee of your competence and care for them.

[1] See also Lauren Whitman, "What Does a Good First Session Look Like?," *Journal of Biblical Counseling* 28, no. 1 (2014): 53–63.

Preparing Yourself[2]

No session preparation is more important than preparing yourself. You are God's instrument in the counseling room. So, how can you be most fit to serve the Lord and your counselee? In addition to making sure you are exhibiting the godly qualities we saw in chapter 11, consider these steps:

1. Renew your commitment to the ministry task God has given you (Matt 9:35–36; Rom 15:14). Remind yourself of its importance. You are dealing with someone's eternal soul and its disordered struggles.

2. Pray that you will reflect Christ, display the fruit of his Spirit (Matt 5:16; Gal 5:22–23; 1 Tim 4:12, 16), and entrust your fears to the Lord (2 Tim 1:7; 1 Pet 5:7). Latch on to one of these verses, and ask God to help you minister wisely and compassionately.

3. Pray for your counselee, remaining aware of fears they might bring to the session (especially if they had a previous negative counseling experience): "What if my counselor doesn't understand me? What if they minimize my problem or put Bible-Band-Aids on me? What if they open old wounds or expose unseen sins? What if they don't guard my privacy and break confidentiality? What if they judge me, reject me, or deem me hopeless? What if the counseling doesn't work? Or makes me worse?" Before the session, sit where your counselee will sit and pray for them Paul's prayers for those to whom he ministered (e.g., Eph 1:15–21; 3:14–21; Phil 1:9–11; Col 1:9–12).

4. If you know the presenting problem(s), be prepared with two or three basic resources, passages, and assignments you might use in the session. You might find it helpful to consult with a supervisor, mentor, or experienced biblical counselor.

---

[2] See also Powlison, *Speaking Truth in Love*, 49–54 (see chap. 1, n. 5), who notes eight healthy preparation practices he seeks to make: (1) I follow through on my commitments; (2) I check out my own attitudes and life; (3) I read and study the Bible; (4) I think hard about those whom I'll meet; (5) I pray for each person, asking God to work; (6) I set a rough agenda for our meeting; (7) I often review basic principles of counseling to orient myself; (8) I do things that orient me to the ministry task.

Preparing Your Materials and Forms

If possible, send in advance or make available on your website your standard forms and ask your counselee to complete them and to either email or post them in advance or bring them to the first session. We recommend three forms: (1) an information and agreement form that describes your ministry and the counselor-counselee mutual responsibilities and expectations, including an informed consent agreement; (2) a brief overview form that summarizes the problem issue(s) to be discussed; and (3) a longer personal information form.[3] Here's a checklist of other items you might need:

- Your Bible. (Having it lying open in the counseling room can symbolize your biblical commitments.)
- Your case file folder, notepad, and pen.
- Other counseling tools you might use, including help lists and pertinent resources. (Keep any books or booklets you might assign hidden until you need them.)

Preparing the Room

Location

While we can counsel people in any setting—we aren't limited to formal offices—knowing the pros and cons of different locations can allow you to make appropriate adjustments if needed.

Most counselors prefer a private room or office (e.g., their workspace or a room in their church) where they have full control of the setting and can better maintain confidentiality. Others prefer the efficiency of counseling out of their home, assuming they can provide a quiet, private room without interruptions from children or pets. (This is especially helpful for stay-at-home moms who can hold sessions during nap times.) But while the privacy and informality of the latter might help fearful counselees feel

[3] For sample forms, see https://www.faithlafayette.org/counseling/get-help/get-started-today or www.robertdjonescounseling.com.

safer and might convey greater warmth, it might seem too informal to some and make counselees feel afraid to leave should they feel awkward. Moreover, most counselors report not having had good experiences in environments they can't control. Maybe a child cried after waking early, the dog barked, or the doorbell or telephone rang during the session.

Some counselors who lack home or office space prefer meeting in restaurants. Quiet restaurants allow either party to leave when they want and provide an informal place for an initial meeting with a reluctant counselee. The downsides of such a setting include public visibility and the added financial cost and time to order food or interact with servers. Coffee shops are a quicker and cheaper option, but their seating might be too cramped and the atmosphere too noisy for private conversation over delicate subjects.

Furniture Setup

Some counselors prefer to sit behind a desk opposite their counselees. Others prefer a table where counselor and counselee share table space and have room to set their Bible, notes, and assignments. Still others prefer no desk or table in the counseling room, just chairs facing each other. There is no one right way to set up your space. Just evaluate the potential cons of each option. While the third option removes physical barriers, some counselees might prefer a table as a little bit of barrier.

Seating Options

Typically, it's best to sit across from your counselee, with their back to the door so they won't feel boxed-in and can easily exit. This also allows you to see anyone who might inadvertently enter the room. (Note: Counselees with law enforcement or military training may prefer to sit where they can view the door.) Consider also cultural practices in cross-cultural ministry settings.

Room Décor and Provisions

Setting matters, so consider these factors:

- Wall decorations, paint colors, and plants can contribute to creating a warm, undistracting setting.
- A wall clock (or two) in your sight line can help you inconspicuously monitor the time.
- Fluorescent lights (especially those that flicker) or bright sunshine through a window can be hard for counselees who suffer headaches. Prepare appropriately.
- Book titles and other items are visible on your tables and shelves. Look at the visible wording in your counseling space. Consider what your counseling space visually communicates.

Having these room provisions handy might help:

- Water bottles
- A stocked coffee and tea station.
- A tissue box and pump bottle of hand sanitizer.
- Blank copier paper and pens for drawing diagrams the counselee can take home. (Some counselors prefer a mounted marker board for diagramming.)
- Small pads of paper and pens to encourage counselee note taking, especially to record Bible instruction, practical counsel, and growth assignments
- Printed materials like forms, homework sheets, articles, booklets, books.
- Extra Bibles, ideally in a duplicate edition to give page numbers of passages without embarrassing counselees who don't know their Bibles well.
- A photocopier in the room or nearby, although camera phones can help with many tasks.

Goals for Session One

How can you best enter your counselee's world, understand both their felt and real needs, and bring them Jesus and his answers in session one? We suggest five goals:

1. Welcome. Immediately initiate a warm, welcoming, and caring relationship so your counselee knows you care. Let them experience that care by your words and actions throughout the session.
2. Know. Get to know your counselee by gathering information about them and showing them you are beginning to understand their unique struggles. This includes discussing and assessing their relationship to Christ.
3. Hope. Present Jesus Christ and the hope he offers through his Spirit and Word. Help your counselee hear from God's Word that Jesus can help them. Biblical counselors offer people a sure foundation of hope, for this life and the next.
4. Plan. Explain the counseling process and propose a tentative plan—an initial direction—you and your counselee can follow. Explain that you will tailor it as you move forward.
5. Invite. Assure your counselee of your desire to help and invite them to commit to counseling and the growth assignments between sessions.

My Typical Session One Procedure

In time, you will develop your own style. Here is what I (Bob) do when meeting with an individual adult.[4] I arrive early to greet my counselees when they arrive. I ask my co-counselor, assistant, or trainee to come early to discuss our plan and to pray. (This person is a man when I counsel men and a woman when I counsel women or couples.) The following example is

[4] Meeting with a couple requires added dynamics beyond the scope of our book. For counseling children, see chapter 37.

based on a seventy-five-minute first session with my counselee, a Christian woman named Ashley.[5]

Welcome (approximately 10 minutes)

- *I greet Ashley warmly.* I give her a firm handshake and engage in brief small talk, e.g., "I'm glad you are here today. How did you hear about us?" Importantly, I don't ask, "How are you?," since I don't want to hear that answer yet.
- *As we sit, I immediately take the initiative.* I say to Ashley, "Let me share a couple things up front that I think will encourage you and help put you at ease. First, I'm really glad you're here. Thank you for giving me the privilege of meeting with you. I'm looking forward to helping you find and apply God's answers for your struggles. I'd also like to commend you for seeking Christ-centered help. People are often too ashamed or too proud to seek help. Second, I'm going to assume you might be a bit nervous, and I want you to know it's OK. Talking about personal issues can be hard. But God is here with us, through his Spirit, and he is committed by his grace to help us today."
- *I preview the process.* I say, "Let me share what we usually do in a first session. I'll begin by telling you a little about myself and my background and why I'm here, and I will introduce my co-counselor, assistant, or trainee. Then I'll lead us in prayer, asking God to meet with us and help us. Then I'd like to spend the bulk of our time together getting to know you and understanding your situation and the struggle you're facing. Near the end of our time, I'll suggest ways I can help you and give you some practical things you can do. How does that plan sound to you?"
- *I introduce myself.* Assuming Ashley agrees with the plan for the session, I continue, "Let me tell you a little about me and why I'm

[5] Many variables determine session length. For a first session, I typically allot an hour to an hour and fifteen minutes for an individual and up to ninety minutes for a couple or family. For subsequent sessions, I allot about one hour for an individual and up to seventy-five minutes for a couple or family.

here today. . ." I give my brief life story, including an overview of my relationship with Christ, my desire to help Ashley, and a hope-giving Bible truth or verse (e.g., 2 Pet 1:3). I will also introduce any co-counselor, assistant, or trainee I might have invited.

- *I lead in prayer.* I typically include three requests: (1) I thank God for his provisions in Christ of three things both my counselee and I need: forgiveness, wisdom from his Word, and power through his Spirit. (2) I ask God to help us recognize his presence. (3) I ask God to help me listen well and reflect his grace and wisdom.
- *I collect the agreement and information forms.* I ask, "Did you have an opportunity to fill out the forms we sent you? It would be helpful for me to look at them."[6] I collect the forms, thank Ashley, and summarize the main points on the agreement form, especially confidentiality and its limits, to make sure she is comfortable. I then take a minute to read the overview form. I glance at the personal information form but will read it more thoroughly before we meet again.

Know *(approximately 40 minutes)*

- *I transition to listening to and interviewing Ashley.* I say, "Ashley, help me get to know you. Give me the ten-minute *Reader's Digest* or YouTube version of your background. Include where you were born, a bit about your childhood family, and anything significant about your childhood or teen years, and then lead me chronologically to the present." (I may have to keep her moving if she gives too many details.) I jot this information down because it becomes part of box 1 in our six-box model discussed in chapter 10.

Let's pause here to elaborate on a few points. First, counselors use intake forms in different ways. Some use them to guide the discussion,

---

[6] If Ashley hasn't completed the agreement form, I ask her to read it there in my office so we can discuss it and she can sign it. If she hasn't completed the Overview form, I usually ask her to take a few minutes to do so. If she hasn't completed the Personal Information form, I ask her to complete it when at home and send it to me before we meet again.

referring directly to them, making comments on them, and inviting the person to elaborate on what they wrote. Others skim the forms and keep them visible but give the person freedom to talk about whatever they want, even topics not on the forms. Focusing overmuch on the forms can detract from face-to-face, conversational dynamics, making papers rather than the person our focus. But if counselees fail to mention in the session something on the forms that seem important, I ask about it. The point is that you should feel free to use them as you see fit.

Second, if after explaining her background, Ashley does not mention her present problem(s), I transition the conversation by saying, "Tell me what's going on in your life now," or, "What brings you here today?" This segment of the first session, after all, occupies the bulk of the meeting time and should be used wisely. Depending on your preferences, you might limit things by asking for just the big picture, assuring the counselee they will have time to unpack more details during the next meeting.

Third, most biblical counselors take notes—especially in the early sessions. Doing so helps us retain and summarize session information as we reflect afterward. It also shows counselees we value their words. It adds accountability by allowing us to cite previous session discussions. It can also help counter any false reports that might come up against us since contemporaneous, in-session counseling notes have probative value in legal proceedings. Writing down homework assignments adds another level of accountability; it tells the counselee they are not merely suggestions. Even so, notetaking can detract from making eye contact, and some counselees find it distracting. We can minimize these problems by using abbreviations, writing down some things without looking, and angling our postures and notepads to maximize eye contact.

There is no one right way to take notes. Counselors vary in what they note, but here's how I do it. I use one yellow lined pad for each case so that I have all my session information regarding any particular counselee at my fingertips. On this, I include the names of the counselee(s) and any others present at a particular meeting, the date, location, session number, a running record of conversation—I include key quotes, a list of topics I might want to explore in future sessions, the counsel given, homework assigned, the next session's date, and a brief summary of the session as well as suggested direction for the upcoming session that can be reviewed beforehand.

Now, let us return to the sample session with Ashley.

Hope and Plan *(approximately 15 minutes):*

- *I offer Ashley Christ-centered hope.* Having heard her story, I say, "Thankfully, Ashley, I have good news for you: God has answers in his Word for everything we've talked about today. I'm confident we can find them together, and my co-counselor and I *want* to walk with you through the process." (Don't underestimate the hope-giving power of making such personal assurances.)
- *We agree on a problem to address.*

By the end of the first session, it's usually best for you and your counselee to identify and agree on one topic to address together (knowing you can agree to shift in future sessions). This allows you both to focus on one problem, to move wisely and caringly toward the counselee's heart, and to bring Christ-centered answers to the table early on rather than circling around different problems and hoping to eventually get to the center of things. In biblical counseling, all roads lead to and from Christ and the heart, so we can usually start with any issue the counselee wants to address. Some others might resolve themselves as a counselee draw nears to Christ and learns to apply Scripture. A changed heart will impact all areas of a counselee's life.

Which issue should we address? Counselees usually come with one presenting problem, or one issue clearly emerges during the first session. On occasions when the counselee discusses multiple possible issues, I briefly summarize the various issues I'm hearing and the ways we might approach each. Then I allow the counselee to choose one. It's her life and her counseling session, after all; she has voluntarily sought my help.[7] Since counselees will invest their time and effort in addressing what they think

---

[7] This might look different if a church elder has directed a member to meet with me to discuss a specific problem.

is most pressing or important, their buy-in, ownership, and motivation is often more vital than which topic they select. Occasionally, however, I might suggest at starter topic, especially if the person seeks my input, if I see something urgent or serious, or if I see how addressing one root problem might help resolve other symptom problems.

Now, back to our example.

- *I suggest a tentative plan to address her problem.* As time permits, I share an initial biblical perspective or briefly share a Bible passage to give some basic hope and direction. But I also remind Ashley we are early in the process and the focus might shift as we go forward.

Invite (approximately 10 minutes).

- *I offer to meet again.* As I prepare to close my session with Ashley, I say, "If you'd like to meet again, I'd love to. I look forward to talking again and working with you to help you. We can schedule something, or you can let me know later today or tomorrow."[8]
- *Whether or not Ashley commits, I offer a growth assignment:* I say, "Let me go ahead and give you a couple things that I think will help get you started." (See chapter 17 on growth assignments.) I make sure to explain the purpose, the importance, and the details of these as I record them in my notes too.
- *I ask for questions:* I then deal with them if I can or postpone time-consuming matters to the next session.
- *I pray and end the session:* I say, "I've enjoyed meeting you and getting to know you, and I look forward to helping you further and to seeing what the Lord will do in your life. Let me lead us in closing prayer, and I'll hope to see you next week." Then I pray. thank

---

[8] Some biblical counselors orally state at the end of the first session or include in their informed consent agreement something like this: "If we were to meet again, there are three things I'd ask of you that will help us make the process best go forward: a learner's spirit, a commitment to do homework, and some time—your problems didn't develop in a day and won't be solved in a day; but given some time, I think you'll see progress."

God for Ashley, for the opportunity to work with her, and for his grace and promises, and I ask God to help her in the upcoming week. After that, I stand (signaling the end of the session), extend my hand for a handshake, walk with her to the door, and warmly say goodbye.

Conclusion

Amid your understandable first-session nervousness, remember that your counselee will likely be even more nervous. How can you offset that double problem? By remembering that you and your counselee are not alone. God himself is with you. Yes, the same God who was with Moses (Exod 3:12), Joshua (Josh 1:9), and Paul (2 Tim 4:17) in their ventures will be with you.

13

The Counseling Process, Step One: Enter Their World

Within any field of evangelical ministry (e.g., evangelism, discipleship, leadership), though the biblical-theological foundations and Christ-centered goals are similar, specific practical approaches typically differ. In the same way, biblical counselors vary in how they describe and carry out the actual counseling process.[1] No one procedure is the right one, including ours.

[1] Other writers conceptualize the process similarly. Paul David Tripp, *Instruments in the Redeemer's Hands: People in Need of Change Helping People in Need of Change* (Phillipsburg, NJ: P&R, 2002), 125–276, outlines a four-step process of love, know, speak, and do. As his former student, I (Bob) acknowledge my debt to Tripp in this and the next two chapters. Wayne Mack, "The Practice of Biblical Counseling," in MacArthur, *How to Counsel Biblically*, 101–200 (see chap. 2, n. 12), uses seven "I's" to summarize his approach: develop involvement, instill hope, take inventory, interpret data, provide biblical instruction, induce counselees to change, and implement biblical instruction. Randy Patten, "The Central Elements of the Biblical Counseling Process," in Kellemen and Viars, *Christ-Centered Biblical Counseling*, pp. 321–36 (see chap. 1, n. 2), presents six key elements: gather pertinent information, sort out the problems, gain involvement, instill hope, provide instruction, and give homework. Pierre, *Dynamic Heart in Daily Life* (see chap. 1, n. 11), uses read, reflect, relate, and renew as a guide.

Overview of Our Model

Building on Jesus's frequent pattern of ministry, our counseling model involves a simple three-step process: Enter, Understand, and Bring (EUB).[2] We enter a counselee's world, understand their needs (both felt and real), and bring them Christ and his life-changing provisions.

In the Gospels, we see our Lord Jesus doing this throughout his earthly ministry, both on a big-picture level (incarnation, earthly ministry, and cross–resurrection–ascension) and in personal, specific ways with individuals. We see his pattern in Matt 9:35–36:

> Jesus continued going around to all the towns and villages, teaching in their synagogues, preaching the good news of the kingdom, and healing every disease and every sickness. When he saw the crowds, he felt compassion for them, because they were distressed and dejected, like sheep without a shepherd.

The passage doesn't describe our Lord's occasional practice but his *usual* practice. It summarizes his typical pattern as a model counselor. While we can learn from his flexible methods with various individuals like Nathanael (John 1), his own mother (John 2), Nicodemus (John 3), or the Samaritan woman (John 4), we shouldn't build our model on specific encounters. Instead, understanding Jesus's usual approach provides a foundation from which we can exercise needed flexibility.

What was Jesus's common ministry practice, and what should it look like in our counseling ministry?

Enter

First, Jesus entered their world. While this began with his incarnation, it continued with his earthly ministry of "going around to all the towns and villages" (v. 35), having personal contact with needy individuals.

---

[2] We use "steps" to describe specific, progressive movements in the counseling process, but it's not mechanical. In moving to step two, we don't disregard step one. We do all three tasks in each session.

In an analogous way, we enter a counselee's world. We warmly welcome a person and invite them to sit with us and share their lives with us. We express sincere care, display Christlike fruit, and seek to build a relationship of love, trust, and concern. In all this, God's grace propels us to "accept [them], just as Christ also accepted us" (Rom 15:7 NASB). In turn, this breeds hope and invites people to entrust themselves to us and share their struggles.

Understand

Second, Jesus understood the people's needs. He diagnosed their problem: "distressed and dejected, like sheep without a shepherd" (v. 36). They were burdened by their sin and misery, receiving no help from the Jewish religious leaders. Note too that our Lord's understanding of their struggle elicited his compassion.

Similarly, having entered our counselees' world to begin a welcoming relationship, we seek to understand each person's needs, both their felt and true needs. Through wise interviewing and skillful listening, we get to know a person—their situation, problems, perceived needs, how they think, and what they feel, value, and desire. We then organize and interpret that information through a biblical lens to discern the person's true needs. Understanding their felt needs and presenting problem(s) is necessary but insufficient. As Prov 20:5 observes, "The purposes of a person's heart are deep waters, but one who has insight draws them out" (NIV). Furthermore, amid our active listening, we convey Christlike love, compassion, and commitment to help. As was experienced by our Lord, seeing the sin and suffering of those we serve moves our hearts emotionally.

Bring

Third, Jesus brought them God's answers as he taught the gospel and healed people of their diseases and illnesses (v. 35).

Based on our understanding of the person, we bring Jesus and his provisions to those we counsel. We share God's Word to comfort them to the extent they suffer in this fallen world, and to confront them to the extent they respond sinfully. We address both inner-person (root) and outer-person (fruit) issues, that is, both the heart and the behavior. As we bring God's Word, we direct people to specific root and fruit changes through practical, application-oriented instruction in the sessions and homework assignments between sessions. As we see progressive growth, we guide and coach our counselees until they can continue to follow Christ without our direct help.

The rest of this chapter and the next two unpack this Enter-Understand-Bring process. However, at the outset, we must recognize our weakness and cry out to the Lord for the help of his Spirit to work in our lives and in the lives of those we counsel. Apart from him, we can do nothing; with him, we all can flourish (John 15:5; Phil 4:13).

Step One: Enter the Counselee's World

Our Goal

We begin by entering a counselee's world. This involves a purposeful, three-part movement. We want to (1) build a warm, welcoming, godly relationship with the person, (2) *so that* they will gain hope and trust us as God's instrument to help them, (3) *so that* we can lead them to a saving or growing relationship with Jesus amid their problems. This is true whether the person is a non-Christian who needs an initial saving relationship with Jesus or a believer who needs an ongoing or renewed growing relationship with Jesus.

Notice the flow. We don't build warm relationships to get people to like us but to be effective instruments of ministry. We don't provide a caring setting merely to give them a comfortable experience but to love them well and to provide an undistracting, trusting, godly atmosphere (Prov 16:7; 20:5; Eph 4:29–30) in which the Holy Spirit can open up their hearts. None of us will share our lives with people we don't trust or whose acceptance of us we doubt. Neither will those we counsel.

Two Theological Analogies

Two analogies underlie this counseling goal. First, consider God's plan of redemption, particularly the initial act of justification.[3] Romans 15:7 calls us to "accept one another . . . just as Christ accepted [us]" (NIV). God's acceptance of us—his act of justification—becomes the model and motive for us accepting others. The Westminster Shorter Catechism describes justification as "an act of God's free grace, wherein he pardons all our sins, and accepts us as righteous in his sight."[4] While in our day the verb "accept" connotes amoral tolerance, it's a historically-rich theological synonym for justification. God *accepts* us as we are, in Christ, to *transform* us progressively into what he wants us to be. Justification is not compromise; it requires the bloody death of Jesus our substitute to bear our sins. In this context, radical change can occur. God declares us righteous and adopts us as his own sons and daughters so that he can progressively transform us. To use Paul Tripp's illustration, God sees each of us as a broken-down house. To repair us, he first buys and owns us.[5]

By analogy, we form welcoming relationships with our counselees. We see that they need help in handling life. But before offering it, taking our cues from the Lord, we accept them as sinners and sufferers in need of change. From that posture of justification-like acceptance, we can function as God's instruments to help people change.

The second analogy for entering a counselee's world is Christ's incarnation. Historical theologian Thomas Oden observes the importance of the incarnation:

> Much of the energy of empathic engagement in the classical pastoral tradition has come from the special dynamic of the comparison of God's care and human care. The incarnation was viewed

[3] Tripp, *Instruments*, 133.

[4] Westminster Shorter Catechism, Q. 33.

[5] Paul David Tripp, *Broken-Down House: Living Productively in a World Gone Bad* (Wapwallopen, PA: Shepherd Press, 2009).

> as the overarching pattern of the willingness of God to enter fully into our human situation of alienation and suffering. God's self-giving incarnate love calls for energetic human response, for entering the situation of suffering of the neighbor to redeem, show mercy, heal and transform, so as to manifest Christ's love amid the world.[6]

For the Christ-centered counselor seeking to enter someone's world in a caring way, Christ's incarnation remains indispensable.

When considering the incarnation, we think primarily of the second Person of the Godhead becoming human: "The Word became flesh and dwelt among us" (John 1:14). That event was history-shattering. But once enfleshed, Jesus didn't remain aloof. He moved among people, interacted with people, and touched people—often literally. "Jesus continued going around to all the towns and villages. . . . When he saw the crowds, he felt compassion for them" (Matt 9:35–36). So closely did Jesus connect with the common people that opponents called him "a glutton and a drunkard, a friend of tax collectors and sinners" (Matt 11:19; also Luke 15:1–2).

Hebrews 2:5–18 masterfully connects Christ's incarnation and his compassionate care. In verses 5–8a, the writer reflects on God's glorious design for humanity and quotes part of Psalm 8. That design placed humankind a little lower than the angels and crowned us with glory and honor. But the Hebrews author laments in verse 8b that this is not what he sees in his world. However, there is hope: there is indeed one man made a little lower than the angels who is now crowned with glory and honor (compare v. 9 with v. 7). Christ accomplished this by being made like us and by suffering death in our place.

In verses 10–18, the writer assures us God also will bring his chosen sons and daughters to that appointed honor and glory, fulfilling the vision of Psalm 8. How? By making Jesus, the source and pioneer of our salvation, like us in every way; he experienced our humanity and

---

[6] Thomas C. Oden, *Pastoral Counsel*, vol. 3 in Classical Pastoral Care series (New York: Crossroad, 1989), 12.

understands for himself our daily struggles. Through faith in Jesus, we believers are now of the same family: God is our Father and Jesus is our brother (vv. 11–13). In fact, for this salvation to be realized, Jesus "had to be like his brothers and sisters *in every way*" (v. 17, emphasis added). We find this same phrasing in Heb 4:15, where Jesus our high priest empathizes with our weaknesses because he has been tempted "in every way" as we are. This made-like-us, tempted-like-us, human nature of Jesus (cf. Heb 5:1) enabled him to become our "merciful and faithful high priest," "to make atonement for" us, and to "help those who are tempted" (Heb 2:17–18).

How might these Hebrews 2 and 4 insights impact your counseling? While you can't physically incarnate yourself into a counselee's life, you can recognize your common humanity—that you are no different from them. Hebrews 2:11 states it powerfully: because we are of the same family and have the same Father, "Jesus is not ashamed to call [us] brothers and sisters." Our Lord's incarnation produced a new shared humanity and relational connection with us. By analogy, to the extent that you view yourself as different from your counselee, or your counselee views you as different from them, you will lack empathy. They will find it harder to trust you and open up to you.

Christlike Relational Qualities

To create a warm, welcoming, godly relationship with a counselee, there are key qualities counselors must cultivate. Let's note three overarching questions any of us would ask, at least implicitly, in assessing any would-be helper: (1) Do you care about me? (2) Can I trust you? (3) Can you help me? A "no" to any of these would effectively disqualify someone from being our dentist, doctor, or attorney—much less our counselor with whom we share the confidential, personal details of our inner life.

Colossians 3:12–14 and 1 Cor 13:4–7 together provide at least fifteen relational graces for us to cultivate: compassion, kindness, humility, gentleness, patience, forbearance, forgiveness, love, lack of envy, respect, refusing to delight in evil but rejoicing with the truth, protectiveness (we address confidentiality in chapter 20), trust, perseverance, and hope (see chapter 16 on giving hope).[7] Dwelling on these passages is a wise lifelong pursuit for every counselor.

The rest of this chapter stresses three relational graces we especially need to enter the counselee's world: compassion, humility, and gentleness.

Compassion

As we saw in Matt 9:36, "When [Jesus] saw the crowds, he felt compassion for them, because they were distressed and dejected, like sheep without a shepherd." So, what is compassion? Compassion is that inward, deeply felt emotional response of pity for the plight of a suffering person, coupled with a desire to alleviate that suffering. Compassion *sees* the suffering person, *feels* tender pity for the sufferer, and seeks to *alleviate* that suffering where possible and prudent.

To what should we respond compassionately? Victimization, oppression, and neglect elicit tears from every normal, caring, just person. To that list we could add general life hardships, economic downturns, and various forms of poverty, natural disasters, and diseases and injuries. Believers might also respond tearfully to the effects of spiritual lostness, false teaching, and demonic attacks. In short, people typically show compassion to those who suffer innocently.

But Scripture goes beyond that. It pictures God showing compassion even to those whose suffering was self-induced. Consider this moving account in Nehemiah 9 where the Levites confess Israel's wickedness and praise God's compassion during the golden calf incident:

> Our ancestors acted arrogantly; they became stiff-necked and did not listen to your commands. They refused to listen. . . . They became stiff-necked and appointed a leader to return to their slavery in Egypt. But you are a forgiving God, gracious and *compassionate*, slow to anger and abounding in faithful love, and you did not abandon them. Even after they had cast an image of a calf for

[7] Consider also the relational qualities in Matt 5:3–12; Eph 4:2–3; 1 Pet 3:8; Gal 5:22–23; and 1 Thess 2:1–12.

> themselves and said, "This is your god who brought you out of Egypt," and they had committed terrible blasphemies, you did not abandon them in the wilderness because of your great *compassion.* (Neh 9:16–19, emphasis added; cf. 9:31)

Few places in the Bible deliver a more devastating description of Israel's evil. Yet God showed them compassion. The Hebrew term for compassion used here (*raḥûm)* carries the sense of undeserved grace and the emotional nuance of pity, care, and tender love (see also Ps 103:13–14; Isa 63:7; Mic 7:19).

In counseling, we often find that a counselee has both sinned and been sinned against. While we will need to sort out and address both strands, we must convey godly compassion and its proper emotive aspect for each.

How can you develop compassion toward those who have sinfully brought suffering on themselves? First, focus on the cross of Christ. Remember your own massive guilt before God that God in Christ fully forgave you (Matt 18:21–35). Remember what you were like before God set his saving love on you and changed you forever (Eph 2:1–10; Titus 3:3–8).

Second, study the compassion of our Lord Jesus. Consider his compassion toward shepherdless people (Matt 9:36), people with disabilities (Matt 20:34), diseased people (Mark 1:41), hungry people (Mark 8:2), demon-possessed people (Mark 9:22), grieving people (Luke 7:13), victimized people (Luke 10:33), and guilty, lost people (Luke 15:20; the father here represents God).

Third, reflect on how God has comforted you in the hardships you have faced. Paul opens this path of thinking in 2 Cor 1:4: "[God] comforts us in all our affliction, so that we may be able to comfort those who are in any kind of affliction, through the comfort we ourselves receive from God." The Father of compassion does not comfort you merely for your sake, but so you can compassionately comfort others.

Humility

Several passages invite our meditation as we prayerfully humble ourselves before the Lord and enter a counselee's world. Isaiah 66:2 tells us God looks favorably on the person "who is humble, submissive in spirit, and trembles at [his] word." And Jas 4:6 reminds us that "God resists the proud but gives grace to the humble."

One of our Lord's most striking parables appears in Luke 18:9–14, the parable of the Pharisee and the tax collector. In verse 9, Luke introduces the story and summarizes its thrust: "[Jesus] also told this parable to some who trusted in themselves that they were righteous and looked down on everyone else." Here we immediately see the tight tie between self-righteousness and judgmentalism: self-righteousness breeds judgmentalism; judgmentalism betrays self-righteousness. In verses 10–14, Jesus tells the story. The Pharisee prays about his own righteous conduct; the tax collector confesses his sin and pleads for mercy. In the end—which would've been a surprise twist for the original hearers—the tax collector and not the Pharisee is said to be justified and exalted in God's sight.

The Pharisee offered a self-righteous prayer: "God, I thank you that I'm not like other people—greedy, unrighteous, adulterers, or even like this tax collector." (v. 11). From this, we get a powerful takeaway: the only thing worse than being a greedy, unrighteous, an adulterer, or a tax collector is *being proud that you are not one*. The implications for counseling are staggering. This means that the only thing worse than being (fill in counselee's problem) is being proud that you are not (fill in counselee's problem). Imagine the most repulsive act someone might do and fit that into the formula; for instance, the only thing worse than being a cocaine dealer or child molester is being proud you are not one.

So, what does humility look like in a counselor?

- "I am no better than you. I know this, and I want you to know it as well. Except for God's grace, I'd be where you are, and maybe in a worse place."
- "I need the same help you need: the same gospel, same Savior, same Bible, same Holy Spirit, and same church ministry and support. I desperately need help from above."
- "I who am helping you today might need someone—maybe you—to help me tomorrow."
- "My position as your helper might deceive you into thinking I am above you. I am not."

Gentleness

Scripture frequently and profoundly pairs humility with gentleness (e.g., 2 Cor 10:1). Our Lord Jesus combines them in Matt 11:28–29: "Come to me, all you who are weary and burdened, and I will give you rest. Take my yoke upon you and learn from me, for I am gentle and humble in heart, and you will find rest for your souls" (NIV). Amazingly, this is the only place in the Gospels where Jesus self-describes his inner person: he is gentle and humble in heart toward those in need. In this, Jesus reflects the heart of his Father: "[God] protects his flock like a shepherd; he gathers the lambs in his arms and carries them in the fold of his garment. He gently leads those that are nursing" (Isa 40:11).

What does gentleness look like as you build a counseling relationship? Scripture couples it with humility, patience, and forbearance (Eph 4:2); with good conduct (Jas 3:13); and with being peace loving, compliant, and full of mercy and good fruit (Jas 3:17). In 1 Thess 2:7–8, Paul likens his own ministry to a gentle nursing mother nurturing her own children (NIV). Care, consideration, tenderness, and kindness—in content and tone—must mark our attitude toward those who seek our help. In 1 Tim 6:11, Paul exhorts Timothy to pursue gentleness along with five other qualities.

Yet gentleness doesn't nullify the need for faithful biblical counselors to admonish, warn, and rebuke when needed. Jesus sets the standard: "As many as I love, I rebuke and discipline" (Rev 3:19). Love, then, lovingly confronts those it loves. So, when a brother or sister is overtaken in sin, we who walk by the Spirit should not be a party to self-destruction; we should restore them. Yet we should do so gently (Gal 6:1). Moreover, when challenged about our beliefs, we must be ready to explain and defend our views, but with gentleness and respect (1 Pet 3:15–16). When confronted by opponents, we must not quarrel but must gently and patiently teach, entrusting the results to God (2 Tim 2:24–25).

What can motivate you to grow in gentleness? First, meditate on the examples above of Jesus, Paul, and the Father. Ask God to make you like them. Second, since gentleness is a fruit of God's Spirit (Gal 5:16–26), consciously seek to depend on and live by the Spirit. Ask God to fill you with fresh measures of his Spirit daily as you dwell on his breathed-out words in that passage. Third, rehearse the gospel's riches. Recall God's undeserved grace toward you. In Titus 3:2, Paul implores us to show "gentleness to all people." Why? Paul gives a reason in verses 3–5 of that same chapter: "For we too were once foolish, disobedient, deceived, enslaved by various passions and pleasures, living in malice and envy, hateful, detesting one another. But when the kindness of God our Savior and his love for mankind appeared, he saved us." Paul then proceeds to unpack the gospel. God's gracious treatment of you in your times of need should move you to be gentle toward others.

Conclusion

While Jesus alone perfectly possesses these qualities of compassion, humility, and gentleness, God's Spirit can grow these relational graces in each biblical counselor. Cultivate them; don't counsel without them. We need these qualities to form warm, welcoming relationships with our counselees that enable us to enter their world.

The Counseling Process, Step Two: Understand Their Needs

Having begun to enter a counselee's world by forming a warm, welcoming relationship (Step One), our next step is to understand their felt and true needs. Biblical counselors know the truth of Prov 18:13: "The one who gives an answer before he listens—this is foolishness and disgrace." We must seek to understand those we counsel.

Goals for Step Two

What are our goals in this second main step? First, we must seek to understand the person, not merely the problem. "Image bearers," as Bob Kellemen reminds us, "cannot be analyzed, dissected, examined, or studied. They can only be known, experienced, and loved."[1] If we can understand the person, we can understand their problem. This includes understanding the person's

- situation—the hardships and the common grace blessings they have or are experiencing;

[1] Robert W. Kellemen, *Spiritual Friends: A Methodology of Soul Care and Spiritual Direction* (Taneytown, MD: RPM Books, 2005), 96.

- behavior—how they are responding to their situation, in words, actions, emotions, and conscious thoughts; and
- heart—their core beliefs, motives, affections, desires—"the source of life" (Prov 4:23).

Our desire as counselors is to view each counselee's life the way they do.

Second, we must convey to each person that we understand them. For counseling to be effective, you must not only understand your counselee; your counselee must *feel* understood by you.

Third, we must lead each person to biblical self-understanding. Apart from Scripture, counselees are confused and self-deceived (Rom 12:3; Eph 4:22–24; Titus 3:3; Heb 3:12–13). We want to help them don biblical glasses to see the Lord, themselves, and their situations in new and accurate ways.

How will we achieve these goals? Through skillful interviewing, active listening, and wisely interpreting the information.

A Case Example

To see the importance of this step, imagine Mandy calls your church's office seeking counseling. Your pastor contacts you, informs you that Mandy's husband left her yesterday to move in with another woman, and invites you to counsel her.

So, what is Mandy experiencing? The answers might seem obvious:

- Shock. "My world has crashed."
- Fear. "What will happen to me? What will he do next? How will others respond to this news?"
- Shame, embarrassment. "What will my friends and family think about me?"
- Sadness, depression, despair, hopelessness, even suicidality.
- Anger. At her husband, the other woman, herself, and even God.

- Revenge. "I'll show him. I'll throw his stuff to the curb. I'll hire the best attorney in town and take him down. He'll never see his children again."
- Guilt. "I was not a good enough wife. I drove him into her arms."
- Jealousy. "Why her? What does she have that I don't?"

Yet all these answers are wrong. When thinking about Mandy's situation before meeting with her, the right answer is, "I don't know." Because while any of these answers *might* be correct, you won't know what Mandy is experiencing until you sit with her and listen.

In fact, the above list misses another possibility: perhaps Mandy is relieved. Maybe her husband has been violent, and she's glad he's gone. Maybe she suspected his infidelity, but he flatly denied it and called her paranoid. Or maybe she has her eyes on another man and sees her husband's infidelity as an exit ramp from her marriage. You don't know how Mandy is experiencing this situation until you get to know Mandy.

Several implications flow from this. First, we biblical counselors focus on people, not categories. We don't counsel abandoned people, alcoholics, or anxious people. Rather, we counsel Mandy, whose husband abandoned her; Joe, who drinks too much; and Meredith, who is filled with anxiety.

Second, we don't counsel Mandy who has been abandoned by her husband, but Mandy who has been abandoned by her husband *and is responding to that experience in a specific way*—a way we must labor to understand.

Third, we recognize there are no one-size-fits-all Bible verses. To suggest, "This is the best verse for abandoned people," ignores individual responses to circumstances. Each one who has been abandoned might warrant a different approach and different biblical truths. Don't assume that passage X is best for all abandoned people, passage Y for all alcoholic people, or passage Z for all anxious people.

Getting to Know Your Counselee

How should you approach the task of getting to know a person?[2] Let's begin with some overall perspectives and then consider the interplay between asking wise questions and active listening.[3]

General Perspectives

First, avoid unfounded assumptions. We often approach significant relationships with assumptions based on one or more of the following:

- personal experience: "I know what this rejected person is feeling. The same thing happened to me . . ."
- general knowledge based on counseling training, books, and so on: "I know what this rejected person is feeling. I read about it. My professor or training supervisor told me that rejected people typically feel . . ."
- previous counseling experience: "I know what this rejected person is feeling. I've worked with three cases like this in the last two years."

Remember, your counselee is not you; he is not the person your professor or textbook described; and he is not the person you counseled last time.[4] Instead, you must base your interpretations on sound conclusions gained through careful interviewing and dialogue.

---

[2] While some biblical counselors call this step "data gathering," others simply prefer "getting to know" or "interviewing" the person since that sounds warmer and more personal.

[3] Secular experts in counselor training have produced numerous resources that, when read discerningly, can help biblical counselors grow in their attending and listening skills. For a brief, starter book, see William R. Miller, *Listening Well: The Art of Emphatic Understanding* (Eugene, OR: Wipf and Stock, 2018); or Allen E. Ivey, Norma Gluckstern, and Mary Bradford Ivey, *Basic Attending Skills: Foundations of Empathic Relationships and Problem Solving*, 6th ed. (San Diego: Cognella Academic, 2019).

[4] See Robert D. Jones, "You Don't Know What You Don't Know: Three Wrong Assumptions," Biblical Counseling Coalition, March 5, 2018, https://www.biblicalcounselingcoalition.org/2018/03/05/you-dont-know-what-you-dont-know-three-wrong-assumptions/.

Moreover, you should seek to move progressively from understanding a counselee's situation (external circumstances) to their behavior and then their heart (internal roots). Constantly work to understand a person's inner beliefs and motives.

Further, as you begin to understand a person, respond with appropriate Christlike emotions and actions. Recall again our Lord's model: "When he saw the crowds, he felt compassion for them" (Matt 9:36). Continue to express the relational graces we saw in Step One as the process proceeds and added information emerges. Demonstrating those specific qualities and attending skills most appropriate to how a *particular* person feels amid a *particular* situation becomes your relational inroad into that person's life.

Asking Wise Questions

Asking wise questions is indispensable for getting to know a person. But not all types of questions are equally valuable. Here are seven guidelines:

1. Prefer Open-ended Questions to Closed-end Questions

Closed questions can be answered with yes or no and require little to no information disclosure. Open questions require counselees to select and self-disclose information. They must scan their mental menus and choose what information they want to volunteer. Below are examples of both types:

- Closed: "Do you have a good marriage?"
- Open: "How would you describe your marriage?"
- Closed: "When your boss said that, did you become angry?"
- Open: "When your boss said that, how did you feel?"

Closed questions begin with words such as *is*, *are*, *did*, *do*, *will*, *would*, *have*, *has*, *can*, or *could*. Open questions start with *who*, *what*, *where*, *when*, *why*, or *how*. They invite a counselee to share more information. Of course, wisdom is required in using open questions. Asking a sinned-against person, "How did that person's action make you feel?" wrongly assigns determinative power to that person ("make you"). Instead, you should simply ask, "How did you feel about (or respond to) that person's actions?"

Importantly, closed questions can help when a person (e.g., a child or teen) seems unable or unwilling to open up or to answer open-ended queries or when you simply want to get a topic on the table. An example of the latter is, "Do you ever feel depressed?" If the person says yes, then you can follow up with open questions, such as "How often? When? How would you describe those times?"

2. Avoid Either/or Questions (Also Known as Binary or Menu Questions)

These questions lock your counselee into your catalog of choices. For example, asking "When you said that to your wife, were you angry or were you sad?" presumes you only supply two options. Just ask, "When you said that to your wife, how did you feel?"

3. Move from Extensive to Intensive Questions

Extensive questions ask a little about many areas and scan the counselee's whole life. Intensive questions ask a lot about one area and probe that one aspect. Extensive questions survey broadly, skim the surface, and use a wide-angle lens. Intensive ones focus narrowly, dive deeply, and use a zoom lens.

Both methods can be profitable in getting to know your counselee and moving toward their heart. Extensive questions uncover common heart themes or behavioral patterns. Asking questions about the person's friends, family, church, job, or health might reveal common themes about financial worries or fearing people. Asking intensive questions would reveal causes and connections. As you explore a counselee's job fears, you might go from the facts of a work incident to their behavioral response and then to their beliefs and motives (e.g., "What were you hoping to gain from that?").

The counseling process typically progresses from extensive to intensive questions, both within each session (start with a general overview then move toward the focused area) and from session to session (more extensive questions in the early sessions as we move toward the focused area of change). In time you will learn to develop your own rhythm for when to dig and when to relax, when to press and when to pause.

4. Use Searching Questions to Move toward the Heart

"Insightful people are insightful," writes Paul Tripp, "not because they have the right answers but because they have asked the right questions."[5] Wise questions not only gain information, they teach counselees to think biblically. When counselees unload their life problems but make no reference to God, asking them "Where do you see God in all this?" brings two benefits: it seeks valuable information about their view of God but also reminds them there is a God involved in their life. Consider these heart-searching examples from the Bible.

- Where are you? . . . Who told you that you were naked? Did you eat from the tree that I commanded you not to eat from? (Gen 3:9, 11)
- Why do you spend silver on what is not food, and your wages on what does not satisfy? (Isa 55:2)
- Why should you die, house of Israel? (Ezek 18:31)
- Why do you look at the splinter in your brother's eye but don't notice the beam of wood in your own eye? (Matt 7:3)
- Why are you looking for the living among the dead? (Luke 24:5)
- Who are you to judge another's household servant? (Rom 14:4)

What might this technique look like in typical counseling settings?[6] You might ask questions like these:

- Where do you see God in this situation? (Or what do you think God is up to?)
- How do you think God looks at you?

---

[5] Tripp, *Instruments*, 284 (see chap. 13, n. 1).

[6] For a list of thirty-five "X-ray questions," with commentary, see Powlison, *Seeing with New Eyes*, 129–43 (see chap. 6, n. 14).

- What were you hoping to accomplish?
- What was going on in your mind?
- If you could change your situation in some way, how would you?
- What do you most want to see happen (or not happen) in this situation?
- What are your biggest concerns about this situation (or relationship)?
- How would you like people to pray for you?
- What do you think might be at the root of your behavior?

5. Ask Simple, Not Compound Questions

Asking, "What did you say to your boss and how did your boss respond?" is one question too many. Ask one simple, clear question at a time. Then close your mouth and listen.

6. Don't Settle for Nonspecific Answers; Go Deeper

If you ask, "How did the conversation with your son go?," and the person says, "It went well," then go deeper: "In what way did it go well?"

7. Let One Question-and-Answer Exchange Lead You to the Next

While it's wise to enter a session with a prepared list of questions, view that list as a menu to select from, not a script to obey.

In summary, ask one simple, open-ended question at a time to move toward a person's beliefs and motives.

Active Listening

Excellent communication requires skillful speaking. The other half of communication—arguably the most important, yet most neglected—is skillful listening.

Where should biblical counselors begin? With God. He is our model and motivator for good listening. We see it within the Godhead as the three Persons listen to each other: the Father listens to his Son (John 11:41–42), the Son listens to his Father (John 8:26; 14:24), and the Spirit listens to the Father and Son (John 16:13). Among God's countless activities before and since creation, there is nothing *more* Godlike than listening. God listens to God.

Furthermore, God listens to us, his people. Genesis 16 records one of the most moving stories in the Bible. Hagar was a woman of no cultural stature or importance, one who had just experienced severe mistreatment (though she was not entirely innocent) and was fleeing back to Egypt, her homeland. Yet the angel of the Lord met her and ministered to her. How?

1. He sought and found her, though she was not looking for him (v. 7; cf. Luke 5:31–32; 19:10).
2. He spoke to her, addressing her by name (vv. 8–10; like our Savior in John 10:3). He asked her an open-ended, heart-searching question, gave her direct counsel, and promised to bless her.
3. He listened to her: "You shall name him Ishmael, for the LORD has heard of your misery" (vv. 11–12 NIV; cf. 21:17–18).
4. He saw her with the eyes of compassion (v. 13; like our Savior in Matt 9:36).

This is what our Redeemer does: he finds, speaks, listens, and sees. And this is what Christlike counselors do, in the name of Jesus and empowered by his Spirit: we meet with those in need, we listen carefully, we see our counselees' struggles, and we speak God's Word to them.

Exodus 2:23–25 describes the same dynamic. Israel's exodus out of Egypt didn't start with the splitting of the Red Sea, the ten plagues, or even God's burning-bush appearance to Moses. It began with God's ears: "The Israelites groaned in their slavery and cried out, and their cry for help because of their slavery went up to God. God heard their groaning and he remembered his covenant with Abraham, with Isaac and with Jacob. So God looked on the Israelites and was concerned about them" (2:23–25 NIV, cf. 3:7–10).

The Psalms in particular speak of the God who hears us, especially amid our suffering:

- For he has not despised or abhorred the torment of the oppressed. He did not hide his face from him but listened when he cried to him for help. (22:24)
- The eyes of the LORD are on the righteous, and his ears are open to their cry for help. . . . The righteous cry out, and the LORD hears, and rescues them from all their troubles. (34:15–17; cf. 1 Pet 3:12)
- I waited patiently for the LORD, and he turned to me and heard my cry for help. (40:1)
- I love the LORD because he has heard my appeal for mercy. Because he has turned his ear to me, I will call out to him as long as I live. (116:1–2)

The pattern in these passages is clear and the lesson unmistakable: God first listens, then helps; counselors should first listen, then help. As Dietrich Bonhoeffer observed, "Christians have forgotten that the ministry of listening has been committed to them by Him who is Himself the great listener and whose work they should share."[7] In Scripture, God furnishes a stirring model of what good listening entails. It means listening actively and attentively. The apostle James exhorts us to be "quick to listen, slow to speak, and slow to anger" (Jas 1:19). Proverbs 18 reminds us that speaking to a matter before listening is foolish and disgraceful (v. 13) and that there is more than one side to every story (v. 17, "The first to state his case seems right until another comes and cross-examines him").

Consider pastor Francis Schaeffer's practice as an example of active, attentive listening. Referring to a hard case that Shaeffer described, Jerram Barrs writes:

> This kind of situation broke [Schaeffer's] heart, and he would devote himself to listening for hours to the struggles and questions of those who came to his home. He would say, "If I have only an hour with someone, I will spend the first 55 minutes asking questions and finding out what is troubling their heart

[7] Dietrich Bonhoeffer, *Life Together*, trans. John W. Doberstein (New York: Harper & Row, 1954), 98–99.

> and mind, and then in the last 5 minutes I will share something of the truth."[8]

While we might not follow Schaeffer's extreme time allotment, the vignette underscores the centrality of active, attentive listening.

Godly listening also means listening caringly and compassionately, as we see God do in Genesis 16 and Exodus 2–3 above. Paul spent three years ministering to the Ephesians "with great humility and with tears" (Acts 20:19 NIV), warning each of them "night and day with tears" (20:31). The same apostle encouraged his readers to care for each other in ways that assume empathic listening: "Rejoice with those who rejoice; weep with those who weep" (Rom 12:15; cf. 1 Cor 12:26).

While in one sense we should listen to every word our counselees utter, some topics warrant special attention. These include

- requests for help;
- topics leading them to become anxious, upset, sad, or withdrawn;
- struggles with God, doubts, and/or inability to pray;
- superstitious religious beliefs ("I know God *will* [give me a husband, bring back my prodigal son, change my wife, heal my cancer, etc.])";
- self-talk and identity statements ("I can't do anything right; everyone seems mad at me; I'm a firstborn; I'm a 2 on the Enneagram");
- attempts to secure agreement with their view or sympathy for their behavior ("Don't you think that . . . ?" "Wouldn't you have . . . ?");
- how they answer questions (answers such as "Yeah, but . . ." are essentially "no" answers; replies such as "I couldn't do that" might tell you more about their willingness than their ability; answers such as "I don't know if this is right, but . . ." usually means it's wrong);
- their explanations and underlying assumptions ("I responded sharply to my spouse *because* I was tired");

[8] Jerram Barrs, "Francis Schaeffer: The Man and His Message," Covenant Seminary, https://www.covenantseminary.edu/francis-schaeffer-the-man-and-his-message/.

- exaggerations, globalizing, or catastrophizing ("This was the *worst* day of my life"; "My husband is *always* angry at me and *never* nice to me");
- goals, wants, felt needs, desires; and
- metaphors, images, illustrations, and word pictures.

Consider also these dozen don'ts for wise listening:

1. Don't be afraid to interrupt the conversation for some silent reflection: "What you're saying, Jenn, is very significant. Give me a moment to think about it."
2. Don't be afraid to admit a concentration lapse or a lack of understanding: "I'm sorry, Jenn, I didn't hear what you said. Could you repeat that?" or "I'm not tracking with what you just said. Could you help me understand a little better?" It demonstrates respect, care, and honesty.
3. Don't trivialize or bypass problems the person regards as important. Take their concerns seriously and deal with them respectfully and caringly.
4. Don't be shocked by the person's admission of sin. The doctrine of remaining sin recognizes that even Christians can do horrible things. Your willingness to calmly listen and bring Christ-centered hope will help them address it honestly.
5. Don't be offended by crude or rude language. Counselees, especially in crisis, might not guard their speech as much as even they know they should.
6. Don't judge motives: "You only said that because you wanted. . . ." Instead, ask, "When you said that to him, what were you hoping for?" (Ask, don't assume; ask, don't accuse; ask!)
7. Don't fill in the person's answers or complete their sentences. Some counselees speak slowly. Resist the temptation to speed along the conversation.
8. Don't settle for not understanding your counselee or some aspect of their experience. Instead, work harder to grasp aspects that seem foreign to you.

9. Don't mix your thinking and the person's thinking: "Yeah, I know what you're saying. In fact, I often respond this way."
10. Don't ignore your counselee's answer to your previous question as you prepare your next question. Frame your follow-up comment or question only *after* you listen. If you need to pause first, do so.
11. Don't become passive with a talkative person or seek to wait out their needlessly long story. Instead, lean forward, increase your active listening, and get on board with their monologue so you can interrupt less abruptly and steer the conversation.[9]
12. Don't fear times of silence when the counselee doesn't immediately answer your question or respond to your comment. View these as providential opportunities to pray for the person and to allow the Spirit to work in a more direct way.[10]

Other Methods of Gaining Information

While the best way to get to know a counselee is through private conversation in the session, other ways might help.

- Written intake forms. Even if you know the person previously, the forms will provide information you didn't know.
- Informal conversations outside of sessions.
- Nonverbal cues; for instance, eye contact, clothing, nervous habits, appearance, seating position, posture, facial expressions, and gestures.
- Your relational experience with the person—real-time information you gain as the sessions progress.
- Written assignments, especially those involving self-disclosure; for instance, journaling, inventories, and personal application components in Bible studies.

---

[9] See Robert D. Jones, "Handling the Nonstop Talker," Biblical Counseling Coalition, December 12, 2016, http://biblicalcounselingcoalition.org/2016/12/26/handling-the-nonstop-talker/.

[10] See Bekka French, "The Art of the Pause: Learning to Be Counselors Who Are Slow to Speak," Biblical Counseling Coalition, https://www.biblicalcounselingcoalition.org/2019/05/13/the-art-of-the-pause-learning-to-be-counselors-who-are-slow-to-speak/.

Confirming Your Understanding of the Person

It's not enough to understand your counselee; he must feel understood. To accomplish this throughout each session, you should listen to the person actively, attentively, caringly, and compassionately. Along the way, ask clarifying questions. For example:

- ask for definitions of terms: "What do you mean by an 'unhappy marriage'?" "What do you mean by 'bipolar'?"
- ask for examples: "Could you give me an example of what your anger looks or sounds like?"
- ask for reasons he did X, believes Y, or wants Z: "Why were you upset?"

Then, at key points, summarize what you hear. Capture content and emotion: "Let me make sure I understand. I hear you saying . . . You seem a bit . . ." Finally, seek confirmation: "Do I understand you correctly?" If the counselee hesitates to answer, assure them you want to understand accurately and ask them to help you understand them better. Then summarize your revised understanding and seek confirmation for that, using reflective statements. Don't repeat verbatim the person's words; instead, weave in some of their key phrases.

Organizing and Interpreting the Information You Gain

Gathering information does not complete our understanding step. We need to interpret it accurately. And to interpret it accurately, we need to think biblically—to view people and their situations through the lens of God's Word.

The Six-Box Model

In chapter 10 we introduced our six-box model, a conceptual model that summarizes how change happens in those we counsel. We unpacked each box and described how they function together to explain the person and the flow of Christ-centered change. (Please review chapter 10 as needed.)

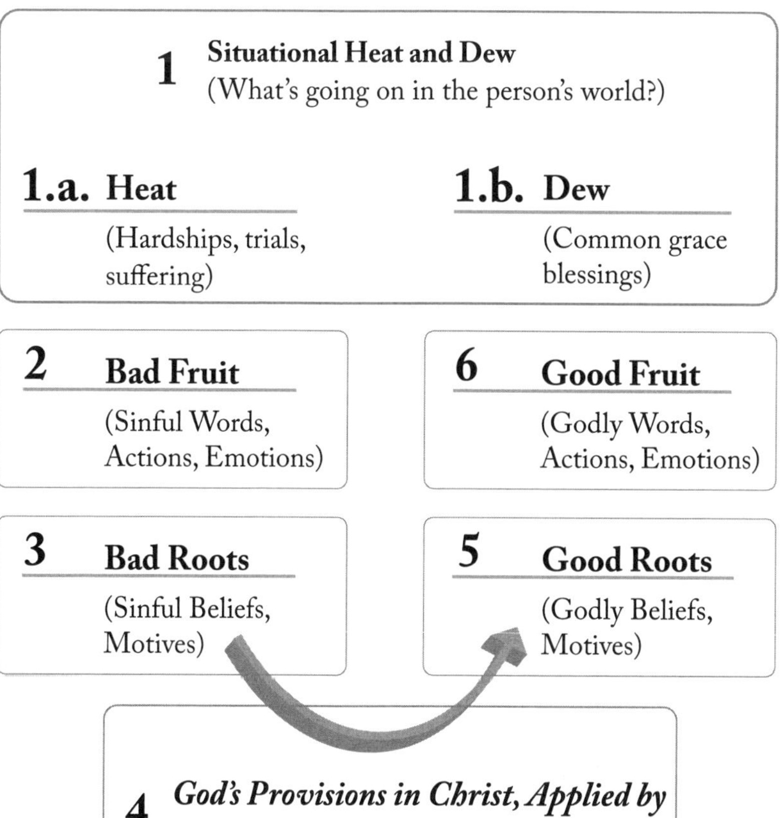

Thankfully, this model can also help us organize and interpret the information we learn about a counselee and help us envision our goals. During session one, we learn a lot about a counselee. When that session ends, I (Bob) take my private session notes and intake forms, combined with my short-term memory, and enter into the six boxes pertinent information—including words and phrases—from the session. As I note the box 1 heat, my compassion increases. I'm reminded afresh that counselees often face difficulties and sometimes suffer. As I enter into box 2 any ways they have fallen short of handling their problem God's way, I also begin to envision how God wants them to handle it and I pencil in what should be box 6 responses (recall the put-off/put-on change dynamic discussed in chapter 10). I won't have much information for boxes 3 and 5 yet, though I begin to pencil in some possibilities. I note in box 4 any Bible passage(s) or theme(s) I introduced, though it might not yet be the primary passage or theme the person needs. I am yet to understand the box 3 heart issues.

At the same time, as I use this tool to reflect on this first session and prepare for the next, I will often see

- categories I missed; for instance, I didn't ask about their job life
- details about categories I included; for instance, I learned about his church attendance but not about how active he is there or his understanding of the gospel
- how much I don't know yet but need to pursue

This model provides a simple, practical tool—built on a biblical view of Christlike change—to record and assess the information I progressively gain in each session. Therefore, I update it after each session, based on my increasing understanding of my counselee. The visual forces me to think biblically about each box and grasp the relationships among them while also recognizing what information I lack.

The Summary Interpretive Question

What is our end goal for Step 2, understanding our counselees' needs? To be able to sufficiently answer The Summary Interpretive Question:

> *How and why is this person responding to this situation (in which God has placed them), and what heart and behavior changes are biblically indicated?*

Each term above is important and each aspect maps on to the Six-Box Model: (Note the explanatory brackets.)

> *How* [box 2] *and why* [box 3] *is this person responding to this situation (in which God has placed them* [hence you must know their situation; box 1], *and what heart* [box 5] *and behavior changes* [box 6] *are biblically* [box 4] *indicated?*

Having satisfactorily answered this complex question in your own mind, you are ready to move to Step Three: Bring Them Christ and His Answers.

Conclusion

We close with the prayer of the twelfth-century British monk, Aelred of Rievaulx (AD 1110–1167). It's a model prayer for all who wish, as Thomas Oden introduces it, "to engage empathically" in ministering to people:

> Teach me your servant, therefore, Lord, teach me, I pray you, by your Holy Spirit, how to devote myself to them and how to spend myself on their behalf. Give me, by your unutterable grace, the power to bear with their shortcomings patiently, to share their griefs in loving sympathy, and to afford them help according to their needs. Taught by your Spirit may I learn to comfort the sorrowful, confirm the weak and raise the fallen; to be myself one with them in their weakness, one with them when they burn at causes of offence, one in all things with them, all things to all of them, that I may gain them all. Give me the power to speak the truth straightforwardly and yet acceptably; so that they all may be built up in faith and hope and love, in chastity and lowliness, in patience and obedience, in spiritual fervor and submissiveness of mind. . . . Teach me, therefore, sweet Lord, how to restrain the restless, comfort the discouraged, and support the weak. Teach me to suit myself to everyone according to his nature, character, and disposition, according to his power of understanding or his lack of it, as time and place require, in each case, as you would have me do. (Aelred of Rievaulx, *Treatises, The Pastoral Prayer*, CF 2, 114–15)[11]

[11] Thomas C. Oden, *Pastoral Counsel*, vol. 3 in Classical Pastoral Care series (New York: Crossroad, 1989), 11–12.

The Counseling Process, Step Three: Bring Them Christ and His Answers

In our previous chapters we explained the first two steps in our Enter-Understand-Bring counseling model. Having entered the person's world and understood both their felt and real needs, let's consider our third step, bringing them Christ and his provisions. We want to help counselees understand their suffering, see their fruit and root sins, repent and believe the gospel, and adopt and live out a new godly pattern of life. This involves speaking God's Word to the person, helping them understand and apply it personally, and guiding and coaching them in walking out that new pattern. We must minister the Word wisely—with confidence, skill, and compassion—not merely dispense it.

Our Ministry Aim: Christlikeness

What does this godly pattern of life look like, the pattern toward which our counseling ministry aims? Consider these outcome goals the apostle Paul consciously labored to produce in those to whom he ministered:

- We are workers with you *for your joy*, because you stand firm in *your faith*. (2 Cor 1:24)

- In the sight of God we are speaking in Christ, and everything, dear friends, is *for building you up*. (2 Cor 12:19)
- My children, I am again suffering labor pains for you *until Christ is formed in you*. (Gal 4:19)
- I know that I will remain and continue with all of you *for your progress and joy in the faith*. (Phil 1:25)
- We proclaim him, warning and teaching everyone with all wisdom, *so that we may present everyone mature in Christ*. (Col 1:28)
- As you know, like a father with his own children, we encouraged, comforted, and implored each one of you *to walk worthy of God*. (1 Thess 2:11–12)
- We sent Timothy . . . to *strengthen and encourage* you concerning *your faith*. (1 Thess 3:2)[1]

Like Paul, biblical counselors should consciously aim to help counselees become like Christ, live worthy of God, be strengthened and encouraged in their faith, and experience Christ's true joy. Our goal is not for them to become self-actualized, be what they want to be, merely find temporal happiness, or measure up to some cultural ideal. Our goal is Christlikeness.

Our Ministry Tool: God's Word

How will Christlikeness happen? As we help people deal biblically with their personal and relational counseling problems, we must remember, as we saw in chapters 1 and 3, that they need the ongoing entrance and wise application of God's Word into their lives. Second Timothy 3:14–17 must be foundational and formative for our ministry. Paul writes to Timothy to encourage him in his ministry:

> Continue in what you have learned and firmly believed. You know those who taught you, and you know that from infancy you have known the sacred Scriptures, which are able to give you wisdom for salvation through faith in Christ Jesus. All Scripture is inspired

[1] All emphasis in these passages has been added.

> by God and is profitable for teaching, for rebuking, for correcting, for training in righteousness, so that the man of God may be complete, equipped for every good work.

From this passage we draw two simple yet profound conclusions about our Bibles.

First, we learn what the Bible is: it is God's "breathed out" Word to us. The Greek term translated above as "inspired by God" is a compound term best translated as "God-breathed" (NIV). This doesn't mean God breathed into an existing set of words but that the words themselves are the product of God's breath. Hebrews 4:12 reminds us the Bible is a "living" Word from God—active, dynamic, pulsating, electric. In 2 Pet 1:21, the Scripture writers "spoke from God as they were carried along by the Holy Spirit." So, though he worked through individuals and their experiences and personalities, the Spirit ultimately wrote the Bible, illumines us and those we counsel to understand the Bible, and enables us and them to believe and obey it. The Bible is a Spirit-ual book, comparable to no other counseling resource.

Second, we learn what the Bible does: it changes our lives. The Spirit uses his Word to save (2 Tim 3:14–15) and sanctify people (3:16–17), enabling biblical counselors who use it to carry out fully the ministry aims God designed his Word to accomplish. The Bible makes this point in many ways:

- Psalm 19:7–8 tells us God's Word renews our lives, and gives us wisdom, joy, and light. The very components every counselee longs for, the Bible guarantees.
- Deuteronomy 29:29 informs us that hidden knowledge is what God alone possesses, but in his Word he gave us revealed knowledge. He gave it not for knowledge's sake but "that we may follow all the words of [it]." Unfollowed truth aborts God's purpose for giving us his truth.
- Isaiah 55:10–13 compares the agricultural impact of life-giving physical rain with the spiritual impact of God's life-giving Word upon our souls: it brings us joy, peace, and stability.

- In Matthew 4:4, Jesus reminds us of our true source of life: "It is written: 'Man shall not live on bread alone, but on every word that comes from the mouth of God'" (NIV). We need God's Word, we need all of God's Word, and we need all of God's Word more than we need anything else.
- In John 17:17, Jesus asks the Father, on behalf of his disciples, to "sanctify them by the truth; [God's] word is truth."
- First Thessalonians 4:1–2 tells us how we can and should live in God-pleasing ways—through the instructions the apostles received from Jesus Christ.

God gave us the Bible to transform our lives.

Selecting an Appropriate Passage

Which passage from this God-breathed, life-transforming book should we bring to our specific counselees? Of the 31,000-plus verses in the 1,189 chapters in the 66 books of the Bible, which should we choose? What Scripture text would be most "timely" (Prov 15:23) and "good for building up someone in need, so that it" helps (Eph 4:29)? How can we skillfully, confidently, and compassionately minister the Word?

Let's consider three marks of a timely counseling passage.[2]

1. A Timely Passage Addresses the Person's Struggle

While there might not be a one-to-one correspondence between specific situations in the Bible and in a counselee's life, there should be a clear approximation we can see and show. Using our six-box model from Step Two (understand), it speaks to the counselee's heat, bad fruit, and bad roots (boxes 1–3). Your answers to the Summary Interpretive Question (from the previous chapter) should guide you: "How, and why, is this person responding to this situation and what heart and behavioral changes are biblically indicated?"

[2] Adapted from Powlison, *Speaking Truth in Love*, 64–66 (see chap. 1, n. 5).

2. A Timely Passage Brings Jesus Christ and His Provisions of Grace, Truth, Promises, and Presence

It presents a specific Christ-centered (box 4) truth that speaks to some key aspects of the counselee's personal and relational problems.

3. A Timely Passage Invites Change and Calls for Some Response by Your Counselee

It's a passage that helps your counselee envision the kind of biblical heart and behavioral changes in boxes 5 and 6. In other words, what passage—if the counselee were to grasp and apply it—might best help them right now? Ideally, such a passage reflects the previously discussed indicative-imperative dynamic (e.g., 1 Pet 5:7) or at least shows that dynamic in its context (e.g., Rom 12:18 with 12:1).

Before considering examples, let's insert several qualifications. First, we are not necessarily talking about general hope-inviting verses (e.g., 2 Pet 1:3) we might share in a first session when we don't yet know the problem well. At this point, we need Scripture that specifically addresses the main problem we have agreed to discuss.

Second, we need not labor to find the perfect passage. Don't place yourself under that pressure. No doubt Jesus would have a perfect passage; you are not Jesus. You simply need to bring a passage that meets our above criteria. While some passages fit better than others, many can work for any given counseling problem.

Third, among several passages that could fit, consider one you know well. Maybe you have studied it previously and feel greater confidence in sharing it. Maybe your pastor or Sunday School teacher recently unpacked it. Maybe it's a passage that impacted you and in sharing it you can offer personal testimony about how the Lord has used it in your life.

Fourth, bring one main passage at a time to the session. A counseling session is not a Bible study or a topical discipleship lesson. It's a time to bring God's life-changing Word to speak directly to the counselee's problem. It's a time to go deep, not broad.

Case Examples

Let's consider three case vignettes and a key passage I (Bob) used with each, followed by a discussion of how the verses fit our three criteria.

Case One

Jim was new to my town, having transferred there from another state to manage a struggling branch of his nationwide company. He felt lonely. His wife and children had stayed behind to finish school and sell their house. Jim visited our church and after the service he shared his situation with a member who referred him to me. It turned out his job was more stressful than he expected. He found himself becoming very anxious about it, even experiencing minor panic episodes. His employees seemed slow to embrace him, resenting that corporate had placed a new manager over them. Jim also felt the stress of an upcoming visit from his boss who was often critical.

After the process of entering Jim's world and understanding his felt and real needs, we looked together at Paul's words in 2 Tim 4:16–17: "At my first defense, no one stood by me, but everyone deserted me. May it not be counted against them. But the Lord stood with me and strengthened me."

- Criterion 1: Indeed, Jim's struggle was somewhat like Paul's. Jim felt alone, was under pressure and facing criticism from his superiors and his subordinates, and his career was in jeopardy.
- Criterion 2: Like Paul, Jim needed to know that he was not alone, and that Christ was both with him and would provide him strength.
- Criterion 3: Paul's testimony posed an implicit call for Jim to believe this as Christ's promise to him, to see the unseen Christ sitting with him as he drove to work and standing with him throughout his challenging workdays. The apostle's purpose—to encourage Timothy in difficult ministry—makes this passage especially helpful for counselees like Jim.

Case Two

Todd and Caitlin are believers who were having severe marital conflict. This often resulted in episodes of yelling, followed by both individuals retreating and offering lame apologies until the next round. After entering their world and understanding their felt and real needs, I discussed with them Col 3:12: "Therefore, as God's chosen ones, holy and dearly loved, put on compassion, kindness, humility, gentleness, and patience."

- Criterion 1: The broader context of 3:5–15 includes anger and relational conflict, making verse 12 an appropriate fit for this couple's situation.
- Criterion 2: Todd and Caitlin's threefold identity (chosen, holy, loved)—plus being forgiven (3:13)—brings assurance and motivation to change. The five relational graces provide a vision for what a Christian marriage can look like.
- Criterion 3: The text calls to this couple to grasp their identity and to commit to pursuing compassion, kindness, humility, gentleness, and patience with each other. (Subsequently, we found the entirety of 3:1–17 valuable in their individual and marital growth.)

Case Three

Jill's unsaved father disapproved of her marriage choice and had essentially rejected her. When he visited her and her family, he treated them rudely and left a day early. Jill was heartbroken. After entering her world and understanding her felt and real needs, I shared with her Ps 27:10: "Even if my father and mother abandon me, the LORD cares for me."

- Criterion 1: Whether actual or hypothetical, David recognizes the hardship of rejection. (I have used this passage frequently with various rejection or abandonment cases, not just those involving parents.)
- Criterion 2: As in David's case, God offers himself to Jill as the One who will care for her when others abandon her. (I followed up verse 10 with news of God's abundant promises and attributes that

are embedded in the whole Psalm so she can get to know the God who promises to care for her.)

- Criterion 3: The passage implicitly calls Jill to trust in/rest in/seek the Lord and to cease trusting in/resting in/seeking her dad. (We later widened our lens to include all fourteen verses in Psalm 27, which helped her focus on who this Lord who cares for her is.)

Steps for Bringing a Passage

Having considered some sample passages and case situations, let's consider an approach for delivering Ps 27:10 to Jill:

1. Segue with something like this: "May I share something from God's Word that I think speaks to your situation and that would help you?"

2. Invite Jill to turn to the passage. (Be sensitive to her ability to locate it.)

3. Briefly explain the verse's context—don't assume Jill (even if a mature Christian) knows the passage. Then ask her to read it or to follow along in her Bible as you do.

Encouraging counselees to read the words of God with their own eyes connects them directly to God. We want those want those we counsel to see, understand, believe, and obey God's words, not root faith and obedience in what might be mistaken for our own words (1 Cor 2:1–5, 13; 1 Thess 2:13). It's not enough to tell counselees God's truth. We should show it to them from an open Bible, pointing to the actual passages and explaining how we drew applicable truths from those passages so they can see it with their own eyes and grasp it in their own minds both in the session and later.[3] We want both our counsel and the changes people make to emerge explicitly and unmistakably from the Bible text.

---

[3] Consider this wise counsel from the Westminster Assembly's 1645 Directory for the Publick Worship of God. It was intended for pastors. They were not only to preach truth but truth "contained in or grounded on that text, *that the hearers may discern how God teacheth it from thence*" (emphasis added), https://www.apuritansmind.com/westminster-standards/directory-of-publick-worship/.

James 1:22–25 supplies a powerful metaphor—the Bible as a mirror. The apostle wrote:

> But be doers of the word and not hearers only, deceiving yourselves. Because if anyone is a hearer of the word and not a doer, he is like someone looking at his own face in a mirror. For he looks at himself, goes away, and immediately forgets what kind of person he was. But the one who looks intently into the perfect law of freedom and perseveres in it, and is not a forgetful hearer but a doer who works—this person will be blessed in what he does.

This perspective can prove useful when we bring to a counselee a truth that will challenge, confront, or rebuke. In that case, we can come alongside them as a fellow reader of God's Word and simply hold it up as a mirror for them to gaze into. We allow the Bible to put God's finger on the life issue that needs attention. Passages like this remind us counselors we are not the King, but merely ambassadors delivering his message to those we serve.

4. Invite a response. "Jill, what do you think? How might these verses apply to you?" Your goal is to guide Jill inductively to see for herself what God says to her in his Word. Resist the temptation to declare the meaning and application of the passage; labor to help Jill experience the joy and impact of self-discovery.

5. If Jill seems confused or unresponsive about the passage, summarize its meaning and ask a searching question or suggest how the passage applies. "Jill, based on verse 10, how would you describe David's relationships to his parents and the Lord?" Steer her to accurate understanding. If you summarize the passage's meaning, ask her to summarize what she heard you say to make sure she understands the passage.

6. Lead Jill to respond with personal application. In some cases, you might relate it directly to the problem you discussed earlier in the session or give an example from your life of how this truth applied specifically to you.

7. Seek to secure commitment to change based on the passage and the personal application Jill sees. We want people to change based on an accurate understanding and application of God's words, not ours (1 Cor 2:1–5; 1 Thess 1:4–5; 2:13).

Be aware that while in some cases you might turn to another passage to reinforce a truth, that can inadvertently dilute your counseling focus. It's usually best to reserve additional passages for a homework assignment or the next session. A counseling session is not a time for broad topical Bible study but for deep, focused application.

Establishing and Implementing an Action Plan

As your counselee grasps the truth of a passage and its application, you should help them develop a growth plan and coach them as they seek to live it out. At this stage of the counseling process, you are moving from the primary roles of listener and teacher to coach, guide, and accountability provider. Here are key ingredients in this process:

1. Use the six-box model to think concretely with your counselees about their specific situations, behaviors, and hearts, along with God's provisions in Christ and the paths of change God desires. Explaining the boxes provides your counselees with a big-picture assessment.

2. Instill and reinforce in your believing counselees a firm grasp of their biblical identity in Christ, its implications for growth, and God's provisions of grace. Consider passages like Luke 12:32; Rom 6:1–14; Gal 3:1–14, 21–29; 4:1–7; Eph 1–2; Phil 2:1–4; 4:11–13; Col 3:1–17 (especially 3:12–14); 2 Tim 4:17; 2 Pet 1:3–9; and Jude 1:1.

3. Deepen their grasp of God's Word and its application by bringing in additional passages in subsequent sessions that fit with the direction you have begun.

4. Work with your counselees to determine specific, concrete steps of needed change. What does God want them to stop believing/desiring (box 3) and doing/saying/feeling (box 2), and to start believing/desiring (box 5) and start doing/saying/feeling (box 6)?

5. Use appropriate growth assignments. (For ideas, see chapter 17.)

6. Stress the need for the person to commune constantly with the Lord in prayer. Prayer expresses dependency on the Lord. Make it part of both your session time and your growth assignments.

7. Discuss with your counselee ways to invite other mature believers—for instance, small group leaders or members—to come alongside them, care for them, and support your biblical counseling goals. The church is a ministering community.

8. As much as possible, communicate with and work with the person's pastors—their God-given shepherds. This includes securing informed consent upfront to talk with a pastor or offering to go with your counselee to talk with a pastor as needed.

9. As the process continues, watch for and deal with any remaining or new issues that might arise in the course of implementing godly change. Common secondary sins during the counseling process include self-resentment, bitterness, judgmentalism, self-pity, selfishness, self-indulgence, fears, and doubt.

10. At every step, keep Jesus Christ central. Remember the goal of Christlikeness at the start of this chapter. Continue the Enter/Understand/Bring model in each session as you show your counselee Christ's box 4 provisions and see God's Spirit create box 5 and 6 change.

Conclusion

The three-step Enter/Understand/Bring model outlined in these three chapters (13–15) gives you a process—a methodology—to do Christ-centered biblical counseling. Many of the common problems encountered in counseling can be mapped on to this model process, even though our introductory-level treatment of those problems in later chapters won't allow us to do this explicitly. Each counselor will develop their own style and practices. While some of the detailed techniques in these chapters are suggestive, inexperienced counselors should consider following them, at least initially, until they develop their own approaches. The Enter/Understand/Bring flow reflects the movement of Christ himself; he enters our world, compassionately understands our problems, and brings us himself and his gospel answers.

16

Giving Hope to Those We Counsel

Experienced counselors know counselees often feel hopeless. Burdened by seemingly insurmountable problems, they are weary and intensely self-focused. Self-preoccupation breeds despair. Some have been told they are failures. They might be embarrassed for having sought help. Perhaps their churches have failed them, preaching platitudes or dispensing abstract concepts instead of practical, life-changing hope. Some even feel burned by previous counselors or Christian leaders.

Worse, our counselees frequently carry misconceptions about God and his promises, ways, and character. They presume God has promised things he has not—health, wealth, a good marriage, a better job, obedient kids—and he has let them down. They don't find contentment in the far richer blessings God actually has promised. And with that comes confusion about the normal Christian life: "No one but me has this problem"; "If I were a good Christian, I wouldn't be in this mess"; or "I need to clean up my act before I go to God."

Like its causes, signs of hopelessness can vary widely. Obvious indicators include despair, giving up, and suicidal thinking. But other symptoms might appear: denial or blame-shifting; works-based righteousness or performanceism; preoccupation with things; lack of spiritual activity, reduced Bible reading, and lower church involvement; various forms of anger; or people-pleasing.

Bringing hope is vital for counseling success.[1] As we saw in chapter 12, we especially want to generate hope at the start of the counseling process. Yet we also need to infuse hope throughout it, including times when the counselee's progress seems slow to the counselee.

How do we give counselees hope? Let's consider fourteen ways. We begin with a general answer and then numerous specific methods.

1. Proclaim Clearly the God of Hope and His Rich, Hope-Giving Provisions

Root your counselee's hope in the Lord. He is "the God of hope" who promises to fill believers "with all joy and peace"—what counselees understandably long for—"as [they] believe so that [they] may overflow with hope by the power of the Holy Spirit" (Rom 15:13). The same Spirit who yanked Jesus from the grave (Rom 8:11) has resurrected us from the dead (Eph 2:5; Col 3:1) and brings us his daily transforming grace (2 Cor 3:17; Eph 3:16). By his divine power God has given us everything we need to live godly, abundant lives now (John 10:10; 2 Pet 1:3); he also guarantees fuller grace when Christ returns. We love our counselees by undercutting any false hope they might place in their own strength or wishful thinking or in ungodly counsel. Their hope for joy and peace and for growth and change is fulfilled in Jesus Christ alone.

2. Study and Memorize Key Hope-Giving Verses to Share

In an initial counseling session you might not yet know the best specific biblical truths a counselee needs. But that doesn't mean you should delay bringing them God's Word. A passage like Ps 46:1, 7; Matt 11:28; Rom 15:13; 1 Cor 10:13–14; Phil 4:13; 2 Tim 3:16; 4:17; Heb 4:16; or

---

[1] For a biblical counseling resource on this, see Wayne A. Mack, "Instilling Hope in the Counselee," in MacArthur, *How to Counsel Biblically*, 114–30 (see chap. 2, n. 12). For a secular resource supporting the importance of hope for counseling success, see Mark A. Hubble, Barry L. Duncan, and Scott D. Miller, eds., *The Heart and Soul of Change: Delivering What Works in Therapy* (Washington, DC: American Psychological Association, 1999), chap. 1, 6.

2 Pet 1:3–4 gives tremendous hope for all sorts of problems, even in a first session. Studying these passages' contexts and memorizing them will bring you confidence as you share them.

3. Apply Relevant Bible Stories and Characters to Your Counselee and Their Situation

Our God delights in delivering his people from hopeless situations. One of the Bible's explicit purposes is to provide hope-giving historical examples of God's work. In Rom 15:2–4, Paul holds forth Jesus as an example of living sacrificially for others, and then adds this rationale: "For whatever was written in the past was written for our instruction, so that we may have hope through endurance and through the encouragement from the Scriptures." He tells us twice in 1 Corinthians 10 that Israel's idolatrous pursuits and God's subsequent judgments on Israel ". . . took place as examples for us, so that we will not desire evil things as they did. . . . These things happened to them as examples, and they were written for our instruction" (10:6, 11). Commenting on the faith displays of a crowd of Old Testament figures in Hebrews 11, the writer concludes in Heb 12:1, "Therefore, since we also have such a large cloud of witnesses surrounding us, let us lay aside every hindrance and the sin that so easily ensnares us. Let us run with endurance the race that lies before us."

Ideally, we should use Bible narratives where a character's situation approximates the counselee's situation and where the Bible character manifests basic faith and obedience. We should also pay attention to the broader context and the story's place within the Bible's redemptive-historical story line. While moralistic approaches neglect this bigger redemptive picture, this is no reason to avoid the proper use of biblical narratives to give counsel.

4. Give Appropriate Testimony of God's Work in Your Life

By testifying to how God has and is helping us, we give people hope that God can likewise work in their lives. These five guidelines can make your testimony effective in giving hope:

a. Be sure your testimony applies in some way to the counselee's situation. The more similar the respective situations, the more you can pinpoint God's faithfulness and the response God wants from your counselee. At the same time, be careful not to imply the Lord must work in your counselee's life the same way he worked in yours. Limit discussion to areas in which the Lord has given you victory, not those in which you still struggle, lest you risk being hypocritical.
b. Be careful not to gossip or betray confidentialities. Unless it's necessary to achieve your ministry purpose *and* you have permission, don't reveal identifying information about others.
c. Be timely. Don't interrupt a person's story to insert yours—especially if it might seem competitive or display one-upmanship ("You think you've got it hard? Let me tell you what I had to deal with. . . ."). This hijacks the session by diverting the focus to you.
d. Be brief; don't divulge too much detail. Practicing your testimony might help your efficiency. You can expand it if the counselee asks for more.
e. Spotlight God as the hero. Build your counselee's hope on God's Spirit, God's Word, God's promises, God's actions—not on your wisdom, efforts, or favorable circumstances. Make you the subject of sentences when describing your failure and the Lord the subject when describing godly responses. Instead of saying, "I failed this week in these specific ways . . ., but I turned back to the Lord," we might say, "I failed this week, but the Lord was faithful. He turned my heart back to him." While both renditions are true, the latter recognizes that the Lord enables our work (Phil 2:12–13; 1 Cor 15:10) and deserves our praise.

An effective testimony gives hope to the counselee that they too can seek and receive the Lord's help.

5. Describe God's Successful Work in Other Believers

Here you might consider famous Christians—living or deceased—who have been the subject of biographies and autobiographies but also living, local believers that you and even the counselee might know. The Bible abounds with exhortations to imitate more mature believers (e.g., Prov 13:20; Phil 2:29–30; 3:17; Heb 6:12). In some cases, you might not only tell a counselee about some other brothers or sisters but also connect them so that the counselee might hear an inspiring story firsthand. When possible, you might also seek to gather written testimonies of God's work in your "graduated" counselees (removing identifying information first).

6. Don't Minimize Your Counselee's Sin; Rather, Maximize God's Grace—God's Power to Forgive and Change Them

Just as diamonds sparkle best when set against a black velvet background, so the gospel shines brightest in contrast to sin. Scripture presents a fascinating, almost paradoxical dynamic: "The law came along to multiply the trespass. But where sin multiplied, grace multiplied even more" (Rom 5:20). "This saying is trustworthy and deserving of full acceptance: "Christ Jesus came into the world to save sinners"—and I am the worst of them" (1 Tim 1:15).

As biblical counselors we can easily be tempted, out of fear of offending or out of a distorted notion of compassion, to try to soothe a counselee's conscience by minimizing that counselee's sin: "There, there, don't be so hard on yourself. Don't beat yourself up over what you said or did or didn't do; it's not that bad." Yet we do our counselees no favor when we downplay their sin because that robs them of the thrilling grace of the gospel. Let's remind them instead that we have a big Savior for big sinners.

I seek to emphasize a counselee's need for *both* God's forgiving grace and God's empowering grace. Hebrews 4:16 brings them together: "Therefore, let us approach the throne of grace with boldness, so that we may receive mercy and find grace to help us in time of need." In Christ we find both forgiving grace ("mercy") and empowering grace ("grace to help us in our time of need")—his enabling, sustaining grace.

Instead of downplaying a counselee's sin, we should lead them to Jesus in a fresh way: "Tanya, what you said to your husband was wrong and was not the way God wants you to respond to him. But the good news is that this is exactly why Jesus came—to save sinners like me and you. So, let me remind you that if you go to Jesus and confess your sin, he will not only forgive and cleanse you (adding perhaps 1 John 1:9) but will also give you renewed power through his Spirit to fight against that sin and respond differently to your husband. And I am here to help you."

7. Remind Your Counselee that Change Happens Incrementally

Hopelessness might come from over-expectations people place on God or themselves. When we see Christ face-to-face, "we will be like him" (1 John 3:2). But the corollary is equally true: until we see him, we will not be like him—at least not completely. Remaining sin will plague us believers. Growth is a process—three steps forward and two steps back. Theologians call this progressive sanctification.

Practically, that means we need to celebrate with counselees even small signs of God's work in their lives. For a start, their willingness to seek your help and your willingness to provide it both display God's grace. Thank God for that as you pray with your counselee. It also means setting realistic, obtainable goals and highlighting progressive growth. Consider the F.I.D.O.T. model.[2] A counselee struggling with anger exhibits growth when there is a decrease in any of the following:

- *frequency* of outbursts (three episodes this week instead of five last week)
- *intensity* (controlling their urge to punch the wall instead of making a new hole in it)
- *duration* of their rants (fifteen-minute tirades instead of thirty-minute tirades)
- *occasions* for anger displays (of the five typical situations that have historically provoked anger, only three did so this week)
- *time* interval before repenting (how quickly the counselee owns his sin and turns back to the Lord)

[2] For a further explanation of the first four categories, see Robert D. Jones, *Anger: Calming Your Heart* (Phillipsburg, NJ: P&R, 2019), 10–11.

Any of these decreases should cause rejoicing. Christian growth means that while we are not yet what we one day will be (perfected, per 1 John 3:2), we are no longer what we once were (lost). We are new creations (2 Cor 5:17). Praise God for his grace in Christ.

8. Spot and Affirm God's Work in Your Counselee

Counselees who lack hope often live unaware of God and blind to what God has been and is doing in their lives. Pointing out God's hand at work in your counselee's situation, as well as any progress in their soul, can bring newfound encouragement. We see this pattern in the New Testament letters where the apostles frequently highlight the faith and other graces evident in their readers (e.g., Rom 1:8; 1 Cor 1:6–7; Phil 1:3–8; 1 Thess 1:2–3). And we see this in the affirmations the Lord Jesus brings to the seven churches in Revelation 2 and 3, even when he concurrently rebukes them (2:3–4, 9, 13, 19; 3:1, 8, 19).

What might this look like? It begins in session one. "Tyler, the fact that you have sought God's help through biblical counseling shows us God is up to something. That God has connected us and that you're willing to let me help you is evidence that God is on-site in your life and working to bring you his help." And it continues as you hear your counselee share their problems and respond in faith to the biblical directions you give.

9. Where Prudent, Use Biblical Categories and Biblical Labels to Describe Problems and Answers

Flowing from the above, we rejoice in the gospel message that "Christ Jesus came into the world to save sinners," not codependents (1 Tim 1:15). As the angel directed Joseph in Matt 1:21, "you are to name him Jesus, because he will save his people from their sins," not a psychiatric or cultural label. Whether stemming from euphemisms or from unbiblical categories, secular labels lack the profundity of God's Word. For example, the label "social anxiety disorder" shallowly focuses only on the horizontal level, excluding

God and failing to address the core issues of what it means to love, fear, and trust God more than others.

Of course, we must exercise prudence. It's unwise to prematurely correct the terminology of psychologized counselees until you have won both their trust in you and their commitment to God's Word. You might win the battle but lose the war.

That doesn't mean we shouldn't wisely address unbiblical language, especially when counselees cling to it. Words have meaning. Cultural and psychiatric labels often use medical-sounding language but typically lack scientific consensus for physical etiology. Moreover, when Christian counselees allow a label ("I am an alcoholic"; "I am bipolar") to define them, they saddle themselves with a discouraging, deterministic diagnosis that can both excuse their sin and rob them of gospel hope. We are wise to focus them on Christ's redeeming power and their glorious identity in Christ: "I am a child of the living God, forgiven by Christ and empowered by his Spirit; therefore, he can help me handle the problems I'm facing."

10. Help Your Counselee See God's Purposes in Trials

As we help counselees know the sovereign, wise, and good God of Scripture, we can help them see how all their problems became opportunities to become more like Jesus. For example, God uses hardships to . . .

- enhance and deepen our relationship with God. Christians in hardship tend to become more God-conscious and turn to him.
- experience a measure of Christ's sufferings (though our sufferings are light compared to those of our suffering Savior).
- expose our remaining sin. God uses trials to burn away our dross, including blind-spot sins.
- engage us more actively in the body of Christ. Suffering can draw us closer to others and make us more properly dependent on them for support and prayer.
- exhibit to others Christ's work in us (Matt 5:13–16). Hardships give us opportunities to reflect Jesus to others.

- equip us for wiser, more compassionate personal ministry. God comforts us in our trials so we can comfort others.[3]

11. Help Your Counselee Discern Their Specific Responsibilities amid Their Overwhelming Concerns

Paul Tripp's "Circle of Concern and Circle of Responsibility" diagram,[4] coupled with passages like Rom 12:17–21; 1 Pet 2:21–23; 4:19; and 2 Tim 2:22–26, can help people distinguish between what they can't control (their concerns, the larger circle) and what they can control (their responsibilities, the smaller circle).

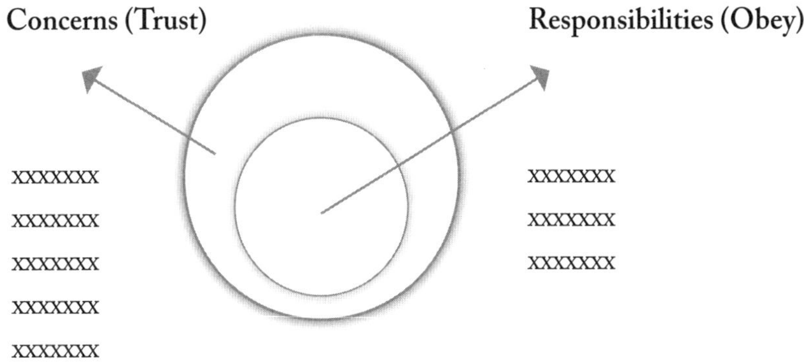

You can help a person overwhelmed with worry by listing their multiple concerns on the left column and then working with them to list in the right column what God calls them to do about them. The latter includes praying for the concerns when they arise—casting them upon the Lord (1 Pet 5:7)—and doing whatever concrete steps of obedience are proper in the specific situation. From this we can help them specify where they must learn to *trust* God to be and do all that God promises to be and do and to *entrust* to God those people and things we are

[3] Robert D. Jones, *When Trouble Shows Up: Seeing God's Transforming Love* (Greensboro, NC: New Growth Press, 2013).

[4] Tripp, *Instruments*, 250–57 (see chap. 13, n. 1).

concerned about to do whatever God wants to do. Hope comes when a counselee sees that the inner circle is much smaller and, with God's power and our help, is doable.

12. Provide Practical Resources

(See chapter 17, "Using Growth Assignments in Counseling.")

13. Pray with and for Your Counselee

Few things give a struggling believer hope more than being prayed for, particularly at the end of a session. It not only brings the counselee the benefits God promises to give due to prayer (2 Cor 1:10–11; Phil 1:18–19; Jas 5:14–16) but demonstrates your care for them and models how to think biblically and how to approach God. It's usually wise to begin and end sessions with prayer. Sometimes you might even insert prayer within a session, especially if the counselee faces a crisis.

At the same time, it's helpful to remind counselees that while you will try to pray for them between sessions, you might fail, though there is One who prays for them *continually*. Jesus "always lives to intercede for them" (Heb 7:25).

14. Assure Your Counselee of Your Hope in God for Them and Carry That Hope for Them

A commercial for a retail chain featured the store's greeters, purporting to show how warmly you would be welcomed into their stores. It ends with the camera zooming in on a stately older employee. "If you come in here without a smile," he tells viewers, "I'll give you one of mine." As cheesy at that commercial is, it offers a valuable insight for wise soul care. Here's my (Bob's) parallel application in counseling: "If you come to me without hope, I'll give you some of mine." As we grow in knowledge of and confidence in God and his Word, we biblical counselors can say to those we counsel, "I know you might not have much hope right now, but I have more than enough for both of us. God's divine power has given us everything we need to live satisfied, godly lives (alluding to 2 Pet 1:3)."

As one biblical counselor told my friend who sought help, "I'm gonna put you on my shoulders and carry you." That one line brought my friend immense hope. To similarly help a counselee know she intends to bear their burden with them, my co-author Kristin uses the imagery of walking shoulder-to-shoulder with a counselee to carry a fifty-pound sack of rice between them.

But what if a counselee overly depends on you? Do we really want people hoping on us? Three responses seem wise. First, we recognize this possibility, though biblical counselors presumably experience it less than other counselors since we constantly direct our counselees to the Lord. Second, for a hope-*less* person who has no hope in the Lord, hoping initially in us is better than in no one. Third, we should use our privileged position to lead the person toward Jesus. By leveraging the trust the person gives us, we can show them where our trust lies and how they too can trust in Someone more trustworthy. A biblical counselor serves as a beggar who can show other beggars not only where to find bread but how to eat and enjoy it.

Conclusion

Don't underestimate the power of hope—not of wishful thinking or of the kind proposed by worldly therapies, but the hope grounded in God's Word. Work hard to impart it, using the strategies above.

> *Now may the God of hope fill you with all joy and peace as you believe so that you may overflow with hope by the power of the Holy Spirit.*
> —Romans 15:13

17

Using Growth Assignments in Counseling

Growth assignments form an essential part of our biblical counseling methodology.[1] While not exclusive to our approach, the value of these between-session progress assignments has been stressed by biblical counselors historically. Because we believe God is the one who changes people, we don't rely primarily on the session as some magic hour for dramatic change. Instead, we recognize God works in people progressively, during the 167 hours between weekly sessions. Moreover, few factors predict counselee growth and fruitful case outcome more than successful homework completion. That calls us to design our assignments well and to give counselees clear direction on how to apply his Word daily.[2]

The Benefits of Growth Assignments

Why should we assign homework? Consider four reasons:

---

[1] In this chapter we use the term "growth assignments" more often than "homework" because of the positive purpose these assignments serve in the growth process.

[2] For helpful resources on concepts and methods of growth assignments, with examples, see Tripp, *Instruments*, 318–54 (see chap. 13, n. 1); Wayne A. Mack, *Homework Manual for Biblical Living*, 3 vol. (Bemidji, MN: Focus, 2005); and Jay E. Adams, *The Christian Counselor's Manual: The Practice of Nouthetic Counseling* (Phillipsburg, NJ: P&R, 1973), 294–343; and Adams, *Ready to Restore: The Layman's Guide to Christian Counseling* (Phillipsburg, NJ: P&R, 1981), 72–76.

1. Growth assignments direct counselees to Scripture and Scripture-based resources so they can see God biblically and can respond with godly change. We want to help them become doers of the Word, not hearers only (Jas 1:22–25; Matt 7:24–27). We also want to highlight the value of self-discovery. People grow best when they discover and apply life-transforming truths from God's Word.

2. Growth assignments extend the session's focus into daily life. A one-hour session is not enough; homework reinforces and helps apply the session content, giving counselees opportunity to implement concrete change and report that in the next session. Too often inexperienced counselors focus their preparation energies on the session itself and treat the assignment as an afterthought. Wise counselors view both the upcoming session and assignment as a whole package of help—as when piano instructors provide assessment and instruction but also give assignments because they know students only develop actual skill through daily practice.

3. Growth assignments prepare counselees for the next session. While most assignments aim to apply the truths of the latest session, some might lead counselees to where you plan to go next. For example, if you plan to address relational conflict in your next session, you might assign the person to memorize and meditate on a passage such as Jas 4:1–2.

4. Growth assignments place responsibility for change on the person, not the counselor. By making homework a vital part of a counseling process—not an add-on—you minimize excessive counselee dependence. Like the piano instructor who cannot create musicians, you cannot change counselees. Rather, each must desire and work at proficiency. Counseling is not like going to a dentist where the patient lies passively and the professional fills the cavity. Biblical counselors are agents of Christ, not fixers; life change occurs when counselees depend on Christ and actively apply his truth in the power of his spirit.

These four benefits suggest we should always give some form of homework, however minimal and even if we send it a day or two later (e.g., when we ran out of time or a session ended abruptly). We want our counselees to do *something* to follow up each session, however informal or light that might be.

Types of Growth Assignments

What kind of homework should we assign? Growth assignments must be clear, doable, beneficial, and in keeping with counseling goals. We should determine what specific assignments would most help a particular counselee at a particular time. Each assignment should specify what the counselee must do to apply it concretely; for instance, "Write down three takeaway points from chapter 3 of this book and talk to God about them," or "Talk this week to your pastor about joining a small group." Wise counselors start thinking about the next assignment even before the current session begins, note homework ideas during the session, and then at the end of the session shape a wise assignment for the counselee.

One standing assignment—which might need to be stated to the counselee each session—involves having them review each session's discussion and insights before the next meeting. You might provide a pad and pen at the start of each session to encourage counselees to take notes.

In selecting assignments for your counselee, assess your stage in the counseling process and what each assignment is meant to accomplish. If you seek to give biblical instruction or generate biblical hope, journaling about feelings won't help. Journaling about a Bible passage will help, however, if you want to learn how the counselee thinks or is processing and implementing God's Word. In all cases, aim for practical change—not merely imparting knowledge of God's truth but helping counselees know *and* do it (John 13:17; Gal 5:6; Jas 1:22–25).

Consider the following categories of assignments to choose from, along with related recommendations and examples:

Scripture to Read, Study, and/or Memorize

- Decide what Bible passage(s) to include. Usually this means any passage(s) discussed in the session that can help the person apply the content. Sometimes you can include additional passages that reinforce the central idea. Assigned passages need not be new each time; sometimes it's best to review and reflect more deeply on texts previously presented.

- Decide what counselees should do with each passage. Merely asking the person to "think about" or "meditate on" a passage is too nebulous. Provide actionable, measurable steps, such as prayer journaling or writing down specific insights and how they concretely apply to the problem. Encourage them to look for specific truths. Consider questions to ask, applications to make, and action steps to take.
- Depending on the counselee's level of Bible knowledge, you might need to explain the textual background or key terms. But be careful not to remove the counselee's joy of self-discovery.
- If the counselee has a consistent Bible reading plan, encourage that to continue, adding to it additional Scriptures that focus on their specific problem. Or they might put that plan on hold for a season and use a devotional guide that focuses on the problem instead.[3]
- If assigning verses to memorize, ask counselees to read and study the context, write the verses on 3x5 cards, and review them ongoingly. Striving for word-perfect memorization in their preferred translation builds confidence.
- Be conscious of lower literacy levels, especially for counselees whose primary language is not yours. Encourage counselees to read the Bible in their heart language.

Reading Scripture-based Books, Chapters, Minibooks, or Articles[4]

- Any assigned reading should be biblically driven, in keeping with the gospel and its application to the person. Ideally, it should connect thematically with the Scripture you discussed or assigned. (Note: If there might be a questionable minor point within the resource, state a disclaimer.)

[3] For example, see P&R Publishing's thirty-one-day devotional series dealing with topics such as pornography, grief, and anger: https://www.prpbooks.com/series/31-day-devotionals-for-life.

[4] See the many biblical counseling books and minibooks published by P&R (e.g., in n. 3, above), New Growth Press, and Shepherd Press.

- Know the resource yourself. Just because others recommend it does not mean it will fit your counselee. Skim-read it through their eyes, as best as you can anticipate.
- Consider whether your counselee's literacy level can handle a resource before you assign it.
- Encourage counselees to "own" the reading. In a book, they should mark compelling thoughts, note three or four specific truths and takeaway applications, write an application summary, and/or compose a prayer to the Lord based on what they learn.
- If your counselee disagrees with some part of a reading assignment, seek to understand why. Discern what primary biblical truths might be at stake without defending a writer's style or secondary points. Focus on how the uninspired, fallible writer nevertheless reflected God's inspired, inerrant Word.

Specific Action Steps

- Use action verbs: visit your dad, call your friend, set your alarm clock, talk to the person, make a doctor's appointment, go to an event, start (or stop) an activity, buy a specific item, sell your truck (the one that sits in the garage most of the time and costs $300 a month).

Biblically Based Audio or Video Resources, Such as Sermons, Lectures, and Podcasts

- Consider the teaching ministry of your own pastor. A recent sermon might nicely supplement other assignments. Also consider the wealth of resources from biblical counseling conferences and websites.
- Ask counselees to take notes or at least write some kind of interaction response or personal application.

Free Journaling

- Help counselees journal their thoughts and feelings related to the session discussion and in response to God's Word. In some cases it is best to delay journaling until they understand how Scripture addresses their problem, lest their journaling merely be the hopeless ruminations of their flesh and lead them to dwell on their struggles rather than Christ-centered answers.

- If counselees are willing, encourage them to talk to the Lord via a prayer journal. (Think "Dear God" rather than "Dear Diary."). Help them thank the Lord, lament their hardships, confess their sins, and seek the Lord's help by writing to him in it. The Psalms, especially lament psalms, provide superb examples of how to get started. Lament psalms give words to those who suffer, capturing and voicing a range of difficult emotions; they frame those struggles within a God-centered perspective, modeling for us how to talk to God about hardships and doubts. You might even ask counselees to study a lament Psalm, note its flow and themes, and then compose their own personalized lament to discuss with you.[5]
- To encourage honesty with God, it is usually best not to ask counselees to allow us to read their journaling. (Assure them up front that you won't.) They might be tempted to write for our eyes or to omit embarrassing entries. Instead, you can invite them to share excerpts if they like.

Guided Journaling, Assessments, Lists, and Inventories

- Guided journals help counselees think about a specific problem in an organized way. For instance, you might ask them to structure their journaling like this:
  - *Initial Situation:* What happened? What was going on?
  - *Behavior:* How did you respond? What did you feel (emotions), say (words), or do (actions)?

[5] For example, see the use of Psalm 77 with a sexual assault victim in Robert D. Jones, *Angry at God: Bring Him Your Doubts and Questions* (Phillipsburg, NJ: P&R, 2003), 19–23.

  - *Heart:* What were you thinking (beliefs)? What were you wanting or desiring (motives)?
  - *What should you have done, or should you do next time?*
- Ask counselees to list five aspects of their marriage (or other difficult relationship) they would like to change, to list ten self-judgments that make up their "low self-esteem" or other contributing issues in that relationship, or to complete an inventory of their perceived rights and needs that are being denied or unmet (being sure to help them think biblically about those perceived rights and needs).
- Ask counselees to list concrete put-off and put-on action steps (per Paul's approach in Eph 4:25–5:2 and Col 3:5–17).
- Use the Evaluating Problem Patterns chart (in chapter 28) to track occurrences of the problem.

Prayer

- Include prayer as a separate assignment when possible. Encourage counselees to have direct dealings with God.
- Make sure your homework doesn't terminate merely on renewed thinking or changed behavior but concludes with conversations with God. In other words, don't settle for "biblicized" versions of cognitive behavioral therapy that merely call counselees to think and act biblically but neglect active communion with Christ. After all, he said, "You can do nothing without me" (John 15:5).
- Perhaps model for the counselee in the session how to pray through a psalm or another portion of Scripture.

Reminder Cards

- Assign counselees to write on three-by-five-inch cards. They can use these to jot down Bible verses, a biblical truth, and a model prayer related to their specific problem. For example,

(Side 1)

My Goal Is to Please God

"Therefore, whether we are at home or away, we make it our aim to be pleasing to him" (2 Cor 5:9). "And he died for all so that those who live should no longer live for themselves, but for the one who died for them and was raised" (2 Cor 5:15).

(Side 2)

Pleasing God Prayer

My goal in life, at all times, must be to please God, not myself or others. Father, help me, in response to your grace, to please you in all my thoughts, words, actions, and desires.

(Side 1)

When Tempted to Get Drunk

Stop! Don't! Pray! Call Jake: 555-327-0174!

1 Cor 10:13: "No temptation has come upon you except what is common to humanity. But God is faithful; he will not allow you to be tempted beyond what you are able, but with the temptation he will also provide the way out so that you may be able to bear it."

(Side 2)

Am I pleasing or grieving God? Do I want a frowning Savior? Do I want . . .

- to be mentally and spiritually out of control?
- to embarrass the name of Jesus and my church?
- to ruin my health and suffer a hangover?
- to risk my job or driver's license?
- to hurt others?

What does God want me to do instead?

Christ-centered Songs

- Assign songs (through whatever media) with words you want them to hear. Quality music can reinforce gospel themes that complement counseling.
- Even if a song's style isn't their preference, they might begin to like the music if it is skillfully performed and they listen to it three or four times to reflect on the lyrics.

Church Worship, Adult Education or Training Classes, and Small Group Participation

- Ask counselees what congregational gatherings they attend and encourage them to increase their participation if it seems insufficient. For example, you might ask them to share with you a sermon takeaway, to attend Sunday school, or to inform their small group leader that they are meeting with you.

Connecting with Other Believers (for Support, Encouragement, Accountability, and Prayer)

- You or your counselee might invite a mature, same-gender Christian friend or couple to meet with the counselee between sessions or even to attend one or more sessions. Sharing biblical truths about modeling and one-another, mutual ministry can motivate the parties you'd like to involve.
- In guiding counselees to meet with another believer, consider who they should meet with (is the person a mature, exemplary Christian?) as well as the purpose of their coming (prayer, training, accountability, Bible study). Establish up front how often and for how long the person's attendance would be needed.

Addressing Health or Medical Issues

- You can urge a counselee to make a medical appointment for possible physical problems.

- Encourage counselees to prioritize exercise, proper nutrition, rest, and getting out and enjoying nature.

Serving the Church or Individuals in Need

- Counselees enmeshed in personal problems live in a confined world. Helping them find ways to serve others can help both them and those they minister to.

Other Assignments

- Use your creativity to design your own assignments.
- If a counselee is progressing well, you can invite them to help you craft an assignment in keeping with what they believe God wants them to be and do. Ask, "Where does God want you to change? How might you practically apply God's Word in specific ways this week?" Involving counselees increases their ownership of the homework and therefore their likelihood to complete it.

Presenting Growth Assignments

How should we introduce homework? Consider a simple three-step movement to use near the end of a session. (Be sure to allow time for it.)

1. Ask: "May I give you some something to work on this week that I think will help you?" Resist the temptation to give many assignments in the first session; a passion for wanting people to change can make you impatient. Know too that even in informal friendship counseling, you can offer assignments; for example, "If you're interested and willing to work at it, I can give you some things to do that I think will help."

2. Assign: "Let me ask you, first, to read . . ." Orally dictate each part of the assignment as you concurrently write it down and ask counselees to do the same, so they take responsibility for owning the homework. You might also choose to take a cell phone picture of the assignment and send it electronically later. Some counselors even develop a standard assignment form to fill in and hand to counselees. If time is tight or you need to think about the assignment, you can promise to email it. However, recognize the

downsides: you won't be able to explain it, ascertain they understand it, or adjust it if they raise a concern; it takes extra time to compose and email it later; and in your busyness you might forget to do so.

3. Ascertain that the counselee understands and agrees to the assignment: "How does that sound? Does it make sense? Seem doable?" Feel free to do a quick sample of an assignment with them to get them started.

Discussing Assignments in the Next Session

When and how should we review homework in the next session? Some counselors prefer to start with it to be sure they will indeed get to the homework and have sufficient time to discuss it. Others start with general conversation, including an update on the person and their problem, and only ask about the growth assignments after that. This approach fosters reconnection and seems less like a schoolteacher checking up on students, though it takes effort to guard adequate time to discuss the homework.

To broach a homework discussion, you might ask, "Did you have opportunity to work on the growth assignments? Can we talk about them?" Even if you might want to focus only on one component, be sure to ask about each one lest you subtly imply the rest are unimportant. (As educators know, savvy students do not do what is expected but what is inspected.)

In discussing a reading assignment, some counselors treat it as supplemental to the main session's focus and merely want to know the counselee has read it. A better approach asks counselees to report their top two or three takeaways so you spend some session time on those takeaways but not the bulk of your time. It's generally unwise to devote the whole session to the reading material; it's best to focus the majority of the session on the person and the Bible's application to their life.

Dealing with Failure to Complete Assignments

Counseling doesn't always progress the way we want. Here is one suggested way to handle counselees who fail to do assignments (for no legitimate reason):

On the first occasion, ask what happened. Remind them that God wants to use your assignments to help them and that real growth happens between sessions as counselees daily apply God's Word. Ascertain their understanding of and commitment to complete the work and encourage them to do so this week.

On the second such occasion, remind them again of the importance of homework. But this time ask, "Since this is the second time, can you help me understand what your intention was after the last session?" Did the counselee plan to do the homework? If so, why did their plan fail? You might point out that when assignments aren't done, you feel like a medical doctor who prescribed a medication the patient didn't take and thus returns with the same symptoms.

On the third occasion of uncompleted assignments, remind them that these growth assignments are an essential part of the counseling process. (You may even refer to your agreement form, assuming you mentioned homework completion there.) After that, humbly question their commitment to counseling: "Joe, to be honest, it's not clear to me that you're committed to the biblical counseling process. I wonder if you really want my help and if we should continue. What do you think?" Then, assuming they voice a renewed commitment, propose, "Let's do this: Let's shorten today's session and let you go home early and work on the homework. Then, when you have completed it, contact me and we can schedule our next session." (Of course, this assumes you have clearly defined the counseling process as including both the sessions and the completion of growth assignments.)

This approach doesn't mean you are dismissing the counselee or terminating the case. Rather, you are providing the best possible help, as you both agreed at the outset. If they choose not to do the assignments, then the counselee—not you—has ended the counseling. Counselees should understand that biblical counseling requires successful assignment completion.

Conclusion

Nothing thrills a biblical counselor more than hearing a counselee explain how God used the assignments we gave to change them. Designing well-crafted assignments and presenting them clearly might be the most valuable function you perform as a counselor. In fact, given our confidence that God's Spirit uses God's Word, wise, biblically-driven homework might be more valuable than the session discussion itself!

18

Concluding a Counseling Case

While the Lord himself changes people through his Word and his Spirit, biblical counselors are stewards of the ministry he entrusts to us. In previous chapters we considered how we should start wisely and progress faithfully through the counseling process. Yet knowing when and how to conclude a case can challenge us. This chapter develops a strategy for ending well when genuine growth has occurred. We will also consider how to end a case wisely when that has not happened. We begin with a fundamental question: How do we know whether the case is ending well?

Indicators that Counseling is Ending Well

Counseling is not designed to last forever. Jesus commanded the church to make disciples (Matt 28:19–20). Counseling is a component of discipleship where hurting people can speak about specific issues and challenges with the goal of honoring Christ.[1] Therefore, counselors should look for the following six indications that the counseling has successfully met that goal and the counselee is ready to continue growth through the other discipleship ministries of the church.

[1] Steve Viars, "Let Me Draw a Picture: The Discipleship River," *Journal of Biblical Counseling* 20, no. 3 (2002), 58–60.

1. The Counselee's Relationship with the Lord Is Improving

Many counselees seek help when their relationship with Jesus is strained. They feel spiritually dry, disconnected from the grace and mercy available in Christ, and unconvinced the Lord is for them in any meaningful way. As counselees rest on the presence and promises of the Lord, including freedom from the power and penalty of sin (Rom 6:1, 11; 8:1), their attitude toward God changes. They lean into him instead of running from him. They rely on his strength rather than struggling to handle things alone. They believe the Lord loves them and they, in turn, grow in their love for him. Growing counselees believe Jesus has given them a new identity and a new purpose. This reminds them that they can live hopefully and purposefully in the life the Lord gives them, even if they must wait for eternity for every tear to be wiped from their eyes (Rev 21:4).

2. The Counselee Is Growing in the Areas That Encouraged Them to Seek Help

Counselors will know counseling can end well when they see a counselee pursuing the right goal of Christlikeness, appropriately handling their past and looking forward to their future (Phil 3:12–14), and applying biblical truth properly to their struggle. You should not expect perfection of a counselee (Gal 5:13–26), but rather declining frequency and intensity of the struggles that brought them to counseling.

Some struggles, though, might have long-lasting effects. A couple seeking help due to regular conflict will unlikely experience a conflict-free life after counseling. However, before graduation we would expect the conflicts to be less intense, less frequent, and more quickly resolved in a God-honoring way. In addition, counselees suffering with cancer will be ready to steward their cancer more effectively even should the Lord allow that cancer to take them home.[2]

---

[2] John Piper, *Don't Waste Your Life* (Wheaton, IL: Crossway, 2018). We are thinking specifically of the cancer patient who uses their trial not only for personal growth, but for evangelizing and encouraging others.

3. The Counselee Applies the Scripture to Areas Not Discussed

While the Bible applies to every aspect of our lives, we don't have time in the counseling room to discuss how Scripture applies to every area of a counselee's life. So, what counselors want to observe is the counselee taking the Word of God discussed in one area and applying that same truth to other areas (2 Tim 3:16–17).

For example, Paul Tripp wrote, "A marriage of love, understanding, and unity is built on worship, not romance."[3] The reason that statement works is because life is built on worship. We are commanded to love the Lord with all of our being (Matt 22:37–40), to value, treasure, and worship him above all else. If our counselees who seek help for marriage issues have come to understand worship in our sessions and assignments, they will apply that truth to other areas as well. When such a counselee speaks about how worship influenced a moment at work, or changed a response in parenting, then you know that the counselee has connected Scripture to their life (Ps 119:105).

4. The Counselee Has Genuinely Repented and Has a Worldview Large Enough to Respond to Suffering

Every counselee sins and suffers. They rebel, make excuses, and want to see themselves as better than they are (Rom 12:3; 1 Cor 1:26–29). While we are not able to judge the hearts of counselees, we know they must repent of their sin against the Lord and others. Several signs of genuine repentance include admitting wrongdoing, acknowledging a past refusal to respond to the Spirit's conviction, accepting consequences, confessing sin before God and the appropriate people, requesting forgiveness, and visible change that's evident to those closest to the situation.[4] Counselors who graduate

---

[3] Paul David Tripp, *What Did You Expect?: Redeeming the Realities of Marriage* (Wheaton, IL: Crossway, 2015), 33.

[4] Jared C. Wilson, "Genuine Repentance," Gospel Coalition blog post, March 18, 2014, https://www.thegospelcoalition.org/blogs/jared-c-wilson/genuine-repentance/. Wilson lists twelve helpful signs of a repentant heart. See also our chapter 7.

counselees without seeing repentance and without knowing they understand how to suffer biblically may be trusting in behavioral change.

Remember that some counselees erroneously believe that counseling "works" if consequences diminish. A counselee might say that since their family is getting along, since they have not looked at pornography, or since they are staying on a budget, their life is good and they are ready to graduate from counseling. While we should celebrate successes, we must realize that genuine change may not have occurred. Without repentance, patterns of worship did not change and counselees thus may quickly return to old patterns of thinking and behaving.

Moreover, as counseling progresses, we should determine if the counselee has a worldview large enough to properly understand how to suffer biblically. Is our counselee prepared to live out their suffering with Christ, in community with his people, and in light of all the Lord might want to accomplish in and through them?

5. The Counselee Understands How Their Struggles in Behavior and Motivation Resulted in the Need for Counseling and Is Able to Explain How to Self-Counsel in the Future

Counselees want solutions—fast. In fact, the faster the solution the better. This mindset is dangerous; giving them exactly what they want won't help them understand their problems or the heart attitudes that led to those problems. It won't help them repent or equip them for the future. Counselors should help their counselees understand biblically how they arrived at their place of need.

Let's consider a couple who comes to counseling due to regular conflict. They will likely say they have communication problems and need communication skills. Counselors who accept this explanation miss the larger and deeper heart issues (Jas 4:1–2). Conflict is merely an opportunity for counselees' sinful inner-person motives, treasures, affections, and love to exert influence. Counselors must go beneath the surface. They must show that such people have a worship problem because they do not love the Lord first. They need help seeing the ruling desires in their hearts that make them insensitive to the spiritual issues involved (Ps 115:1–8).[5] After all, the more a counselee is able to understand their heart, repent of their wrong motives, and seek to please Christ, the more they will be ready for the communication skills that will build relationships (e.g., Prov 15:1; Eph 4:25–32).

When counselees understand how their affections, desires, motivations, behavior, and emotions work together, they are properly equipped to counsel themselves through future challenges.

6. The Counselee Is Well Connected to Their Local Church

Whether the counselee receives counsel from a friend, their local church, or from a counseling center, they must be committed and connected to the church family. Sometimes counselees don't want their own church involved or to know about the counseling. We think this is unwise for many reasons. First, God gave them pastors who not only care for them, but also must give account for them (1 Pet 5:1–4; Heb 13:17). Second, the local church is the place where our counselees will receive ongoing care and give care to others (Heb 10:24–25; Eph 4:11–16). Third, the reasons they seek counseling are the most important growth opportunities in their lives. Fourth, God designed each of us to be part of a local body of believers where the normal discipling process will help our counselees continue to grow after formal counseling ends.[6]

Final Steps to Ending a Successful Case

Assuming the counselee has satisfied the six characteristics above, let's consider five practical steps to end your case successfully.

---

[5] Psalm 115 is particularly powerful because it not only explains the problem; namely, that the counselee will be like the lifeless idols (v. 8), but it also provides the solution: trust in the Lord (vv. 9–10). For a more detailed explanation of the subject of idolatry, see G. K. Beale, *We Become What We Worship* (Downers Grove: InterVarsity Press, 2008).

[6] See Jonathan Leeman, *Church Membership: How the World Knows Who Represents Jesus* (Wheaton, IL: Crossway, 2012). See also our chapter 2.

1. Review and Summarize the Problems and the Progress

In your final regular session (the "graduation session"), consider using the following questions as guides: (1) What have you learned? (2) How did you previously handle your struggles? How would you handle them now? (3) What are some of the passages we've discussed that helped you most? (4) How are you seeking to live for the Lord today?

You might also want to ask (but not require) your counselee to summarize the counseling on paper and submit a copy to you. It will serve as a written record for them and will help you know how the Lord worked. A counselee's summary could be one data point for helping the next counselee more effectively.

2. Work with Your Counselee to Produce a Six-Month Growth Plan

Over the course of counseling, the Lord has used you, the counselor, to direct your counselee's path for spiritual growth. As you understood your counselee and encouraged them to find hope and help in Christ, you were the one, humanly speaking, who chartered the path forward. After the counselee graduates, they will apply God's counsel to their own lives. In preparation for that, help them develop an action plan.

This could involve many different components, such as the type of personal Bible study and application to be done next, reading particular biblically based materials, developing a meaningful accountability relationship, ensuring ongoing and appropriate Christian fellowship, and being part of meaningful ministry opportunities. Help them know what to do next.

3. Encourage the Counselee to Communicate the Same Truths to Others

Those who have been changed are most excited to share what the Lord has done. It may help the counselee to write down two names of those with whom they could share what they've learned as well as some of the Christlike personal care God used to change them.

4. Help Counselees Engage in Training Opportunities at Their Churches

Your counselees might be in the next counseling training class offered. Maybe your counselee could assist another counselee or even co-counsel with an experienced counselor. Maybe they can serve in other areas of ministry they would be qualified and equipped to do.

Perhaps your counselee is ready to share what the Lord has done in front of the entire local church body. Testimonies, after all, provide reasons to rejoice and serve as catalysts. If the counselee is not ready to share, maybe their story—with their permission and appropriate details changed—could be used in your ministry contexts.

5. Schedule Appropriate Follow-Up

Ending counseling abruptly can be a challenge for some counselees—especially those who have enjoyed the process. Some might fear ending.[7] One way to mitigate those fears and ensure that your counselee is doing well is to schedule an appointment four-to-six weeks after the final regular session and perhaps another one a few months later. Check-up sessions provide an opportunity to continue to celebrate, offer advice, and potentially restart counseling if necessary.

When Counseling Ends for Less Positive Reasons

Our focus to this point has been ending cases successfully. But every counselor knows that not every case ends that way. This section will identify a few reasons why.[8]

---

[7] Some think they need counseling and hope it never ends. As kind and encouraging as that sentiment might be to hear, we must emphasize the discipleship river (see n. 1 of this chapter). Counseling is designed to help people get to the place where they are ready to grow through the normal ministries of the church. Reviewing the discipleship river diagram, expressing confidence in the Lord's work (Phil 1:6), and helping them serve will help them realize that ending counseling is best.

[8] Jeremy Pierre and Deepak Reju offer two additional answers: (1) they do not trust you, and (2) they need more help than you can offer. Jeremy Pierre and Deepak Reju, *The*

Life Gets in the Way

Sometimes childcare needs become overwhelming or challenges at work no longer make counseling possible. Vacations, church events, or similar activities might halt counseling. Job changes might require a relocation. Wise counselors pay attention to life changes that may necessitate the end of counseling, making the best use of the time available (Eph 5:15–16).

The Counselee Does Not Really Want to Change

Some people who seek counseling want different circumstances, but they do not want to be different. More challenging is the person who attends counseling in hopes you take their side and validate their opinion about their situation. In a marriage case, for instance, both parties might come believing the other is mostly at fault. Sometimes cases end because no one is looking for help.[9]

The Counselee Refuses to Complete Growth Assignments (Homework)

We believe the counseling room is an important place for thinking, praying, and strategizing, and that what happens when we meet is an important part of the change process. However, we also believe it is important for the counselee to continue to pray, think, and act in ways consistent with biblical truth between sessions. Scripture must impact their work, their family relationships, their friendships, and wherever else they live out their lives. Those who refuse to do homework refuse to connect the Scripture to where they live. A persistent unwillingness to do this gives counselors

---

Pastor and Counseling: The Basics of Shepherding Members in Need (Wheaton, IL: Crossway, 2015), 90–92. Further, Jay Adams reminds us of the problem when counselees become more dependent on the counselor than on the Lord. See Jay Adams, "How Can I Know When?," http://www.nouthetic.org/nouthetic-counseling/adams-answers/69-you-talk-about-nothing-else-but-sin.html.

[9] In some cases, counselees are forced to counsel either through family requirements or government involvement. In these situations we should explain the benefits of our ministry and see what the counselee decides.

reason to end the case or suspend the sessions until assignment completion occurs. (See also chapter 17.)

Steps to End Counseling When the Goals Were Not Achieved

The worst-case scenario that arises is when the counselee leaves and does not give you an opportunity to speak with them. There is not much you can do with or for the counselee then. Thankfully, this is rare. Here are three actions you can take as a counselor to end well even if the goals were not achieved.

1. Communicate That You Are Willing to Meet in the Future

Providing an opportunity for a future session allows us to show kindness (Eph 4:32), patience (1 Thess 5:14), and loving care (Acts 20:31). Even if you are the one to initiate a three- or six-month break, the very fact that counseling can resume demonstrates the counseling is not ending on adversarial terms. Second chances abound in the Bible. Abraham, Jacob, David, Peter, John, and Paul all found God to be gracious beyond measure. Many who serve as counselors can remember times that God, in his grace, also gave them undeserved second chances.

2. Communicate That What the Counselee Has Been Given Can Still Be Helpful

We biblical counselors always hope some truth we shared or example we gave will prick a dissatisfied counselee's conscience and lead them to the Lord or back to us to resume counseling. Maybe one morning as they drink coffee, they will see their Bible, open it, find a homework assignment completed three years earlier, look up its suggested Scripture passage, and turn to the Lord or contact us.

3. Seek to Learn All You Can from Every Failure

It is easy to blame others. Many counselees have developed skills in deflection, justification, self-righteousness, and blame shifting. But counselors can do the same thing. Instead of looking at ourselves when counseling fails, we quickly rehearse reasons a counselee did not want to change.

Matthew 7:3–5 encourages us to consider ways we did not counsel wisely. No counselor enjoys failure; but God uses it, as he uses success, to help us become more like Christ. Counselors should consider ways the counseling might have failed due to their own errors.[10] In some cases we should humble ourselves and seek forgiveness from a counselee for a failure—whether or not the counselee resumes sessions.

Conclusion

Concluding a case successfully is an occasion to celebrate God's goodness. Your counselee can rejoice that God has grown them and that God will complete the work he started in them (Phil 1:6; 2:13). You can rejoice that God has used you to serve him and to help one of his dear sons or daughters become more like Christ. Yet even when a case ends for less positive reasons, you can have hope and confidence that the Lord will do his will.

Concluding a case is a counseling skill. The basic ideas found here should be applied in each case. When they are ending successfully, then you want to help long enough to prepare the counselee for a more faithful life before the Lord without keeping them so long that they miss stewardship opportunities the Lord gives them. When cases end unsuccessfully, look first to your own possible failures, keep the door open for future ministry, and remain humble and dependent on the Lord who desires to use you for his honor and glory.

---

[10] Jay Adams says counselors may fail because they reach conclusions before hearing the situation fully (Prov 18:13), they side with one person because they emotionally relate better to one counselee than another (Prov 18:17), they give in to temptation, or they don't provide the hope available in Christ (1 Cor 10:13). Adams concludes his discussion with these words: "It is sufficient to say that counselors may fail in exactly the same ways that their counselees have failed." Jay E. Adams, *Competent to Counsel* (Grand Rapids: Zondervan, 1970), 59. Adams also lists fifty possible failure factors in his *Christian Counselor's Manual* (Grand Rapids: Zondervan, 1973), 459–61.

19

Counseling Non-Christians

From its inception, Christianity has been missional, an evangelistic movement to win people to the Lord Jesus Christ.[1] While the prophets before Jesus and the apostles after him consistently taught this, our risen Lord issued what we call the Great Commission: "Go, therefore, and make disciples of all nations, baptizing them in the name of the Father and of the Son and of the Holy Spirit, teaching them to observe everything I have commanded you" (Matt 28:19–20).

How does our Lord's Great Commission inform biblical counseling? The modern biblical counseling movement began by focusing on counseling Christians. This was largely definitional, with some early leaders defining counseling specifically as helping *believers* change in God-pleasing ways. They correctly observed that unbelievers cannot do so apart from Christ and his Spirit's regenerating work (Rom 8:5–8; 1 Cor 2:14). These biblical

[1] This chapter has been adapted from Robert D. Jones, "Biblical Counseling: An Opportunity for Problem-Based Evangelism," *Journal of Biblical Counseling* 38, no. 1 (Spring 2017): 75–92. See also Kevin Carson and Randy Patten, "Biblical Counseling and Evangelism," and Rob Green and Steve Viars, "Biblical Counseling, the Church, and Community Outreach," in Kellemen and Carson, *Biblical Counseling and the Church*, 314–48 (see chap. 1, n. 2); and Lambert, *Theology of Biblical Counseling*, 300–303 (see chap. 3, n. 15).

counselors thus sought to evangelize or "pre-counsel" non-Christians and then counsel them after conversion.

Sharing the same theology of salvation, most biblical counselors today define counseling to include evangelism. We seek to win to Christ people who struggle with life and seek counseling help for their personal and relational problems. We help each person know and follow Jesus—the unbeliever is presented initial ways to do so, and Christians are presented deeper, ongoing ways. In this sense, we point every counselee to Jesus and his Word within their specific, problem-filled situation. We teach both unbelievers (Acts 4:2; 5:21, 42) and believers (Acts 11:26; 18:11; 20:20), proclaiming the gospel and its implications to both groups (Rom 1:14–15). As in the case of Christians, we enter the non-Christian's world, understand their struggles, and bring them Jesus and his gospel-soaked answers; the main difference is that we adapt our goals, strategies, and methods to their spiritual condition. We might call this problem-occasioned evangelism.

So, how can and should biblical counselors lead unbelievers to Christ in the counseling process?

Our Evangelistic Opportunities

Aside from informal contacts with unsaved friends, family members, and coworkers that might lead to counseling opportunities, four avenues for problem-occasioned evangelism sometimes open.

First, some unbelievers might seek a biblical counselor. They might have a genuine desire to explore biblical Christianity or hear a Christian perspective on their problems. Maybe they want a free (church-based) option or to please their Christian friends who recommended one. Or maybe they are desperate—since other therapies failed—and have some flickering hope God might help.

Second, as we participate in the outreach ministries of our churches, we encounter people who need Christ. In particular, churches that start counseling ministries for the community will get evangelistic opportunities.

Third, we sometimes counsel those who profess faith; but as we get to know them, we find reason to question the genuineness of their salvation.

Maybe a conversion testimony is unclear or a counselee demonstrates inconsistencies between their professed faith and daily living.

Fourth, we sometimes counsel those whom we believe are followers of the Lord but are crippled by doubts about their faith. While such counseling is not evangelistic in the traditional sense, we bring fresh and focused measures of the gospel—"the evangel"—to address their uncertainties so they can experience deepening assurance.

Assessing a Counselee's Relationship to Christ

Knowing a counselee's spiritual state helps us decide which gospel emphases to bring and when and how to do so. When we counsel those in our churches, we often have some idea of their spiritual condition. Yet even those cases might be unclear—to say nothing of the uncertainty that arises when we counsel those we have never met previously. Do they truly belong to Christ? If not, are they near or far from him? Spiritually hungry or disinterested? What aspect of their fallen condition should we first address? Biblical counselors want to know.

Four categories of questions help us assess a counselee's spiritual commitment to Christ in the counseling process.

Appointment Setup Information

1. Were they referred to you by someone (e.g., a church leader) who described their spiritual state?
2. Do they know you are a *biblical* counselor, and are they willing to seek biblical counseling?

Intake Form Information

1. Did they complete the presession agreement and intake forms?
2. Are they active church members? Does their church teach the gospel clearly, require a premembership course that explains the gospel, and interview potential members concerning their testimony and walk with Christ?

3. Did they give you permission to contact their pastor?
4. How did they answer questions like these (assuming your intake forms ask such):
   - Do you believe in God? Do you consider yourself saved?
   - How frequently do you pray?
   - What is your view of the Bible? How frequently do you read it?
   - Have you come to the place where you know for certain that if you were to die tonight you would go to heaven? Suppose you were to die and stand before God and he were to say to you, "Why should I let you into my heaven?," what would you reply?
   - Why do you desire counseling that is Christ-centered and biblical?
   - Explain any recent changes in your religious life.

Session One Discussion

1. In telling their story, do they volunteer testimony about any kind of conversion, church involvement, or religious practice? (Omissions can be revealing.) How do they respond to your inquiry?
2. If you inquire about or explain the gospel, how do they respond?
3. Do their responses and behaviors in the session suggest a sound Christian conversion and commitment? Even in their confused, struggling, or guilty state, do they show interest in Christ and evidence the Spirit's fruit?

Next-Session(s) Information

1. Did they complete the growth assignments? If not, why? If so, did their responses evidence faith and obedience?
2. If an assignment sought to assess their spiritual condition, what did it reveal?
3. As the sessions continue, what spiritual fruit appears?

While none of these criteria are foolproof—the Lord alone knows those who are his, and the Bible records false conversions—they paint an unfolding picture of a counselee's genuine relationship with Jesus or lack thereof.

Limitations in Counseling Unbelievers

At least two factors challenge us when counseling non-Christians. First, they lack the proper desire and ability to change. Jesus stated it directly: "I am the vine; you are the branches. If you remain in me and I in you, you will bear much fruit; apart from me you can do nothing" (John 15:5 NIV). Apart from Christ and his Spirit's regenerating work, unbelievers cannot please God or even embrace his truth (Rom 8:7–8; 1 Cor 2:14).

Second, non-Christians don't submit to Scripture as their final authority. While some might respect Jesus and the Bible, their failure to heed the gospel's call to repent, believe, and follow Jesus exposes their unsaved condition. When counseling Christians, we can appeal to God's Word as our shared standard. With unbelievers, we share no objective standard—no agreed-upon, final counseling authority; this results in disparate definitions, diagnoses, goals, and remedies.

These two limitations must not stop us from ministering to unsaved counselees. Nevertheless, they explain why some of them seem unable to grasp the gospel and might resist our counsel. These realities drive us to plead for God's help—to depend prayerfully on Christ's Spirit, who alone opens blind eyes.

Handling Evangelistic Opportunities in Counseling

Four truths can help motivate and guide us in counseling non-Christians. (To personalize these guidelines, we refer to a counselee named Katie, although there is nothing gender-specific here.)

1. Know with Certainty that What You Have in Christ is What Katie Most Deeply Needs

Although non-Christians face the same suffering we do in this groaning creation, they do so "without hope and without God" (Eph 2:12). Their lives are also intertwined with those of other lost people, a humanity described by Paul as "foolish, disobedient, deceived and enslaved by all kinds of passions and pleasures. . . ., being hated and hating one another" (Titus 3:3 NIV).

Katie's felt needs might include the usual: relational peace, freedom from guilt, internal stability, life purpose, material provisions, approval from others, and the like. But more than anything, Katie needs Jesus, the One "who came from the Father, full of grace and truth" (John 1:14 NIV). She needs his Word that refreshes the soul, makes wise the simple, gives joy to the heart, and gives light to the eyes (Ps 19:7–8 NIV). While Katie's presenting problems are important to her and should be important to you, you must not allow them—even if severe—to obscure your gospel-centered counseling vision. You must resist the temptation to divide the "spiritual" from the "practical," "emotional," or "psychological." The all-sufficient Bible speaks robustly to Katie's heart condition.

For example, consider how the Old Testament Wisdom literature connects unsaved people to the God who understands the gamut of their human experience and who came in person to redeem them.

- For those who have suffered undeservedly, the book of Job moves past the short-sighted, popular opinions of Job's friends, to a God of ultimate sovereignty, wisdom, and goodness, and to an ever-living Redeemer who brings hope, justice, and final vindication to his people.
- For those whose lifestyles have left them unsatisfied, Ecclesiastes provides an odyssey demonstrating the futility of life apart from the Lord. As the author traverses the landscape of human -sophies, -logies, and -isms, he leads them back to their Creator and his Word.
- For those who face hard circumstances but mishandle them and reap unpleasant consequences, Proverbs delivers concrete direction

about money, marriage, sex, work, addiction, communication, eating, friends, temptations, priorities, authorities, parenting, and a dozen more areas of relentless pressure and daily decisions. Those answers lead to the fountainhead of life: the fear of the Lord and a right relationship with him.
- For those feeling an array of disordered emotions, the Psalms give voice to anger, fear, worry, grief, loss, sadness, and depression, yet frame these experiences within a personal relationship to God. Here our unbelieving counselees, amid the torrent of disturbed emotions, meet our Shepherd-King who can lead them beside quiet waters.

Only an encounter with Christ and the gospel can save and satisfy Katie. This is the life-changing provision and the calling entrusted to biblical counselors.

2. See Yourself as One of God's Instruments to Offer Jesus to Katie

As Paul reminded Timothy, God gave us the Bible to make people "wise for salvation" and for our public and private ministries of "teaching, rebuking, correcting, and training in righteousness" (2 Tim 3:15–17 NIV). Katie needs gospel-centered counseling, not secular therapy. In problem-occasioned evangelism, the person's difficulties become opportunities to present Jesus as relevant to their presenting problems and as the transformative answer to their deeper ones. When Katie comes to you, know that God has led her to you so you can lead her to the Savior who will bring her new life.

3. Move toward Katie with Compassion and Humility

Like Jesus, you must enter Katie's world, understand her needs, and bring her his saving help. Consider Jesus's attitude toward the rich young ruler in Mark 10:21: "Jesus looked at him and loved him" (NIV). Note his personal, caring-but-pointed engagement with both Simon the Pharisee and the sinful woman in Luke 7:36–50, with the little children and the blind beggar in Luke 18:15–17, 35–43, and with Zacchaeus in Luke 19:1–10.

Or consider his skillful listening and flexible style with his mother, with Nicodemus, with the woman at the well, and with the disabled man in John 2, 3, 4, and 5, respectively.

How should you show care, compassion, and presence? Encourage Katie to share her story and voice her struggles. Ask wise questions and listen for open doors into her heart beliefs and motives. Pray for the Spirit to move in her life. As you build relational rapport and trust, you bring those specific truths about Christ most suited to her particular need. We look at lost people not merely as *lost* but as *people* who are lost. The harvest field Jesus calls us to enter abounds not with generic lost people but with specific individuals with detailed personal problems.

4. Bring Christ-Centered Truth to Address Both Katie's Presenting Problem and Her Deeper Problem

We must always address the person's presenting problem. If Katie wants to talk about her marriage, you must not hijack the agenda by inserting a disconnected evangelistic presentation. At the same time, you must not hold back the ultimate answer she needs both in this life and the life to come. So, give Katie practical help based on general biblical wisdom *and* show Katie how Jesus addresses her presenting problems and also the wider, deeper dynamics beneath them. As one counselor puts it,

> The next step is to take every opportunity we can to demonstrate their need for Christ. We will attempt to give them some skills to handle some of their problems, but only in the context of seeking to help them understand that they have a much larger problem—they remain under the power and penalty of sin. In terms of process that means our unbelieving counselees are hearing the gospel message every time we meet with them.[2]

[2] Rob Green, "How Do You Counsel Someone Who Is Not a Christian?," BCTC Questions and Answer Series, October 19, 2011, http://blogs.faithlafayette.org/counseling/2011/10/bctc-question-and-answer-series/.

Giving Katie some life skills to handle some of her felt-need problems while simultaneously pointing her to the ultimate Redeemer blends timely care with Christ-centered truth.

For example, you might listen empathetically to Katie about her disappointing marriage, bear that relational burden with her, and pray for her in the session. You can suggest practical steps to communicate better with her husband or what to do when X or Y happens. But along the way you should communicate to her that the only true and lasting solution to any human problem is found in Jesus. And for Katie, solutions begin with her knowing him as her Lord and Savior. You can voice his personal, timely invitation to her: "Come to me, all you who are weary and burdened, and I will give you rest. Take my yoke upon you and learn from me, for I am gentle and humble in heart, and you will find rest for your souls" (Matt 11:28–29 NIV).

Since the Gospel of John was written to bring people to faith (20:31), it provides winsome, captivating pictures of our Savior. You might find John 10:1–18 particularly valuable:

- The words come from Jesus himself, a voice Katie might respect and respond to more than other voices in the Bible.
- Jesus knows his sheep by name and cares for them in ways that transcend the care of the hired hands.
- Jesus speaks to those who have experienced hardships and the misleading voices from thieves and robbers around them.
- Jesus offers life to Katie—abundant, full life.
- Jesus points to his cross and resurrection as the ground for redemptive hope. Unlike anyone else in Katie's life, Jesus self-sacrificially laid down his life for her.
- Jesus gives Katie a clear invitation to come to him.

With whatever specific passage we use, we must communicate a relevant invitation to our non-Christian counselees. For example,

> Katie, the only lasting hope and true help for the problems you face is in a personal relationship with Jesus Christ. He alone is the Good Shepherd of our souls. No counselor (including me), psychologist, or psychiatrist can give you the ultimate help we both

> desperately need. Apart from him we are lost, without hope. With him there is rich and lasting hope. I invite you to believe in the Lord Jesus Christ—to commit yourself to him as your Lord and Savior.

Whether Katie turns to Christ or not, you need to be ready to answer her questions and engage in wise follow-up.

What assignments might you give? Let the same "both/and" aim guide you. Give Katie assignments to address her particular marriage problem *and* her fundamental need for Christ. For the latter, she could reflect on John 1:19–51, a narrative of different people meeting Jesus and beginning to follow him. People like narratives.[3] You could ask her to read the story a few times on different days and record five titles, names, or descriptions of Jesus to discuss at your next session. In this passage Jesus is called the Lord, the Son of God, Rabbi/Teacher, the Messiah/the Christ, the King of Israel, and the Son of Man. Moreover, he is twice called the Lamb of God—"who takes away the sin of the world!"—providing a clear gospel path to discuss next time (vv. 29, 36). You can ask Katie how a relationship with this Jesus might change the way she views God, herself, and her husband. Katie might also be helped by theologically-sound evangelistic literature and recordings.

By keeping this both/and perspective in counseling lost people, we provide both the immediate help they have sought *and* the greater help they ultimately need.

When Non-Christian Counselees Don't Turn to Christ

Don't fret. There is value in giving unsaved people practical counsel about presenting problems, even if there is no immediate conversion and it only results in a better *non-Christian* life.

---

[3] While we could assign the entire chapter, the 1:1–18 prologue section might be too conceptually dense for some non-Christians, at least initially. Non-Christians are more open to reading a narrative than another style of biblical writing.

- We demonstrate integrity. If you agreed to meet with Katie, you must address her concerns.
- We increase the likelihood Katie will come back. Biblical principles generally make life work better, at least in this life. Doing good to our neighbors is a good thing.
- We pray that in her attempt to follow our practical advice, Katie will recognize her inability to change and admit her need for Christ to forgive and transform her.
- We pray that God will water the gospel seeds we plant and eventually convert Katie. Who but God knows the later fruit that your evangelistic biblical counseling might bear?

Two assurances give us confidence. First, God will save those he chooses to save. By his Spirit he will draw his chosen sheep to himself. Rather than excusing inactivity, this encourages our efforts. Second, God will use his Word and his people—including you—in salvation's work.

True, we have no assurance God will save Katie. We love, labor, pray, and persevere in showing Christlike care and providing gospel-centered counsel. But at the end of the day, Katie might reject Jesus. Even the greatest evangelist, our Lord Jesus, knows what this feels like. While he "came to seek and save the lost" (Luke 19:10 NIV), not everyone got saved: "From that moment *many* . . . turned back and no longer accompanied him" (John 6:66, emphasis added). Jesus wept over Jerusalem's rejection of him (Matt 23:37; Luke 19:41); most of that city—his chosen city—wanted nothing to do with him. The rich young ruler (Mark 10:17–22), Simon the Pharisee (Luke 7:36–50), and the unrepentant thief on the cross (Luke 23:39–43) resisted his counsel.

This means we must entrust our unsaved counselees into God's hands, praying that *God* will make our gospel ministry effective in their lives. We must remember, "The Lord's servant must not quarrel, but must be gentle to everyone, able to teach, and patient, instructing his opponents with gentleness. Perhaps God will grant them repentance leading them to the knowledge of the truth" (2 Tim 2:24–25). Our hopes for their salvation depend on him. As long as our Bibles speak of the transformations of wicked kings like Manasseh (2 Chronicles 33) and Christian-persecutors like Saul of Tarsus (Acts 9), dramatic conversions can happen.

What should we say when counselees opt to discontinue our Christ-centered counseling (John 3:16–18; 6:35–37; Rom 10:9–10)? Faithful love for our non-Christian counselees requires us to issue a warning to all who turn away from the Lord. We must lovingly remind them of both the sweet consequences of faith *and* the grave consequences of unbelief:

- Many are the woes of the wicked, but the LORD's unfailing love surrounds the one who trusts in him. (Ps 32:10 NIV)
- Whoever believes in the Son has eternal life, but whoever rejects the Son will not see life, for God's wrath remains on them. (John 3:36 NIV)

Notice in these texts how God pairs his appeals with his promises. Along with giving warnings and invitations we should ask God to make a counselee willing to talk again with us or another gospel-centered counselor. Meanwhile, as they experience the inevitable woes of their non-Christian lifestyle and the weight of God's disfavor, we keep our counseling doors open and pray and long for them to come back.

Conclusion

Biblical counseling as problem-occasioned evangelism provides a unique way to reach people for Christ and fulfill his Great Commission. Seeing beyond the felt needs and presenting problems of unsaved counselees—without bypassing or ignoring them—allows us to point to their ultimate and greatest need and motivates us to seek and seize opportunities. May God open doors for us to counsel lost people, and may he grant us the love and wisdom to do so well. Personal and relational problems provide timely occasions to offer the good news of Jesus.

20

Ethical and Legal Issues

The Enter-Understand-Bring method in chapters 13 through 15 encourages you to biblically love your counselees (Matt 22:37–40) and to practice the golden rule of treating others the way you would like to be treated (Matt 7:12). One way to practice that love is by treating the knowledge of your counselees' thoughts, actions, and feelings ethically and confidentially.

As you seek to do that, you also want to obey our governmental leaders (Rom 13:1–7; 1 Pet 2:13–17). This chapter, though, is one of the riskiest to include in an introductory book on biblical counseling because laws vary from state to state and can change quickly (e.g., the legal definition of marriage and laws relating to counseling transgender children). At the time of this writing, biblical counseling remains a largely protected enterprise in our society.[1] However, that could change. Therefore, readers must not view this chapter as a replacement for legal counsel or as an authoritative document.

[1] Grace Community Church in Sun Valley, California, counseled a man but was sued by his parents after he committed suicide. The case went to the California Supreme Court, which ruled in favor of the church. See https://law.justia.com/cases/california/supreme-court/3d/47/278.html. It since has helped provide legal protection for church-based biblical counseling.

Instead, allow it to orient you to the subject, provide questions, and raise some issues involved in wisely serving the Lord and following the law.[2]

Ethical Issues

Ethics is concerned about honesty, integrity, and the fulfillment of commitments. It involves explaining who you are and what you seek to accomplish. Biblical ethics demands truth telling and an openness about a situation, since we do every aspect of ministry before the eyes of God to keep our conscience clear before him and others (Acts 24:16). Below are issues related to ethics.

Limited Confidentiality and Informed Consent

The Bible clearly tells us what we should do with personal information. Proverbs 11:13 says, "A gossip goes around revealing a secret, but a trustworthy person keeps a confidence." Similarly, Prov 20:19 records, "The one who reveals secrets is a constant gossip; avoid someone with a big mouth." These verses remind us that issues of confidentiality are associated with trust on the positive side and gossip on the negative. We want our counselees to freely share about their struggles so that we can give wise counsel (Prov 18:13). Providing a safe place for them to talk is part of loving our counselees well. After all, the counseling enterprise is unique. The counselee shares personal information that the relationship would not normally allow. That information can be viewed as a trust. A counselee chooses to entrust a counselor with information they would not want shared or discussed with others because they view it as potentially shameful, painful, or embarrassing.

---

[2] For more on legal and ethical issues, see Bob Kellemen, "Ethical and Legal Issues in Biblical Counseling in the Church: Caring Like Christ," in Kellemen and Carson, *Biblical Counseling and the Church*, 290–312 (see chap. 1, n. 2), originally published in Robert W. Kellemen, *Equipping Counselors for Your Church* (Phillipsburg, NJ: P&R, 2011), 304–23. See also the many resources at https://biblicalcounseling.com/til-196-legal-issues-and-abuse/.

Biblical counselors are committed to keeping in confidence what they are told because it is a God-honoring and loving thing to do. It also builds relationship and suggests honesty, care, and compassion. However, we must also consider some limits to confidentiality.

Since 1973, my (Rob's) congregation, Faith Church in Lafayette, Indiana, has operated a counseling ministry that serves people in our church and community. While we never want to be guilty of the sin of gossip, we communicate in writing six ways the confidentiality commitment does not apply.[3] We must be able to take the following actions:

1. Seek Advice from Other Professionals

Throughout this book, we encourage you to adopt Scripture as your system of knowledge and to study it carefully to develop your model of care. We also encourage you to be a good listener and to understand your counselees properly. However, no one is all wise or all knowing. Sometimes we listen to our counselees, but we are not sure what to do. We might not know where to go in our Bibles or know how to wisely counsel the issue. In such cases, we should communicate to our counselees that we want the freedom to ask other counselors or professionals for advice. We must acknowledge our own need for counsel even as we counsel. When we seek advice from those more experienced or gifted, our goal is to improve our service and ministry.

2. Seek Advice from an Attorney

At times we might have a situation that warrants a conversation with an attorney. The most common situations involve the next category, but we ask for permission to contact a trusted attorney if we believe the situation requires it. In this and the above situation, we normally would need to divulge the counselee's name.[4]

---

[3] This information should be part of the informed consent to counsel agreement every counselee signs before their first appointment. The six reasons listed herein are not exhaustive; you may apply additional exclusions.

[4] We sometimes counsel people ordered by a court to seek counseling. In these situations, the court normally asks for progress reports or a summary of the counseling

3. Accommodate Mandated Reporting

Every state has guidelines on what must be reported and who must report it. A counselor should know their state laws and check that understanding with an attorney licensed in that state. Indiana, for example, mandates everyone to report child abuse. Some states have elder abuse mandated reporting. We should clearly communicate with our counselees that we cannot hold in confidence what the authorities require we share.[5]

4. Address Suicidal Intentions

Another exclusion to our informed consent regards a counselee's stated intent to commit suicide. Some individuals believe ending their lives is the only path to end their suffering. The counselor must, therefore, take claims of suicide very seriously (see Chapter 26). In fact, we would rather limit confidentiality and be part of protecting a person from self-harm than keep it quiet and learn a counselee took their life. While some counselees have found this exclusion troubling, the vast majority have appreciated our commitment to take proactive steps to provide safety if needed.

5. Report Crime as Necessary

Counselors are not law enforcement officers. Our job is not to investigate crimes, conduct interrogations, prosecute those who have done wrong, or declare a verdict. Rather, we help our counselees understand how to have a saving and growing relationship with the Lord. People sin in numerous ways that remain solely a part of the counseling process. For example, some counselees abuse illegal drugs. This confession might not automatically

---

provided. At times, a counselee requests a character letter or a summary of counseling letter in hopes of proving to the court they are taking steps toward change. For such cases, you may contact an attorney for advice.

[5] Some authorities may bring charges against a counselor for withholding information they were required to report. See also chapter 26.

result in a call to law enforcement. However, if a counselee states they plan to physically harm another person, we should call law enforcement and follow their direction. While counselees rarely confess to a plan to harm another, reading confidentiality exclusions that address this matter reminds them of the seriousness of their words and actions.

6. Communicate with the Counselee's Local Church

Sometimes counseling fails and the local church must decide whether to move forward with steps of restorative church discipline (see Matt 18:15–17; 1 Cor 5:1–13). Whether a counselee comes from my (Rob's) local church or from a different church, my colleagues and I reserve the right to speak with their pastor(s). By informing counselees up front that we practice limited confidentiality, not absolute confidentiality, we avoid having to break our word. We can't, after all, break a promise we never made in the first place.

The above statements about confidentiality do very little unless there is an informed consent that counselees read and sign before counseling starts. In fact, it is good practice to discuss the limits of confidentiality during the first session. Such openness and honesty about who we as biblical counselors are, what we are going to do, and how we approach personal information is one way we build trust with our counselees. It is also one way to protect against legal challenges.

Clear Communication

Everyone hates fine print because it has been used to hide important information (e.g., some lenders use fine print to hide the true cost of borrowing). Ministries certainly should not be known for hiding important information. In your written, electronic, and personal communication, then, be clear about who you are and what you plan to do.

Years ago, a man called to explain that his estranged wife had called our ministry (at Rob's church) for counseling. He since had read the information on our website and concluded that we were focused on helping every counselee have a saving relationship with Jesus and that the Bible served as our authority for counsel. I agreed he had read our information correctly. He responded by saying that he was not interested in that. After the call, I reflected. I was sad that he was not interested in a relationship with Jesus and that his worldview had no place for the Bible. At the same time, I was glad that we were able to speak honestly with one another, that our office website is so clear, and that our information empowered him to make an informed decision and to know that we intend to function with integrity. (I (Rob) still hope that one day he will be willing to come, to consider the claims of Christ, and to obey the gospel.)

Even clear written and electronic communication is not always enough. It is also wise to confirm the understanding personally. I recall one man who came to counseling and signed the consent form. His said his intake form was essentially blank because he wanted to explain his situation personally. Discussion revealed that he was upset because his boyfriend had left him. Although our ministry's written and electronic communication had been clear, I still needed to personally explain our understanding of the Bible's view of homosexuality and give him the option to decide to speak with us further or seek a different type of counseling. It is always important to use part of the first session to confirm the counselee's understanding of your counseling philosophy.

What We Promise and What We Ask Them to Promise

Another ethical concern is the agreements we make with our counselees. As a counselor, I (Rob) like to promise them two things. First, I promise that I will listen to them, seek to understand them, and seek to explain what they have told me. That does not mean I will agree with everything they say because there is a difference between listening and agreeing. I also give them freedom to confront me if I have not understood them. Second, I promise to do my very best to connect whatever they tell me with the truth of Scripture.

I also ask my counselees to make some commitments. First, I ask them to be honest. Amazingly enough, I have had counselees who wanted agreements not to talk about certain things. Such cases have never gone well, because the things we needed to discuss most were the very things they wouldn't discuss. Honesty is a *crucial* component of counseling.[6] Second, I ask each person to be a willing learner. This means I want them to allow me to speak with them about them without their trying to direct my attention to any other person. Third, I ask for regular appointments and time. I remind them that the problems did not occur overnight and neither will the solutions. We need regular appointments to maintain counseling effectiveness and focus. Fourth, I ask for a willingness to do growth assignments. I look for a commitment to work hard.

Commitments provide the basis of relationship; they are the rules of engagement so each party understands what they are to contribute. Some counselors include them within the intake forms.

Counselor in Over Their Head!

A third ethical issue involves attempting to match a counselee's struggles with a counselor's competency. While the Scriptures are sufficient, counselors have various levels of skill. All ministries should provide excellent initial training for their counselors and ongoing education to continually improve them. Additionally, if multiple counselors are available, a ministry should seek to match a counselee with the counselor in the best position to help. Asking every potential counselee to submit an intake form in advance will help you discern the complexity of the case. If the counselee shares very little on the intake form, though, you might not discover the true complexity of a case until the personal sessions begin. So, what does quality biblical ethics look like then?

First, know that counselors should reserve the right to ask for help at any time. Our confidentiality policy (where Rob serves)

[6] However, we should not confuse asking for a commitment to be honest with actual honesty. If you counsel, some people will deceive and manipulate you. When this happens, remember that you got involved in counseling because you believed the Lord wanted you in personal ministry. Counselees who deceive and manipulate will hurt you, but you do not have to become cynical. The Lord will use even those hurts in your life and perhaps in their lives at the proper time (Rom 8:28).

allows for counselor-to-counselor interaction for prayer, counsel, and encouragement. This action may be sufficient to help a counselor prepare for counseling sessions.

Second, a counselor could speak to the counselee about either asking another counselor to join the process or for the counselee to be reassigned. This is an act of care and concern for the counselee. We never want a transition to result in undue shame and embarrassment. Should that happen, the blame is on the counselor.

Partnership with Physicians

Many counselees are involved with their personal or family physicians before seeking counseling. A biblical counselor should care about the medical issues of counselees, can speak about the spiritual implications of suffering and struggle, and can partner with physicians. Biblical counseling recognizes the place of medical science and welcomes the understanding that is available. We should partner well with physicians seeking objective answers to the health concerns of counselees.

A challenge arises when some biblical counselors want to go further than they ethically should. Biblical counselors, in most cases, are not physicians. Even those that are do not typically function as physicians when counseling—especially if the counselee is not the physician's patient. We should leave medical advising to those with the training, expertise, and authorization to give it.

The most common question among newer counselors relates to psychiatric medication. When this topic comes up, we should lovingly encourage counselees to discuss it with their physicians.[7] When our counselees ask if taking medication displeases the Lord, we must emphasize that this is a matter of conscience.[8]

---

[7] We address this in chapter 36. See also Michael Emlet, *Descriptions and Prescriptions: A Biblical Perspective on Psychiatric Diagnoses and Medications* (Greensboro, NC: New Growth Press, 2017).

[8] For a detailed explanation of the conscience, see Andy Naselli and J. D. Crowley, *Conscience: What It Is, How to Train It, and Loving Those Who Differ* (Wheaton, IL: Crossway, 2016).

Legal Issues

There are four legal issues that those beginning counseling ministries should consider.

Charging Fees or Accepting Donations

Currently, state governments set the rules for how organizations receive funding for counseling services. Centers with state-licensed counselors have the opportunity for insurance reimbursement. Ministries have the option of charging a fee or requesting a donation depending on individual state laws. Some local church ministries offer free counseling to all interested people;[9] others provide free counseling to members but suggest or perhaps request a donation from outsiders. Since the services are free, those ministries do not have to rely on insurance reimbursements or offer licensed counselors. This does not prevent a counselee from supporting the ministry. Some ministries encourage those who have been blessed to be a blessing in return; thus, many counselors and churches have received generous gifts from grateful counselees.

There is, however, a significant concern in the biblical counseling movement for graduates to be able to earn a living in their area of study. Thus, organizations and individuals have to think through these matters thoroughly. Some practitioners secure positions in larger local churches. On occasion, a group like a Baptist association or a Presbyterian presbytery will support a person to be the primary counselor for the collective of churches.[10] These days, biblical counselors are opening their own private practice ministries or joining with larger biblical counseling practices.[11] Issues of state licensure, employment, and donation versus fee structure will play a role in the possibility of life-sustaining work in biblical counseling. Whatever method a person, church, or independent center uses

[9] For example, see Faith Church, Lafayette, IN, https://www.faithlafayette.org/counseling#free.

[10] For example, see Sue Nicewander, *Building a Church Counseling Ministry without Killing the Pastor* (Leominster, UK: Day One Publications, 2012).

[11] For example, see Fieldstone Counseling, https://fieldstonecounseling.org.

should be explored thoroughly and then communicated clearly to counselees in advance.

501(c)(3) Versus LLC Versus Ministry in the Church

A common matter pastors want to understand is how to legally organize ministry. One option allows a counseling ministry to be one ministry under the church. For many years, for instance, Faith Biblical Counseling Ministries was simply a ministry of Faith Church. Some churches find that to be the best option. However, other ministries might have reasons to separate the formal counseling ministries from the church in the form of an LLC, an auxiliary 501(c)(3), or an independent 501(c)(3). Each option has its own requirements, responsibilities, risks, blessings, and opportunities. We recommend your leadership team think, pray, and seek advice from ministries and an attorney authorized to practice in your state.

Liability Insurance

We live in a litigious society. While we cannot allow the fear of being sued to prevent us from ministering, it is wise to secure liability coverage for everyone counseling. In some cases, depending on the company and the nature of counseling, a church policy might already include coverage or offer a separate rider. We encourage being sure the policy covers both staff and laypersons who are part of the counseling ministry.

Disclosure of Counseling Files

It is possible that a person or attorney will request various kinds of documents as part of a legal process involving a counselee. When appropriate, it may be wise to comply with those requests willingly. For example, an attorney might want a letter stating the times and dates of the counseling sessions to confirm the counselee fulfilled their commitment. However, a person is not entitled to see all records and private notes simply by asking for them.[12] When a counselor or ministry is concerned about fulfilling a request, we recommend you contact trusted legal counsel for advice. This is especially true if you receive a court subpoena.

Conclusion

Every counseling ministry and counselor should understand the various issues involved in ethical and legal matters. We want to serve the Lord with excellence, love people well, and be wise stewards of the ministries he has given us. It is wise to have an attorney licensed in your state ensure your policies, organizational structure, and practices conform to current legal standards.

---

[12] Those counseling in church settings might not fall under HIPAA rules. See "Some—Not All—Ministries Are Subject to HIPAA Requirements," Brotherhood Mutual, https://www.brotherhoodmutual.com/resources/safety-library/risk-management-articles/administrative-staff-and-finance/some-not-all-ministries-are-subject-to-hipaa-requirements/.

State-licensed therapists and those working for ministries or organizations required to follow the guidelines should familiarize themselves with the distinction within the HIPAA Privacy Rule between psychotherapy (a.k.a. process or private) notes and progress notes. See "The Differences between Psychotherapy Notes and Progress Notes," ICANotes, June 8, 2018, https://www.icanotes.com/2018/06/08/the-differences-between-psychotherapy-notes-and-progress-notes/; "Health Information Privacy," HHS.gov, updated November 2, 2020, https://www.hhs.gov/hipaa/for-individuals/medical-records/index.html; and Dana Taylor, "Special Protections and Frequently Asked Questions for Psychotherapy Notes," January 17, 2019, https://www.magmutual.com/learning/article/special-protections-and-frequently-asked-questions-psychotherapy-notes/. Reading Internet articles, however, should never take the place of consulting legal counsel.

PART FOUR

COMMON INDIVIDUAL PROBLEMS AND PROCEDURES

21

Anger, Resentment, and Bitterness

Perhaps no problem more frequently plagues people than anger. It's a universal tendency, prevalent in every culture, experienced by every generation. It permeates society and affects our most intimate relationships. Anger is a given in this fallen world. People might not call it anger. We might label it as being upset, hurt, frustrated, troubled, or irritated. But as we will see in the definition below, there is a common thread in all those terms.

The good news biblical counselors bring is that the Bible says much about anger and gives us answers for anger problems.[1]

Understanding Anger

A Working Definition

We begin by defining anger as a whole-person response of negative moral judgment against perceived evil. Consider several elements:

[1] For expansion on this and various portions of this chapter, including growth assignments, see Robert D. Jones, *Uprooting Anger: Biblical Help for a Common Problem* (Phillipsburg, NJ: P&R, 2005); Jones, *Anger: Calming Your Heart* (Phillipsburg, NJ: P&R, 2019); Jones, *Pursuing Peace: A Christian Guide to Handling Our Conflicts* (Crossway, 2012), 57–73; see also David Powlison, *Good and Angry: Redeeming Anger, Irritation, Complaining, and Bitterness* (Greensboro, NC: New Growth, 2016); and Edward T. Welch, *A Small Book about a Big Problem: Meditations on Anger, Patience, and Peace* (Greensboro, NC: New Growth, 2017).

- Anger is a response. It's an activity, not a thing, substance, force, or fluid. It's something we do, not an "it" or some substance we have.
- Anger is a whole-person response. It engages our cognitions, affections, volitions, and bodies. While we call anger an "emotion," it involves more than an emotive component. Our beliefs and motives play an active, formative role in this response.
- Anger responds to some provoking stimulus. That provocation might be what someone just said or did or our current memory of what someone previously said or did.
- Anger responds to something we perceive that offended us. We see that past or present event as wrong. Anger is "an active stance you take to oppose something you assess as both important and wrong."[2] It's a moral judgment we make about something we value. Of course, my personal perception that your action was wrong might be accurate or inaccurate, based on my fallible beliefs and values.

Let's add one more vital perspective to our description: like all behavior, we do our anger before God. He sees and weighs it, and when it's sinful it incurs his negative judgment. As Jesus declared, "anyone who is angry with a brother or sister will be subject to judgment" (Matt 5:21–22 NIV; cf. 1 John 3:15).

Four Biblical Categories

Scripture presents four categories of anger: First is God's righteous anger. Our sin deserves God's judgment (Ps 7:11; Isa 34:2; John 3:36; Rom 1:18), but Christ's sin-bearing, substitutionary death bore the wrath believers in Christ deserved. God's righteous anger and our sin met at the cross (Rom 3:21–26; 1 Pet 2:24; 3:18). Second is the righteous anger of Jesus, the God-man, discussed in the next section. Third is the righteous anger of other humans, such as Moses (Exod 32:19–20), Saul (1 Sam 11:1–6), Jonathan

[2] Powlison, *Good and Angry*, 39.

(1 Sam 20:33–34), and the psalmist (Ps 119:52–54, 103–104, 113–116, 127–128, 135–137, 139, 157–159, 162–164).

This chapter focuses on the fourth category, the sinful anger of humans.[3] In terms of sinful anger expression, some people reveal their anger through harsh words or hurtful or destructive actions—something many Bible characters display and that Proverbs (12:18; 14:16–17, 29–30; 15:1, 18; 16:32; 19:11, 19; 22:24–25; 25:28; 29:11, 22), Jesus (Matt 5:21–26), and the apostle Paul (Eph 4:29–32) warn against repeatedly. Others express their anger in colder ways, avoiding or distancing themselves from an offender (Luke 15:25–30). Still others might conceal their anger, acting normally on the outside but inwardly retaining angry thoughts and attitudes (Lev 19:17; 1 Cor 13:5) that might lead to outward actions.

Distinguishing Righteous and Sinful Anger

We sometimes meet counselees who admit their anger but defend their innocence. "Sure I was angry," such a person states, "but I had a right. After all, Jesus got angry. My anger was righteous." So, how do we discern whether human anger is righteous or sinful?

Consider three marks of righteous anger. *First, righteous anger responds to actual sin*, not against someone inconveniencing us or violating personal preferences. *Second, righteous anger focuses on God and his kingdom, rights, and concerns*, not on one's personal kingdom, rights, and concerns. It centers on God, not self. *Third, righteous anger expresses itself in godly, self-controlled ways.* It doesn't scream, rage uncontrollably, or wallow in self-pity. It doesn't ignore, snub, or withdraw from people. Christlike mourning, joy, and obedience attend it. Righteous anger produces godly ministry: it defends the oppressed, seeks justice for victims, rebukes transgressors, and pursues repentance, reconciliation, and restoration.

---

[3] Two subcategories of sinful human anger are anger against God and anger against self (a confused notion involving biblical and unbiblical self-judgments). For biblical perspectives on the first, see Powlison, 219–232, and Jones, *Uprooting Anger*, 113–128. On the latter, see Jones, *Uprooting Anger*, 129–138, and Powlison, 202–18.

Consider the two places where the Gospel writers describe Jesus's anger.[4] In Mark 3:1–6 Jesus met a disabled man on a Sabbath day. The Pharisees opposed the Lord's intention to heal him. In response, Jesus looked at them in anger (v. 5). Note the three marks of righteous anger at work here: (1) Jesus accurately perceived their sins of not loving the man and rejecting his own lordship over the Sabbath. (2) Jesus didn't take personal offense—think of the many ways the Jewish leaders lied to and about him, mocked him, called him a glutton and a drunkard, whipped him, beat him, pressed a crown of thorns on his head, and crucified him, yet he didn't express anger. But here they opposed his ministry mission as God's appointed Messiah (cf. 2:12, 27–28). (3) Jesus maintained Spirit-given self-control. He kept his head, not venting rage. He didn't need to storm off to regain composure. Instead, he did God's will and healed the disabled man.

Similarly, in Mark 10:13–16 Jesus responded angrily to his own disciples who rebuked some parents who sought to have Jesus touch their children. Here we again see the marks of righteous anger: (1) The disciples sinned by rebuking the children. (2) Their action opposed God's kingdom: "Let the little children come to me. Don't stop them, because the kingdom of God belongs to such as these" (v. 14). Seeing such mistreatment against others, our Lord became indignant. (3) Jesus's anger didn't derail his ministry. He took the children in his arms, laid his hands on them, and blessed them. We could likewise analyze the righteous anger of others, like Jonathan or the psalmist noted above.

We can help counselees discern whether their anger is righteous by turning the three marks into three searching questions: (1) Did the other person sin against you, or were you merely inconvenienced? (2) Did that person hinder God's agenda or hinder yours? (3) Did you display Christlike grace, self-control, and ministry, or did you lose control, pull away, or make matters worse?

---

[4] Likely Jesus was angry on other occasions; we are merely observing biblical terms. He certainly exercised righteous judgement against the moneychangers in the temple in John 2:13–17 and against the Pharisees in Matthew 23.

What counsel should we give counselees who claim their anger is righteous but fail the above tests? First, beware self-deception. Based on the number of godly versus ungodly examples of human anger throughout the Bible and the frequency of biblical warnings (along with our experience as counselors), we can conclude that while some human anger is righteous, most is not. The classic case of self-deception is Jonah in Jonah 4, but we also see New Testament warnings in Eph 4:22; Heb 3:12–13; and Jas 3:14–15. (Note that admitting your tendencies to justify your anger gives counselees permission to do the same.) Second, study the Bible passages above, pray, and seek honest feedback and accountability from those closest to you. Third, own your anger as sinful, confess it to God, and seek his forgiveness and help to change. Fourth, ask God to cultivate righteous anger within you, to help you emulate our Lord Jesus who "loved righteousness and hated lawlessness" (Heb 1:9).

The Causes of Sinful Anger

In helping angry people, we need to address not only their behaviors but also the causes behind them. Outward "anger management" approaches fall short. Even if we could control angry expressions with behavioral techniques it would not bring about the whole-person Christlike change God wants.

Common Answers

Why do people express sinful anger? Counselees offer assorted reasons:

- Past mistreatment or bad modeling (e.g., past abuse, dysfunctional families of origin, angry dads, abandonment)
- Present failures by others (e.g., unmet felt needs, disappointed expectations, perceived rights denied)
- Situational pressures (e.g., work demands, parenting challenges, traffic, in-laws)
- Worldly influences (e.g., ungodly friends, social media lies, sinful cultural trends)
- The Devil, (e.g., so-called territorial spirits, demons of anger)

- Physical factors (e.g., disease, injuries, imbalanced hormones, illegal drugs, fatigue, poor nutrition)

How should we view these explanations for anger? These factors can exert enormous impact and be extremely hard to handle. Caring counselors must listen compassionately, "weep with those who weep" (Rom 12:15), reflect God's tender care, assure counselees this is not the way God originally designed the world to be, and acknowledge the hardship they suffer.

As difficult as these factors might be, however, they don't cause anger. As we saw in our six-box model in chapter 10, these box 1 heat factors are important, significant, and influential but not causative, determinative, or ultimate. Loving counselees means not allowing them to excuse their anger or blame other people or events for it. But it also means giving them good news: "While you can't blame your situation, you don't need to! These factors don't make you angry. You are not doomed or destined to anger. Even amid these very real hardships, you can learn to handle things in godly ways. Jesus did so and through his Word, his Spirit, and his church, you can too."

God's Answer

If not from the factors above, where does sinful anger come from? The apostle James answers:

> What causes fights and quarrels among you? Don't they come from your desires that battle within you? You desire but do not have, so you kill. You covet but you cannot get what you want, so you quarrel and fight. You do not have because you do not ask God. When you ask, you do not receive, because you ask with wrong motives, that you may spend what you get on your pleasures. (Jas 4:1–3 NIV)

While the apostle described angry behavior (fights, quarrels, murder), his focus was not behavioral or to simply get readers to "stop it!" Instead, he rooted human anger in our sinful desires. Like other sins, then, anger comes from the heart. James's point is simple yet profound: you cannot get what you want, so you're angry. Indeed, the angry heart declares, "I want what I want when I want it. And when I want it, it had better be there. If you don't give me what I want, I'll be angry at you." As Paul Tripp observes, "James encourages us to examine our desires because it is the only way to understand our anger. Desire lies at the base of every angry feeling, word, and action."[5]

Note that what is likely in view in the James passage is not desires for evil things but for good things. After all, James holds out the possibility that if we asked God properly, he might give them to us (v. 2). Since God would not give evil items, we infer that the problem lies in the demanding of our good desires.[6] In other words, there are two ways desires can be evil. We can desire an evil object (something God forbids) or, as it seems in this passage, a good object too much—that is, with a selfish, inordinate, ruling desire. Counselees often desire acceptance, affirmation, or affection (all good things) but they desire them too much, making them sinful demands. When unmet, those demands inevitably produce angry responses.

How can we help counselees identify and expose their anger-causing demands? Encourage them to consider these self-examination questions:

- Is it consuming your mind? or Do you think about it often, to the point of obsessing over it?
- Do you manipulate, nag, pressure, or guilt-trip others to get your desire met?
- Do you attack or separate from others when you don't get your desire met?

Another helpful technique is asking counselees to complete a key sentence when angry. Consider these suggestions:

---

[5] Tripp, *Instruments*, 79 (see chap. 13, n. 1).

[6] James's terms—desire(s), covet, want, pleasures—were used in the Bible and other ancient Greek literature for good or bad desires, depending on the context. For example, the word "want" (*epithumia*) carries a negative sense in 1:14–15 and Gal 5:16–17; but a positive sense in Luke 22:15 and 1 Tim 3:1. Desires are wrong when they become entrenched ("battle within you") and lead to fights and quarrels.

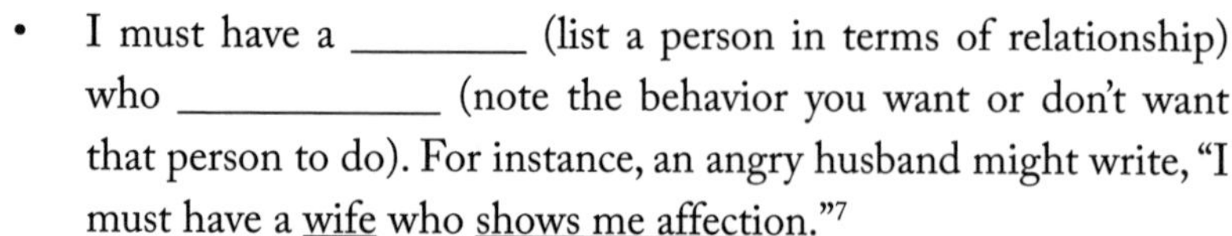

- I must have a ________ (list a person in terms of relationship) who ____________ (note the behavior you want or don't want that person to do). For instance, an angry husband might write, "I must have a <u>wife</u> who <u>shows me affection.</u>"[7]
- What I think I need[8] from you or desperately want from you is ______________.

- You must give me __________ or I'll be angry at you.

A helpful visual tool that illustrates how legitimate desires become ruling demands is "The Throne-Staircase Heart Diagram":[9]

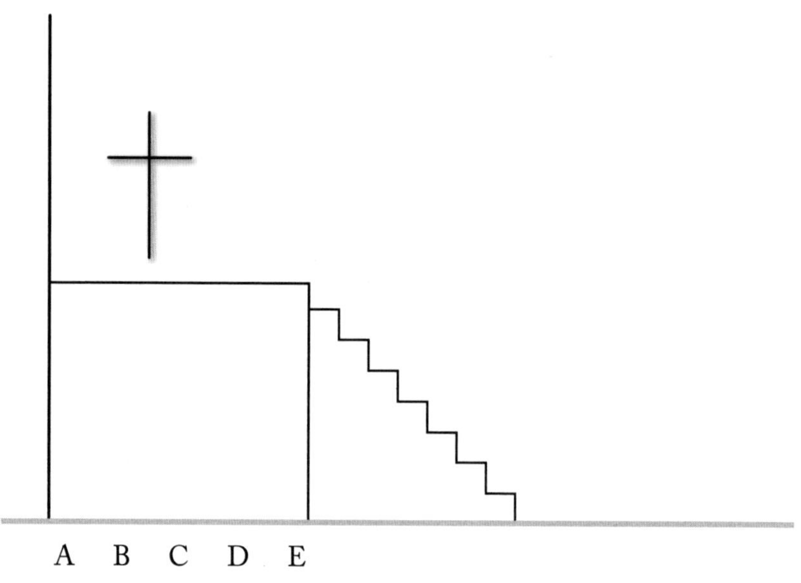

The letters beneath the throne represent legitimate but unmet desires properly submitted under the lordship of the enthroned Christ. This is a picture of a healthy heart at rest in Christ. We see it in Jesus himself in

---

[7] Note that this same model can be applied to those who are worried and anxious or depressed and despairing.

[8] For a biblical view of "needs," see 2 Pet 1:3 and Luke 10:38–42 (cf. Pss 27:10; 73:23–28; Matt 4:4; Phil 4:11–13; Hab 3:17–19). What our psychologized society calls "needs" is more accurately called "felt needs" or "desires."

[9] For a fuller treatment of this diagram, see Jones, *Pursuing Peace,* 57–73 (see chap. 7, n. 2).

the garden of Gethsemane (Matt 26:39–42) as he submitted to his Father his legitimate desire not to drink the cup of God's wrath on the nations. We see the same kind of heart in Paul (Phil 4:11–13), David (Ps 27:10), Habakkuk (Hab 3:17–19), and others.

Problems arise, however, when desires don't remain submitted but become steroidal. They sprout legs, ascend the staircase, and compete with Christ for the functional lordship of a soul. No longer mere desires, these newly elevated demands produce anger, worry, depression, and all sorts of disordered behaviors. Godly change requires dethroning those demands and resubmitting them under Christ's sovereign, wise, and loving lordship.

Helping Counselees Change Sinful Anger

Assuming you have caringly entered a counselee's world and compassionately understood both their felt needs and real ones, including ways they have been sinned against, consider leading them through a four-step process of recognizing, repenting, refocusing, and replacing.

1) Help Them Recognize the Source of Their Anger

As we've noted, anger is not caused by past or present hardships but by demanding hearts. So, ask counselees to journal anger incidents by identifying (a) the situation (who, what, where, when), (b) their behavior (what they said, did, felt), (c) their beliefs and motives (what they thought or wanted, especially desires that became demands), and (d) how God wanted them to respond differently.

2) Help Them Repent on Both the Heart and Behavioral Levels

The larger contextual unit of Jas 3:13–4:12 gives multiple pictures of humble heart repentance over the following sins:

- envy and selfish ambition (3:14–16),[10]

[10] Note the earthly and demonic undertones and their fruits of disorder and evil practice.

- ruling desires, including those expressed in self-centered prayer (4:1–3),
- spiritual adultery, friendship with the world (4:4),
- participating with the devil in what he wants to accomplish (4:7), and
- playing God (4:11–12) by judging others; this is the most heinous root of sinful anger.

Heart repentance should in turn produce behavioral repentance over the many ways we reveal or conceal our sinful anger. (Recall our discussion on repentance in chapters 7 and 10.) We must guide our counselees to own, confess to God, and turn from their anger.

3) Help Them Refocus on God and His Grace, Provisions, and Promises in Christ

For those who repent, God offers these promises: "He gives greater grace. . . . God resists the proud but gives grace to the humble. . . . Draw near to God, and he will draw near to you. . . . Humble yourselves before the Lord, and he will exalt you" (Jas 4:6, 8, 10).

As we saw in chapter 10, the Lord provides both pardoning grace and enabling grace (Heb 4:16; 2 Pet 1:3–4) to those who repent. The Christian man who demands (box 3) his wife and children serve him and yells at them (box 2) when they don't meet his demands needs Christ and the truths of his Word and the help of fellow believers (box 4). As the Spirit uses God's Word in the context of the church (including you as a biblical counselor), this man can repent of his demanding, God-playing heart and begin to see himself as a forgiven, Spirit-empowered son of God (box 5). From his renewed sense of identity, he is ready to be helped to get rid of his angry words, to learn to speak words that build up his family and demonstrate Christlike kindness, compassion, and forgiveness toward them (box 6, Eph 4:29–32).

4) Help Them Replace Sinful Anger with Christlike Attitudes and Actions

Recall the put-off/put-on dynamic we saw in chapter 15 (Eph 4:17–32; Col 3:1–17). What kind of Christlike attitudes and actions should replace sinful anger?

- Prayer, learning to ask God humbly, with a submissive heart, for good things we legitimately desire, without any demanding (Phil 4:6–7; Jas 4:3).
- Contentment, even if desired blessings don't come and people don't give us what we want (Phil 4:10–13).
- Patience, forbearance, and forgiveness toward those who provoke us (Prov 19:11; Matt 18:21–35; Eph 4:1–2, 31–32; Col 3:12–14).
- Self-control when tempted to respond angrily (Gal 5:22–23; Prov 16:32; 25:28; 29:11).
- Godly listening and godly speaking, learning to communicate in Christlike ways with those who tend to provoke us (Exod 2:23–25; Prov 12:18; 15:1; 18:13; Eph 4:29).
- Biblical peacemaking and conflict resolution, learning to handle our conflicts in nonangry ways (Matt 5:9; Rom 12:18; Eph 4:3)
- Christlike ministry toward those who sometimes deserve the opposite (Mark 10:45; John 13:1–5; Phil 2:1–4)

Resentment and Bitterness—Settled Anger

Let's consider two other aspects of anger, namely, resentment and bitterness. We will use these terms as essential synonyms, with the latter being a more severe form of the former. We typically think of anger as a response to a provoking incident, something someone says or does. But it's possible for someone to sin so repeatedly or severely against a counselee that their anger is no longer related to an incident or two; rather, it is directed at the offender. The initial anger has settled down into bitterness—an opposition to that person. If anger responds to an event, bitterness responds to a person. And once a person reaches a point of bitterness, the offending person can do nothing right in their eyes. They even view with suspicion or cynicism any attempt to apologize, change, or make things right.

God calls us to get rid of bitterness and to forgive others: "Let all bitterness, anger and wrath, shouting and slander be removed from you, along with all malice. And be kind and compassionate to one another, forgiving one another, just as God also forgave you in Christ" (Eph 4:31–32). Ultimately, only the gospel can teach and move us to do so. Consider six gospel-driven truths God's Spirit can use to help your counselee fight against bitterness:[11]

1) The enormity of God's love was displayed in the cross. Bitter believers forget the massive size of the sin debt God forgave them (Matt 18:21–35; Eph 4:32; Col 3:13).

2) We all desperately need God's forgiveness. Bitter people essentially declare they don't (Mark 11:25; Matt 6:12–15; 18:21–35).

3) Our ultimate need is God's mercy. Bitter people essentially declare they don't need God's mercy on the day of judgment (Matt 5:7; Jas 2:13; Luke 6:36; Mic 6:8).

4) We must understand God's role is not ours. Bitter people assume God's role as judge and executioner (Jas 4:12; Rom 12:19; Gen 50:19).

5) There is a dual nature to an offender's sin. Bitter people forget that an offender, as a sinner, is in one sense deceived and enslaved by sin (Luke 23:34; John 8:34; 1 Cor 2:7–8; Col 3:12–13).

6) We are fallible. Bitter people forget that they are capable of the same behavioral sins that hurt them; in fact, the same heart sins might already reside in them (Jer 17:9; 1 Cor 10:12; Prov 16:18; Heb 3:12–13).

[11] Jones, *Pursuing Peace,* 137–50. For a minibook version applying these points, including a built-in assignment, see his *Freedom from Resentment: Stopping Hurts from Turning Bitter* (Greensboro, NC: New Growth, 2010).

Conclusion: Why Deal with Anger?

Why must we help counselees put off their sinful anger and put on Christlike replacements? First, their anger ruins their health—both physically[12] and spiritually.[13] Second, their anger damages their relationships.[14] Their children, for instance, breathe the secondhand smoke of their anger. Third, and most importantly, their anger dishonors, offends, and grieves God.[15] Ephesians 4:30–31 connects grieving God's Spirit to a half dozen forms of anger. James 1:19–20 tells us human anger doesn't produce godliness. When helping counselees deal with their anger, remember there is no higher motive than honoring God.

---

[12] See Psalms 32; 38; Proverbs 3; 14:30. See also chapter 5 on the heart-body interaction.

[13] See Acts 24:16; Ps 66:18; 1 Tim 2:8; and Matt 5:21–22.

[14] See Eph 4:1–6; 4:25–5:2; Col 3:15–17; Jas 3:13–4:12; Luke 15:28; Matt 7:3–5; Prov 22:24–25; Eph 6:4; Prov 16:17; and Rom 12:18.

[15] See Matt 5:21–22; 1 John 3:15; Eph 4:26–27, 30–31; Col 3:5–10; 1 Tim 2:8; Jas 1:19–21; 4:11–12; and Heb 13:20–21.

22

Worry, Anxiety, and Fear

We live in a challenging world, one full of threats and uncertainties that tempt us to be fearful, worried, and anxious. A woman reflects on the possibility of being a young widow after her husband is diagnosed with stage 4 cancer. A student speaks of paralyzing fear before tests. A father does not know how he will provide for his family if he is part of the company's next layoff. A weary wife explains her husband's ongoing controlling, oppressive actions over the last twenty years. These situations and many more provide fertile ground for worry, anxiety, and fear.

In response to these issues, some counselees spend significant time weeping. Others sit and think about possible outcomes. Still others become emotionally and relationally distant. In this chapter, we will explain how to use the biblical foundations and procedures we outlined earlier to minister to such hurting people.[1]

[1] An excellent annotated source is Bob Kellemen, "23 Biblical Counseling Resources on Anxiety, Fear, Panic Attacks, and Worry," Biblical Counseling Coalition, March 18, 2020, https://www.biblicalcounselingcoalition.org/2020/03/18/23-biblical-counseling-resources-on-anxiety-fear-panic-attacks-and-worry/.

Definitions

Since the concepts of worry, fear, and anxiety are similar, some counselees and dictionaries use them interchangeably. All three words describe an emotional condition based on the belief that an unpleasant situation is occurring or will occur in the immediate future. One counselee might say, "I am afraid I will lose my job," while another might express the same thoughts with the words, "I am worried (or anxious) about the status of my job." Yet another counselee might say, "I am concerned about my job." In every case, the goal is to help your counselees think biblically about whatever terms they use.

But to complicate matters more, the Bible uses some terms with a wide range of meaning. For example, fear is used more than one way in the Bible. "The fear of the LORD is the beginning of knowledge" (Prov 1:7), yet we are told "do not fear" hundreds of times in the Bible. The New Testament Greek words *merimna* and *merimnaō*, typically translated "worry" or "anxiety/anxious" (depending on the English Bible translation), can also indicate positive, godly care or concern.[2] Paul commends Timothy for expressing *merimna* (godly concern) in Phil 2:20, yet commands readers not to have *merimna* (worry) in 4:6–7.

In view of these observations, counselors must carefully evaluate their counselees to help them respond biblically.[3] After all, a counselee's admission of "fear," "worry," or "anxiety" might not express a sinful thought, action, or condition. They may describe understandable responses to their circumstances and conditions that the Lord simply wants counselees to deal with his way. In that case, we should encourage them to think biblically, continually use the challenges and future uncertainty to grow in their dependence on the Lord, and to pursue community for encouragement and support.

---

[2] The Greek terms appear twenty-five times in the New Testament. Some interpreters believe the words "worry" or "anxiety" describe negative heart conditions that are to some degree sinful and need to be changed and words like "care" or "concern" describe positive conditions God commends or commands. Others are less certain this line is so clear, believing some passages are broad enough to encompass both conditions.

[3] To use the paradigm from chapters 13–15, fear, worry, and anxiety often describe box 2 material. It is the counselor's job to understand what this represents at the box 3 heart level.

In this chapter we will address the sinful aspects of fear, worry, and anxiety, and how to help counselees handle them. For just as it is possible to wrongly lump all aspects of fear, worry, and anxiety into the category of sin, it is also possible to minimize the significance of the sinfulness of fear, worry, and anxiety.[4]

Therefore, consider the following indications that a counselee is expressing sinful fear, worry, and anxiety: (1) They function as if the possible future event has already occurred; they are not living according to what is true. (2) They fail to pray, rely upon God's grace, or believe God is working in the midst of their struggle; they exercise unbelief in the Lord's promises. (3) They refuse to accept that the Lord may allow suffering and hardship for his own divine reasons; they demand the Lord's will conform to theirs. (4) They neglect the responsibilities God has already given them—whether in terms of their personal time with the Lord, their involvement in community, or their willingness to serve their spouse or help raise the children. In this case, they fail to steward what the Lord called them to do. They focus on the possible bad outcomes and neglect what is true for today. Wise ministers will remember that counselees are rarely either entirely sinful or entirely godly as they express their worries. We should encourage a godly fear of the Lord, support their biblical concerns, and help them address sinful expressions of worry.

To avoid saying, "worry, anxiety, and fear" repeatedly, we henceforth will use the term *worry* except when other terms are more appropriate to the context.

Biblical Theological Categories

Suffering and a Rightful Place for Fear and Concern

Some counselees tell heartbreaking stories. They describe childhoods full of hardship, lost relationships, broken dreams, and dangerous situations. Wise

---

[4] See Jerry Bridges, *Respectable Sins* (Colorado Springs: NavPress, 2007), who argues that every culture and society has sins they deem acceptable and unacceptable based on man-centered definitions.

biblical counselors seek to understand their stories. A person's worry has developed over real concerns and real consequences from past events. We understand why those abused as either children or adults could continue to fear the reappearance of former abusers or people like them. We respect the wishes of a wife in an abusive relationship who needs us to move at her pace, knowing she faces real and present dangers. Caring counselors also prioritize safety for those in danger. Even mighty David hid from Saul and from David's own son Absalom.

We take parents seriously when they speak about their teenage children walking in the path of rebellion and destruction. We know their love for the children and their concern for their salvation are right where they should be. The apostle Paul, after all, speaks with great love and compassion for his people and of his concern that they have rejected Christ (Rom 9:1–5).

Sometimes counselees correctly describe their circumstances in the language of fear, worry, and anxiety. As fellow sufferers in this world, we can show them the Bible has a significant place for grief, sorrow, and intercessory prayer (e.g., Psalm 13). The Bible encourages us to be concerned about the very things that concern God and to eagerly desire the Lord's work in each counselee's life. Part of our counsel involves affirming their concerns, joining them in prayer, and encouraging them to suffer in godly ways while waiting for the glory yet to be revealed (Rom 8:18).

Emphasize the Character and Promises of God

Those who worry need to spend significant time thinking about God since they often expend much mental energy on the threats and uncertainties they face. They can break the cycle by thinking about things that are true, excellent, and worthy of praise (Phil 4:8–9), that they have a God who is for them (Rom 8:31), who loves them (1 John 4:11), and who cares deeply for them (1 Pet 5:7). This puts their worries in the proper context. Offering them these four truths can help:

1. God is gracious and compassionate. Exodus 34:6–7 provides one of the clearest statements about the character of God found in the Bible: "The LORD passed in front of [Moses] and proclaimed: The LORD—the LORD is a compassionate and gracious God, slow to anger and abounding in faithful love and truth, maintaining faithful love to a thousand generations, forgiving iniquity, rebellion, and sin." These words come in the context of Moses interceding for the people of Israel regarding the golden calf incident.

While the characteristics of God the passage mentions may seem difficult to believe in times of suffering or danger, a counselee can be powerfully helped in facing their circumstances by hanging on to these truths. Christ followers have a God predisposed toward grace, compassion, covenantal love, and truth! Those who worry need to grasp these qualities. One potential growth assignment for a counselee struggling with worry, then, is journaling evidences of God's grace or compassion. While their circumstances might not change and their concerns might continue, meditating on such truths and looking for ways God is working in the midst of trials encourages a counselee to trust the Lord, to use their circumstances for growth, and to conform their will to his.

2. God is faithful, and he provides strength to endure. First Corinthians 10:13, a popular biblical counseling passage, contains precious promises from our Lord. The text becomes even more significant when read in its larger context. The Lord encourages his church to learn from the failures of the nation of Israel (vv. 6, 11): they committed idolatry (v. 7), immorality (v. 8), put the Lord to the test (v. 9), and grumbled against him (v. 10). The Old Testament context for these sinful choices reveals that issues of worry, fear, and/or anxiety were involved. The quotation in v. 7 comes from Exodus 32:6, where the people were wondering whether Moses would ever return. They decided they needed a new leader.[5] Worshiping security, they pursued false gods they thought would give it to them. They grumbled against the Lord for not providing in advance. When gripped by certain desires, people will worry whether they can achieve them, be anxious about losing them, and fear what life will be like without them.

---

[5] For a wonderful exposition of Exodus 32–34, see R. W. L. Moberly, *At the Mountain of God: Story and Theology in Exodus 32–34* (Sheffield, UK: JSOT Press, 1983).

What is the overall truth of 1 Cor 10:13? God is faithful. When all else seems lost, he remains committed to his character and promises. Counselees can rely on the fact that God will not give them more than they can handle with his help, even if it seems like they cannot take one more minute.[6] To those who are suffering, such words may sound trite or dismissive of their pain. Therefore, counselors should engage counselees in discussions to address questions as they communicate them and to encourage them to freshly consider the Word of the Lord.[7]

Endurance, by the grace of God, requires going through difficulty, but it yields good results. It proves the genuineness of faith (1 Pet 1:6–7), produces godly character (Rom 5:3–5), encourages unity (Rom 15:5), and sets a positive example for others (2 Thess 1:4). Assigning counselees to explain ways God has given them endurance for past difficulties can benefit them and give them hope.

3. God wants to hear our concerns and provide his peace. Not everyone who experiences similar difficulties responds to them in the same way. While it may seem that difficulties don't bother some, their sense of peace in trial often occurs because they have learned biblical ways to handle struggles. First Peter 5:7 says, "Cast all your anxiety on [God] because he cares for you" (NIV), and Phil 4:6–7 remind us, "Don't worry about anything, but in everything, through prayer and petition with thanksgiving, present your requests to God. And the peace of God, which surpasses all understanding, will guard your hearts and minds in Christ Jesus." Peter wrote to a group of people who are suffering, and Paul wrote from prison. Yet, instead of worrying or living in sinful fear, they just reminded their audiences God wanted to hear from them. And God was not simply interested in

---

[6] Note the words "with his help." In 2 Cor 1:7–9 (NIV), the apostle Paul mentions having faced overwhelming challenges "far beyond [his] ability to endure." It is untrue, then, that God will not give a believer more than they can handle. Sometimes he allows us to face more than we can bear so "that we might not rely on ourselves but on God, who raises the dead."

[7] My (Rob's) colaborers, Randy Patten and Bob Kellemen, often speak about this concept. Patten calls this ministering the Word, not dispensing it. Kellemen calls this a trialogue between the counselor, counselee, and the Lord (through his Word).

listening; he wanted to provide peace, the peace that surpasses understanding. Counselees can remain confident during storms because God provides the kind of peace that guards hearts and minds.

One practical exercise is to discuss Phil 4:4–9 and help a counselee think about how that passage specifically and practically impacts their greatest fear, worry, or anxiety. After discussing it, you can assign a homework project in which they do the exercise on their own. Have them write out (1) their anxious thought(s), (2) what each thought reveals about their heart, (3) a couple of Bible passages or truths that speak to it, (4) the true or correct thought/motivation/desire, and (5) a resulting action if acting in obedience to God's Word.[8]

4. God knows about our needs and desires to meet them. The Sermon on the Mount emphasizes righteousness. On the one hand, it is impossible to fulfill the requirements of the sermon (cf. Matt 5:48). Reading it, in fact, brings us to our knees in dependence. On the other hand, it is impossible to miss the practical steps it offers for dealing with various problems. In Matt 6:25–34 Jesus commands his audience not to worry. The basis for that command is that God already knows about and cares for our physical needs, valuing us even more than the flowers and birds he provides for. As D. A. Carson explains, "Jesus' disciples must live lives qualitatively different from those of people who have no trust in God's fatherly care and no fundamental goals beyond material things."[9]

As you work with a counselee, remember this has not always been their experience. Asking careful questions and using counseling skills are vital. Counselees often define needs differently than Scripture does. Even so, God still cares for them and still provides for them, sometimes in surprising ways.

---

[8] Many thanks to my (Rob's) coauthor Kristin for this excellent example of ministering the Word to encourage counselees to rest in the peace of God when tempted to worry.

[9] D. A. Carson, "Matthew," in *The Expositor's Bible Commentary*, vol. 8, ed. Frank E. Gaebelein (Grand Rapids: Zondervan, 1984), 181.

Teach Trust in God's Sovereignty

The reason for difficult circumstances that lead us to various worries, anxieties, and fears is not always available. The Lord, for his own purposes, does not choose to answer every question we might have regarding the difficult things that come into our lives.[10] That is why our counselees must learn to trust in the sovereignty of God. It is theologically wrong and of no practical value to think God is missing from our circumstances. After all, the earth is the Lord's and everything that is in it (Ps 24:1). The Lord owns everything, and all was designed for his glory (Colossians 1). God tells us believers that everything works for our good (Rom 8:28–29). Counselees might struggle to hear that, though, and we can understand; after all, even we (the writers) have lost unborn children, carried the caskets of toddlers, wondered where a next meal is coming from, lost jobs, and experienced other hardships that seemingly came out of nowhere.

Some counselees question God's sovereignty, but it's a truth they need to process. Other counselees don't like God's sovereign choices, but every Christ follower must learn to be like Job who asked, "Should we accept only good from God and not adversity?" (Job 2:10). One counseling exercise that can help involves asking the counselee to read about certain events in godly David's life (like the Goliath incident in 1 Samuel 15–17, the massacre at Nob in 1 Samuel 22, or the conflict with both Nabal and Saul in 1 Samuel 24–26). Then they can evaluate them using these questions: (1) What circumstances did David accept? (2) How did he choose to respond? (3) What circumstances are you struggling to accept? (4) How would accepting those circumstances change your responses?

---

[10] Not only are some questions unanswered, but it's possible to overinterpret suffering. See Ed Welch, "What Is God Up To?: The Temptation to Overinterpret Suffering," May 21, 2020, https://www.ccef.org/what-is-god-up-to-the-temptation-to-overinterpret-suffering/?mc_cid=ba137737b7&mc_eid=6a7de6cd01.

Encourage Repenting of Wrong Standards

Earlier in this chapter we highlighted the distinction between sinful worry and concern, between sinful fear and godly fear. While the vast majority of our counseling plan focused on the character of God, his ongoing work in the lives of our counselees, and encouraging trust, we also have to deal with the sinful realities that exist.

Counselees have hearts that love, desire, and crave. It is easy to worry or fear when items we value are threatened or to be anxious when we fear never having them again. Many parents, for instance, worry about their children. They see a path before them that looks rough, dangerous, and full of heartache. They want children who love Jesus, obey, and do the right thing. Many families want financial security, and they worry when they do not see a path to that location. Everyone wants something. So, as we work with counselees, we need to think with them about the things they value most or fear losing. Worry, anxiety, and fear are clues to determine when a good desire has become a ruling one (Jas 4:1–2).

Identifying ruling desires leads to repentance, and repentance leads to change.

Emphasize Courage and Action

Those who struggle with sinful worry often become unproductive. They focus on their fears and their troubles, and they fail to accomplish the things the Lord has given them to do. A counselee might have a son who creates havoc and becomes the focus of attention. Church attendance changes for the entire family because the parents are embarrassed that someone might know what he's doing. They neglect their other children to give mental energy to the son creating problems. When counselees understand the character of God and his promises and their own ruling desires, they repent of their sinful worry and fear; then they can live courageously, accomplishing the will of the Lord.

The story of Saul and David (1 Samuel 8–31) includes the themes of self-preservation and undaunted courage. In it, Saul is afraid to lose his power. He makes life and the kingdom about him. The more he does so, the more he fears losing what he has. On the other hand, David repeatedly spares Saul—even to his own peril—because he refuses to touch the Lord's anointed. David is absolutely convinced that the Lord has a plan for him and that his job is to do exactly what the Lord has given him to accomplish. Our counselees must follow David's example: they must reinvest the time they spend on worry into doing the will of the Lord (Matt 6:34).

Evaluate with your counselees the things they have neglected or not done with courage. Help them list the responsibilities God has given them. Work with them to courageously accomplish those works by the grace of God. This will change their prayers. It will change their daily schedules. It will change the time given to specific events and tasks.

Conclusion: Extreme Forms of Worry, Anxiety, and Fear

We close this chapter with some brief perspectives on extreme forms of worry, anxiety, and fear: obsessive-compulsive disorder (OCD),[11] perfectionism,[12] and panic attacks.[13] Each represents a more developed version of the struggles discussed. Those who deal with one of these extreme forms face not just fear, but fear that has been practiced over years. None of these extreme forms are simply a fear of danger; they largely reside in the mind of a fearful person, and others see these fears as irrational. The more such counselees have dwelt\led on and responded to their extreme thoughts, the more habits they have built around them. Perfectionism, for example, is not only an enemy to accomplishment; it is inner pride

[11] See Michael Emlet, *OCD: Freedom for the Obsessive Compulsive* (Phillipsburg, NJ: P&R, 2004), and Jeffrey M. Schwartz, *Brain Lock: Free Yourself from Obsessive-Compulsive Behavior* (New York: HarperCollins, 1997).

[12] See Amy Baker, *Picture Perfect: When Life Doesn't Line Up* (Greensboro, NC: New Growth Press), 2014.

[13] See Andrew H. Selle, "The Bridge over Troubled Waters: Overcoming Crippling Fear by Faith and Love," *Journal of Biblical Counseling* 21:1 (2002): 34–40; Chuck Sigler, "Panic Attacks: Listen to the Messenger," *Journal of Biblical Counseling* 24:2 (Spring 2006): 14–20; and Jocelyn Wallace, *Anxiety and Panic Attacks: Trusting God When You're Afraid* (Greensboro, NC: New Growth Press, 2013).

accompanied by the worry and fear of disappointing someone else. Such versions of worry, anxiety, or fear are deeply entrenched.

Sadly, these problems often bring significant physical realities. Panic attacks, for example, mimic the signs of a real heart attack. They are scary events. Those who experience them for the first time are often shocked by their severity. Those struggling with OCD have an exceedingly difficult time giving up whatever thought captures and dominates them.

Since these issues are well practiced, have real physical symptoms, and tend to drive their victims a little differently than other issues, counselors need to be aware that these cases will require more time and patience from them than do other cases.

23

Fear of People, Social Anxiety, and Human Rejection

This chapter addresses twin counseling problems. First, we discuss the fear of people,[1] popularly called "social anxiety." This is *anticipated* rejection, the fear that people will disapprove of us, reject us, or not accept us somehow. Second, we discuss human rejection, the fact that people have disapproved of us, rejected us, or not accepted us. This is *experienced* rejection.

These two can feed each other. If we fear disapproval or rejection and then experience it, we will fear further instances. While we address these topics separately below, we include them together because Scripture provides similar, overlapping explanations and solutions for each. Counselors helping people who present with just one will benefit from reading this entire chapter.

[1] While many English Bibles use the phrase "fear of man," we will use the generic wording, "fear of people," lest anyone limit the concept to fearing males. Related popular labels include "people-pleasing," "being an approval junkie," "codependency," "social phobia," and sometimes "shyness."

Biblical Perspectives on the Fear of People

We might define the fear of people as an inordinate, enslaving desire to gain the approval or avoid the disapproval of some person or persons, more than God or instead of God, along with the positive or negative consequences that follow that approval or disapproval. How do we think biblically about the fear of people? Consider five truths.[2]

1. The most vital difference between the secular and biblical perspectives on the fear of people is God.[3] From the Bible's perspective, people don't merely fear people. They fear people *more than they fear God* or fear people *instead of God*. These passages show the repeated contrast between fearing God versus fearing people:

- Proverbs 29:25, "The fear of mankind is a snare, but the one who trusts in the LORD is protected." (Note the parallel words "fear" and "trust," and the contrasting results.)
- Psalm 56:11, "In God I trust; I will not be afraid. What can mere humans do to me?"
- Psalm 62:8–9, "Trust in him at all times, you people; pour out your hearts before him. God is our refuge. . . . Common people are only a vapor; important people, an illusion. Together on a scale, they weigh less than a vapor." (God is a secure refuge to whom we can run; people, being vaporous, are unsuitable refuges.)
- Matthew 10:28, "Don't fear those who kill the body but are not able to kill the soul; rather, fear him who is able to destroy both soul and body in hell."
- Hebrews 13:6, "The Lord is my helper; I will not be afraid. What can man do to me?"

---

[2] The best starter book on the subject is Edward T. Welch, *When People Are Big and God Is Small: Overcoming Peer Pressure, Codependency and the Fear of Man* (Phillipsburg, NJ: P&R, 1997). His shorter version also includes interactive components, *What Do You Think of Me? Why Do I Care? Answers to the Big Questions of Life* (Greensboro, NC: New Growth Press, 2011). See also Lou Priolo, *Pleasing People: How Not to Be an "Approval Junkie"* (Phillipsburg, NJ: P&R, 2007); and Zach Schlegel, *Fearing Others: Putting God First* (Phillipsburg, NJ: P&R, 2019).

[3] See *DSM-5*, 202–3 (see chap. 9, n. 7).

Unlike the horizontal-only label "social anxiety," a deeper scriptural diagnosis views it as a "fear-of-people-more-than-God," capturing both its horizontal and vertical dimensions. Biblical counselors should continually assess a counselee's functional relationship with God.

2. People fear the specific individuals or groups whose approval they crave or disapproval they avoid. Apart from extreme cases, we rarely fear every person all the time. We don't fear people who unconditionally approve of us, only those who don't and whose approval we especially treasure. The workaholic husband typically fears his boss's disapproval not only more than God's disapproval but also more than his wife's. Counselors should probe this selectivity—why counselees fear one person or group and not others.

3. The counselee's desire is inordinate, beyond the legitimate desire to be approved or not disapproved. Desires become *ruling* desires—demands and needs others must meet. Since a fine line runs through every heart, you will often see expressions of the fear of people in many counseling cases, even when it's not the presenting problem. Counselors should affirm the legitimacy of the desire for approval while exposing the sinfulness of craving or demanding it.

4. This inordinate desire enslaves people. It brings bondage, misery, and sadness. Preoccupation with what people think or say about us cripples us and drains vitality. It paralyzes decision-making and produces unwise choices. Moreover, it keeps relationships shallow. It tempts us to flatter rather than use honesty; we tend to say what we think others want to hear. Instead of wisely confronting others when needed, we tolerate unrighteousness as it urges. In fact, when something other than Jesus rules my heart, everyone in my world becomes either an ally helping me gain my goal or an adversary blocking me. If I live for your approval, then you're my ally when you like me (until you inevitably fail me) and my adversary when you don't. And when you become my adversary, I am quick to write you out of my life.

5. This chapter's definition of the fear of people encompasses various forms that the problem might take. For example,

- avoiding your disapproval might matter more to me than gaining your approval: "I don't care if you don't like me; just don't hate me."

- gaining your approval might matter more to me than avoiding your disapproval: "It's not enough that you don't hate me; I need you to like me."
- the positive consequences of your approval might matter more to me than your actual personal approval: "I don't care if you like me or not, just give me the good thing I want from you (e.g., a party invitation or a job recommendation)."
- the negative consequences of your disapproval might matter more to me than your actual personal disapproval: "I don't care if you like me or not, just don't give me some bad thing I don't want from you (e.g., spreading gossip about me or job demotion)."

Subtle forms of the fear of people include adopting or rejecting the values and practices of others (e.g., caving to peer pressure, fitting in with the crowd) or wanting to be only with those who like us.

One insightful self-diagnosis of fearing people came from a successful young woman:

> Visible signs of my fear of man are when I will exaggerate or minimize details in a story, or tell "white" lies to my friends, to make myself look better; when a friend confronts me about a sin, I get very defensive and I am not willing to be vulnerable with them and admit my sins and weaknesses; when I am with a group of friends, I will one-up my friend's stories so the attention will be on me and my story; and I will talk about my accomplishments a lot because I want people to be impressed with me.

Biblical Examples of Fearing People

Scripture provides many examples of people who succumbed and people who succeeded when facing the fear of people.

Category 1: People Who Sinfully Feared People More Than God

In Exodus 32, in response to Moses's delay in coming down from meeting with God on the mountain, the people became impatient and pressured

Moses's assistant Aaron to create a golden calf for them to worship. Sadly, Aaron caved to the peer pressure and committed idolatry. When Moses heard about it, he confronted Aaron—who offered a lame, false explanation (vv. 22–24).

In John 12:42–43, John describes a group of Jews, including even some rulers, who "believed" in Jesus in some sense, although it's unclear if their belief was authentic since John notes instances of false faith in other passages (e.g., 2:23–25; 6:66; 8:30–37). Regardless, we learn in John 12:42–43 that "because of the Pharisees they did not confess him, so that they would not be banned from the synagogue. For they loved human praise more than praise from God." This incident nicely illustrates our definition above. They didn't openly confess Jesus because they wanted to both gain the positive benefit of human praise and avoid the negative consequence of synagogue excommunication.

Category 2: People Who Rightly Feared God More Than People

While Hebrews furnishes several examples of men and women who feared God more than people, the example of Moses shines brightest. He

> chose to suffer with the people of God rather than to enjoy the fleeting pleasure of sin. For he considered reproach for the sake of Christ to be greater wealth than the treasures of Egypt, since he was looking ahead to the reward. By faith he left Egypt behind, not being afraid of the king's anger, for Moses persevered as one who sees him who is invisible. (Heb 11:25–27)

The contrasts Moses faced are striking: (1) suffering with God's people versus enjoying sin's pleasure; (2) treasuring reproach for Christ's sake and the reward Christ will bring versus enjoying Egypt's material treasures (cf. Matt 6:19–21); and (3) choosing which of two kings to serve—Christ the Messiah or Pharaoh. Thankfully, Moses prioritized the unseen Christ and his future rewards more than visible, present treasures.

In 1 Cor 4:3–5 the apostle Paul discusses his identity as God's ambassador in the face of criticism. "It is of little importance to me," declares Paul, "that I should be judged by you or by any human court." It's not that we shouldn't care at all what people think or say about us; we bear the name of Christ. But we must not let others' judgments—or even our self-judgments—to define or control us. Instead, we should entrust ourselves to the Lord our Judge. For the believer who follows Paul's path that verdict is certain: we will receive God's praise. Both Moses and Paul endured the hardship of foregoing human acceptance in favor of God's.

Category 3: A Mixed Case with a God-Fearing Outcome

The apostle Peter's life provides a fascinating case of someone who alternated between fearing people and fearing God.

We meet Peter in the Gospels as a fearless but immature man. He boldly voiced his opinions, even to the point of opposing the prospect of Jesus being arrested and crucified (Matt 16:22–23) and overconfidently asserting his unflagging loyalty to Jesus (Matt 26:31–33).

But when Jesus went on trial, Peter denied him three times, fearfully cowering before the possibility of also being put to death.

Yet after Jesus's resurrection, he restored Peter to ministry and commissioned him afresh (John 21). A different Peter emerged. Filled with the Holy Spirit, he preached boldly (Acts 2), fearlessly condemning those who killed Jesus and courageously proclaiming him despite the threat of prison (Acts 3–4).

Sadly, though one might hope Peter's fear of people had been conquered given such a success, Gal 2:11–13 records a setback. He "withdrew and separated himself" from fellowship with the Gentiles "because he feared those from the circumcision party." Peter's fear of people drove him to compromise the gospel of God's grace toward both Jews and Gentiles.

Yet finally, a mature and fearless man emerged. Peter's ups and downs end on an up note in 1 Pet 3:14–15, where it is clear he had learned his lesson: "But even if you should suffer for what is right, you are blessed. 'Do not fear their threats; do not be frightened.' But in your hearts revere Christ as Lord" (NIV). Peter, then, came to realize that fearing Christ means not fearing people. Indeed, history tells us Peter was persecuted for his faith and executed by crucifixion.

Peter's story can comfort a counselee in their ongoing fight against fearing people. It reminds them that this sin is not uncommon—it even plagues an apostle. It shows that Christian growth is progressive. Amid their ups and downs of often succeeding but sometimes succumbing they can have hope that God's Spirit will help them revere Christ more than people.

Biblical Examples of Human Rejection

Closely related to the problem of fearing people's disapproval or rejection is having been rejected. Let's consider three examples of biblical individuals who experienced rejection.

David in Psalm 27:10

In Psalm 27 David addressed the severe heat not only of persecution from enemies (vv. 2–3, 6, 11–12) but also of rejection by parents: "Even if my father and mother abandon me, . . ." (v. 10). We looked at this passage briefly in chapter 15 as we applied it to Jill, who was rejected by her dad. While we lack details of David's situation, the verb "abandon" is a strong word, elsewhere translated "leave" or "forsake." Yet rather than responding to it with the bad fruit of despair, depression, anger, bitterness, rejection, fear, hopelessness, or a dozen other possible sinful responses, David found hope. ". . . the LORD cares for me," he concluded (v. 10).

As counselors we must help rejected counselees focus their trust on God, not on their parents (or anyone else).[4] They must let God their Father parent them. Sticking with the language of Psalm 27, we should help them gaze upon, seek, and make the LORD their one thing (v. 4) and also wait on him to provide (v. 14). Having a counselee study the many descriptions of the Lord in the psalm yields many riches.

---

[4] For an excellent minibook on this topic, see David Powlison, *Life beyond Your Parents' Mistakes: The Transforming Power of God's Love* (New Growth Press, 2010).

Jesus in John 16:32

In his private ministry to his disciples on the evening before his death, Jesus continued to teach them (John 14–17). In John 16:30 they voiced a mini-breakthrough of understanding that he indeed came from God. Jesus affirms them in verse 31 but then issues this sober warning in verse 32: "Indeed, an hour is coming, and has come, when each of you will be scattered to his own home, and you will leave me alone. Yet I am not alone, because the Father is with me." How was it possible for Jesus's closest earthly friends to abandon him—to leave him all alone—yet for him not to be alone? Someone more important to him—Someone whose presence trumped their absence—was with him. Jesus knew God as his ultimate source of help and hope.

In one sense, Jesus's entire earthly life can be summarized as one of rejection by people (John 1:11; Isa 53:3; Matt 23:37). Yet the rejection in this passage was perhaps worse since it came not from unbelievers, but from close friends.[5] Judas had already rejected him (Matt 26:14–16, 20–25). Here Jesus addresses the other eleven disciples, including Peter, James, and John. He *predicted* their rejection in Matt 26:31–35; it was *fulfilled* in Matt 26:36–75 when they all deserted him.

Hagar in Genesis 16

In Gen 16:1–6 we learn that Hagar, though not entirely innocent, was "mistreated" at the hands of Sarai.[6] We don't know the details of the mistreatment—the Hebrew term used can mean afflict, mishandle, oppress—but it was so serious that she fled back toward her homeland, Egypt. In verses 7–14, the LORD seeks and finds her (cf. Luke 19:10), appearing in a theophany as an angel. He speaks to her by name, counsels her to return, and promises to bless her. He sees her, hears her, and draws near to her in grace to comfort and assure her.

---

[5] For other biblical cases of rejection by friends, see Ps 55:12–14; 2 Cor 6:11–13; and 2 Tim 4:9–11, 16–17.

[6] See also our comments on this passage in chapter 14. For other biblical cases of masters rejecting slaves, see Gen 39:13–23 and Exod 1:8–14.

The Two-Reality Rejection Chart

When counseling, I (Bob) often use the "Two-Reality Rejection Chart" below, selecting for it Ps 27:10 or another passage above. On a blank sheet, I draw a "T" chart and write *Seen Reality* and *Unseen Reality* atop the columns this creates. I explain the passage I want to focus on and inductively lead my counselee to complete the two columns. I lead them to see that both realities are present at the same time; we need not deny the rejection column while concurrently focusing on the reality of God's love and care. I then set the goal of progressive growth: "Be controlled increasingly by the right column so that the Unseen Reality defines you and occupies more and more of your focus."

	Seen Reality	*Unseen Reality*
Ps 27:10 (David)	Parents abandon him.	The LORD cares.
John 16:32 (Jesus)	Disciples leave him alone.	The Father is with him; therefore, he is not alone.
Gen 16:6–16 (Hagar)	Sarai mistreats her.	The Lord finds and ministers to her.

Helping Counselees Handle Fear of People and Human Rejection

Let's consider five practical guidelines to help those who fear people or who have experienced rejection, recognizing some points will pertain to one issue more than the other.

Help Counselees See How God in His Word Speaks to Their Situation

Expand their vision of the Bible's breadth. Besides the biblical examples above of fearing people and facing rejection, Scripture records many more examples of real-life people facing pertinent struggles. Bringing in stories of lesser-known Bible figures (e.g., Exod 1:17; Heb 13:35–38) who feared God more than people can assure counselees of the Lord's help in their daily lives.

Show Compassion and Empathize with Counselees Who Have Experienced Mistreatment or Rejection

It's hard to handle being sinned against by anyone, but especially by people we value. God recognizes such hurt and weeps for those counselees. Moreover, he hates and promises to judge the sins of those who reject his people. Even if your counselee provoked rejection, they didn't cause it; rejecters remain fully responsible for their choices. We must also show compassion when a counselee's fear of people and of their disapproval and rejection has led to relationship breakdowns, job losses, social isolation, or significant physical symptoms related to anxiety.[7]

Teach Gospel Truths Continually

God declares and swears that he will never reject his people, based on his covenantal promises of saving grace (1 Sam 12:22; Ps 94:14; Matt 26:28; Heb 6:13–20). His promises, in turn, are based ultimately on the death and resurrection of Jesus Christ, who bore God's wrath that we deserved (2 Cor 5:21; 1 Pet 2:24; 3:18; Rom 8:1, 31–34; Jer 31:3, 31–34). We can assure a Christian counselee, "God will never reject you because, for one hideous moment in history, he did reject his own Son in your place! Your sins demanded divine rejection. Jesus, your substitute, absorbed that wrath, the lightning strike you deserved."

Help counselees find their core, controlling identity as sons or daughters of God, who has accepted them forever (see, e.g., Ps 27:10; 73:23–28; 94:14; Heb 13:5–6). The world won't reinforce these messages, so be sure you do.

---

[7] For information on handling these issues, see chapter 22 on worry, anxiety, and fear; chapter 21 on anger, bitterness, and resentment; and chapter 29 on grief.

Lead Counselees to Confess Any Sins They Need to, Repent of Them, and Seek to Please and Fear God More Than Anyone Else (2 Cor 5:9; Eccl 12:13)

It's insufficient to prize God's acceptance if counselees prize other people above him. So, encourage them to pray over, meditate on, and personalize gospel-saturated passages (e.g., Gal 4:4–7; Eph 1:3–14; Col 3:1–17). Idolatry must be uprooted and exposed before God's withering light. We must exalt God and dethrone people; the Lord tolerates no rivals. God's smile must become the believer's greatest delight and his frown their greatest disappointment. Ask counselees to study fear-of-people passages and to journal prayers to the Lord. For example, for those who fear their peers, a prayer journal entry based on Prov 29:25 might look like this:

> Father, I am doing it again, right now. I am tempted to automatically do what my friends want me to. But that is not pleasing to you, and it only ensnares and enslaves me. Help me to find true safety right now in trusting you and not my friends. And help me to do the right thing here—not to live for them or even for myself but for you as the One who loves me, chose me, sent his Son to die and rise again for me, watches over me, and will send Jesus back for me. Help me, right now, to prioritize and live out my new identity as your child.

In cases of rejection God offers, along with his compassion, forgiveness for any ways a counselee sinfully provoked rejection or responded wrongly to it. The Lord also provides wisdom and power to endure righteously the undeserved rejection they face (1 Pet 4:12–19).

Guide Counselees to Properly Love Those Whom They Have Feared or Those Who Rejected Them

With renewed repentance and with faith fueled by the gospel (as discussed above), counselees are positioned to produce new, godly attitudes and actions toward others. While secular approaches exclude God and focus only horizontally, a biblical approach starts vertically and then extends horizontally. It encompasses both our Lord's first and second great commandments, to love him and to love our neighbors (Matt 22:36–40). God calls us believers to actively extend his deliberate, focused love to those who reject us (Luke 6:27–49; 23:34; 1 Pet 2:18–23; 3:9; 4:19; Rom 12:12–21).[8]

For example, in contrast to offering self-protective "boundaries" approaches or encouraging counselees to love themselves better, we can teach them to love others selflessly and fearlessly. If we live in light of the grace we have received in Christ, we can afford to be radically others-centered in a positive way (Phil 2:1–4). Ed Welch helpfully presents this agenda: "Regarding other people, our problem is that we *need* them (for ourselves) more than we *love* them (for the glory of God). The task God sets for us is to need them *less* and love them *more*. Instead of looking for ways to manipulate others, we will ask God what our duty is toward them."[9]

Biblical counseling seeks to liberate people-pleasers to experience the freedom and delight that God-pleasers enjoy and to become true people-lovers.

Conclusion

Whether your counselee has experienced disapproval or rejection, fears such, or both, the gospel holds out the beauty of Christ's acceptance. God's Word assures us of his love and provisions for all who trust and fear him more than people. In turn, the gospel enables us to need people less and love people more. It helps us become more like Jesus, who feared neither friends nor enemies, but God alone, and gave himself wholly and self-sacrificially for others.

---

[8] For extreme cases of rejection or mistreatment, see Jones, *Pursuing Peace*, 182–95 (see chap. 7, n. 2); Ken Sande, *The Peacemaker: A Biblical Guide to Resolving Personal Conflict* (Baker, 2004), 247–57; and Jay Adams, *How to Overcome Evil: A Practical Exposition of Romans 12:14–21* (Phillipsburg, NJ: P&R, 1977).

[9] Welch, *When People Are Big*, 19.

24

Sadness and Depression

Sadness and depression run rampant in our culture. Clinically, the latter is the most common "psychiatric disorder" diagnosed in the United States, affecting between 5 and 10 percent of the population.[1] Though most English Bible translations don't use the word *depression*, mentions of sadness, being downcast, despair, and hopelessness appear throughout. Such feelings, when amplified, lead to depression. In other words, we can think about sadness as the umbrella term, and a common human experience; but as sad feelings increase in intensity and impact and hope decreases, depression emerges.

While the term "depression" can be used to describe many different situations, in this chapter we view depression as a more extreme form of sadness, rather than a technical diagnosis. Counselors must be mindful of using the term "depression" in the counseling room because of what it might imply (e.g., freedom from personal responsibility) or might lead the counselee to assume about themselves (e.g., "I *am* depressed" or "I must have clinical depressive disorder").

---

[1] "Major Depression," National Institute of Mental Health, updated February 2019, https://www.nimh.nih.gov/health/statistics/major-depression.shtml.

Understanding Sadness and Depression

Let's begin with the general concept of sadness. It often comes in response to disappointment. That may be disappointment over loss, such as the death of a loved one, or over unmet expectations. In the Scriptures David experienced deep sadness or grief for a variety of reasons. He was sad over the loss of his sons (2 Sam 12:16; 18:33), he felt grief over his sin (Psalms 6; 32), and he was in despair as he fled from his attackers (Psalm 69). Godly Elijah (1 Kgs 19:4), Job (Job 3:26), Jeremiah (Jer 20:14, 18), and others had similar experiences. David wrote repeatedly in response to his troubles or trials. He acknowledges in Ps 143:4, "My spirit is weak within me; my heart is overcome with dismay," and in Ps 102:4, "My heart is suffering, withered like grass; I even forget to eat." These descriptors closely align with someone struggling with deep sadness or despair.

Since God experiences sadness (over sin) and our emotions as image bearers flow from his, we also experience sadness. Yet despair and hopelessness, magnifications of sadness, don't mark God's character. When Jesus experienced sadness, he did not grieve with despair. In other words, God does not "get depressed." So, while we can understand the proper place of sadness over sin and loss, we must also acknowledge that sadness is not always sinless.

Depression as an amplification of sadness might appear in different forms: isolation, loss of interest, gloominess, melancholy, despair, hopelessness, suffering, debilitation or an inability/unwillingness to function, and a host of others.[2] We might demonstrate it this way:

[2] Three helpful resources for understanding depression from a Christian perspective are Charles D. Hodges, *Good Mood Bad Mood: Help and Hope for Depression and Bipolar Disorder* (Wapwallopen, PA: Shepherd Press, 2012); Edward T. Welch, *Depression: Looking Up from the Stubborn Darkness* (Greensboro, NC: New Growth Press, 2011); and Zack Eswine, *Spurgeon's Sorrows: Realistic Hope for Those Who Suffer from Depression* (Geanies House, UK: Christian Focus, 2014).

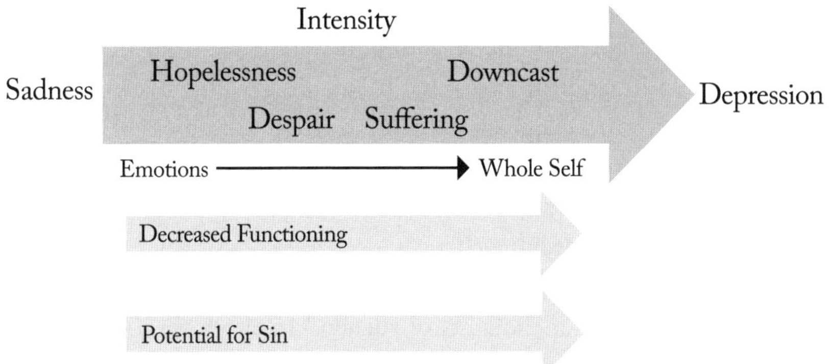

While it is difficult to narrow depression to one descriptor, a proper understanding of depression is wholistic: it involves both heart (beliefs, motives, affections, thoughts, and emotions) and body. It includes thoughts and feelings of sadness, hopelessness, isolation, emptiness, muted emotions, or apathy, often alongside physical symptoms such as muscle pain, sleeplessness, lack of appetite, or significant fatigue or loss of energy. In the struggle with depression, sufferers might find they are unable to care for themselves or concentrate on a task, or fail to find pleasure in things they used to enjoy. Many have described their depression as a heavy cloud that is difficult to lift or see through, a deep pit they are unable to climb out of, or a tunnel with no light at the end. Further, depression quite often carries with it a connection to sinful expressions (including beliefs, thoughts, feelings, and behaviors), while an experience like grief or sadness may not. This does not mean we should assume a person dealing with depression is in sin, but we should be on the lookout for any sinful roots or responses.

These descriptors help us understand what it is like to experience depression. It is more than just a deep sadness; it is an intense sense of being downcast. It makes people feel they have little hope, little energy, and little motivation or ability to pull themselves out. It is, then, deep sadness paired with intense suffering. A sufferer might feel like David did in Ps 6:6: "I am worn out from my groaning. All night long I flood my bed with weeping" (NIV).

While our definition of depression is not equivalent to the secular term, noting the observations of common experience from the *DSM-5* can help us ask thoughtful questions based on how depression typically presents.[3] For a formal diagnosis of major depressive disorder (MDD), several common experiences must be evident. For instance, the person might experience a depressed mood or irritability, decreased interest or pleasure in daily life, weight or sleeping changes, decreased physical activity, fatigue, feelings of excessive/inappropriate guilt or worthlessness, diminished concentration, or feelings or thoughts of suicide.[4] In short, the *DSM* echoes our observation that depression is a wholistic phenomenon with heart and body components.

We should add a final note concerning postpartum depression (PPD). While the expression of PPD might be in line with the criteria above, this form of depression is directly linked with hormonal and physical changes within a mother following childbirth. Many times, as hormones and situational stressors level out, so will the PPD. So, while some biblical counsel might help a sufferer, a conscientious counselor should vocally acknowledge the physiological realities present within new mothers and refer her early on to her physician alongside continued counsel.[5] Note too that situational stressors also come into play for new mothers, such as a lack of adequate sleep, potentially lower levels of self-care, and the demands of caring for a baby.

Biblical-Theological Perspectives

Since Scripture presents humans as complex beings (see chapter 5), we must address the whole person, both body and soul. A proper, biblical

[3] *DSM-5*, 155–88 (see chap. 9, n. 7). For more on the *DSM*, see our chapter 9.

[4] This *DSM-5* list includes a mixture of body and heart issues, including some within the domain of biblical counseling—e.g., guilt, worthlessness, and suicidal ideation. Unlike previous editions, the *DSM-5* added (not without controversy) responses to grief events into the category of depressive disorders, even though such responses should be viewed as expected and not necessarily disordered.

[5] See Welch, *Counselor's Guide to the Brain* (see chap. 5, n. 7).

understanding of depression must do the same; the Bible has sufficient responses to each facet of the experience of depression.

Scripture is full of examples of deep sadness and despair; at the same time, it is full of encouragement to someone in that state. Psalm 34, for instance, presents a hope-filled perspective in the midst of David's deep sadness and suffering. Throughout the psalm David continually turns to the Lord: "I sought the LORD, and he answered me and rescued me from all my fears. Those who look to him are radiant with joy; their faces will never be ashamed. . . . The righteous cry out, and the LORD hears, and rescues them from all their troubles. The LORD is near the brokenhearted; he saves those crushed in spirit" (Ps 34:4–5, 17–18). While David had been downcast and afraid, he trusted in the Lord's presence and provision. Amid his struggles, he had hope: God heard him, God would respond to him, and God would save him. While these realities didn't remove David's struggle or change his hard circumstances, they brought him God-given joy, confidence, and hope.[6]

Lamentations 3:19–26 provides further hope to those experiencing depression. In verses 19–20 the prophet Jeremiah, the author, describes his affliction and his ensuing depression. He apparently thinks on them constantly and can't find relief. Yet, as he moves through verses 21–26, he says, "Yet I call this to mind, and therefore I have hope: Because of the LORD's faithful love we do not perish, for his mercies never end. They are new every morning; great is [his] faithfulness! I say, 'The LORD is my portion, therefore I will put my hope in him.' The LORD is good to those who wait for him, to the person who seeks him. It is good to wait quietly for salvation from the LORD." Here Jeremiah recognizes that despite his hardships, God is still faithful, merciful, and good. God remains the same, therefore we can have hope.

Further, Jas 1:2–4 speaks of an important purpose behind a believer's struggles: "Consider it a great joy, my brothers and sisters, whenever you

---

[6] For more on the connection between suffering and depression, see D. Martyn Lloyd-Jones, *Spiritual Depression: Its Cause and Its Cure* (London: HarperCollins Publishers, 1998), or William Bridge, *A Lifting Up for the Downcast* (Louisville, KY: GLH, 2014).

experience various trials, because you know that the testing of your faith produces endurance. And let endurance have its full effect, so that you may be mature and complete, lacking nothing." He addresses both one's attitude in the midst of the trial (choosing joy) and a proper understanding of the purpose of trial (it is producing something God-honoring).

We must also consider the possible role of personal sin (see chapter 6) in the experience of sadness and depression. Several times in Scripture, the condition of the heart (sadness or despair) is sinful. Consider the first instance of deep sadness in Scripture, Cain in Gen 4:1–7. Cain is "despondent" because God does not accept his wrong offering. A close read reveals that his heart is the problem that led to his sadness. Soberingly, when he rejects God's answer to his sadness, murder soon follows. Or consider the disciples in Luke 24:13–24, who were discouraged on the road to Emmaus after the death of Jesus. They were downcast (v. 17 NIV) because their picture of who the Messiah would be seemingly had gone unfulfilled (v. 21). Their hearts were focused on their own understanding of the Savior rather than on who Jesus had already declared himself to be. Thankfully, Jesus addressed their remnant unbelief, revealing himself to them from the Scriptures and in breaking bread with them, restoring their hope and joy in him as their Messiah (Luke 24:25–53). In the cases of both Cain and the Luke 24 disciples, the beliefs, desires, and expectations of the heart were pivotal in their sadness and despondency, and ultimately they were sinful. So, in our understanding of sadness, despair, hopelessness, and ultimately depression, we must consider whether sin is present, and to what degree. While Scripture affirms normal, righteous experiences of sadness, it also provides examples in which sin is present and must be addressed.

The Example of Job

Let's consider Job's story. He experienced severe loss, grief, physical affliction, poor counsel, and spiritual questioning as part of his suffering. All of these might be components of a modern-day believer's struggle with depression. In the midst of his suffering, Job says,

> My spirit is broken. My days are extinguished. A graveyard awaits me. . . . [God] has made me an object of scorn to the people; I have become a man people spit at. My eyes have grown dim from grief, and my whole body has become but a shadow. . . . My days have slipped by; my plans have been ruined, even the things dear to my heart. They turned night into day and made light seem near in the face of darkness. If I await Sheol as my home, spread out my bed in darkness, and say to corruption, "You are my father," and to the maggot, "My mother" or "My sister," where then is my hope? Who can see any hope for me? (Job 17:1, 6–7, 11–15)

Many counselees feel the same. They are discouraged, they hurt, they believe their lives should end, they feel rejection and shame, and they are hopeless. They question where God is and why he let all this happen. But the book of Job teaches that God is still sovereign and good despite hardship—even when the purpose for our troubles seems incomprehensible. Like Job, we may wrongly feel entitled to a satisfactory explanation for our trials. It helps to know that in God's response to Job, his experience of suffering was not diminished, though his understanding of his suffering found correction in light of God's perspective on reality.

Counseling Strategies and Assignments

When counseling those with sadness and depression, several strategies are helpful.

First, we must listen well and encourage. Ephesians 4:29 gives a pertinent reminder: we believers should continually build one another up, encouraging others in their struggles. A wise counselor, then, listens well, seeks to truly understand, and encourages often. This foundation presumes an appropriate empathetic response; as Rom 12:15 reminds us, we are to grieve with those who grieve. Many counselees benefit from someone simply listening and committing to walk with them.

Next, we must reiterate the gospel. Not only has the finished work of Christ given us believers immeasurable hope, combating feelings of hopelessness and despair, but the Spirit is continually at work in us to conform us to Christ's image. This includes producing spiritual fruit, like joy and peace, both of which run contrary to depression. As Paul notes in 2 Tim 4:17, the Lord stands with us and strengthens us; these realities are of utmost importance in the midst of sadness and despair.

We also must aid counselees by exploring their underlying heart issues and helping them think biblically. The counselor should be alert to wrong motivations or desires as well as problematic thought patterns (those that are false, distorted, or intrusive), which are indicative of what is going on in the heart. It may help to ask, "When you are experiencing periods of distress, what are you thinking? What do those thoughts reveal about your desires?" and "What are you living for, wanting to see happen, or hoping will change?" Then we can think about how a specific untruth or distortion can be corrected with God's truth. Moreover, we should listen for anything a counselee might need to repent of and turn from.

The Bible speaks about being transformed by the renewing of the mind (Rom 12:2), thinking about what is true (Phil 4:8), and taking thoughts captive (2 Cor 10:5). A depressed person struggles with thought patterns, whether that be incorrect thinking, repeating messages of hopelessness, or misunderstanding God's role in their trials. Counselors must focus on a counselee's thoughts, including underlying desires, demands, and expectations, so they may correct them to line up with the truth of God's Word.

One helpful exercise involves asking a counselee to track specific thoughts that arise throughout the week that are most connected to feelings of hopelessness or despair and then to evaluate them in light of Scripture and take them before the Lord in prayer. When they find that a thought is not true or right, a counselee can write out a parallel truth from the Bible as well as the implication of that truth (i.e., what it looks like to live in light of it). They can then ask God to help them do so. When the recurring thought arises again, the counselee should focus their thoughts on the truthful reality rather than their perceived or felt reality, then live out the practical implication they determined with the help of the Spirit. Their notes can be discussed and evaluated in session to make sure they are on track.

It is also important to remind the counselee of their purpose. When depressed, counselees often seek help to alleviate symptoms. Understandably, they want to feel better. While feeling better is not a bad goal, it is insufficient and should not be a believer's ultimate aim. As counselors, we should help people rely on the Lord for his strength rather than their own. We should help them evaluate not just how to feel better in a day but how to live for his glory amid their suffering.

We should also assess them for suicidal thoughts. The wise counselor asks often whether their depressed counselee has had any suicidal thoughts or is at risk (see chapter 27).

The counselor should also seek to reduce any situational or environmental triggers for the counselee, where possible. For instance, if the counselee is struggling with stress from work, and a feeling of hopelessness that things will not get better, the counselor might explore ways counselees might change the situation, offer them a different perspective on their job, or suggest stress-reduction techniques such as setting aside time for relaxation and self-care. While these approaches will not cure, they can aid in growth and change.

We must also help counselees connect faith and action. Quite often, depression prompts spiritual questions regarding the nature of God, personal guilt or shame, or how we might struggle to obey despite the weight of our sinful condition. Help the counselee dive deep into the truths of Scripture and patiently work through any such struggles, reminding them that their battle with depression and those questions does not negate salvation nor alleviate the responsibility to obey. Similarly, we should encourage a counselee to obey God even when they might not feel like it. After all, one is not required to be happy or be in good circumstances to choose joy (see the psalms of lament). Even in the midst of despair, a believer can rejoice in the Lord's goodness and faithfulness, remembering how he has been good and dependable throughout the generations and in their own life. Additionally, the counselor should encourage the counselee to act in line with Scripture rather than their own feelings (which are subjective and influenced by sin). We can point out that God's Spirit enables people through his power rather than their own.

We must also encourage spiritual disciplines, particularly prayer. A counselee should continue to commune with God often through prayer, presenting needs to him and thinking on God's truth (Ps 34:17; Col 3:2; 4:2; Rom 8:5–6; Psalm 1). For some, depression feels like an insurmountable wall between the believer and God, so much so that prayer and reading Scripture feels impossible. Yet we must encourage it, even if by prompting a person simply to pray the Lord's name and read a selected verse or two. Small victories turn into larger ones; the Lord is faithful to his children.

Engaging with the Psalms often proves particularly helpful to those struggling with sadness. Therefore, we should direct counselees to pay special attention to those that speak to their struggles. This often includes Psalms 34; 69; 88; 102; or 143, as well as the psalms of lament (e.g., 13; 22; 44). Help a counselee notice each writer's honesty before the Lord and how they invoke his help, yet are not overcome. In most cases—particularly with the laments—the psalmists close their work by reminding themselves of God's goodness and faithfulness to deliver them, praising God and proclaiming their confidence in him. Such reminders are key for a counselee struggling in the midst of depression. Correction by God's Spirit (including through the wise, caring biblical counselor) is effective. A counselee might read, meditate on, pray through, and journal about particular passages that connect with their experiences or write their own lament.

Equally critical for those battling despair is to connect with other believers. A counselee should connect with others in their local church, under the oversight of their pastor/shepherd, specifically because doing so fights the tendency toward isolation. When someone struggles with hopelessness and despair, they tend to think they are the only one who suffers; such Christians tend to think they will be judged for their lack of faith. Pointing to Heb 10:24–25, the counselor should encourage the counselee to engage once or twice each week with other believers and to share their struggles in some degree within a small group setting in order to receive accountability and encouragement.

Counselees struggling with deep sadness should also be encouraged to focus outwardly rather than inwardly. The counselor should encourage a focus on Jesus and others through service, which helps fight the tendency to turn inward. Our Savior serves as a primary example; despite situational stressors and the weight of what he was to endure on the cross, he continued to serve others consistently throughout his ministry. A counselor can bring direct instruction from Scripture here: "Only fear the Lord and serve him faithfully with all your heart. For consider what great things he has done for you" (1 Sam 12:24 ESV). Serving the Lord through serving others acknowledges what he has done on our behalf.

We counselors should also urge care for the body. Given the whole-person nature of depression, the counselor should address the counselee's care for their own physical being. This might include helping them establish a regular pattern for sleeping, eating healthy meals, exercising, and resting. Regulating the body can help with addressing thought patterns and might alleviate part of the struggle.

If the counselee's depression is severe, medical treatment might be needed. (In fact, that should not be surprising given the fallenness of both body and soul.) A referral to a physician for evaluation and possible medical treatment might set a counselee up to receive needed help. While medication should not be viewed as a cure for depression (see chapter 36) unless the cause is primarily organic, it might help them function more effectively in life and in the counseling process.[7]

Conclusion

Sadness and depression are common experiences, laden with potential for ungodly responses but also for growth and change. In seeking to understand the complexity of a particular counselee's struggle, you can bring the hope of God's Word to bear on that unique situation, as the Bible says much to those who are sad or depressed. Help those you serve grow in Christlikeness amid their struggles; this brings honor to God and will help them learn how to comfort others in their struggles as well (2 Cor 1:4).

---

[7] For more regarding treatment, see Hodges, *Good Mood Bad Mood.*

Infertility and Pregnancy Loss

Infertility and pregnancy loss are quite common, yet neither is a topic of regular conversation. Even the church often reserves mention of these difficult matters for either Mother's Day or an occasional women's Bible study. As a result, infertile couples sometimes have no one to talk to and lack clear teaching on how to rightly understand and grieve their lack of children or the loss of a baby.

Understanding Infertility and Pregnancy Loss

It is estimated that of known pregnancies, 10–15 percent end in miscarriage. However, true miscarriage rates might be as high as 50 percent, if unknown pregnancies are included.[1] Additionally, approximately 12 percent of women have some sort of impaired fertility, including recurrent pregnancy loss.[2] This means that of the childbearing-aged women in churches, one in eight has fertility struggles and the number that has experienced a miscarriage is likely higher, since not all miscarriages are reported

[1] www.marchofdimes.org/complications/miscarriage.aspx

[2] https://www.cdc.gov/nchs/fastats/infertility.htm#:~:text=Infertility.%20Data%20are%20for%20the%20U.S.%20Percent%20of,15-44%20who%20have%20ever%20used%20infertility%20services:%2012.0%.

or even known. Churches must openly discuss these topics so men and women know where to go for help, for compassionate counsel.

The medical community defines infertility as the inability of a woman under thirty-five to get pregnant within twelve months of regular unprotected sex.[3] It might be caused by the lack of a viable egg or sperm, a genetic anomaly in one or both partners, or the woman's body not sustaining a fertilized egg. Many times the cause is unknown, and sometimes the infertility comes after the birth of a healthy child. The infertility umbrella also includes the topic of recurrent miscarriage, when a couple has experienced three or more. The reasons for this are generally less clear than with typical infertility. Known causes include hormonal imbalances in the woman, clotting issues, genetic factors, anatomical anomalies, immune differences between mother and child, poor egg quality, and infections.

Despite these nuances, counselors must recognize that any type of infertility or pregnancy loss, even one miscarriage, can tremendously impact a couple. While not all couples will seek medical treatment for their infertility or their loss, many do seek to determine both the causes for their struggles and their options for moving forward. As counselors, we must try to understand the individual circumstances of each couple if we are to walk with them through their struggles.

How Do Fertility-Related Struggles Present in a Counselee?

While every person will respond differently to infertility or a miscarriage, we can expect some commonalities. Primarily, we'll likely see some form of grief in them. Remember that grief looks different for each person (see chapter 24). For some, it looks like a search for answers, such as going to a fertility specialist. For others, it involves inward or outward mourning, clear expressions of the emotional struggles that come along with loss. Still others experience feelings of failure and disappointment, including a sense of failure to fulfill one's role as a father or mother. Feelings of grief and

---

[3] "What Is Infertility?," Centers for Disease Control and Prevention, last modified January 16, 2019, https://www.cdc.gov/reproductivehealth/infertility/index.htm.

disappointment are likely worsened on holidays such as Mother's Day or Father's Day, or when those close to them celebrate a pregnancy or birth.

Though there are physical components to infertility and miscarriage, most responses to them will be inner-person responses. Understandably, a woman or couple might experience great sadness or disappointment. This grief might be in part over the tangible loss of a child (miscarriage) or with the intangible loss of the idea of children or a perceived future as a parent (infertility). In either case, it's often quite difficult for people to imagine life without having children. Couples might grieve even this change in what was their view of the future. Alongside grief might come hopelessness or a fear that no answers will be found or that there are no options to move forward. For recurrent losses, fear might arise with each new pregnancy. And it is not uncommon for those struggling with infertility or pregnancy loss to experience anger at themselves, their spouses, others, or even God.

I (Kristin) have experienced five miscarriages: three before our first full-term pregnancy, then two more before our second full-term pregnancy. Unfortunately, no medical reason has been given to explain what happened, further complicating my grief after each loss and adding fear during pregnancies. The last two paragraphs noted a myriad of emotions; I have felt all of them, at different times. What has been made clear, at least in my experience, is that no loss is the same. What I felt after the first loss was different from the third or the fifth. And it never gets easier. This is a strong reminder to us as counselors that no woman feels the same way from loss to loss or from month to month of failing to conceive. Emotions are complex and highly individual. We must, therefore, take great care to understand each woman and her experience.

Some common threads of thought might be present. A woman or couple might find themselves concluding that they are never going to have a baby. They might feel isolated, that no one understands what they are going through. And they may regularly ask questions like "How could God let something like this happen?"

Further, a woman or couple might feel as if God has grown distant or doesn't hear their prayers. They might be angry at God for withholding a "good gift" from them, his children. They might struggle with reconciling the idea of God as a "good Father" given their bad experiences—particularly if they are grieving the death of a child they desired greatly.

For those struggling with infertility or pregnancy loss, a myriad of responses might be present and might even shift from day to day. Various triggers, such as seeing a pregnancy announcement on social media, getting a negative pregnancy test, serving in the church nursery, hearing about a family member or close friend who is expecting, or even simply having a tough day might turn a relatively good day into a sad one. Therefore, counselors must be sensitive to where each such counselee is at the moment of counseling and be patient in approach.

Biblical Perspectives

We must lay some theological groundwork for how to properly understand both infertility and pregnancy loss.[4] As we saw in chapter 5, the impact of sin on the human person has particular importance in this discussion, namely the brokenness of the physical body, which can leave a couple physically unable to have children.

Another important biblical theme for counselors to consider in relation to this topic is identity. For all people, identity *in part* is related to who one's family is; after all, even our names are directly tied to other people. For many, parenthood is a highly anticipated aspect of their identity. Most people simply assume they will be parents one day. In the Old Testament, one's identity was almost inextricably linked to one's family. The Jewish people, for instance, were descendants of Abraham and proud of it. Yet the coming of Christ shifted the notion of identity away from being based in our earthly families to being a part of God's spiritual family. For Christians, our new identity as sons and daughters of God comes through our adoption into God's family as his children. The biological family becomes secondary to one's spiritual family (Luke 14:26; Matt 19:29; Mark 3:31–35).

---

[4] See Matthew Arbo, *Walking through Infertility: Biblical, Theological, and Moral Counsel for Those Who Are Struggling* (Wheaton, IL: Crossway, 2018); and Kimberly and Philip Monroe, "The Bible and the Pain of Infertility," *Journal of Biblical Counseling* 23, no. 1 (Winter 2005): 50–58.

Scripture describes several instances of infertility and pregnancy loss, but people often misunderstand those passages in relationship to those currently suffering in those ways. In 1 Samuel 1–2, Hannah is barren but cries out to the Lord for a child. After she promises to devote the first son she receives to the Lord's service, he opens her womb. Likewise, in most cases of infertility or barrenness described in Scripture, the woman conceives in the course of time. This might lead readers to assume that one simply must pray enough, promise enough, or have enough faith, and she will get pregnant. But the purpose of the biblical passages dealing with fertility issues is not to demonstrate a formula for having a healthy child. Rather, they describe instances of the Lord carrying out *his plans*—often as part of the Bible's redemption narrative.

In some of the struggles involving fertility that the Bible reports, another theme appears: relationship problems between husband and wife. For instance, Hannah's husband tries to console her, yet she remains in anguish. This tension is a reminder that fertility struggles have the potential to either build up a marriage or cause division, whether because of blame, isolation, a lack of understanding, or a difference in emotions or responses. Nevertheless, the husband's biblical call to lovingly lead his wife remains. At all times, spouses should continually build one another up (Eph 4:29) and speak words of encouragement (1 Thess 5:11) rather than withdrawing from one another.

Lastly, counselors should "rejoice with those who rejoice" and "weep with those who weep" (Rom 12:15). But without intentionally seeking to have conversations about whether a counselee is rejoicing or weeping and why, we simply cannot do this. For many women (and men) who have deeply desired to have a child, the inability to have a baby or carry one to full term can be devastating. So, to understand and weep with them over this devastation, we must be willing to dive into their pain.

Quite often Western Christians believe that God is good because their circumstances are good. Their experiences become their authority over the Word of God. This wrong thinking may not even be recognizable until negative experiences arise to test them. This is where I (Kristin) found myself after my three losses before our son was born. That's when I was confronted with the reality that God's Word must be true regardless of what I think; if it says he is good, he is—no matter what my experiences might suggest. Ultimately, the deaths of my children cannot determine if God is good or bad. *He is good.* And all the bad is a tragic side effect of our living in a world now cursed by sin. In fact, God himself is deeply saddened over death, as evidenced by Jesus weeping over Lazarus's passing before raising him (John 11). We must remember—and help counselees remember—that the effects of sin are not the fault of our good God. God's Word, not our circumstances, must determine truth. If not, we will view God as ultimately weak and insufficient. So, while we grieve with our counselees experiencing fertility struggles, we must listen for sinful desires and wrong beliefs coming into play so that we can help counselees draw right—that is, biblical—conclusions about God.

Counseling Steps and Practical Procedures

To counsel a woman (or couple) walking through infertility or pregnancy loss,[5] consider these practical reminders.

Recognize the Sense of Isolation Your Counselee Might Feel

A counselee dealing with infertility most likely thinks about it on a day-to-day and also month-to-month basis; to cope, she may be isolating herself, perhaps even from her spouse. Each menstrual cycle makes her feel more

[5] On infertility, see Chelsea Patterson Sobolik and Russell Moore, *Longing for Motherhood: Holding On to Hope in the Midst of Childlessness* (Chicago: Moody, 2018); Amy Baker and Daniel Wickert, MD, *Infertility: Comfort for Your Empty Arms and Heavy Heart* (Greensboro, NC: New Growth Press, 2013); and Sandra Glahn and William Cutrer, MD, *When Empty Arms Become a Heavy Burden: Encouragement for Couples Facing Infertility,* rev. ed. (Grand Rapids: Kregel, 2010). On pregnancy loss, see Stephanie Green, *Miscarriage: You Are Not Alone* (Greensboro, NC: New Growth Press, 2014); Ryan Showalter, *Grieving the Loss of Your Child: Comfort for Your Broken Heart* (Greensboro, NC: New Growth Press, 2014); and Nancy Guthrie, *Holding On to Hope: A Pathway through Suffering to the Heart of God* (Carol Stream, IL: Tyndale Momentum, 2015).

and more like a failure, so she withdraws from others. Help such women, and their husbands when possible, identify and respond properly to both forms of isolation.

Recognize the Difficulty of Discussing Fertility Struggles

It is uncommon for counselees to invite outsiders into their private struggles. It is not easy for a woman or a couple to discuss the very personal struggle with infertility. If a counselee does open up about her struggle, affirm her transparency and assure her that you respect her for seeking help.

Be Sensitive to the Uniqueness of Each Counselee's Struggle

If you have walked through a struggle in your own marriage, you might be tempted to try to encourage a counselee by saying that you understand what they are going through or to assume they will struggle the same way you did. Yet, as with any other situation discussed in your counseling room, you must recognize that experiences and feelings differ. Moreover, a husband and wife might respond and struggle differently from each other, even though they are walking through the same hardship. So, make sure to communicate to both that they might grieve differently from one another. Point out that there is little that is "right" or "wrong" about grieving the loss of a child or the hope of future children.

Share Pertinent Truths from Scripture with Wisdom, Grace, Compassion, and Boldness

The following themes especially relate to infertility and pregnancy loss:

- Death and loss are sad, often truly heartbreaking. Jesus even wept over the passing of his friend Lazarus, whom he was about to raise (John 11:35). Therefore, it is appropriate to grieve an inability to conceive or carry a child to term. We can find hope in knowing God "heals the brokenhearted" (Ps 147:3).

- God is faithful despite our circumstances or experiences; what the Bible says about him does not change based on our experiences (1 Cor 1:9; Heb 10:23).
- God sees every tear his people cry; in fact, he lovingly records and bottles them (Ps 56:8).
- Believers' bodies will one day be restored, which means that the present reality of brokenness is not an eternal one. We can look forward with hope to the day of restoration (Rom 8:18; Rev 21:4; John 16:22).
- A believer's identity is found in Christ, not in what one does, has, or whether one bears children. Neither family ties nor medical diagnoses can define us (Eph 1:11–16).
- God's plan for each believer is good, even if its unfolding involves pain (Rom 8:28). The close of the book of Job in particular reminds us that even in cases of great loss, the Lord manages to work all things together for our good. He is most wise (John 16:33).
- While Christians differ on the subject of the eternal destiny of a deceased infant, many believers carry the hope of seeing their deceased sons and daughters in the new heaven and earth.[6]

Encourage Counselees Not to Assume Something Is Wrong with Them

Assumptions can lead them to the belief that infertility or loss is something they can control or could have controlled, and therefore it is their "fault."[7] That might bring a false sense of shame or helplessness. More specifically, it can add embarrassment to hurt each time they have to answer questions about when they are having children, as if it is something they can easily control.

[6] For this discussion, see Grudem, *Systematic Theology*, 499–501 (see chap. 3, n. 13).

[7] This doesn't mean past decisions can't directly affect the ability to conceive or to carry a child to term. Past abortion, obesity, an eating disorder, and drug use all raise the risk of future infertility. Counselors should consider potential connections to past decisions yet remain compassionate and delicate toward current suffering.

Grieve Openly with Them

Acknowledging someone's pain might include weeping alongside them. Be sensitive to a counselee's struggle as well as any past behaviors that they think might have contributed to their fertility struggles or pregnancy loss. Also, remember to be patient with each counselee's grief and to walk at their pace (see chapter 24). As a growth assignment, you could have a counselee read and meditate on various psalms of lament, such as Psalms 6, 13, or 31, and then progress toward reading and meditating on psalms of praise like Psalms 30 and 34. Such selections will remind them of both the need to cry out to the Lord in grief as well as the importance of choosing hope and praise.

Offer Encouragement and Support When Counselees Express a Desire to Pursue a Legitimate Path Forward

Some people dealing with the issues discussed in this chapter may choose to supplement or follow counseling with the pursuit of medical intervention or adoption. Occasionally, they may ask that you accompany them to related appointments. (This is part of why it's wise for a female to counsel a female, or a couple to counsel a couple.) In such cases, we must be sure not to step outside our ethical roles as biblical counselors, yet we should offer appropriate support as requested.

Pray about Even the Most Sensitive Issues

By lifting counselees' thoughts, desires, hopes, motivations, and potential letdowns up to the Lord outside the counseling room, you can express more heartfelt sensitivity within it. Keeping in mind the wisdom of same-gender counseling and appropriate boundaries, be aware that in some instances it might be appropriate to offer to pray for a counselee particularly around the key days of her cycle or on the anniversary week of her miscarriage. You might choose to reach out to a counselee after a doctor's appointment you know she's been fearing.

Lovingly Confront Sinful Responses

The types of losses discussed in this chapter are tragic side effects of the curse of sin at work in the world, but they are not at all sinful. Sometimes, however, responses to loss might be. For instance, a counselee may be operating under false beliefs such as God is punishing them or has abandoned them. They may feel they "deserve" children for one reason or another. They may harbor bitterness or unrighteous anger toward God, their spouse, or themselves. They may find themselves drifting into hopeless and despair. You must lovingly—and with great compassion—confront and correct any sinful beliefs, motives, or behaviors that manifest, seeking to lead counselees toward repentance.

Continually Present the Idea of Grieving with Hope

Explore with your counselee what it looks like to grieve with an eye on eternity (1 Thess 4:13–18; 2 Cor 4:7–18). Help them learn to intentionally keep heavenly biblical truths foremost in their minds; these can keep sinful hopelessness from creeping in. Once we reach heaven, even the worst of what we experienced here will seem only "light and temporary" by comparison. This perspective, coupled with the idea that God can renew and strengthen our hearts in the meantime (see chapter 35), can help counselees avoid getting bogged down in despair. Living by it might also give them opportunity to extend Christ's hope to others. Importantly, Rom 15:13 describes the Lord as "the God of hope."

Encourage a Counselee and Their Family to Connect with Their Local Church

As counselors, we should urge couples to seek the loving support a church family can offer. The church can pray for them and weep with them, and potentially rejoice with them when the time is right. A counselee might choose to share their story with only one or two people, like a mentor in the faith and a small group leader; the point is that in reaching out, they are letting people know they need help in bearing their load and giving them opportunity to step up. Also, it may be helpful—drawing from the principle in 2 Cor 1:3–4—to offer a growth assignment intended to connect your counselee with a believer who has walked through a battle similar to theirs. This, in fact, might help a counselee shift their focus from self to others.

Conclusion

Struggles with infertility or pregnancy loss are difficult to walk through and difficult to speak to because of the depth of pain and grief involved. These realities would not exist had sin not entered the world.

As biblical counselors, we must keep in mind and help others see that even when facing such intensely personal tragedies as these, the believer is not without hope. The Scriptures repeatedly declare God's faithfulness to his children, his provision in seasons of plenty and of want, and the hope of future restoration—and deliverance from the current brokenness—because of the gospel. Biblical counselors must bring this hope to those who are infertile or who have lost a baby to miscarriage. Even these are struggles Christians can walk through victoriously because the Lord is with them.

26

Suicide and Self-Harm

Since the struggles of suicidal thoughts and self-harm can overlap, we will address them both in this chapter. Yet they are not the same. One does not indicate, necessitate, or exclude the other. Therefore, we will consider them under separate headings.

Suicide

Description of the Problem

Suicide is the intentional act of taking one's own life. Suicidal ideation is the thought pattern that precedes or surrounds that event, and a suicidal attempt is a (failed) intentional effort at ending one's own life. Typical means include firearms (the use of which is most prevalent among males), poisoning (most prevalent among females), suffocation/hanging, or less common approaches such as cutting or drowning. Tragically, suicide is consistently listed among the top ten leading causes of death in America. The highest demographic for completed suicide attempts is middle-aged white males. While four times as many men die by suicide as women, females attempt suicide more often.[1]

---

[1] "Suicide Statistics," American Foundation for Suicide Prevention, modified March 1, 2020, https://afsp.org/suicide-statistics.

While no clear set of criteria can determine suicidality, common risk factors include

- prior suicide attempts or self-harm behaviors;
- expressed feelings of hopelessness or helplessness, or that life feels "out of control";
- comorbid struggles such as depression, substance abuse, or ADHD;
- a history of abuse; and
- family history of suicide.

Significant life stressors and a lack of consistent support further this risk. The presence of any of these factors should precipitate an intentional conversation around suicidal thoughts.

It is difficult to determine clear symptoms of someone's suicidal thoughts since counselees often hide their distress. However, indicators include the person talking about their intentions directly or indirectly, perhaps by making statements about not being around, being a burden to others, feeling trapped, having no reason to live, getting their affairs in order, giving things away, or writing a will. They might withdraw from others or show significant mood changes, including sleep changes, acting anxious or depressed, or being aggressive or reckless. Sometimes substance use or abuse indicates a sufferer's attempts to deal with problematic, overwhelming feelings.

Counselees express numerous reasons for desiring to end their lives. Most often attempts are related to situational stressors involving relationships, finances, jobs, or physical health. They typically involve some sort of internal emotional distress like feelings of despair, hopelessness, deep sadness, or unrelenting suffering with no prognosis for positive change. A counselee might express feelings of guilt or shame over a particular event or personal failure. (Some cultures view suicide as an honorable option over bringing shame to one's family.)

Other counselees might want to end their lives because they feel some unmet "need," like the desire for love or acceptance, or a physical need for income or protection. Some might admit their suicidal thoughts come from anger or bitterness; they may think of taking their lives as an opportunity to seek revenge or to hurt another person. Older adults might have suicidal thoughts after the loss of a loved one, feeling so empty they don't want to live without a certain person.

Biblical counselors should explore the underlying motives for any suicidal thoughts presented to them. Treating someone with deep emotional distress will look different than treating someone who feels lost without their spouse of fifty years. Understanding motives involves spending significant time listening to the counselee's reasoning for wanting to take their life and responding accordingly.[2] It also means exploring what brought them to counseling as it relates to their motivation and desire to change. For instance, did the counselee approach you because they were frightened by their own thoughts or because their family made them?

Risk Assessment

While evaluating a counselee, the counselor should listen well, assessing the person's situation and intentions. We can ask questions like these:

- On a scale of 1 to 10, with 1 being very low and 10 being very high, what is your distress level?
- What circumstances are contributing to your thoughts?
- Why do you believe you would be better off not living?
- What emotions are you experiencing?
- Do you have a plan to take your life and a means to carry it out?
- Have you made a recent attempt?

These questions aim to uncover the counselee's internal logic and motivations.

Asking such questions also helps the counselor evaluate suicide risk, an important first step.[3] Wise assessment considers intent, plan, and means, as

[2] For more, see Jeffrey S. Black, *Suicide: Understanding and Intervening* (Phillipsburg, NJ: P&R, 2003); and David Powlison, *I Just Want to Die: Replacing Suicidal Thoughts with Hope* (Greensboro, NC: New Growth Press, 2010).

[3] For more on risk assessment, see "Suicide Prevention and Grieving a Suicide," Biblical Counseling Coalition, May 4, 2013, https://www.biblicalcounselingcoalition

well as contributing risk factors such as any history of suicidal thoughts or suicide attempts, problematic emotions or relationships, life stressors, and any emotional, behavioral, or thought patterns indicating intent. Several available tools can help counselors assess risk.[4]

Suicide in the Bible

While we see examples of suicide in Scripture, those who chose it were either clearly not walking with the Lord, faced imminent death from mortal injury, and/or evidenced great fear.[5] Since these situations don't typically align with what we see in biblical counseling encounters, we glean little from these accounts.

However, several key theological themes speak to the issue of suicide and suicidal ideation. First, Scripture affirms the value of human life. Humans are God's image bearers, precious and valuable to God, and their value is not based on capacity or ability (Gen 1:26–27). Therefore, human life should be upheld as tremendously valuable. Second, Scripture presents God alone as Creator and Author over life; he gives and sustains it, so he alone has authority over when a life begins and should end. Third, the Bible prohibits murder (Ex 20:13; Gen 9:5–6). Theologians include suicide as murder. Therefore, the topic carries a clear moral component; it is not about honor versus dishonor. It is clearly sinful because it disobeys God's commands, is an act of unbelief (desiring to do things one's own way), and self-centeredly disregards others.

.org/2013/05/04/suicide-prevention-and-grieving-a-suicide/; and Aaron Sironi's lecture, "Assessing and Counseling a Person with Suicidal Thoughts," https://www.ccef.org/shop/product/assessing-and-counseling-person-suicidal-thoughts/.

[4] See, for instance, the Suicide Assessment Five-Step Evaluation and Triage (SAFE-T), available at https://store.samhsa.gov/product/SAFE-T-Pocket-Card-Suicide-Assessment-Five-Step-Evaluation-and-Triage-for-Clinicians/sma09-4432; and the Columbia Suicide Severity Rating Scale (C-SSRS), available at https://suicidepreventionlifeline.org/wp-content/uploads/2016/09/Suicide-Risk-Assessment-C-SSRS-Lifeline-Version-2014.pdf.

[5] See, for instance, the story of Samson in Judg 16:28–30, that of Saul and his armor bearer in 1 Sam 31:4–5, and that of Judas in Matt 27:3–5.

Nevertheless, we don't believe committing suicide costs a true believer their salvation. By God's preserving grace, one act of rebellion cannot undo God's covenantal commitment to his child. Yet we should certainly not take suicidal thoughts or attempts lightly. The wise counselor should hold in tandem both the seriousness of this sin and the grace of God, recognizing that we cannot know with certainty the eternal state of one who professes faith yet commits suicide (Matt 7:21–23).

Counseling Suicidal People

How should counselors proceed with those who seem suicidal, either through open admission or leading behavior? Our first concern should be for the safety of a counselee. We should speak openly with them about any suicidal thoughts/ideations. Talking about suicide won't lead a person to take their life, but avoiding such discussion might lead a counselor to miss clear indicators. Therefore, if any indicators exist, we should raise the topic *at least* in the first session(s) and by continually assessing and responding to a counselee's stressors and risk level throughout counseling.

The informed consent agreement presented to a counselee before treatment should include a note about limited confidentiality, explicitly freeing the counselor to involve others as is deemed wise should suicidal indicators exist. Safety steps might include asking counselees or their family members to remove any means of harm from a residence (e.g., flushing pills, locking or removing weapons), establishing a suicide watch, procuring a verbal or written no-harm agreement, and developing with the counselee a written safety plan that lists potential triggers or warning signs, a list of coping strategies (prayer, Scripture reading, removing oneself from a current context/situation, etc.), and the names and numbers of support people and crisis lines that one might call when suicidal thoughts arise.[6] As much as possible, we should involve a counselee's family members and church to support the person and be part of the safety plan.

---

[6] For helpful templates, see http://www.sprc.org/sites/default/files/resource-program/Brown_StanleySafetyPlanTemplate.pdf and http://socialworktech.com/2017/05/16/safety-plan/?v=f24485ae434a.

Even while establishing safety measures, the counselor must seek to validate and grieve over a counselee's experience of suffering. While we must never affirm a desire to take one's life, and we should do whatever we can to prevent tragic action, we must acknowledge the depth of the counselee's despair and distress. As the psalmist noted in Ps 23:4 (ESV), "Even though I walk through the valley of the shadow of death, I will fear no evil, for you are with me," so too is God with a counselee. We must demonstrate that closeness in our care.

Further, we must show compassion. We must not assume the counselee hasn't already wrestled with the morality of their decision. For the suicidal counselee, taking one's life may seem logical. They have reasons for the course of action they are considering. While those reasons might not make sense to us, they make sense to our counselees. Therefore, we must seek to understand their logic, not dismiss it. Why is the counselee considering suicide? What is driving them to that course of action? One counselee might feel hopeless, scared that things will never change. Suicide is a way of escape. Another might feel out of control and unable to change their sinful ways. Taking their own life is something they can control. Or maybe the counselee desires to exercise control over others, manipulating them through threats or even suicide attempts. For this counselee, suicide is a tool. Counselors must understand and directly address heart motives with the appropriate truths of God's Word.

Throughout our sessions, we must often speak the gospel, graciously and firmly exposing lies and wrong desires influencing our counselees. The following passages can aid us in applying God's Word to someone's unique struggle:

- First Corinthians 10:13–14 assures believers we are never tempted beyond what we can bear. Even thoughts of suicide, or strong temptations toward it, are not beyond what we can battle with the help of the Lord.
- Second Corinthians 4:7–18 prompts us to keep an eternal focus in our suffering. While suffering is real and pressing, it is temporal. It will pass away.

- Hebrews 4:12–16 tells us Jesus sympathizes with us in our weaknesses. Jesus faced immense hardship and knows intimately the suffering of our counselees.
- Lamentations 3:22–23 says God's mercies "are new every morning." Each day, then, the counselee can receive those mercies to face the day ahead, including the struggles it brings.
- Psalm 46:1–2 notes that "God is our refuge and strength" (ESV). Because our strength comes from the Lord of hosts, we need not fear, "though the earth trembles."
- Psalm 73:26 says, "God is the strength of my heart, my portion forever" (ESV). This reminds us that in life he guides believers with his counsel, and afterward he will take us up in glory. He receives his children despite their weaknesses.
- John 10:1–18 reminds us that Jesus is our Good Shepherd. It is he who leads us to safety, rest, and provision. He protects and cares for his own, by name.

Throughout counseling, we should lean on three key themes: (1) the hope-giving assurance that God is present, compassionate, merciful, and forgiving; (2) God's sovereign control over a situation despite the chaos one is experiencing; and (3) God's genuine care and concern over his children's struggles. The gospel speaks directly to each of these: Jesus became present on earth, and the Spirit remains present within believers; God pours out mercy on his children because of the cross; he retains control over all things—even the death of his Son; and the crucifixion and resurrection give us everlasting hope. We must not miss the importance of the gospel for those struggling with suicidal thoughts. We must caringly bring these truths to bear on a counselee's specific thoughts, feelings, and desires.

One common theme with suicidality is a counselee's lack of hope in their situation, their feelings, or their struggle. Ultimately, this hopelessness stems from a failure to understand fully who God is, that his sovereignty is good because he is good, and that we each are valuable to him and others. It might also stem from unfulfilled desires, failed dreams, or real-life losses. The wise counselor should explore any faulty ways of thinking or underlying sinful desires that relate to these areas and then directly, compassionately speak God's truth concerning these beliefs and motives.

To do this, the counselor can lead the counselee to read particular passages from the Psalms that deal with hopelessness and God's response in the midst of it (e.g., Pss 34:17–19; 94:1–16; 13:1–6). The counselee might then even find it helpful to write their own psalm, expressing their emotions and concerns frankly to the Lord while applying God's Word to their situation. The person might benefit from meditating on and then journaling prayers about God's present promises to them in passages like Phil 4:19; 2 Pet 1:4; Isa 41:10; and John 14:27. Additionally, the counselor might ask the counselee to memorize and meditate on passages that directly relate to their underlying fears, worries, or grief. The counselee might also journal their thoughts as they arise, then either with or without the counselor, look for patterns of unbelief or wrong thinking, underlying longings/desires, toppled idols, failed dreams, or losses.

Additionally, we should seek to help a counselee think biblically about and respond righteously to their present troubles. We know that sin and brokenness are present realities in this world; suffering abounds. But this world is not our home (Heb 13:14); rather, we Christ followers seek the heavenly city over temporal comfort. Revelation 21:4 reminds us that "[God] will wipe away every tear from [our] eyes. Death will be no more; grief, crying, and pain will be no more, because the previous things [will] have passed away." On that day, the counselee's suffering will cease. Forever. Yet we cannot usher in that kingdom; God holds authority over life, death, and the restoration of his creation. God's promises and provision are sufficient for this life until that restoration comes. Scripture suggests we should live in a healthy balance between hope and longing.

Further, we must remember that the struggles of a counselee are neither new to God nor something they cannot handle with God's help (1 Cor 10:13). We want to help them think and live rightly in light of God's truth. The counselee seeking escape must realize this should not be his ultimate aim; honoring the Lord in the midst of suffering must be. The counselee feeling out of control must come to see the Lord as the sovereign overseer of all things; God is the one in control, not any individual. The manipulative counselee must see their own sin in trying to exercise power over others. In each case, a sinful heart drives suicide attempts and sadly bypasses God's answers by seeking a permanent "solution" to a temporary problem.

We close with a final reminder: ultimately, counselees are responsible for any decisions they make. This is no less the case should someone you counsel choose to take their own life. You can plead with them not to, you can provide guidance, wisdom, prayer, and care, and in some cases you may be able to help them get committed to a hospital for supervision, but you cannot own anyone's choice to end their own life. There is no guarantee that everyone you counsel will heed even the Lord's words.

Self-Harm

What Is Self-Harm?

Self-harm, also called self-injury, is intentional physical harm caused to one's own body. It may include things like cutting one's arms, legs, or stomach, carving words into one's body, hitting oneself with a fist or a hammer, or burning. Self-harm may or may not be related to suicidal ideation; nevertheless, the counselor should assess for risk of suicide in cases of self-harm.

Statistically, self-injury is on the rise and is most common in adolescent and young adult females. Most people who self-harm begin during their teen or preteen years, and nearly half of them have been abused in some way. Many report learning how to injure themselves from "friends" or pro-self-injury websites. The current teen subculture, in fact, in many ways affirms and propagates self-harm as an acceptable method of dealing with problematic emotions or situations. There is a noteworthy correlation in age (teen/preteen) and developmental realities, such as the influx of emotions without fully developed abilities to regulate them (see chapter 38).

Symptoms and Manifestation

Self-harm commonly involves using a knife, razor, scissors, or fingernails to cut into one's skin. Quite often the wounds are hidden on areas of the body that are easily covered (like the arms, thighs, or stomach), given the level of shame associated with this behavior. Typically, self-harm is a regular occurrence that leads to frequent wounds or bruises, though these may not be noticed since they are also frequently concealed.

Understanding the reasons behind these behaviors is pivotal to helping those we counsel. The most common reasons include

- an attempt to stop or cover negative emotional feelings (since self-harm might give a sense of control over one's feelings),
- a desire to at least feel something or to feel alive if experiencing emotional numbness,
- self-punishment,
- an attempt to relieve feelings of emptiness,
- a way to relax, and
- something to do when alone.

To these reasons we might also add a felt need for attention, which often appears in tandem with one or more of the reasons above. The current youth culture seems to give increased attention to these behaviors, and some teens desire to stand out or be viewed a particular way. Unfortunately, having attention placed on them can reinforce their behavior despite any negative connotations associated with it.

Common risk factors include an inability to cope with negative emotions (i.e., difficulty with emotional expression), prior exposure to self-harm behaviors, low levels of self-control or emotional regulation, a lack of a strong support network, and having comorbid mental health struggles such as anxiety or depression.

Counseling Steps and Practical Procedures[7]

Assessment, including an assessment for suicide, is an important aspect of counseling those engaging in self-harm. The counselor should explore the

[7] See Amy Baker, *Relief without Cutting: Taking Your Negative Feelings to God* (Greensboro, NC: New Growth Press, 2011); Julie Ganschow, *A Biblical Understanding of Self-Injury*, 2nd ed. (Kansas City, MO: Pure Water Press, 2013); Jeremy Lelek, *Cutting: A Healing Response* (Phillipsburg, NJ: P&R, 2012); and Edward T. Welch, *Self-Injury: When Pain Feels Good* (Phillipsburg, NJ: P&R, 2004).

counselee's history of injury, the means, frequency, reasons, openness, any triggers or stressors, and any other struggles like depression or anxiety that might be involved. In particular, we should seek to grasp the reasons and motives behind the behaviors, because only when we understand motivation can we get at the heart of the problem. As counselors, we don't want to just stop the behavior, but deal with underlying issues. Typically, conversations with those who harm themselves will focus on the underlying struggles (emotions, motivations), teaching godly means of dealing with stress or emotions, and removing or minimizing stressors when possible.

Specifically, we should address the underlying struggles, feelings, or stressors in a way that understands them rightly and responds to them appropriately in light of God's Word (per boxes 4, 5, and 6 discussed in chapter 10). Self-harm is a sinful response (box 2) to heat (box 1) that reflects sinful underlying heart issues (box 3). We must address all three of these to move counselees toward a response that honors the Lord. While this will look different for each counselee, the progression is the same.

Further, the counselor should urge the person and their family to reduce any access to tools of self-harm, such as knives, razors, or pencils, while acknowledging that this offers limited protection (for instance, the counselee may use her fingernails to inflict wounds). The counselor also can encourage supervision, when possible, and should involve parents with any underage counselee by encouraging them to disclose to their parents directly. The counselor should also document disclosures of self-harm or any suicidal thoughts that might accompany self-abusive actions.

A counselor must be patient since the behaviors mentioned typically won't stop overnight. Like an addiction, self-harm can become a habitual, seemingly "effective" way to cope with stressors/heat the counselee cannot handle. Counseling involves helping the counselee handle their struggles in new and better ways that honor the Lord. Therefore, we must uphold God's Word (John 17:17) as being authoritative over all emotions. What God says about their struggles matters more than how they feel about them. We all must trust the Lord, rather than our own understanding or feelings, as our rest and peace (Matt 11:28–30). The counselor should talk openly and frequently about submission to the Lord and repenting of wrong ways the counselee has handled life. It is sinful to harm oneself, and the counselee must work toward both thinking and acting in ways that please God. In 1 Pet 2:24, we believers are reminded that Jesus Christ bore our sins on the cross so that we might live *and live righteously*. He did the work and it is finished. The Bible reassures the believing counselee engaging in self-harm that living rightly is possible because of what Christ already accomplished on the cross.

Lastly, the Bible speaks at length about the struggles between the flesh and the spirit. In particular, Paul writes in Rom 8:6, "Now the mindset of the flesh is death, but the mindset of the Spirit is life and peace." When we follow the (sinful) desires of our hearts, it only leads to destruction and death. Yet, when our minds are set on the things of God, led by his Spirit, we find life and peace. For the self-harming counselee, life and peace are often missing, but God provides the solution in his Word: setting the heart on him rather than self. The counselor should continually share gospel truths pertinent to this struggle: God is near to the brokenhearted; he gives comfort, hope, and peace; and by his power sinful patterns can be broken. There is hope.

Suggested Growth Assignments

A variety of growth assignments might help those struggling with self-harm. First, a counselee should keep a log of self-harm incidents between sessions. What they record should include setting, triggers, feelings before and after, any coping mechanisms in place, thought patterns, and any discernible motivations or desires. This will allow for better assessment and discussion in the counseling sessions, particularly related to underlying heart issues.

Second, the counselee should meditate on passages such as 1 Cor 6:19–20 ("You are not your own, for you were bought at a price") and Isa 53:5 ("We are healed by his wounds"). In light of Phil 4:8, the believing counselee might benefit from listing biblical truths related to their triggers; for example, "I am his, not my own" (1 Cor 6:19–20) and "Because the Son has set me free, I am free indeed!" (John 8:36). We should also help counselees learn to pray—to talk to the Lord in light of his Word and seek the Spirit's help in fighting temptations. Lastly, growth assignments might involve having a counselee practice other methods of managing their stressors: reading a psalm, praying, and thinking on truthful thoughts as explored above.

Conclusion

We close with a sobering caution. In view of the seriousness of suicide and self-harm, we recommend inexperienced counselors consult with more experienced counselors or supervisors to be better equipped to walk with those who struggle with these life-threatening issues. Counseling in suicide and self-harm cases is often complex and requires patience, compassion, and wisdom, yet also direct, loving confrontation. Ultimately, the aim is to help the counselee move toward a proper, God-honoring response to their struggles.

Addictions and Enslaving Sins

Counseling involves verbal communication. The language we use matters. How we label a presenting problem carries implications for how we both assess the problem and counsel the person. No counseling issue illustrates this dynamic more clearly than "addiction." Besides the word *addiction*, our culture uses an array of terms: *disease*, *chemical dependency*, *substance abuse*, *codependency*, and a variety of words ending with -*aholic*, -*aholism*, or *mania* (e.g., *shopaholics*, *kleptomania*). The *DSM-5* devotes over a hundred pages to a wide range of "Substance-Related and Addictive Disorders," including gambling.[1] While these cultural and psychiatric terms sometimes add descriptive value, they largely proceed from unbiblical anthropological assumptions, they carry unwarranted connotations of medical causality, and they evoke unbiblical counseling strategies.

Biblical Perspectives

While not using the term "addiction," the Bible addresses its dynamics through the concept of enslaving sin. At the same time, given the popular use of addiction language, wise biblical counselors don't prematurely correct a counselee's words but instead show them how Scripture provides a

[1] *DSM-5*, 481–589 (see chap. 9, n. 7).

better way to understand and solve the problem.[2] Given its prominence, we focus in this chapter on slavery to alcohol, but we recognize the principles below (e.g., lack of self-control and destructive impact) apply to all forms of addiction (e.g., gambling, gaming, shopping, and tobacco).

Biblical View of Alcohol

Let's begin by distinguishing between alcohol use and abuse.[3] Scripture does not prohibit the moderate, self-controlled use of alcohol (Col 2:16–23; 1 Tim 4:1–5). It was a standard beverage in the biblical world, its provision often seen as a blessing from God (Deut 32:14; Ps 104:14–15; Isa 55:1; Joel 2:24; Amos 9:13; Matt 11:16–19; Luke 7:33–34; John 2:1–10), including as a medicinal treatment (1 Tim 5:23). At the same time, believers must limit their liberty when it might hurt the sensitive consciences of weaker brothers and sisters (not pharisaical believers) who might imitate stronger believers and thereby violate their own consciences (Rom 14–15; 1 Cor 8–10).

Yet the same Bible condemns the abuse of alcohol. We find biblical examples of drunkenness (e.g., Noah in Genesis 9; Lot in Genesis 19; Nabal in 1 Samuel 25), biblical prohibitions (Isa 5:11; Luke 21:34; Rom 13:13–14; 1 Cor 5:11; 6:10; Gal 5:21; Eph 5:18; 1 Pet 4:3); and biblical descriptions of its destructive impact (Prov 20:1; 23:19–21, 29–35; 31:4–7; Isa 28:7–8; Hab 2:15). These latter passages sound eerily like the descriptions in addiction literature. For this reason, counselors should urge addicts to abstain from all forms of an addictive substance. Believers must be filled with the Holy Spirit, not intoxicating substances, and bear the Spirit's fruit of self-control and sober-mindedness (Prov 25:28; Gal 5:22–23; Eph 5:15–18).

---

[2] To think biblically about addiction, start with Edward T. Welch, *Addictions: A Banquet in the Grave: Finding Hope in the Power of the Gospel* (Phillipsburg, NJ: P&R, 2001). See also Mark E. Shaw, *The Heart of Addiction: A Biblical Perspective* (Bemidji, MN: Focus, 2008); Richard Baxter (1615–1691), *The Practical Works of Richard Baxter*, vol. 1, *A Christian Directory* (Ligonier, PA: Soli Deo Gloria, 1990), 309–30; and David R. Dunham, *Addictive Habits: Changing for Good* (Phillipsburg, NJ: P&R, 2018).

[3] On the Bible's view of alcohol and its implications for Christians, see Wayne Grudem, *Christian Ethics: An Introduction to Biblical Moral Reasoning* (Wheaton, IL: Crossway, 2018), 675–96.

Defining Addiction

How should we understand addiction? Ed Welch provides a theologically rich definition: "Arising out of our alienation from the Living God, addiction is bondage to the rule of a substance, activity, or state of mind, which then becomes the center of life, defending itself from the truth so that even bad consequences don't bring repentance, and leading to further estrangement from God."[4] This definition captures six dynamics:

1. The root problem is alienation from God. Addiction is primarily a vertical problem, a worship disorder, an attempt to live independently from the Lord.

2. Addiction includes bondage to any substance, activity, or state of mind, including human praise, bodily thinness, or work productivity. While our culture predominantly uses addiction language for substance abuse, the term covers addictions to sex, food, exercise, love, sports, politics, sleep, work, the lottery, gambling, pornography, TV, video games, and shopping.

3. The addictive behavior becomes "the center of life." Biblical counselors sometimes refer to addiction as a "life-dominating" sin, affecting every aspect of daily living. That treasured substance, activity, or state of mind magnetizes hearts.

4. The enslaving sin "defends itself from the truth," resisting the life-giving entrance of God's Word. It repels all biblical truths that might shrivel and kill it. Passages like Romans 6 become paradigmatic for the struggle of the kingdom of sin, darkness, and slavery versus the kingdom of righteousness, light, and freedom. It also presents the vital interplay between initial sanctification (e.g., our new identity in Christ) and progressive sanctification (e.g., putting to death our remaining flesh).

5. This stubborn resistance to God's truth becomes shockingly irrational when "even bad consequences don't bring repentance." Despite arguments and evidences we might (and should) marshal to persuade counselees to turn from sin, they love their addiction more than their health, family, reputation, and job, and sadly, more than their God.

---

[4] Welch, *Addictions*, 35. The first clause, "Arising from our alienation from the Living God," comes from Gary S. Shogren and Edward T. Welch, *Running in Circles: How to Find Freedom from Addictive Behavior* (Grand Rapids: Baker, 1995), 27.

6. The opposition to God's truth in turn leads to "further estrangement from God's kingdom." Addictive behaviors typically degenerate and spiral downward.

Of course, in our alcoholism-as-disease culture, biblical counselors might find even their Christian counselees resist the biblical view of addiction as sin. This calls us to broaden and deepen a counselee's understanding of sin as more than deliberated willed choices (see chapter 6).

Why does the unbiblical alcohol-as-disease viewpoint seem so inviting, even for those who understand they are making moral choices? Welch helpfully alerts us to two metaphors for sin that express the experience of addiction: (1) sin as an attacking beast crouching at the door ready to spring on you and maul you (Gen 4:7; 1 Pet 5:7), and (2) sin as an illness or disease (Isa 1:5–7).[5] Recall in chapter 6 the images that describe the active, degenerative, predatory nature of sin. It enslaves, overtakes, and burdens people. Addiction can feel like "something outside [us] has taken over [us]."[6]

A biblical dynamic that captures an addict's experience is their simultaneous condition as willful rebels and unwilling slaves. The following table describes these dual, concurrent realities:

God sees addicts as both willful rebels and unwilling slaves, and he responds with both anger and compassion. For those who turn to Christ in faith, God graciously justifies and forgives and regenerates and progressively sanctifies (cf. Rom 5:6–11).

Counseling Strategies

How should biblical counselors help those who seek counsel for their addiction problems, whether they involve substance abuse or other forms of behavioral sin? Several methods can be employed:

[5] Welch, *Addictions*, 60–61.

[6] Welch, 33.

The Twofold Condition of Addicts: Rebels and *Slaves*

REBEL	SLAVE
The Addict's Felt Experience	
Willful, "I want to"	"Against" my will, "I can't help it"
In control	Out of control, controlled
Choosing, calculating, premeditated	Blind, confused, spontaneous, "victimized," seized
Overreactions in Our Culture and Sometimes in the Church	
Moralism, superiority, behaviorism	Disease models, victim models
Instantaneous change, "Just Say 'No!'"	"Incurable sickness," lifelong therapy, "once an addict, always an addict"
God's Attitude and Response	
Divine anger, righteous wrath	Divine pity, sympathetic compassion
Addicts as responsible, disobedient	Addicts as enslaved, mastered
God justifies and forgives	God regenerates and progressively sanctifies
Key Passages	
1 Cor 6:9–11; 1 John 3:4; Isa 53:6	1 Cor 6:12–20; 2 Tim 2:22–26; Titus 3:3–8
Both dynamics appear in Prov 5:21–23; John 8:12, 31–36; Rom 6:15–23; 7:14–25; Eph 2:1–3; 4:17–24	

View Counselees as Fellow Strugglers and Fellow Sinners

Effective addiction counseling begins with you recognizing that you wrestle with sin's enslaving power too; thus, you need the same Savior and same grace your counselees do. So, counselor, ask yourself these questions:

- *How well do I admit my sin patterns?* While your sinful habits might not be as severe in consequences and may even be socially acceptable, the difference between you and even the most troubled counselee is one of degree, not kind.
- *How well am I fighting in the power of God's Spirit against my addictive temptations? What success am I experiencing?*
- *To what degree do I look at myself as being no better than my addicted counselee? Do I really believe the only reason I am not similarly enslaved is God's mercy?*

The following passages powerfully challenge any sense of moral superiority or self-righteousness we might inadvertently bring to sessions:

- Luke 18:9–11: Self-righteousness produces judgmentalism and disdain. The only thing worse than being a robber, evildoer, adulterer, or tax collector—or an addict—is being *proud* you are not one.
- Titus 3:1–3: Show gentleness to all people—including addicts—because ("for," v. 3) you too were once "enslaved by various passions and pleasures."
- 1 Corinthians 10:12: Don't arrogantly assume you are immune to every form of addictive temptation.
- 2 Timothy 2:24–26: Only God can grant repentance and free people from sin.

Give Counselees the Abundant Hope Jesus Provides

Jesus provides every addict with hope through his Word, his Spirit, and his church. Working through John 8 with a counselee struggling with addiction can bring that powerful hope right into the counseling room:

- 8:1–11 offers a simple one-two message: sinful behavior is indeed sinful, but the Lord offers forgiveness and calls people to stop their sin.
- 8:12 presents Jesus as "the light of the world." Addiction, with its inherent evil and its denials and lies, reflects moral darkness (cf. John 1:1–18; 1 John 1:5–10).
- 8:31–36 brings four crucial truths that prove especially useful in a first and second session: (1) True discipleship involves persevering in gospel truth. (2) This gospel truth frees people from slavery. (3) All sin has enslaving force. (4) Christ the Son of God brings true freedom. Both God's Word (v. 32) and God's Son (v. 36) liberate addicts from enslaving sin. As Paul puts it in 2 Cor 3:17, "Now the Lord is the Spirit, and where the Spirit of the Lord is, there is freedom."

Labor to Create an Atmosphere of Hope, Love, Acceptance, and Honesty

Such an atmosphere encourages counselees to be honest about their addiction. Emphasize the Bible's stress on truthfulness (Exod 20:16; Lev 19:11; Ps 15:2–4; Prov 6:17, 19; 12:19; 17:7; 21:6; John 8:44; Eph 4:25; Col 3:9) and on God as the One who does not lie (Ps 33:4–5; Num 23:19; Titus 1:2; Heb 6:18). Like all sinners, addicts cover their sins. To help them, we must value honesty and truthfulness even above the behavioral "success" of outward sobriety or purity. We might tell them, "It is better for you to be honest with me, even if you stumble or relapse, than to pretend all's well. If you minimize the extent of or hide your relapses, I can't help you. If you let me in, I won't reject you. We can work *together* to help you fight against temptations."

First John 1:5–2:2 speaks powerfully to this reality, offering a glimpse of what honest ownership of sin looks like and promising gospel hope. Note within the passage below my (Bob's) added *bracketed* insights for biblical counselors:

> This is the message we have heard from him and declare to you: God is light, and there is absolutely no darkness in him. *[Start with God's character as light, with no darkness.]* If we say, "We have fellowship with him," and yet we walk in darkness, we are lying and are not practicing the truth. [*Hidden sins are incompatible with walking in God's light.*] If we walk in the light as he himself is in the light, we have fellowship with one another, and the blood of Jesus his Son cleanses us from all sin. [*We should walk in the light, with the promise of one-another fellowship and cleansing from our sin.*] If we say, "We have no sin," we are deceiving ourselves, and the truth is not in us. [*Walking in the light requires honesty, not sinlessness.*] If we confess our sins, he is faithful and righteous to forgive us our sins and to cleanse us from all unrighteousness. [*This includes confession, aided by the assurance of forgiving and cleansing grace.*] If we say, "We have not sinned," we make him a liar, and his word is not in us. [*Again, honesty, not sinlessness.*]
>
> My little children, I am writing you these things so that you may not sin. [*God commands purity and sobriety.*] But if anyone does sin, we have an advocate with the Father—Jesus Christ the righteous one. [*God knows the presence and power of our remaining sin, so he provides a Savior who pleads his righteousness, not our goodness or sobriety.*] He himself is the atoning sacrifice for our sins, and not only for ours, but also for those of the whole world. [*That Savior's sacrifice continues to supply grace to all who belong to him.*]

Understand the Nature of the Enslaving Substance, Habit, or Practice

While the Internet can provide information, it's more helpful to have a medical professional or addictions expert to contact. In some cases, the physical addiction or medical complications are so severe that inpatient, medically-supervised treatment is required (e.g., for substance abuse, disordered eating). If so, biblical counselors should continue to provide spiritual oversight and guide counselees in inpatient and outpatient choices.

In the psychiatric world, substance abuse is considered a brain disease. However, while addictive behavior involving substances can produce medical consequences, to argue for biological causation ignores our dualistic (heart and body) nature (see chapter 5).[7]

Understand the Specific Patterns of Your Counselees' Addictions

Gather a lot of information. When do they indulge? What do they consume? How often? For how long? At what times in the day? On what occasions? When alone or with others? Who knows about the addiction? What motivates them? What are their emotional moods before, during, and after indulging? To what degree are they conscious of God's presence? Assigning and discussing an Evaluating Problem Patterns chart (provided at the close of this chapter) can help. Our six-box model in chapter 14 can aid in organizing information.

Help Counselees See Their Addictions Accurately

To successfully fight against sin, addicts must personally own several key truths:

- My addictive behavior is something for which I am morally responsible. It's not a disease or sickness, although it might feel that way and voices in my culture tell me that.
- My addictive behavior comes from my heart, what I worship, treasure, and live for.

---

[7] In the article "What Is a Substance Use Disorder?," the American Psychiatric Association states this starkly: "Changes in the brain's structure and function are what cause people to have intense cravings, changes in personality, abnormal movements, and other behaviors. . . . Addiction is a complex, but treatable, disease that affects brain function and behavior," December 2020, https://www.psychiatry.org/patients-families/addiction/what-is-addiction. While genetics might play a role in some cases, there is to date no solid medical evidence for addictions having genetic causes. See "Genetics of Alcohol Use Disorder," National Institute of Alcohol Abuse and Alcoholism, November 4, 2008, https://www.niaaa.nih.gov/alcohol-health/overview-alcohol-consumption/alcohol-use-disorders/genetics-alcohol-use-disorders.

- My addictive behavior reflects both the rebellious and enslaving nature of sin, and that dual dynamic explains why I feel both responsible and helpless.
- My addictive behavior brings destructive consequences on myself and others.
- My addictive behavior put Christ on the cross, but he rose from the dead to offer me forgiveness and power to break my enslaving sin.

Overcoming addictive behavior requires a warfare mentality. It's a long-term fight. We must be active, vigilant, and violent against our sin. This includes removing access to substances and implementing other forms of radical amputation (Matt 5:29–30). We learn to know the Lord more deeply *in* the battle as opposed to growing only *after* we defeat addictive sin.

Present Christ and Lead Counselees to Confess Their Sin, Know Christ's Forgiveness, and Rely on Christ's Spirit and Provisions

Help each person treasure Jesus for daily grace and progressive growth. Despite various problems with the secular recovery approaches, their "one day at a time" mentality reflects the biblical reality of temptation and remaining sin. We must offer Christ-centered hope and the fullness of God's provisions of grace (Romans 5–8; 1 John 1:5–2:2; Exod 2:23–25; 3:7–10; 1 Cor 6:9–11). Help your believing counselee see not only what their sin did to their Savior on the cross, but what their Savior did to their sin.

Help Counselees Address the Root Sin(s) That Underlie Their Addictive Behavior

Since sinful words and actions flow from our sinful hearts, we must not settle for simplistic abstinence, "just-stop-it," or "just-say-no" approaches. Consider five heart demands that might motivate drunkenness:

- Escapism. Counselees seek to anesthetize emotionally-painful realities or conflicted relationships.

- People-pleasing. Ruled by the fear of people, counselees seek to please their peers who pressure them to drink.
- Revenge. Counselees angrily pursue a self-centered path, knowing it will hurt that friend, parent, or spouse who hurt them.
- Pleasure-seeking. Counselees crave the high or other components that go with partying.
- Social rebellion. Counselees know their families or churches forbid drinking, but they do it anyway as a form of protest.

One or more of these, or even several others not listed, might describe your counselee's beliefs and motives. Moreover, their root issues can shift as the enslaving sin increasingly dominates.

Understand How Addictions Can Dominate Every Sphere of Life, and Work toward Helping Counselees Restructure Their Entire Lives

What impact can addictions bring?

- They compromise relationships; addiction affects how addicts relate to others.
- In the case of drugs or alcohol, they jeopardize the addict's health, not only because of the chemicals they are ingesting, but because of sleep disruptions and other physical complications caused by the addiction or even the treatment. Moreover, addicts sometimes pay insufficient attention to their physical well-being, including avoidance of routine medical appointments to hide their addictions.
- Addictions endanger employment. If an addict hasn't lost their job already, then missed workdays, lower productivity, or failed test results soon might place it at risk.
- Addictions hurt finances: the high cost of the addictive substances, treatment expenses, and possible job loss, unpaid leave, etc., coupled with lack of self-control, can take a heavy toll on an individual's financial outlook. Financial safeguards, such as fixed budgets and spending limits, might need to be set or even imposed

to insure provisions for the addict's family (1 Thess 4:11–12; 1 Tim 5:8).

- Above all, an addict's relationship with God suffers.

The life-dominating nature of these sins often requires a greater number of sessions than usual. In severe cases, receiving residential care might give addicts a valuable fresh start.

Care for and Minister to the Addicted Person's Family

While it's wise to help the family members of any counselee, such investment is especially needed in addiction cases because of the extensive, life-dominating impact of an addict's behavior.

Direct Counselees to Full Participation in the Life of Their Local Churches

Urge addicts to participate in God-centered corporate worship, along with small group life and other community means of grace. Rich gospel hymns and songs can fuel their faith and give them a fresh glimpse of Someone more glorious than that substance, activity, or state of mind that competes for their affection. Jesus is bigger than any drug of choice.

Establish a Plan for Accountability and Mobilize the Body of Christ to Help

Counselees need to connect with at least one or two same-gender, mature Christians to provide encouragement and accountability, especially in times of intense temptation. Biblical counselors can help select people, convene them with the counselee in a session, and give direction.

In addition, well-managed addiction support groups and recovery programs can provide a safe place for program members to discuss their habits and temptations and seek help; this makes them a valuable resource for the addicts who come to us. Caring sponsors who are recovered addicts provide accountability, support, and guidance to members. While groups like Alcoholics Anonymous and Narcotics Anonymous provide these benefits and are better than nothing, their secularity or quasi-religiosity can be counterproductive to Christ-centered change. Evangelical Christian versions (e.g., Celebrate Recovery) that present Jesus and encourage Christian spirituality are better, although they might not synchronize completely with a biblical counseling approach. Church-based ministries using biblical counseling resources provide the best option.[8] We pray that local churches committed to biblical counseling will increasingly function as spiritual hospitals for every member struggling with enslaving sin.

Point Counselees to Christ's Ultimate Future Deliverance

Our sufficient Bible recognizes the insufficiency of even the best biblical counseling. Thankfully, it guarantees the full, final, and future transformation the Redeemer will bring to his people when he returns (1 Pet 1:3–5, 13; 1 John 3:1–2; Rev 7:9–17; 21–22; see also chapter 10). Here's the hope we can voice:

> One day, my brother/sister in Christ, your fight will end. When you see him, you will be like him. Your remaining sin will disappear, your heart will be perfected, your sinful cravings will vanish. There will be no more worldly or satanic temptations. Until then, persevere by faith. Bank your ultimate hope on Christ's future, final deliverance, and let that hope fuel your present faith, love, and obedience.

Conclusion

Despite the claims of our culture, at its core addiction is not a medical problem. It's a heart problem, the problem of enslaving sin (John 8:34). We find the answer to it in the freeing power of the Son, his Word, and his Spirit (John 8:32, 36; 2 Cor 3:17)—in this life and ultimately in the better life to come.

---

[8] See, for example, Edward T. Welch, *Crossroads: A Step-By-Step Guide Away from Addiction, Study Guide* (Greensboro: New Growth Press, 2008). A facilitator's guide is also available.

Evaluating Problem Patterns Chart

Name ____

Problem ________________________________ Date __________

In the chart below, place a T (temptation) or O (occurrence) for each temptation or occurrence of the problem. Add a number next to the T or O to reference and evaluate that entry on the next page. (Use additional pages if necessary.) Place the date at the top of each day (e.g., *Mon* – 11/3).

	Mon –	*Tue* –	*Wed* –	*Thu* –	*Fri* –	*Sat* –	*Sun* –
6:00 a.m.							
6:30							
7:00							
7:30							
8:00							
8:30							
9:00							
9:30							
10:00							
10:30							
11:00							
11:30							
12:00 p.m.							
12:30							

1:00							
1:30							
2:00							
2:30							
3:00							
3:30							
4:00							
4:30							
5:00							
5:30							
6:00 p.m.							
6:30							
7:00							
7:30							
8:00							
8:30							
9:00							
9:30							
10:00							
10:30							
11:00							
11:30							

Evaluating Your Incidents Charted on Page One

	Situation, triggers, events	Behavior: What you did, said, felt (emotions), etc.	Beliefs and motives: What you thought, wanted, etc.	Results, consequences, what happened
1				
2				
3				
4				
5				
6				

On a separate page, list your takeaway insights, lessons learned, challenges, and changes you need to make. Then include a written prayer (and pray it) asking for the Lord's help, forgiveness, wisdom, and strength.

Eating Disorders

At fifteen, Tabitha is an accomplished ballet dancer. She's also a perfectionist. Every movement she makes draws attention to her body, so she wants it to look flawless. To maintain what she believes to be perfect, she began skipping meals. After a few months of that, she couldn't remember what it was like to eat a full meal three times a day. Her body began to become ill, physically rejecting food any time she ate "too much."

Derrick is a wrestler, and a good one at that. But to maintain his weight class, he must be conscious of what he eats. As Derrick gets better and better, more pressure comes. He finds himself fasting before matches, then throwing up after the meals he does eat. He has noticed lately he has had less energy, but that seems a fair price to pay to win.

Brittany is seventeen but essentially has been on her own since she was a young child. Her father left when she was an infant, and her mother had a string of live-in boyfriends. Brittany was neglected often, and several of her mother's boyfriends molested her when they were under her mom's roof. She felt out of control and alone. As she grew, she realized that one thing she could control was how she looked; she did this through her eating habits. Today Brittany weighs just ninety-five pounds.

What Qualifies as an Eating Disorder?

In each scenario above, we see an instance of disordered eating. Though the situational heat in each case varies, the disordered eating stems from an improper belief about food (bad root, box 3). In all three cases, the person uses food to achieve something they desire, whether it be perfection, success, or control.

Yet, as we consider the cases, we find that each of them is complex. The experience of disordered eating is wholistic; there are inner- and outer-person issues at play, bad roots leading to similar bad fruit. In the physical realm, there are consequences for a lack of eating: low energy, chronic fatigue, and ultimately a weight that cannot be safely maintained. In the mental and spiritual realm, specific thoughts and underlying motivations and desires contribute to the disordered eating. These often express themselves emotionally, with anxiety or depression over food intake.

Disordered eating, very simply, is the misuse of food to accomplish some sort of goal: a certain body type or weight, control, coping with difficult emotions, a response to trauma, and so on. This misuse might involve undereating or overeating,[1] as well as a form of "compensation" for overeating. Additionally, there is a high rate of comorbidity with other disorders. More than half (56.2 percent) of respondents formally diagnosed with anorexia nervosa, 94.5 percent with bulimia nervosa, and 78.9 percent with binge eating disorder met criteria for at least one of the core *DSM-5* disorders, the most common being some type of anxiety disorder.[2] Another study also showed that over a third of studied ado-

---

[1] For biblical counseling resources relating to undereating, see Ed Welch, *Eating Disorders: The Quest for Thinness* (Greensboro, NC: New Growth Press, 2008); and John D. Street and Janie Street, "Eating Disorder: Anorexia," *The Biblical Counseling Guide for Women* (Eugene, OR: Harvest House, 2016), 135–51. A particularly helpful secular resource for understanding medical ramifications (66–79) and various theoretical approaches, along with suggested treatment plans (83–107, 150–74) is Carlos M. Grilo and James E. Mitchell, eds., *The Treatment of Eating Disorders: A Clinical Handbook* (New York: Guilford Press, 2011). While this chapter focuses on undereating, Scripture says a lot about the sin of gluttony. For a starter counseling booklet, see Michael Emlet, *Overeating: When Enough Isn't Enough* (Greensboro, NC: New Growth Press, 2020).

[2] "Eating Disorders," National Institute of Mental Health, updated November 2017, https://www.nimh.nih.gov/health/statistics/eating-disorders.shtml.

lescents with an eating disorder (ages twelve to twenty-two, 92 percent female) had experienced some sort of traumatic event related to the disordered eating.[3] What does this mean for counselors? Eating disorders are complex and often accompanied by some other significant life struggle, such as anxiety, depression, or a traumatic experience. Our approach to caring for counselees with eating disorders must also be complex and comprehensive.

There are three commonly known eating disorders, though disordered eating goes beyond these three. First, anorexia nervosa (AN) is the practice of restricting food intake; it is characterized by extreme thinness, a pursuit of increased thinness, and a distorted self-image highly influenced by perception of body weight or shape. Alongside the comorbid conditions mentioned above, a significantly higher rate of suicide accompanies anorexia—indeed it's higher than with other disorders. The effects of AN range from health issues like thinning bones, anemia, muscle weakness, and low blood pressure to heart problems, organ failure, fatigue, and infertility.

Bulimia nervosa (BN) is a lack of self-control through overeating large amounts, followed by behavior that compensates for the overeating (vomiting, taking laxatives, fasting, exercising, etc.), with the counselee generally maintaining a relatively healthy body weight. The effects of BN are like those of AN, but also include throat and teeth issues, acid reflux, GI problems, dehydration, and an electrolyte imbalance, specifically because of purging behaviors.

Lastly, binge-eating disorder (BED) is also a lack of self-control through overeating large amounts, but there is no purging that follows like there is with BN. Most counselees in this category are overweight, given the lack of purging. Like AN and BN, BED has significant side effects, though they are less severe than the other forms. They include eating even when full to the point of discomfort, eating alone, and frequent dieting to compensate for weight gain.

---

[3] Ashley A. Hicks White, Keely J. Pratt, and Casey Cottrill, "The Relationship between Trauma and Weight Status among Adolescents in Eating Disorder Treatment," *Appetite* 129 (2010): 62–69.

In all three forms, sufferers will often struggle with issues like distress, shame, guilt, embarrassment, withdrawal, and isolation.

What Does the Bible Say about Disordered Eating?

The Scriptures are full of references to food, from the provision of it in the garden of Eden to the wedding feast in Revelation, and there are important key ideas that the Bible draws out about eating. Most clearly, the Bible indicates that food is given as physical sustenance from the Lord, for our good (Ps 104:14–15; Eccl 9:7; Gen 9:3). For the counselee struggling with disordered eating, these teachings directly contradict any beliefs that food is harmful, toxic, or something to be avoided.

Further, all that we do is done before a holy God, so how we view and eat food can and should intentionally be to honor God. What we eat and why matters. Paul writes in 1 Cor 10:31, "Whether you eat or drink, or whatever you do, do everything for the glory of God." Bringing glory to God is an integral part of being a believer. We should also eat with joy and thanksgiving, rejecting ascetic or legalistic attitudes (1 Tim 4:3–5). For the counselee struggling with disordered eating, the Bible's teaching must be at the heart of counseling.

While Scripture doesn't directly describe anorexia or bulimia, it powerfully addresses the heart beliefs and motives that lead to disordered eating. Consider these common root issues:

A Distorted Sense of Self or the Body

Quite often, counselees struggling with an eating disorder do not view themselves properly. They might distort how they see themselves physically in a mirror or push themselves to be thinner and thinner, placing their value in their appearance or weight. A Christian counselee might view their own body as something to be controlled or used to accomplish some end, rather than seeing it as the dwelling place of the Holy Spirit (1 Cor 6:19–20), bought at a price by Christ (Rom 14:7–8).

Misplaced Identity

Many who struggle with disordered eating place their identity in their physical bodies, rather than seeing themselves as both body and soul. They wrongly believe they have less worth if they do not conform to a desired physical ideal. Scripture is clear: one's identity comes from being an image bearer of God (Gen 1:27); believers are new creations in Christ (2 Cor 5:17).

Self-Idolatry

Ultimately, all sin boils down to idolatry, typically of self. Eating disorders are no exception. The counselee often elevates an ideal self above a healthy, God-honoring self. That ideal self might stem from the counselee's own view of how they should be or might be highly influenced by the thoughts of family members, peers, or cultural or media images.

Fear of People

Many counselees who struggle with disordered eating find themselves driven primarily by what they think others think of them. Yet Heb 13:6 reminds us believers in particular that we have nothing to fear from others (what they think of us or how they might respond to us); rather, "we can confidently say, 'The Lord is my helper'" (ESV). Paul gives us a powerful reminder in Gal 1:10: "If I were still trying to please people, I would not be a servant of Christ." We cannot please both God and others—not even ourselves.

Lack of Control, but a Sense of Being Overpowered

Many with an eating disorder report feeling unable to control their urges, particularly with regard to overeating or purging. While we understand that the sinful nature remains in believers, and therefore the struggle with sin is ongoing, the Bible teaches that believers are set free from that bondage (Gal 5:1). Scripture also speaks at length about being sober-minded

(1 Pet 5:8), self-controlled (Titus 2:12; 2 Tim 1:7), and free from enslavement to sin (John 8:36; 1 Cor 6:12).

Misplaced Contentment

Like many sinful habits, disordered eating stems in many ways from a lack of contentment. That contentment might be found in a desired appearance or weight or in the ability to control one's circumstances, and thus can only be found once those goals are obtained. This misplaced contentment is sinful, as it supplants God as our contentment.

Improper Response to Stress or Anxiety

While stress is a normal part of life, disordered eating might arise in response to what seems to be overwhelming stress or anxiety. This is tied closely, at times, to feeling a lack of control over one's circumstances. A struggling young man or woman begins to habitually use food to cope with difficult emotions instead of dealing with their worries in a way that honors the Lord.

Improper Response to Trauma or Crisis

Since over a third of adolescents with an eating disorder have experienced some traumatic event, your counselee's disorder might have arisen in direct response to a crisis. Rather than running to the Father, the counselee sought to cope with the situation through their eating habits.

While these various sinful beliefs and desires of the heart (box 3 roots) ultimately drive disordered eating, some researchers assert that eating disorders might also have biological underpinning, an underlying genetic predisposition that combines with environmental influences (e.g., adverse life events) as two forms of box 1 heat.[4] Some research

[4] Suzanne E. Mazzeo and Cynthia M. Bullock, "Environmental and Genetic Risk Factors for Eating Disorders: What the Clinician Needs to Know," National Center for

shows that for some who overeat, the brain no longer triggers feelings of fullness, making it more difficult to regulate intake.[5] For others, particularly after long periods of not eating, resuming food intake causes physical discomfort.

As biblical counselors, we should view these studies cautiously, given the limits of research. Yet we should not be surprised if clearer evidence emerges of links between genetics and eating disorders. As we saw in chapter 6, our fallen bodies can play a role in various sin struggles, perhaps even influencing counselees toward disordered eating. However, you should not assume *a particular* counselee has a genetic disposition. Moreover, you must not view it as a *cause* of disordered eating—causation comes from the heart—or view it as something that relieves the counselee of personal responsibility or lessens their ability to change.

Finally, as the gospel declares, the believer has been set free from the bondage of sin. While the effects of sin remain and the battle with sin continues throughout life, the Christian is no longer enslaved (Gal 5:1; 1 Cor 6:12). The counselee struggling with disordered eating need not be controlled by it; rather, there is hope found in the freeing power of Jesus and the Spirit dwelling within.

Counseling Steps and Practical Procedures

Consider Whether the Counselee Needs Medical or Nutritional Treatment

First, recognize that an eating disorder affects all parts of the struggling counselee, the physical and the spiritual. If seeking to care for a counselee with a more significant eating disorder, it is wise to involve a medical

---

Biotechnology Information, https://www.ncbi.nlm.nih.gov/pmc/articles/PMC2719561/. This source discusses growing evidence obtained through family and twin studies that risk factors do not cause but increase the tendency toward an eating disorder and what that means for clinical practice.

[5] Wade Berrettini, "The Genetics of Eating Disorders," National Center for Biotechnology Information, November 2004, https://www.ncbi.nlm.nih.gov/pmc/articles/PMC3010958/.

professional and most likely a nutritionist too.[6] Depending on the severity of their condition, the physician might hospitalize them or refer them to a residential facility, since treatment in a facility can provide consistent oversight, regulation of intake/output, and ongoing counseling. These facilities can address all aspects of the counselee as a part of treatment. This is not to say, however, that you as a biblical counselor must refer and not care directly for your counselee; instead, you should evaluate your potential role based on personal competency level and by also considering who else might contribute positively to the struggle.

Be Aware of Intake and Output

Seek to help your counselee regulate food intake and output *wisely* and *appropriately*. This might include having the counselee eat in the presence of others or be accompanied to the grocery store or to restaurants. Eventually, they might need help with diet regulation or changes in tracking intake and output. It simply will not suffice to tell a counselee to "eat more" or "stop purging." That approach is largely ineffective. Rather, it is wise to exercise great patience in this area, focusing first on thought patterns and beliefs before seeking to radically change behaviors. Only when you address their underlying roots (box 3) will their external fruit (box 2, eating habits) change.

Focus on Motivations and Desires

Given that the biblical counselor will be most equipped to speak to the inner person, to heart issues, we should focus on a few key areas. First, lovingly challenge the believing counselee's misplaced desires and identity, drawing from the discussion above. Focus on who they are in Christ, the role of the Spirit, a biblical perception of self, and progressive sanctification. The counselee can

[6] See Hayley Satrom, "A Three-Pronged Team Approach When Caring for People with Eating Disorders," Biblical Counseling Coalition, March 3, 2015, https://www.biblicalcounselingcoalition.org/2015/03/03/a-three-pronged-team-approach-when-caring-for-people-with-eating-disorders/.

memorize, meditate on, and pray through passages like 1 Cor 6:19–20; 10:31; Matt 6:25–33; Ps 104:14–15; Eccl 9:7; and 1 Tim 4:3–5. You might ask the counselee to keep a journal or food diary to track both external expressions like behaviors (eating, purging, and avoidance of situations) and internal expressions such as thoughts and desires (urges, fears, motivations, and thought patterns). Then you can work through areas of struggle together.

For example, if the counselee struggles with control, you can help them recognize that tendency and learn more appropriate responses. This, however, comes after helping them understand the proper place of control versus trust in the Lord. Or, if the counselee, like Tabitha and Derrick, introduced at the start of this chapter, is aiming to look a certain way and maintain a certain weight to partake in activities they enjoy, gently identify potential heart idols that need to be set aside and repented of. In each case, and countless other examples we might explore, the aim is to get to the heart issues that have led to a particular sinful expression.

Evaluate Struggles Listed above and Work through as Appropriate

Help your counselee identify underlying struggles, such as a fear of people, a felt lack of control, or misplaced identity. Then bring them applicable truths from God's Word, like these:

- We do not need to fear what others think of us; our only aim should be to bring honor to Christ (Gal 1:10; Ps 118:8; Isa 2:22).
- True value comes not from outward appearances but from being adopted into God's family (Eph 1:3–6; Ps 139:13–15).
- Our outward bodies are wasting away, but believers' bodies will one day be restored (2 Cor 4:16–18; Phil 3:20–21).
- Our God is sovereign over all things; we are not (Prov 21:1; 19:21; Job 42:2).

Help the Counselee Think on Scripture Regularly

Given that disordered eating often involves wrong thinking, you can use passages like Phil 4:4–9 to help a counselee think biblically and therefore respond appropriately (boxes 5 and 6). In verse 4, the apostle invites his readers to "rejoice in the Lord." How well does your counselee grasp the gospel and find ultimate joy in Jesus and his saving grace? Verse 5 reminds us that "the Lord is near." How conscious is your counselee of God's presence with her as she faces pressures in her life and is tempted to run to or away from food in disordered ways? Verse 6 encourages her to replace her anxiety—even if connected to eating disorders—with prayer, seeking God's help and thanking God for his grace. Verse 7 then makes her a promise: God's peace will guard her heart and mind, bringing her inner stability amid her confusion. Verse 8 invites her to focus her mind on "whatever is true, whatever is honorable, whatever is just, whatever is pure, whatever is lovely, whatever is commendable," which includes the biblical truths about eating we saw earlier. Verse 9 adds a call to obedience, prompting your counselee to follow Christ in light of gospel realities. She can spend time meditating on and applying this passage to her struggle.

Explore Practical Applications of Proper Beliefs and Desires the Counselee Can Apply Day In and Day Out

Flowing from the last point, you can help the counselee make God-honoring choices one at a time, day by day. Disordered eating impacts every area of life, not just mealtimes: it influences scheduling, social interactions (e.g., avoiding eating around others), and conversations. Together with your counselee you can celebrate each victory, no matter how small, rejoicing in God's work in even the minute details. This includes urging you counselee to invite others into their walk, and your providing accountability and encouragement as they move toward godly living. It also involves calling for regular repentance and offering gospel assurances when the counselee fails to believe and act rightly.

Help the Counselee Move Toward Contentment

While this point applies to many of the struggles this book addresses, disordered eating often flows from a lack of contentment. Counselees might experience discontentment over negative opinions of others toward them, continued stress related to the issues noted above, or a feeling of lack of control. Remember, Paul tells us in Phil 4:11–13, "I have learned to be content in whatever circumstances I find myself. . . . In any and all circumstances I have learned the secret of being content—whether well fed or hungry, whether in abundance or in need. I am able to do all things through him who strengthens me." In other words, in Christ and because of Christ, we believers have all that we need. So, help your counselee learn contentment, resting in the Lord's provision for them, including in his design for their body and their physical sustenance. Additionally, help them accept their life circumstances, including both the blessings and limitations God has given them.

Be Mindful of Comorbid Struggles or Situational Hardships; Evaluate and Care for the Counselee as Necessary

Lastly, keep in mind the risk for comorbid conditions and address them as appropriate, and/or acknowledge that suffering (such as past trauma or abuse) might contribute to your counselee's disordered eating. Watch for struggles such as anxiety or depression, and regularly screen for suicidal thoughts or self-harm behaviors. In a case where the counselee has experienced deep suffering, and the disordered eating arose after that experience, compassionately and patiently explore those potential connections. Suffering does not alleviate responsibility in one's response, but we as counselors must acknowledge and address it.

Conclusion

Eating disorders are complex and often require long-term counseling. We must not reduce a counselee to their eating input and output or to numbers on a scale. Rather, we must understand their situational stressors, their sinful patterns, and their underlying heart roots before patiently bringing God's Word to help them move toward godly eating habits. Change and growth are possible with the Lord's help as he conforms a person to be more like him in all areas, including their eating habits.

Grief

Grief is a normal part of life on our fallen planet and something everyone eventually experiences. While typical, however, it nonetheless often leaves us in a state of confusion or emotional upheaval. And though time might soften the impact, it doesn't make the present grief-filled realities any more bearable. Scripture has much to say on both the situations that bring grief and appropriate responses during grief.

It might be easy to take for granted a proper understanding of what grief actually is, given the multitude of definitions available.[1] For our purposes, we will define grief as a whole-person response of intense sadness or despair to a real or perceived loss of something the person values.

Types of Losses and their Impact

Grief is inextricably tied to some sort of loss, tangible or intangible, real or perceived. Some categories you might encounter when entering a grieving counselee's world include these:

[1] See Robert W. Kellemen, *God's Healing for Life's Losses: How to Find Hope When You're Hurting* (Winona Lake, IN: BMH Books, 2010); and Paul Tautges, *Comfort the Grieving: Ministering God's Grace in Times of Loss* (Grand Rapids: Zondervan, 2015).

- material or physical loss, that is, the loss of material possessions or a person
- abstract loss, which could include the loss of love, hope, ambition, or of a dream or perceived future
- relational loss, that is, the end of a relationship, such as a marriage, due to death or divorce
- role loss, or life changes that result in loss of a social/relational role, such as becoming a widow or an empty nester
- functional loss, that is, the loss of functional capabilities, such as what comes with a physical or mental impairment
- ambiguous loss, which is any loss that brings uncertainty or confusion, such as receiving an Alzheimer's diagnosis

Though the types of loss vary, they are all impactful. Counselors often focus on the more tangible losses, yet the loss of an anticipated future with a loved one might actually bring more grief than losing the person. By understanding not only the type of loss, but its impact on the counselee, we can more sensitively bring them Christ and his answers.

Further, grief is typically proportionate to the counselee's perceived value of the loss. Two people might experience the same grief event yet perceive the impact differently. Many factors contribute to one's perception of loss (e.g., personal resiliency, impact on everyday life, whether expected or unexpected), which directly translates into their experience of grief. The wise counselor should be aware of these factors.

The Presentation of Grief

We might be tempted to believe everyone grieves in obvious outward expressions of sadness, but that is not always the case. Our aim is to minister to all counselees amid *their* experience of pain. We must understand that while sin might be a factor in their expression, people vary greatly in how they experience and express grief.

Grief is both complex and unpredictable; it may or may not follow observed "stages." For instance, Elizabeth Kübler-Ross proposed the stages of denial, bargaining, anger, depression, and acceptance as a typical progression through grief, but not every grieving person follows this process.[2] The biblical counselor's concern is not with the progression itself, but with how the person expresses grief.[3] This could include a counselee continually denying the loss, putting off dealing with their grief, or experiencing more intense or prolonged grief than is typically appropriate. This evaluation understandably brings a level of subjectivity for the counselor. Additionally, the counselor should notice sinful responses, such as bitterness or desires for revenge rather than lament.

A myriad of presentations of grief are typical, yet often unexpected. Alongside sadness might come feelings of despair or hopelessness, of numbness or emptiness. A grieving person might find it hard to focus on mundane, everyday tasks; what used to be automatic is no longer. The counselee might have lapses in memory, particularly short-term memory, or experience nightmares or flashbacks centered on the loss. They might experience changes in sleeping or eating patterns or in how much they want to talk to or interact with others. The physical stress from grief might bring exhaustion, headaches, or even illnesses from a weakened body. Grief is a whole-person experience, not just an outwardly expressed behavior. This is especially true for children who might experience more physical symptoms, like stomach aches or developmental regressions, than emotional or cognitive struggles.

Grief can also raise within a counselee a host of theological questions, particularly if the loss was intensely personal and unexpected: Why did this happen? Is God really good? Is he truly sovereign? Is he worth my trust? Importantly, such questions are normal and should not be feared. They don't necessarily indicate a lack of faith; rather, they may indicate wrestling with one's faith and wanting to hold on to it. We should help counselees distinguish blasphemy and lamentation.

---

[2] Elizabeth Kübler-Ross, *On Death and Dying: What the Dying Have to Teach Doctors, Nurses, Clergy, and Their Own Families* (New York: Scribner, 2011). For a biblical counselor's response, see Kellemen, *God's Healing for Life's Losses*.

[3] Often expressions of grief are culturally directed. What is appropriate in one culture, such as public displays of mourning, might not be in another. The counselor should wisely understand proper expressions of grief for the counselee's culture/sub-culture rather than evaluating them solely from the counselor's perspective.

While blasphemy opposes God, lamentation includes honest questions addressed to God about where he is amid grief and why he sovereignly allowed a loss (Pss 10:1; 13:1; 22:1).

Further, the emotions of a grieving person might come and go, and at times feel contradictory. An adult caregiver, for instance, might feel sadness over the loss of a parent, but relief that the parent is no longer in pain or that the burden of caring for the parent no longer falls on them. That sense of relief can then usher in feelings of guilt, as if the relief from a personal burden indicates something negative about their feelings toward the deceased parent. In this case, the grieving counselee might present with feelings of sadness, relief, and guilt all at the same time. We can help them understand, sort out, and think biblically about mixed feelings and learn to hold them in tandem.

Biblical-Theological Perspectives

In understanding expressions of grief, we should first look to Scripture's descriptions and prescriptions for how we are to grieve. Most important is the reality that we as people are not alone in our experience of grief; God experiences it as well. But as with other emotions, like anger, we must note *under what circumstances* God grieves and *how he responds to grief*. Both are pertinent to counselors and counselees.[4]

God's Expressions of Grief

In Scripture, we see God's grief primarily toward sin or the effects/impact of sin on his creation. In Gen 6:5–6, God grieves over the wickedness of man, including the evil in his heart. In fact, he grieved that sinfulness even to the point of regretting that he made people. Jesus demonstrates grief over the death of Lazarus alongside the grief of his friends Mary and

---

[4] See also Joni Eareckson Tada, *A Place of Healing: Wrestling with the Mysteries of Suffering, Pain, and God's Sovereignty* (Colorado Springs, CO: David C. Cook, 2010), and Paul Randolph, "Grief: It's Not about a Process; It's about *the* Person," *Journal of Biblical Counseling* 23, no. 1 (Winter 2005): 14–20.

Martha in John 11:32–36. And in Eph 4:30, Paul tells us that we grieve the Holy Spirit when we sin. In each of these examples, the resounding theme is that the triune God grieves over sin itself and its impact on his creation, especially on humankind. Ultimately, sin results in death; it is the reason for our physical death, and it also led to the death of his Son. God grieves these things alongside us.

Scripture also speaks at length about God's responses to our grief. Isaiah 53:3–5 connects Christ's own experiences of grief (note that this passage prophesies the Messiah) with our own. Not only was Christ "a man of sorrows and acquainted with grief," he "has borne our griefs and carried our sorrows" (ESV) Jesus carried our grief alongside his own; he experiences and responds to sorrow and even knows our grief personally. Further, Heb 4:15–16 comforts us by assuring us Jesus has experienced temptations, even in grief, just as we have, and we can know the resulting command for us. Lastly, the Scriptures show us that grief is not an eternal reality. Isaiah wrote of the new heaven and the new earth in Isa 65:17–25, and Rev 21:3–4 gives us a picture of eternity: "Look, God's dwelling is with humanity, and he will live with them. They will be his peoples, and God himself will be with them and will be their God. He will wipe away every tear from their eyes. Death will be no more; grief, crying, and pain will be no more, because the previous things have passed away." One day grief will be gone forever because sin will no longer exist. In the meantime, God can both grieve over the suffering of his people and rejoice in the redemptive purposes he will bring about for them (e.g., Isaiah 54–55; Rom 8:17–39). He feels the weight of our suffering yet concurrently envisions the joyful resolution to come. We can do the same.

These passages should bring comfort that God grieves over sin and its impact; thus, we may rightly weep over our own sin and the impact of sin on others. We can grieve when a loved one dies, when injustice is committed, or when we are sinned against—none of which would happen were it not for the fall described in Genesis 3. We may also grieve when something good is lost or taken from us. Yet we should also take comfort knowing that God sees our sorrow; he has experienced it and cares deeply.

How God's Grief Informs Our Own

At the same time, we should distinguish between God's expressions of grief and our typical ones. Although God does not sin, we do, which means our experiences or expressions of grief can be sinful. Seeing how God experiences grief helps us better align our own experiences and expressions with his.

First, God grieves while knowing the rest of the story. He knows history's outcome. Similarly, as Paul wrote, we believers should not grieve as those who have no hope, because we know the eternal hope Christians have through Christ (1 Thess 4:13). Second, God is wise and we are not. As believers, we must rest knowing that biblical truths do not depend on our losses or our experiences of grief. God remains good, sovereign, and wise. Third, God's responses to our suffering—his feelings and actions—are always good and appropriate. While he grieves, he does not sin. He is not anxious, fearful, or hopeless. Yet these sinful emotions often accompany our grief. Therefore, we must be aware that we might sin in our grief and need to repent in order to align ourselves more closely with how God might respond to the same situation.

Scripture's Direct Teachings on Grief

The Bible often explains how God worked in the midst of his grieving people. The story of Job demonstrates God's sovereignty even over loss. Job experienced tremendous loss, more than many of us can fathom. Yet among his experiences we see not only the improper responses of those around him, but God's response at the end of the book. In the last several chapters, God provides the answer to Job's grief: remember my sovereignty, wisdom, and provision. And after Job's repentance, God abundantly reverses and restores his losses (Job 42); this is a picture of the promise that awaits us believers as we persevere in Joblike faith until Christ's return (Jas 5:7–11).

David's grief over his sin provided an opportunity for God's provision and grace. After Nathan confronted David about his sexual sin with Bathsheba and having her husband killed, he was overcome with grief. Psalm 51 shows him pouring out that grief and repenting before the

Lord. In 2 Samuel 12, we see David's outward expressions of grief when he learned of his infant son's terminal illness: refusing to eat, lying on the ground, remaining unwilling to take part in his royal duties. Such responses are typical of grief, even today. Yet upon learning that his son had indeed died, David found strength in the Lord (cf. 2 Sam 12:20–24) and was enabled to rise from the ground, wash, eat, worship the Lord, and minister to his grieving wife. God provided for David and was gracious toward him in each of these situations.

Scripture also encourages those who grieve by reminding them of the Lord's presence. Psalm 34:18 says, "The Lord is near the brokenhearted; he saves those crushed in spirit." Those who grieve can know that the Lord is near to them. Psalm 23 reminds us that even though we walk through the "valley of the shadow of death (ESV)," we need not fear because the Lord is with us. Many who grieve feel like they are walking through a valley of death; again, they can rest knowing that God is ever present. Additionally, Isaiah 40 speaks about needing strength in grief as we grow faint and weary, yet we Christ followers can find comfort in our God.

Finally, passages like 2 Cor 4:17 and Rom 8:18 remind believers we have hope that the future glory will far outweigh current suffering. Death is evil, an enemy, a result of God's earned curse on humanity (Gen 2:17; 3:19; Rom 8:18–39), but God one day will reverse that curse and put death to death forever for his people (1 Corinthians 15; Revelation 21–22). We can encourage our Christian counselees to have a godly, eternal perspective rather than a temporal one—to remember the future outcome that God guarantees, the reality that God will establish his kingdom, one free from guilt and sorrow.

Counseling Actions

Grief and the process of working through it are highly individualized. Loss often magnifies the need for sensitivity and patience. Yet common issues are typically present. While the following actions are good practices for any counseling situation, they are especially valuable in ministering to grieving counselees.

Affirm the Reality of the Counselee's Loss and Grief

While counselors at some point can discuss the appropriateness of the response, you must immediately affirm the reality of each loss, the experience of the counselee, and the resulting emotions. You can also acknowledge potential reminders or triggers and the resulting floods of emotion that might come even well after the loss happened.

Be Patient

Grief is complex and often comes upon people unexpectedly. Reminders of a loss and mentally revisiting grief can also come unexpectedly. No set timeline exists for when grief should be complete.

Weep with Those Who Weep

Empathy is an essential skill for counseling, especially for walking with someone through grief and loss. Counselors must intentionally enter the world of the counselee, understand the loss from their perspective, and feel that loss alongside them. Only when you do can you truly weep with someone with understanding.

Be Quick to Listen, Slow to Speak, and Slow to Respond

James 1:19 reminds all believers to be "quick to listen, slow to speak, and slow to anger." James's larger point is that we are to be self-controlled in our emotional responses, thinking clearly about the appropriateness of our own responses. The same is true for counseling grief: we should listen well, speak with wisdom, and pay attention to our own responses to others' grief.

Serve in Practical Ways

Consider ways you can get the church involved in practically loving a grieving brother or sister—whether through offering meals, running errands, visiting regularly, or presenting gifts of remembrance. Through loving displays like these, the counselee receives the message they are cared for and their pain is not forgotten. Such practical acts of love and service can speak volumes to someone who feels alone in their grief, and they also speak to those around them who observe the church's Christ-centered care.

Encourage Appropriate, Helpful Ways to Memorialize the Loss

It's often hard to think about practical ways to bring closure to a loss. While events like a funeral help in the case of losing a loved one, intangible losses are harder to close. Help your counselee think through appropriate ways to memorialize a particularly significant loss—to communicate that the memory is still there, despite the sense of loss felt.

Remember the Anniversary Date

One way we show continual love is by expressing our care and prayers for the grieving person in the months and years to come. Anniversaries can bring new waves of grief, but connection and remembrance help. Keep pertinent dates related to your counselee's loss (e.g., a loved one's date of death or birthday) on your calendar and send a "thinking of you" card each time such an anniversary nears.

Wisely, Gently Challenge False Beliefs and Sinful Behaviors

We have the capacity to sin in the midst of experiencing and expressing grief, such as when we respond with bitterness or lash out. Thus, in terms of our six-box model from chapter 10, we biblical counselors should listen for any box 2 or 3 responses. In some cases, the grief itself might be sinful, as when mourning the loss of an adulterous relationship. Or the counselee might have a false understanding of where God was in their loss and blame God. They might place undue responsibility on themselves for a loss or grieve the loss of something they inordinately treasured. In such cases, gently seek to correct and free the counselee from false beliefs, encouraging them to grieve and respond in proper, God-honoring ways.

Encourage the Counselee to Look Outward

Paul tells us in 2 Cor 1:3–4 that "the Father of mercies and the God of all comfort . . . comforts us in all our affliction, so that we may be able to comfort those who are in any kind of affliction, through the comfort we ourselves receive from God." He reminds his readers that their suffering is not only about them; they should minister to others out of it. Thus, you can encourage a believing counselee to be the church to another person since everyone experiences grief and suffering and often needs help walking through it.

Ensure Your Counselee Has a Proper Theology of Suffering

While suffering is a reality in this life, God remains sovereign, omnipotent, omniscient, just, merciful, and compassionate. In the midst of grief or trials, a counselee might struggle to hold on to these truths as circumstances appear to challenge these traits. Yet circumstances do not determine the truth of God's Word. You must help counselees affirm biblical truths (box 4) while acknowledging their circumstances (box 1) and encouraging them toward a proper response (boxes 5 and 6).

Suggested Growth Assignments

The following growth assignments may be helpful for the grieving counselee:

- Praying, meditating, and journaling surrounding grief. You can direct counselees to look to the Scriptures for examples of grief, then pray and journal in light of those passages. Some places to start include Isaiah 40; 53; Psalm 23, or various passages where Jesus comforts those who grieve (e.g., Luke 7:11–17; John 11; 14–16).
- Writing a psalm, focusing on both lament and worship. In writing a psalm, primarily following the examples in Psalms 6; 42; or 88, counselees not only express how they feel and their views about God or others, but they encourage themselves to remember God

in the midst of their struggles. Moreover, a counselee can use such psalms as prayers. Lament psalms help us voice our feelings to the Lord and frame them with God's perspectives.

- Preserving helpful memories. A counselee might benefit from practical exercises like creating a memory book or writing a memorial tribute. Such exercises might bring closure and help the counselee accept the permanence of the loss.
- Sharing the loss with someone, transparently and openly. Sharing losses within the body of Christ, rather than just discussing them with a counselor, allows us to both weep and rejoice alongside one another. It minimizes any sense of isolation.
- Connecting with the corporate body. Receiving continual community care can help a counselee feel less isolated in their grief. It can also encourage them to remember biblical truths about grief and loss. Such care can come in multiple ways, for example through small groups, support groups, church-based ministry, or even through reading the testimonies of others who have walked through similar experiences.[5]
- Grief tracking. Daily noting their levels of grief and any expressions of it (emotional, spiritual, or physical) can help counselees more easily understand the impact of their grief. The tracking journal can be discussed in sessions and reviewed over time, revealing the longer-term impact of their loss.

Conclusion

The information in this chapter has simply scratched the surface of ministering to a grieving counselee; after all, love is wonderfully creative. Though

[5] For instance, see the Grief Share curriculum from Church Initiative. www.griefshare.org; Paul Tautges, *A Small Book for the Hurting Heart: Meditations on Loss, Grief, and Healing* (Greensboro, NC: New Growth Press, 2020); Joni Eareckson Tada, *When God Weeps: Why Our Sufferings Matter to the Almighty* (Grand Rapids: Zondervan, 2010); Bob Kellemen, *Grief: Walking with Jesus*, 31-Day Devotionals for Life (Phillipsburg, NJ: P&R, 2018); John Piper, *When the Darkness Will Not Lift: Doing What We Can While We Wait for God—and Joy* (Wheaton, IL: Crossway, 2006).

grief is complex and often messy, it is something no one can escape. At some time or another, we all will experience the loss of something precious. And most of the time, those losses will be unexpected. Counselors must be ready to speak biblical truth with sensitivity and wisdom. The gospel alone can transform a grief experience.

30

Trauma and Abuse

Trauma and abuse are more common than we want to admit, and often the initial events as well as the ongoing effects are hidden. While our English Bibles don't use these terms, the Bible is not silent on abuse and trauma. Not only does Scripture record a myriad of hardships and afflictions, many times describing the response of the godly character involved,[1] but it speaks at length about the effects of sin, suffering in a fallen world, and the future redemption that awaits believers. This chapter will primarily address trauma with a special focus on abuse.

What Are Trauma and Abuse?

Writers vary on how they define trauma and abuse, and how they distinguish or sometimes subordinate the two. We will view abuse as one category that can overlap with the category of trauma, so envision the intersection of a Venn diagram. When speaking of abuse, we will primarily discuss what we might call *traumatic abuse*. Most forms of trauma, including traumatic abuse, follow a typical pattern applicable to many different scenarios.

---

[1] See, for instance, David's responses (both immediate and ongoing) to his hardships (Psalm 31); Paul's responses to his imprisonment and torture (Phil 4:11–13); and Elijah's response to being pursued (1 Kings 19).

The Bible provides a helpful framework for understanding what we might call trauma. It consists of three key components: a triggering event (or events), one's experience of that event, and the possible ongoing adverse effects of that event and experience, which we call trauma.[2] First, there is a precipitating event (box 1 in our six-box model)—a serious or severe trial, hardship, suffering, affliction, or adversity—that brings or threatens harm, whether physically or otherwise. This event might be something like a car accident, house fire, or natural disaster. Or, as we will focus on in this chapter, the event might be an instance of abuse or a violent exchange seen or experienced. To put it simply, in these cases the person is severely sinned against.

Second, there is some sort of experience or reaction. This response usually involves both physical (e.g., a fight-or-flight response) and non-physical (a subjective interpretation and volitional response) aspects. It may be godly, ungodly, or a combination of both based on how the individual understands and assigns meaning to the event (box 2 or 6 behaviors based on box 3 or 5 heart responses).

Third, in cases we call trauma, there are ongoing effects that impact the whole person (emotions, functionality, thought processes, relationships, physiology), commonly in long-lasting ways. In some cases, the precipitating event(s) of severe mistreatment (box 1) can directly produce bodily effects (e.g., brain injuries with cognitive impact)[3] or indirectly invite or provoke psychosomatic responses, such as anxiety, depending on how the person processes the abuse (box 3 or 5). These bodily effects, in turn, become a new, additional box 1 heat/hardship factor, creating a feedback loop and adding complexity to the abused person's response. Over time, these ongoing effects have the potential to

---

[2] This framework is echoed by the US Substance Abuse and Mental Health Services Administration. See "SAMHSA's Concept of Trauma and Guidance for a Trauma-Informed Approach," July 2014, https://store.samhsa.gov/sites/default/files/d7/priv/sma14-4884.pdf.

[3] Discerning the absence or presence of bodily problems, their causes, and how we as counselors should aid a person is not always easy. In the absence of medical evidence about a counselee, we should be cautiously agnostic, neither assuming nor dismissing the possibility of bodily problems. At the same time, we should pay attention to valid, relevant neurological research, despite its limits. (See the discussion that follows.)

lead to ungodly responses like bitterness, wrong beliefs, and desires for revenge, or to godly responses like sanctification, spiritual growth, and ministry to others.

The above threefold understanding does not mean that experiencing a severe event will produce trauma or that the person will become *traumatized*. These precipitating events are only potentially traumatic, depending on how people respond to them. Two people can experience the same event in different ways with different effects. Simply experiencing an event does not necessitate a particular disruptive response or ongoing negative impact. Much goes into the experience and effects of an event; specifically, the human heart is impacted by sin in all its forms yet can also be strengthened by God's empowering grace. Thankfully, Scripture gives multiple examples of people who suffered severely but were not traumatized because of God's grace.

Alternatively, abuse means mistreatment or misuse of something. When applied to a person, it is a set of actions between people that is marked by mistreatment, power, or control rather than mutual honor and value. Typically, a person with relative power or authority mistreats a person in a position of weakness or subordination.[4] One person is severely sinned against or oppressed by another. There are a variety of categories both with respect to age (child versus adult) and type (physical versus nonphysical). For instance, child abuse is the mistreatment of someone under the age of eighteen; it includes neglect or abandonment and falls under mandatory reporting laws in all states.[5] In contrast, domestic violence is violence or abuse within the home, typically happening between adult spouses or partners.

At its core, abuse involves power and control. An abuser exerts improper power and control over another human at that person's direct expense. The abuser directly and significantly sins against the victim.

---

[4] See John Henderson, *Abuse: Finding Hope in Christ* (Phillipsburg, NJ: P&R, 2012); Robert W. Kellemen, *Sexual Abuse: Beauty for Ashes* (Phillipsburg, NJ: P&R, 2015); and David Powlison, *Sexual Assault: Healing Steps for Victims* (Greensboro, NC: New Growth Press, 2010).

[5] See our chapter 20 for the reporting statutes for your state. Also see Brad Hambrick, ed., *Becoming a Church that Cares Well for the Abused* (Nashville, TN: Lifeway, 2019), 181–242.

Abuse fails to treat image bearers with dignity and honor, and it often involves pain and manipulation.

The following list of various forms of abuse is not exhaustive; nevertheless, it gives a starting place for understanding different categories.

Physical Forms	Non-Physical Forms
• Bodily harm such as hitting, punching, or biting • Sexual touching offenses such as rape or molestation	• Verbal attacks such as name-calling, insults, demeaning speech • Attempts to manipulate or coerce for personal gain at the expense of the other • Distortions of religious teaching to elevate self, demean another, or demand submission • Sexual, nontouching offenses such as verbal sexual comments or forced observation

Of course, these forms may overlap; one does not exclude the other. Each instance involves two parties (an abuser and a victim) and an injustice or violation. Psalm 58:2 gives a helpful picture: "No, you practice injustice in your hearts; with your hands you weigh out violence in the land." While the Old Testament idea of justice is to make something right, or as it should be, abusers do the opposite. Instead of living rightly with God and others, abusers violate fellow image bearers. They are crooked, turning away from God in all of their ways. Contrary to what Isa 1:17 says godly people should do, the abuser does not do good, pursue justice, correct their own oppressive behavior, or defend those who cannot defend themselves.

Impact of Severe Hardship on a Person

If not responded to in God-honoring ways, being severely sinned against can have a tremendous, often lifelong, impact on the whole person. For instance, one might begin to have distorted thought patterns, hold wrong beliefs in response to repeated abuse (Stockholm syndrome;

misunderstandings about proper relationships), or live perpetually in a state of fear, worry, and anxiety. Being exposed to trauma, particularly if it is ongoing and/or increases in severity, greatly increases the temptation to respond wrongly. Further, the traumatized person might relationally withdraw or isolate themselves, or fail to understand how to live in right relationship with others. Questions about God's sovereignty or goodness might arise.

Much recent research has focused on the physical and neurophysiological implications of trauma. While we must recognize its limits (e.g., its exclusion of the heart and biblical heart/body interaction) and wisely assess its reliability and relevance to a specific counselee (see chapter 9), we should welcome its valid insights. On a basic level, trauma might include physical injury; but on a more complex level, evidence demonstrates it can affect brain structures, bringing physical changes that impact functioning, behavior, and thought patterns. This reality does not alleviate personal responsibility but demonstrates that the effects of trauma are more pervasive than previously known and calls us to address the whole person rather than simply one's thought patterns or behavior. Biblical counsel must incorporate a proper understanding of both the heart and the body in the counselee's response to suffering. Our bodies, for instance, were not meant to live in a perpetual state of fear or danger. When we do, our sympathetic nervous systems go into overdrive and stay there; adrenaline continues to be released, our hearts continue to race, and the thought centers of our brains (namely, the prefrontal cortex) struggle to function.[6] While we cannot know if such a change has occurred in any individual counselee, being aware of these possible dynamics helps us counsel the *whole person*.

What often complicates abuse is its level of secrecy. Often the abuser uses secrecy to continue inflicting trauma on the victim. Secret abuse by definition is hidden, but it may be present. Maintaining secrecy might involve manipulation ("If someone finds out, you'll be the one in trouble") or outright lies ("This is your fault"). The words of Prov 10:11 ring true:

[6] Bessel van der Kolk misses the spiritual component of trauma but describes at great length its impact on the brain and body in van der Kolk, *The Body Keeps the Score: Brain, Mind, and Body in the Healing of Trauma* (London: Penguin Books, 2015).

"The mouth of the righteous is a fountain of life, but the mouth of the wicked conceals violence." An abuser's words are not life-giving; they hide violence and are life-draining.

Despite the complex impact that severe mistreatment might have, a person's responses to it can also be complex. Numerous "protective factors" can lessen abuse's impact and guard a person against becoming traumatized. These include:

- strong beliefs about God and his sovereignty and goodness;
- a strong support system, including a counselor and a healthy church home;
- past experience with working through suffering;
- overall resilience to challenges; and
- a stable environment (i.e., hardships are not recurring).

While none of these factors guarantee a person will not be initially traumatized, they generally lessen and shorten the impact of precipitating events.

Ultimately, the person who has experienced a horrific event and its effects is suffering; we must anticipate that. While sinful responses can occur (see below), the traumatized counselee likely needs help in many areas of life (spiritually, physically, emotionally, relationally, etc.). Quite often, their life feels out of control; they need help discovering how the Lord speaks to their suffering and offers them his comfort.

Biblical and Theological Perspectives

Scripture gives multiple examples of severe hardships and abuse. Murder, rape, war, genocide, slavery, and other tragic topics fill many pages of the Bible because of the depth and pervasiveness of sin in our fallen world. One brother murders another because of jealousy (Genesis 4), a man rapes his half-sister out of lust (2 Samuel 13), and three men are thrown into a furnace because of a king's desire for total power (Daniel 3). In each instance, a grievous sin happens because one person desires something they should not and severely mistreats another to get what is wanted. The news that the gospel brings is that all of these sinned-against individuals could have responded to their mistreatment in godly ways and many of them did, providing us examples, hope, and a Christ-centered way forward for our counselees.

The Bible is full of teachings pertinent to this conversation:

for instance, many passages show us how to respond well to abuse. Psalms 27 and 55–57, for instance, teach us how to view oppressors and how to cry out to God for help while trusting in his presence, power, and promises. God's power is sufficient for us in our weakness, despite any sin committed against us. In the midst of trials, we can run to and rest in the power of our Father to bring comfort and justice. Jesus often instructed his disciples about how to handle persecution; we see them live that out in Acts. Paul gives us a clear directive in Rom 12:12: "Rejoice in hope; be patient in affliction; be persistent in prayer." The entire letter of 1 Peter teaches us how to handle mistreatment. We should respond to it in God-honoring ways (boxes 5 and 6) rather than self-honoring ones (boxes 3 and 4).

The Bible also tells us how to treat our enemies and clarifies the role of civil authorities. The apostle Paul teaches us how to view enemies and the surprising way God wants us to treat them (Rom 12:14–21). He also sheds light on the proper role that civil government might play in cases where victims should seek law enforcement help (Rom 13:1–5; cf. Acts 16:35–40). We Christ followers have the freedom, and the mandate where directed by law, to involve law enforcement for cases of abuse, as an effort toward justice. However, God commands us not to "repay . . . evil for evil" but to do what is honorable (Rom 12:17). This does not prevent consequences for certain abusive actions; instead, it prohibits retribution.

Wisdom is a necessity when discussing biblical forgiveness and reconciliation. As an example, an older child might forgive his abuser, but that abuser remains under laws that punish abusive behavior. Further, despite forgiveness, it would be generally unwise for a child to spend unsupervised time with an abuser. There are consequences for behaviors, even when forgiveness and reconciliation take place.

Next, the Bible teaches that we have a choice in how we respond to difficulties. People are moral beings. This means we can choose both sinful and nonsinful responses to trials, however severe, though there will always be some sort of a response. As we saw from Scripture in chapter 1 and in our six-box model in chapter 10, our active hearts can produce good fruit or bad in response to the heat of being sinned against. For example, in the face of immense suffering—the loss of his children, his possessions, and his health—Job responded in godly ways (Job 1:20–22; 2:10) while his wife responded in ungodly ways (Job 2:9). When "distressed" by the threatening devastation of an invading army, King Ahaz "became more unfaithful to the LORD" (2 Chron 28:22) while King Manasseh "sought the favor of the LORD his God and earnestly humbled himself" (2 Chron 33:12). Suffering becomes the occasion for, not the cause of, good or bad responses.

Thankfully, Scripture provides many examples of those who responded to ungodly mistreatment in godly ways. In the Psalms David cried out to God in the midst of his affliction; he ran to the proper source of help in his time of need (Psalms 40; 69). Similarly, in the midst of repeated trials discussed in Genesis 37 through that book's end, Joseph consistently indicated that the Lord was near to him, that he depended on the Lord, and that the Lord spoke directly to him. Jesus in his suffering cried out to the Father (Luke 23:34, 46; Matt 27:46). Paul chose to trust the Lord's sovereignty in his afflictions (2 Cor 1:8–10; Acts 14:21–22). In each instance, the person chose to honor the Lord despite grievous sin against them.

Scripture also assures believers that our ultimate hope is in the promise of "new heavens and a new earth" where God will dwell with us (2 Pet 3:12–13). Indeed, part of the gospel message is that one day our Lord will make all things new. As Rev 21:4 reminds us, "He will wipe away every tear from [our] eyes. Death will be no more; grief, crying, and pain will be no more, because the previous things [will] have passed away." That means a time is coming when there will be no more trauma, no more abuse. Thus, we can grieve the effects of suffering on our lives, even the severe effects, and yet hold on to hope (1 Thess 4:13). For example, although Paul faced immense mistreatment, he kept an eternal perspective that brought great hope (2 Corinthians 4; 12:1–10). Based on the description at the end of Acts and his testimony and outlook in his last letter (2 Timothy), these gospel realities apparently kept him from being traumatized.

Finally, Scripture presents Jesus as our perfect example of how to respond to severe mistreatment. Consider the cross: Christ endured intense physical and nonphysical suffering (beatings, verbal assaults) as he was executed in the most shameful way possible at the time. Yet he responded rightly and honorably. No doubt he was in great pain, both physically and spiritually; yet, in the midst of his suffering, he did not sin. Jesus was not traumatized by the severe abuse he received. He even used the occasion to help teach us how to view and treat our enemies (Luke 6:27–36; Matt 27:27–31; 1 Pet 2:21–23). Pointing such things out during sessions can lead counselees to two necessary truths: Jesus knows our suffering, and we are not alone in it. Our Lord's sympathy with us in our temptations and his provision of help as discussed in Heb 4:14–16 become much more touching in light of the cross.

At the same time, this does not mean we should not seek to avoid or escape unnecessary suffering or neglect to seek help. Our Lord's suffering involved some unique aspects—he voluntarily came to earth to atone for our sins and chose to suffer in our place. Nevertheless, when we do face sinful mistreatment from others, the New Testament repeatedly presents Christ as our example who showed us how to handle it in godly ways.

Counseling Steps and Practical Procedures

Before considering some practical counseling approaches in dealing with trauma, including abuse, we must focus on two preliminary points. First, because of the potential complexity of trauma, particularly repetitive abuse, wise counseling requires both competency and wisdom. Helping people who have suffered complex trauma or recurrent abuse, and sometimes even straightforward instances of trauma or onetime instances of abuse, will require more than entry-level skill. Poorly done counseling can do great harm. A counselor needs to be properly equipped to handle such cases, which might require seeking more training or ongoing consultation with more experienced biblical counselors who better understand the complexity of sin and suffering. In some cases, it might also involve consulting with secular professionals.

Second, because of the nature of trauma and abuse counseling, counselors with a personal history of such should be aware of potential triggers when working with traumatized counselees. Failing to sufficiently work through your own trauma or abuse can impact your ministry to a hurting counselee (see chapter 11).

As counselors, we should seek to provide tiers of help. First, we should ensure a counselee is safe and that their basic physical needs are met. If the counselee is not safe or lacks essential provisions, counseling might not be effective.[7] The preliminary aim in such a case is to get the counselee support for daily living, which may require the involvement of the church or community resources. The counselor should also ask about suicidality or self-harm and respond properly. Further, this step involves discerning when to advise a counselee to report abuse to law enforcement (Rom 13:1–6) and to church leaders (Heb 13:17) as well as when to seek medical care or legal counsel.

Next, we should address the trauma/abuse more directly, but in a way that considers the totality of the counselee's experience and the effects of the trauma on their life. As biblical counselors, we should spend a great deal of time hearing each counselee's story, compassionately bearing that burden with them, and continually pointing to scriptural truths about God's goodness, compassion, sovereignty, presence, love, and other characteristics directly related to someone who is hurting. We should grieve the offenses where appropriate and should acknowledge sin where present, in both the offender and offended. We should also work through any heart issues, including temptations, desires, or any spiritual questions or struggles that might arise in our counselees, bringing frequent encouragement and biblical truth (e.g., Ps 9:9, "The Lord is a stronghold for the oppressed, a stronghold in times of trouble" ESV).

Within this step, a counselor should also recognize potential traumatic physiological responses to the mistreatment that are producing additional box 1 hardship(s). God created our bodies to respond in particular ways to experiences, and one of those involves threat and danger. God created

[7] Note that Jesus often met physical needs (through feeding or healing; see Matt 15:29–37) alongside his teaching.

what we know as the "fight-or-flight-system" (our sympathetic nervous system). When employed correctly, it leads us to protect ourselves without relying on logical thought before response. In the case of trauma, though, this system can get overwhelmed. Rather than being a temporary state, the fight-or-flight system remains activated, which it was not created to do. What this side effect of the fall means for counselors is that we cannot ignore the physiological responses of our counselees; instead, we must acknowledge them and help people work toward a restoration of proper functioning in these areas.

A counselor might use several activities to address trauma and its impact on the counselee. For instance, a counselee can read and meditate on Ps 10:17–18: "LORD, you have heard the desire of the humble; you will strengthen their hearts. You will listen carefully, doing justice for the fatherless and the oppressed so that mere humans from the earth may terrify them no more." Such an exercise is a reminder that the Lord is just and hears our cries, and he also brings strength.[8] Other passages to study might include Psalms 3–5; 55–57; and the book of Job. The counselor may also choose to have the counselee note any connections during the week between distressing emotions, problematic thoughts, and resulting behavior so they can explore how past experiences or present motivations and desires are impacting the counselee's struggle. They might also construct together a visual or narrative timeline to help the counselee better understand the event(s) and their impact. To address physiological responses such as the fight-or-flight sensation, the counselor might also teach practical skills, like controlled breathing and relaxation, focused times of prayer or meditation, and mitigating negative emotions' impact on everyday life.[9]

Third, the counselor should help the counselee move toward right attitudes (box 5). Several temptations exist when trauma or abuse occurs. These include embracing a "victim mentality," exhibiting self-righteous anger, and harboring bitterness and/or unforgiveness. These are sinful actions that go

---

[8] For more on using Psalm 10, see David Powlison, *Why Me? Comfort for the Victimized* (Phillipsburg, NJ: P&R, 2003).

[9] Some biblical counselors might want to consider ways to appropriate, with caution, various effective therapy techniques from trauma specialists (e.g., narrative exposure therapies).

against God's directives for us even in the midst of being grievously sinned against (Matt 18:21–22; Eph 4:31; Jas 1:20; Luke 18:9–14). Should we see these tendencies in our counselees, we should address them. Correcting sinful attitudes, however, need not undermine empathy for their suffering; instead, patiently help your counselee become more like Christ who, even in his severe, multifaceted suffering, did not sin (1 Pet 2:21–23).

Fourth and finally, the counselor should help the counselee to live wisely before the Lord (box 6). This means teaching proper responses to the past or present events to counter unwarranted feelings of danger or fear. We should also help counselees learn what God-honoring relationships look like, particularly if these have not been modeled in their lives. Drawing on 1 Cor 13:4–7, for instance, we can walk others through what it means to love one another—what authentic, God-honoring love looks like. We can also work through presenting these struggles to the Lord in prayer while thinking on truth like Phil 4:6–8 rather than uncertainties, taking thoughts captive to think on Christ and his goodness (2 Cor 10:5). In doing all this, the aim is to break the unhealthy or sinful patterns that have developed in response to mistreatment. Finally, with great wisdom and patience, we might need to explore forgiveness and reconciliation between our counselees and their offenders.

Conclusion

While counseling victims of severe abuse is difficult and often draining, it's also an opportunity to see tremendous growth. By God's grace, by the help of his Spirit and the truth of his Word, we can come alongside brothers and sisters in the faith who have been mistreated and comfort them in their affliction. We can point them to "the Father of mercies and God of all comfort," who can offer a level of help like no other in the midst of even the hardest struggles (2 Cor 1:3–6).

31

Pornography and Masturbation

Sex sells. It always has and will until Jesus returns. Maybe that's one reason the Bible teaches about sex so frequently. Tragically, in our culture's lust for all things sexual, issues of pornography and masturbation—sex with oneself—further distort God's plan for sex. These sins typically go together.

Over the years, pornography has become more readily available than in the past. Today people can find it for free on any device that accesses the Internet.

In our counseling ministries we have seen individuals go to elaborate lengths to feed their desires, whether by acquiring a separate device, using a pathway to the Internet that is not readily tracked by Covenant Eyes, or by travelling to a library or university. When it comes to accessing pornography, where there's a will, there's a way.

Sadly, distortions of God's plan for sex and intimacy impact both men and women. While men tend to be the more prevalent advertising targets of pornography and are most often identified with this problem, women struggle as well.[1] Pornography and masturbation are common issues among singles, and their use is rampant among high school and college

[1] We especially appreciate women who help other women fight against these sins. While pastors rightly want to shepherd everyone in their flocks, wisdom dictates that women struggling with sexual sin are served best by godly women.

students—both secular and Christian. They are also surprisingly popular among married couples, even those who are active members of the church. It's heartbreaking to remember the many couples who have sat in my (Rob's) living room to explain how pornography and masturbation impacted their relationships not only with the Lord but with one another.

If you counsel long, you will encounter these issues.

Understanding the Issues

As we begin, know that counselees may be conflicted about the rightness or wrongness of pornography use and masturbation. Some Christians, for instance, sincerely believe that masturbation is God's gift to singles. Yet many struggle with guilt over it nonetheless. We believe their consciences are functioning properly, that their guilt feelings are leading them in the proper direction. We believe that pornography and masturbation distort God's good design for sex and are therefore sinful. So, rather than assuaging anyone's guilt over this kind of indulgence, we hope to address with them its causes so that they might lead lives more pleasing to God.

An Issue of the Heart

It is possible that a counselee's entry point into pornography was unintentional; perhaps they misspelled a word in a Google search or clicked on a misleading ad that then exposed them to inappropriate content. Nevertheless, even that innocent entry set into motion a series of steps that started with experimentation and led to conscious choices. By the time a counselee reaches out to you about the matter, their pornography use can no longer be described as accidental.

Jesus taught, "From the heart come evil thoughts, murders, adulteries, sexual immoralities" (Matt 15:19). That means that the topics of this chapter are fundamentally heart problems, no matter how they got started. Therefore, the more consuming pornography use and/or masturbation have become in a counselee's life, the more questions you need to ask. You also need to be wise in the depth of information you gather. For instance, know that those who look at video pornography and masturbate to it enter a fantasy world they create. In it, they "control" the situation and pretend that what they see is happening to them. Their experience is intense and requires very little work. Today, a counselee can even engage in virtual sexual experiences with another live person via video conferencing. The wide range of sinful sexual experiences accessible to counselees is staggering.

Though such things terribly distort God's design, the physical pleasure associated with them is both enjoyable and intoxicating. Counselees will often say they don't want to be involved in pornography and masturbation, they know it's wrong, and they feel guilty, yet they keep doing it. They won't tell you their hearts crave the pleasure associated with picking the actors, choosing the videos, and enjoying the partially make-believe and partially real scenes. When counselees describe pornography's irresistible draw, know they mean it has a hold on their hearts. What keeps bringing them back to the pit is the sense of pleasure the pit provides.

An Issue of Affections

Humans are thinkers, feelers, and lovers. The Lord encouraged us to love him first and our neighbors as ourselves (Matt 22:37–40). Unfortunately, the counselees in view in this chapter love their sin. Yes, we may hear of guilt and a repeatedly stated desire to change, yet there is nevertheless a love for all that their sin provides. For the single person, it's often the thrill of sexual pleasure without marital commitment. For the married person, it's the joy of easy sexual pleasure without cultivating relational intimacy, or perhaps it's a way to indulge a desire for something/someone different from their spouse. The longer a counselee has been in this type of sin and the more intense their experiences with it, the more they will love what it provides. It will be relatively easy to go back to their sin because they love it.

An Issue of Self and Others Deception

"The Lord is okay with this"; "This is not hurting anyone"; or "No one knows about this" are all statements counselees use to justify their actions and cover up their guilt and shame. In fact, they deceive themselves with these sayings.

Many struggling with the issues mentioned herein also regularly deceive spouses, parents, friends, or accountability partners. We should ask questions about such deceptions and their frequency to better understand each counselee. We should also be aware that some sufferers will even seek to deceive their counselors.[2] I have been in the counseling room with a young man hooked on pornography who looked me in the eye and lied to my face eight sessions in a row—just as he'd done to every person in his past whom he had asked to help him. I was just one more victim of his well-rehearsed deceptions. His lies were only exposed by the hand of the Lord.

As biblical counselors, we must realize that our counselees rarely tell us the whole story at the beginning. This becomes even more obvious with those struggling in this area of sexual sin, especially if they know they face serious consequences if there is no change (e.g., the loss of employment or ministry/missionary service, or the dissolution of a relationship).

An Issue of Habit

Those who turn to pornography and masturbation have often developed a series of habits around their sin. There are structured times for their sin, certain pathways to access their sin, and specific kinds of days or moments that lead to it. Their sin has become part of their routine.

Breaking the sin of pornography and masturbation can be very challenging. Biblical counselors must know what we are up against. The longer and deeper a counselee has gone into this sin, the more difficult it is to break.[3] We thus need to think about the solution through many different aspects.

---

[2] This need not make us cynical. We can choose to believe the best about our counselees without being naïve to their tendencies. Moreover, biblical counselors can wake up each day believing that today could be the one when the Lord works mightily and changes a counselee's heart.

[3] In some cases, residential programs like Pure Life Ministries (www.purelifeministries.org) and Restoration Ministry (www.faithlafayette.org/restoration) can help.

Looking to Solutions

I like to use the analogy of war when speaking with a counselee about pornography and masturbation. Such sins are not going to change because we talk about them or because they feel guilty. The overcoming process involves war. Just as in an actual military conflict one brings every resource into the fight, so also we need every resource to fight against pornography and masturbation.[4] And as in the case of all biblical counseling, counselees should grow in their love for the Lord and desire to honor and glorify him in their lives even as they take practical steps toward overcoming these sins. The theme of Christian growth (Eph 4:17–24; Col 3:5–17) applies to each aspect of the battle.

The Importance of Pursuing the Greater Joys

If the heart has learned to love and enjoy the sins of pornography and masturbation, then the antidote involves seeking a greater joy.[5] God designed us to love, want, and experience joy.[6] He desires that we love him first, want what he wants, and experience delight through relationship with him. Part of the way counselees can fight their sin, then, is to see that God offers something better. Why settle for chicken from the dumpster when God offers made-to-order filet mignon?

It is insufficient to simply talk about the importance of loving God more than an indulgence. Rather, help your counselee "Taste and see that

---

[4] See Heath Lambert, *Finally Free: Fighting for Purity with the Power of Grace* (Grand Rapids: Zondervan, 2013).

[5] Unbelievers can also give up the sin discussed in this chapter, but the desire for change normally results from the thought of losing something. An unbelieving husband, for instance, might give up his pornography because his wife threatens divorce. An unbelieving mom might give up her pornography because her son caught her using it. In such cases, counselees judge something else to be more important than what they are giving up. Remember, mere change in behavior is not the change we seek.

[6] Consider assigning one or more of these resources to be read between sessions: John Piper, *Desiring God: Meditations of a Christian Hedonist*, rev. ed. (Colorado Springs: Multnomah, 2011); Milton Vincent, *A Gospel Primer for Christians: Learning to See the Glories of God's Love* (Bemidji, MN: Focus Press, 2013); J. I. Packer, *Knowing God* (Downers Grove: InterVarsity Press, 1991); and Jerry Bridges, *The Discipline of Grace: God's Role and Our Role in the Pursuit of Holiness* (Colorado Springs: NavPress, 1994).

the LORD is good" (Ps 34:8). Most of us would admit that we take the blessings of the Lord for granted. Rather than look intently for them, we grow accustomed to the fact that God cares for us. Our counselees normally pay little attention to God's goodness. Their desire for their next hit of pornographic pleasure blinds them to the Lord's blessings.

So, part of our job in these cases is to work with counselees to see the many ways in which the Lord loved them first, loves them most, and continually expresses that love. This might include assigning daily journals about the Lord's work during the week, reflections about God's love during various times in their lives, and enlisting the help of those closest to them to help them focus on their blessings from the Lord. A devotional guide can help with this.[7]

The Importance of Repentance, Not Just Guilt

Every person I have counseled regarding this area has expressed guilt. Many say they feel guilty immediately after each session of sin; others describe an overall sense of guilt about their pattern. Such guilt has bothered them and led them to seek help and possibly accountability, but it has not resulted in change. So, why not?

There is a difference between guilt and repentance. Only repentance produces change. Guilt is an objective, judicial state. The feeling of guilt sometimes accompanies that state, but neither the state nor the feeling automatically leads to repentance. People can push away guilt and continue to sin.

As we counsel, then, we need to challenge counselees to repent; we also need to ask God to grant them repentance. Great confessions like those in Psalm 51 and Dan 9:1–19 describe certain characteristics present in those who repent. First, repentant people do not excuse away their sin. The pornography user tends to say, "It does not hurt anyone," but those who repent don't make excuses. Second, repentant people are willing to

---

[7] For example, see Deepak Reju, *Pornography: Fighting for Purity* (Phillipsburg, NJ: P&R, 2018).

see their sinfulness historically. They can see moments in which the Lord was working in their hearts and they refused his work. If they are willing, they can even recount a number of exit ramps the Lord provided and note how responding weeks, months, years, or even decades earlier would have put their lives on a different path. Third, repentant people are willing to accept the consequences of a righteous and just God. They can understand the hurt they have caused the Lord, themselves, and others and are willing to bear the consequences of their sin. Fourth, repentant people depend on the gracious and compassionate nature of God to grant forgiveness. They ask for it because they know their heavenly Father delights in forgiving his children. Fifth, repentant people change. They are willing to do what is necessary to forsake their sin and put on righteousness.

Frankly, it is hard to repent. Apparently, it took David at least a year to repent of his sin with Bathsheba (2 Sam 11:27–12:13). Therefore, go slow and be thorough in encouraging your counselees to repent. And remember that being prompted to repent is different from actually repenting. (Know too that counseling brings pressure, and some counselees will respond positively to the pressure without genuine repentance.) When a counselee has worked through repentance in their heart, then there may be many people who should hear their meaningful and credible confession. Without true repentance, counselees will not change.

The Importance of Transparency and Accountability

Another characteristic of those in sexual sin is their tendency to hide it, even when accountability structures are set in place to help them. Transparency must be a high priority. Also, we must labor to help those we counsel to honestly admit their sexual sins so they can know the Lord's forgiveness (e.g., David in Ps 32:3–5). Then, is not just accountability but transparency.

At the same time, when we think about accountability, we must distinguish it from friendship. Effective accountability occurs when there is something to lose. If a person chooses not to go to work, disciplinary actions follow (e.g., a warning, a loss of pay, even termination). So, where is the loss for those hiding sexual sin? In too many counseling cases there has been none because people confused friendship one-anothering with genuine accountability. In friendship, we do not expect loss; rather, we expect friends to encourage us, cheer us on, and make life easier. That's not accountability.

So, we encourage you to consider some possible losses your counselee should face should they continue to employ a lack of transparency with you or another who is tasked with helping them be accountable. Perhaps it's the loss of a ministry position, a relationship, a privilege, or even membership in the church (1 Cor 5:11–13). Look to bring a sense of genuine accountability to the equation.

The Importance of Reducing Access

Counselees who have seen provocative images or videos do not quickly forget what they have seen. Often they can even replay it in their minds. Yet that should not dissuade us from helping them reduce their access to new material. While televisions, computers, and smartphones are part of daily life, not every counselee needs unrestricted access to them. Greatly limiting the time spent on such devices and even changing the location of a phone and computer will help counselees who want to change—as will adding software that blocks or reports inappropriate sites.

While many counselees find these recommendations frustrating to apply, we believe their use reflects biblical truth. Jesus taught in Matt 5:28–30, "But I tell you, everyone who looks at a woman lustfully has already committed adultery with her in his heart. If your right eye causes you to sin, gouge it out and throw it away. For it is better that you lose one of the parts of your body than for your whole body to be thrown into hell. And if your right hand causes you to sin, cut it off and throw it away. For it is better that you lose one of the parts of your body than for your whole body to go into hell." The language is metaphorical; it emphasizes the radical steps we must take in our battle against sin. While limiting or removing access to a televisions, smartphone, or computer makes certain tasks more difficult, it's another weapon for the war.

The Importance of Hating the Sin

Some counselees tell themselves their lustful sins are harmless. They fail to recognize how a self-centered and image-based view of sex trains a person to connect sex with pleasure sensations apart from a God-given spouse, which can harm present and future marriages.[8] They also ignore the harm done to the models and actors involved in the pornography industry. That industry violates what it means to be a person made in the image of God. How wicked and sad that anyone would watch a sex act being performed and masturbate to it as if included! Such a selfish action reduces the other individuals involved to sexual slaves designed only for personal benefit. This is all the more tragic when done by Christians, who are tasked with helping a world that desperately needs a Savior to hear the good news of Jesus. Counselors should help counselees hate every aspect of this sin.

With this in mind, I have asked sinning fathers, "If that was your daughter in that video, would you want someone to share Christ with her or to continue to exploit her?" I have asked college-aged young men, "If that woman in the picture was your mother, sister, or girlfriend, would you want someone to lust after her or to share Christ with her?" In every case, we should help counselees to hate how the pornography industry mistreats women and damages relationships.

While these matters can challenge the conscience, ultimately counselees learn to hate their sin only by seeing how it offends a holy God. The industry distorts God's design to achieve their own financial gain. Realizing this should produce a productive and meaningful anger that leads Christians in particular away from sin and to the purpose God has for them.[9] The more they grow in their hatred for it, the more likely they will turn away from it when the next moment of temptation strikes.

---

[8] The Bible warns about self-deception that leads to believing lies about the sexual experience (e.g., Prov 5:1–14, 6:23–35; 7:1–27). In recent years, neuroscience has illustrated the enslaving power of sexual sin (Prov 5:21–23) and the self-harming consequences of pornography. See William M. Struthers, *Wired for Intimacy: How Pornography Hijacks the Male Brain* (Downers Grove, IL: InterVarsity Press, 2010).

[9] See Powlison, *Good and Angry* (see chap. 21, n.1).

The Importance of Building a Proper Biblical Theology of Sex

In my counseling, I rarely find counselees who can give a meaningful biblical theology of sex and sexual expression. They received their teaching about sex through their friends, through entertainment, and mostly through pornography. The Bible contains a wealth of information about our sexual lives, so let's highlight three truths.

First, God designed sex to be good and pleasurable. Appropriate sex does not produce guilt and shame. It honors the Lord and produces joy in our bodies and hearts. God designed it as an act of procreation and pleasure. From the beginning of creation, it was a relational matter that was never about the performance. That is one reason God says, "This is why a man leaves his father and mother and bonds with his wife, and they become one flesh" (Gen 2:24).

Second, God designed monogamous marriage as the proper place for sex (Heb 13:4). In 1 Thess 4:3–5 Paul wrote, "This is God's will, your sanctification: that you keep away from sexual immorality, that each of you knows how to control his own body in holiness and honor, not with lustful passions, like the Gentiles, who don't know God."

The Bible, as we know, reveals the will of God. He desires his people to abstain from all forms of sexual immorality. First Corinthians 6:18 says, "Flee sexual immorality! Every other sin a person commits is outside the body, but the person who is sexually immoral sins against his own body." The wonderful gift of sex God gave his created people was designed to exist only within the bounds of marriage. Pornography and masturbation violate this standard.

Third, God designed sex for mutual benefit. First Corinthians 7:2–5 explains the equality in the bedroom. Each line describes mutual service and mutual authority to encourage each person to focus on the other. Pornography and masturbation, by contrast, teach that others are designed for *my* pleasure and *my* satisfaction. Sex with oneself therefore violates God's purposes for sex. It is the fastest way to harm a marriage even before it begins.

Ministering to the Wife of a Pornography User

While a woman can also engage in the sins of pornography and masturbation, the more common counseling experience involves males. Therefore, we want to provide you as a counselor with some initial help and resources in ministering to the wife of a man engaged in the sexual sins discussed.[10] Caring wives are often crushed when they learn of their husbands' sexual sin. They can feel deeply betrayed by their impurity and deceitfulness, rejected and abandoned for images on a screen, and confused about what to do next.

Consider at least five priorities when caring for such individuals.

First, provide access to others who can help. For instance, if you are a male counselor working with not just a sinning man but his hurting wife too, involving a mature Christian woman as a co-counselor or assistant is wise. Most wives appreciate having a supportive female presence in these sessions.

Second, stress that (if she is a believer) her primary identity is in Christ. She is the daughter of a caring Father, united forever to her faithful Savior, whose selfless death for her proved his unfailing love. Keep the gospel before her eyes.

Third, assure her that her husband's porn use is not her fault, despite any attempt he might make to minimize his sin or blame her. Don't let her accept blame for his choices. If you find she has taken responsibility for "causing" his sin, help her forsake that lie and dislodge her confused guilt (recall chapter 7).

Fourth, involve her in the counseling process, taking into consideration her desires. Be aware that some wives prefer to be at every session while others would rather be present for only certain sessions. Allow her to provide input regarding her husband's attitude and behavior, speak with her

[10] For example, see Vicki Tiede, *When Your Husband Is Addicted to Pornography: Healing Your Wounded Heart* (New Growth Press, 2012); and Kathy Gallagher, *When His Secret Sin Breaks Your Heart: Letters to Hurting Wives* (Dry Ridge, KY: Pure Life Ministries, 2019).

about her ongoing role with her husband, and help her as she processes her own motivations and desires. The goal is to care for and minister to her.

Finally, and above all, help her draw near to God and deepen her communion with him. Temptations surround her: to be bitter, seek revenge, pull away from her husband, or give up on her marriage. In fact, weaknesses in her relationship with the Lord might get exposed as a result of her ordeal. So, help her see those weaknesses and build her life on Jesus—his love and promises (Ps 73:23–28; 2 Tim 4:17). Comfort her, help her re-anchor her heart in Jesus, and coach her on how to love, forgive, and assist her husband to fight against his sin.

Conclusion

Counseling those struggling with pornography and masturbation is common. Counselees are at war. Ministering well to them involves understanding the powerful draw of sexual sin at the physical and heart levels, calling counselees to genuine repentance, and teaching them biblical truths about sexual attitudes and actions. Thankfully, the Lord is able to produce lasting change in each counselee (1 Cor 6:9–11). By God's grace, we will see the demand and desire for the things of God increase so that counselees live for Christ, the pornography industry closes for lack of business, those involved are saved, and the biblical truth on sex dominates our hearts and behavior.

32

Same-Sex Attraction and Gender Dysphoria

The current American culture, like most of the West, celebrates individuality and personal happiness. It should come as no surprise that these celebrations also occur in the area of sexuality. Unlike a century ago, or even fifty years ago, our culture now affirms and at times encourages things like homosexuality and a fluid gender identity.

Despite this, the church has remained fairly outspoken about these issues, affirming that while God has created gender and sexuality as good things within proper bounds, sin has distorted them immensely. But where does this leave the Christian struggling with homosexual attraction or gender dysphoria? How might we counsel in a way that faithfully and graciously brings God's Word to the counselee?

Definitions and Descriptions

Clear definitions are essential to this discussion. We must distinguish between *attraction* (or *feeling*) and *identity*—that is, between an internal state versus outward behavior and lifestyle. While this might seem like splitting hairs, it is vastly important. For example, consider the parallel between someone who *desires* to harm another person versus one who *actually hurts* someone versus someone who *identifies* as a murderer. While all three are impacted and ultimately driven by sinful hearts, the behavior and claim of identity matter tremendously.

Same-sex attraction (SSA) is essentially what it sounds like: sexual interest in and attraction to those of the same gender, with or without attraction to the opposite gender as well.[1] This includes those who act on or identify with the attraction (i.e., consider themselves homosexual and live the homosexual lifestyle) and those who do not (i.e., those who feel the attraction but do not identify as homosexual and do not act accordingly). The difference is the willingness to act on and identify with the internal conflict.

Numerous struggles come with SSA, some paralleling the struggles of those without it. These include dealing with impure thoughts, feeling different, feeling ashamed, grief over the inability to be "normal," setting appropriate physical boundaries, and internal conflict from the acceptance of some alongside the rejection of others. Christians with SSA might also wrestle with whether or not the attraction they feel is sinful, why God would allow their SSA, the surety of their salvation, and how to respond when others react poorly.

Gender dysphoria (GD) is a felt incongruence between one's biological sex and one's felt gender, like being born as a female but having an internal sense of being male. Like SSA, GD does not require that someone act on the internal feelings. In other words, gender dysphoria is separate from being transgender (living out and identifying as the opposite gender). It often includes things like disgust for one's body (beyond genitalia), emotional disturbances, feelings of isolation or "feeling different," confusion, and anxiety. While each counselee is an individual, we find that these

[1] For more on same-sex attraction, see Rosaria Champagne Butterfield, *The Secret Thoughts of an Unlikely Convert: An English Professor's Journey into Christian Faith* (Pittsburgh, PA: Crown & Covenant, 2012); Rosaria Champagne Butterfield, *Openness Unhindered: Further Thoughts of an Unlikely Convert on Sexual Identity and Union with Christ* (Pittsburgh: PA, Crown & Covenant, 2015); Wesley Hill, *Washed and Waiting: Reflections on Christian Faithfulness and Homosexuality* (Grand Rapids: Zondervan, 2016); Denny Burk and Heath Lambert, *Transforming Homosexuality: What the Bible Says about Sexual Orientation* (Phillipsburg, NJ: P&R, 2015); and R. Nicholas Black, *Homosexuality and the Bible: Outdated Advice or Words of Life?* (Greensboro, NC: New Growth Press, 2014).

feelings of incongruence generally begin between ages eight and fourteen. The struggles are very similar to those of SSA: internal conflict and suffering (looking one way on the outside but feeling like that appearance is wrong and difficult to change), confusion over boundaries for behavior and dress, feeling different and/or ashamed, grief over those differences and the inability to be "normal," and the spiritual questions mentioned above.

The Bible's View on Sexuality and Gender[2]

Scripture speaks clearly on both homosexuality and gender. We might consider the following passages when we think of both SSA and GD:

- Genesis 1:27, "God created man in his own image; . . . he created them male and female." The creation of Adam and Eve indicates both God's design for marriage (between one man and one woman) and for gender (Adam created as "male/husband" and Eve as "female/wife").
- Leviticus 18:22, "You are not to sleep with a man as with a woman; it is detestable." This passage speaks particularly to God's design for sexual relations between people.
- Deuteronomy 22:5, "A woman is not to wear male clothing, and a man is not to put on a woman's garment, for everyone who does these things is detestable to the LORD." God has established a clear male-female binary; the sexes are not to be confused with one another.
- Romans 1:26–28, "For this reason God delivered them over to disgraceful passions. Their women exchanged natural sexual relations for unnatural ones. The men in the same way also left natural relations with women and were inflamed in their lust for one another. Men committed shameless acts with men and received

[2] See Kevin DeYoung, *What Does the Bible Really Teach about Homosexuality?* (Wheaton, IL: Crossway, 2015); Sam Allberry, *Is God Anti-Gay? and Other Questions about Homosexuality, the Bible and Same-Sex Attraction*, rev. ed. (Epsom, UK: The Good Book Company, 2015); and R. Nicholas Black, *Homosexuality and the Bible: Outdated Advice or Words of Life?* (Greensboro, NC: New Growth Press, 2010).

in their own persons the appropriate penalty of their error. And because they did not think it worthwhile to acknowledge God, God delivered them over to a corrupt mind so that they do what is not right." Phrases such as "dishonorable," "contrary to nature," and "shameless acts" indicate God's position on sexual desires and behavior that fall outside his established norms and bounds.

- 1 Corinthians 6:9–10, "Don't you know that the unrighteous will not inherit God's kingdom? Do not be deceived: No sexually immoral people, idolaters, adulterers, or males who have sex with males, no thieves, greedy people, drunkards, verbally abusive people, or swindlers will inherit God's kingdom." Several of the sins in this list involve sexual misbehavior; its end result is separation from God.

These texts teach that ultimately homosexuality and atypical gender identity are products of sin in the fullest sense of the word: the entire person (whether they fall into these categories or not) is fallen and impacted by it. This includes the physical and nonphysical aspects of one's being (see chapters 5 and 6). All people have passions that do not align with God's desires, and for many these passions are sexual. But even in light of passions, we *choose* whether to act accordingly. Here the gospel brings us good news: In Christ, we have a new identity as a son or a daughter of the living God. We have a new power provided by his Spirit to fight against those sinful passions and to live celibately, even if those desires never change in this life.

Scripture also speaks to several key themes related to SSA and GD in less explicit ways. First, those who struggle with either commonly experience suffering. As I (Kristin) have sat repeatedly with counselees who struggle in these areas, I've been astounded by the depth of their suffering. It may be because of rejection from loved ones, including those in the church, a constant feeling of disconnect from their own bodies, or hopelessness. While SSA and GD are their "presenting problems," their pervasive feelings involve suffering, which the Bible addresses at great length. God knows what it is to suffer (Isa 53:3), he comforts believers in all of their afflictions (2 Cor 1:4), he will restore and strengthen us (1

Pet 5:10), and he guarantees us a future glory that outweighs any current suffering (Rom 8:18).

Further, God's Word must be the believer's authority despite feelings, including in these areas. His Word, not our experiences or any emotions we may have, is truth (John 17:17). His Word speaks to all of life (2 Pet 1:3) as we believers move toward godliness. For the counselee struggling with SSA or GD (or anything else), Scripture must be the voice of truth that counters any internal feelings or desires that do not align with God's design.

Finally, God remains sovereign despite feelings of incongruence within oneself. The counselee struggling with SSA or GD, particularly if they initiate counseling, rarely desires to feel the way they feel or to have the desires they do. They may be tempted to think—or have even been told—that God wouldn't have created them "that way" if they weren't supposed to live out those desires. But these conditions were not part of God's original design for men and women; they are products of sin's pervasive influence on the world. Nevertheless, God remains sovereign over how each person was created, and he has given clear directives for how we should live within his creation.

What does this mean for our counseling conversations regarding SSA and GD? It means that by God's Spirit, believers have the power to obey God despite their passions—even if that means fighting them day in and day out. It means our behaviors and identity matter immensely and that in Christ no one has to be enslaved by wrong desires any longer (Romans 6). Further, while God has the power to change one's passions and other sinful desires in this life, he sometimes chooses not to. Paul, for instance, lived with a "thorn"; and whatever it was, God left it in his life to help remind Paul that when he felt weak, Christ within him would prove strong (2 Cor 12:7–10). The believer's identity is found in Christ. He, rather than our feelings or struggles, determines what we are.

Counseling Steps and Practical Procedures

Before discussing counseling procedures, we should note that SSA and GD are distinct struggles. A counselor should not assume that one who struggles with GD also struggles with SSA. Still, those with GD, who might see themselves as the opposite gender, might be attracted to someone of their own biological gender and that attraction will "feel" appropriate, though it is technically same-sex attraction. While this matter will need to be addressed *at some point* in counseling, the counselee's SSA in these instances is secondary to their GD.

Counseling Same-Sex Attraction

When counseling someone with same-sex attraction,[3] the counselor must first seek to understand the counselee as fully as possible. If the counselor has little or no experience with SSA, it will take extra effort up front to grasp the person's perspectives and struggles. We can demonstrate the love and grace of Jesus by entering the world of the counselee and seeking to understand the weight of their struggle. Not only do we need to listen for evidence of suffering they are experiencing, but we must keep in mind their personal responsibility before a holy God.

Second, the counselor should discuss personal identity and where it comes from. To do that, we might weave in a homework assignment that asks the counselee to initially write out who they are and how they determined each aspect of their identity, and then work with them to challenge wrong thinking or to make any additions or changes in light of what the Bible teaches. In every case, the counselor should bring to light what Scripture says about human identity. We are all image bearers, and followers of Christ should seek to be Christlike. Also, it can prove helpful to a counselee to study what God's Word has to say about sexuality and sexual expression. Having them read passages like Genesis 1, Romans 1, and 1 Corinthians 6, and then record their insights and applications, will give them a starting place to have an informed talk with God about their struggle.

---

[3] See Edward T. Welch, *Homosexuality: Speaking the Truth in Love* (Phillipsburg, NJ: P&R, 2000); David White, *Can You Change If You Are Gay?* (Greensboro, NC: New Growth Press, 2013); David Longacre, ed., *First Steps of Compassion: Helping Someone Who Struggles with Same-Sex Attraction* (Boone, NC: L'Edge Press, 2009); and various resources from Harvest USA (www.harvestusa.org).

Third, the counselor can seek to walk with the counselee to determine how they choose to live in light of their struggle, focusing much more on the response than the struggle itself. Christians are responsible to obey the Lord's directives despite any wrong desires, and we must repent of those desires and actions that do not align with God's design. Christians can obey God by the Spirit of God living within us, but sometimes we first need a little gentle help to see where we are veering off course.

Fourth, the counselor should not give false promises about change. Though God may choose to relieve a counselee of their desires and align their desires with his, he may also opt not to relieve the burden of struggle on this side of eternity. So, while we can encourage the counselee to grieve this aspect of their fallen condition and to ask God to transform their desires, we must not guarantee God will do so. A person might struggle with SSA for the rest of their life. They should focus on walking with Christ and depending on God's power to live rightly in a fallen world.

Fifth, the counselor should discuss with the counselee God's sovereignty and suffering, acknowledging their counselee's suffering while maintaining God's sovereignty in the midst of it. This would include having any necessary discussions about God allowing our suffering, his creation of people living under the impact of sin[4], and his design for prolonged singleness despite a desire for marriage and companionship. It may also involve having a conversation about feelings of having to "prove" oneself by amplifying one's own masculinity or femininity.

Finally, the counselor must proclaim the good news of the gospel, that the Lord Jesus already paid the price for all sin on the cross. Even if a particular counselee is a longtime believer in Christ, they will benefit from a fresh reminder that the gospel impacts life on a daily basis. Christ's followers have suffered and died with Christ; we belong to him—even with our disordered desires. He calls us to mortify the desires of the flesh, and we

[4] Note that humankind was not designed to live under the effects of sin. Adam's disobedience ushered in that tragic state. Christ's obedience, by contrast, offers humans the path out from under the curse (John 3:16–17; Rev 21:3–4). For further study, see our Appendix: Recommended Resources on Suffering.

are to seek to honor him. *All* struggles are temporary; one day they will end. Keeping an eternal perspective is key to living in daily victory.

Counseling Gender Dysphoria

How should biblical counselors approach GD? Since few such counselors have written on this topic to date, we must find help from the wider world of evangelical Christian counseling.[5] In counseling parents of younger children who might express GD, "watchful waiting," combined with positive, nonconfrontational biblical teaching about gender, seems wise.[6] In many instances, the child's gender will work itself out as the child grows up. With older children, adolescents, and adults, the wisest approach seems to be watchful waiting that allows the counselee to explore their struggles without the counselor reinforcing the unbiblical identity. After they have entered the counselee's struggle and sought to understand their suffering, parents or counselors should introduce Christ-centered biblical teaching in wise and timely ways. Of course, each parent might need to decide how much freedom to explore they should give to their older minor children living under their roof. Since the struggle might consume sufferers day in and day out, we should show them grace, compassion, and wisdom. While each counselor can decide what this looks like in practice, some issues to consider are the timing and content of conversations and whether to use the counselee's preferred name or gender identifier ("he" or "she") in conversations with them.[7]

---

[5] For example, see Mark Yarhouse, an integrationist Christian counselor, in his *Understanding Gender Dysphoria: Navigating Transgender Issues in a Changing Culture* (Downers Grove, IL: IVP Academic, 2015). He summarizes four approaches secular counselors use. Biblical counselors might affirm the first two—direct intervention and watchful waiting—but not psychosocial facilitation and puberty suppression. Another helpful resource for counseling those with GD is Andrew T. Walker, *God and the Transgender Debate: What Does the Bible Actually Say about Gender Identity?* (Epsom, Surrey, England: The Good Book Company, 2017).

[6] For resources for parents or youth leaders, see Tim Geiger, *What to Do When Your Child Says, "I'm Gay"* (Greensboro, NC: New Growth Press, 2013); Ben Marshall, *Help! My Teen Struggles with Same-Sex Attractions* (Wapwallopen, PA: Shepherd Press, 2011); and Cooper Pinson, *Helping Students with Same-Sex Attraction: Guidance for Parents and Youth Leaders* (Greensboro, NC: New Growth Press, 2017).

[7] Counselors vary on whether they should use the counselee's preferred name or gender identifier. Some argue doing so condones the preferred gender. A third approach

For those helping people struggling with GD, much of the best counseling advice echoes that listed above in counseling SSA, though it is nuanced for gender struggles. Certainly, the counselor must be quick to listen and slow to speak (Jas 1:19), taking a good bit of time to understand the counselee and their struggle, especially if the counselor has not struggled personally with GD. We must work to understand each individual well, including where they are in the struggle (i.e., when did they first notice the feelings, and have they thought extensively about gender-reassignment surgery?) and what they are wanting out of counseling.

As when counseling those with SSA, counselors should discuss identity and the source of the believer's identity, helping counselees study Scripture's teachings on sexuality and gender for themselves. We also should wisely and graciously affirm Scripture's reality of distorted desires because of the fall. This, of course, would look different for a believer than an unbeliever who will likely not see Scripture as an authority on gender identity. So, early on, we should seek to understand the weight the counselee places on God's Word.

In light of the suggested approach above—watchful waiting balanced with biblical teaching and caring confrontation, the counselor should decide how to follow these principles while taking care not to affirm behavior. In fact, counselors should settle this matter in their own minds, according to their consciences before the Lord, early—even before counseling begins. It is not loving or kind to a counselee to have a counselor unprepared to discuss struggles appropriately, especially such weighty matters as these.

Finally, the counselor should grieve the struggle along with the counselee. No person going through GD or any struggle delights in suffering. Neither does the Lord. He is gracious and kind in the midst of struggles, and uses them to accomplish his purposes, but struggles with gender identity are yet another product of sin in its many expressions, and that is to be grieved. Moreover, we grieve with counselees when they realize that they might deal with these feelings for the rest of their lives, and consequently never marry or have children.

---

avoids the use of gender specific pronouns (instead using *them/their*) or any names to avoid affirming or needlessly offending a person.

In counseling parents of children with GD, the counselor can educate them on their child's struggles (see footnote 6 above). It is about more than just the behaviors or feelings and practical implications (like dressing differently or conflict that arises); emotional struggles come along with it. The counselor should acknowledge the struggle of the parents as well. GD is usually expressed outwardly, which might lead to embarrassment or awkward questions from outsiders. Counselors can help parents think through how to love their children well while not affirming their behaviors; they can aid them in balancing grace and firmness that doesn't stem from their own frustrations, embarrassment, or legalism.

Lastly, the counselor should affirm the gospel. In the midst of struggles over gender identity, we must remember that hope and true identity are found in Christ, that God's saving power is mighty, and that all who trust in Jesus as Lord and Savior will have eternal victory over sin. Even a struggle that might last for a lifetime is not eternal.

Conclusion

The need for counseling those with issues of same-sex attraction and gender dysphoria will likely increase over the next several years, particularly given the current cultural climate. Therefore, biblical counselors must be prepared to enter into these struggles with their counselees, understand both the sin and the suffering dynamics, and bring Christ's gospel power and hope to help them.

33

Sexual Abuse and Assault

In the beginning, God created sexual intimacy to be a good thing expressed in particular ways. He designed sexual expression for a husband and wife within the covenant of marriage (Gen 2:24–25; Heb 13:4). Sin's entrance into creation distorted sexuality and sexual expression; one distortion is the sin of sexual abuse or assault, which appeared as early as Old Testament times.

Counselors must be prepared to address this tragic issue with both children and adults, and with both recent victims and those who have been dealing with the effects of assault for decades. While this chapter will apply to three categories—children and teens recently abused,[1] adults recently abused,[2] and adults abused in the past[3]—we will focus primarily on counseling adults who have experienced sexual abuse at some point.

---

[1] Sometimes parents bring an abused child to us or seek our help in how to care for that child. See chapter 37 for more on counseling children after abuse.

[2] For more on sexual assault, see David Powlison, *Sexual Assault: Healing Steps for Victims* (Greensboro, NC: New Growth Press, 2010); Justin S. Holcomb and Lindsey A. Holcomb, *Rid of My Disgrace: Hope and Healing for Victims of Sexual Assault* (Wheaton, IL: Crossway, 2011).

[3] See David Powlison, *Recovering from Child Abuse: Healing and Hope for Victims* (Greensboro, NC: New Growth, 2008); John Henderson, *Abuse: Finding Hope in Christ* (Phillipsburg, NJ: P&R, 2012); Robert W. Kellemen, *Sexual Abuse: Beauty for Ashes* (Phillipsburg, NJ: P&R, 2013); and Pamela Gannon and Beverly Moore, *In the Aftermath: Past the Pain of Childhood Sexual Abuse* (Bemidji, MN: Focus Publishing, 2017).

As counselors, we might meet counselees at any point relative to their experience of abuse. You might meet a young woman who was recently raped or encounter an adult who just now realizes the impact childhood abuse has been having on her life. In every case, you must pay attention to each person's individual struggle. While much of the below applies to multiple categories, we will note nuances for particular categories when they arise.

Understanding Sexual Abuse

Sexual abuse is any sexually-related action against the will of another person (i.e., without their explicit consent) through force or coercion, often by a person with power or authority over the victim. It includes both physical touching (with or without penetration) and nonphysical, nontouching (speech, forced viewing of sexual activity) sexual behavior. These intentionally broad, umbrella terms encompass a variety of sexual misbehavior. While sexual abuse and assault might include a component of satisfying sexual desire, they primarily involve power and force. The abuser ultimately aims to dominate or control the victim. Other forms of abuse, in fact, often go with it. These include physical violence, verbal abuse, or manipulation.

Most victims are female, and the overwhelming majority of perpetrators (over 90 percent) are male. Approximately 80 percent of the time, a person is abused by someone she or he knows.[4] Sexual abuse and assault are common: one in three women and one in six men will be victims of sexual abuse or assault—usually before the age of eighteen. Experts estimate it's often significantly underreported. Worse, we see cases of sexual abuse arising even within the church.[5]

---

[4] "Statistics . . . Sexual Violence by Any Perpetrator," National Sexual Violence Resource Center, https://www.nsvrc.org/statistics.

[5] See "Sexual Misconduct and Churchgoers: National Survey of Protestant Church Goers," LifeWay Research, http://lifewayresearch.com/wp-content/uploads/2019/06/Sexual-Misconduct-and-Churchgoers-Report-6.14.2019.pdf.

What Might We as Counselors See?

Sexual abuse or assault can be difficult to detect unless the victim reports it. However, certain behaviors should encourage us to inquire about it as a possibility even when it's not a counselee's presenting issue. In adults, red flags include aversions to people or places, sudden withdrawal, or unexplained bruising or physical injury. We might see compulsive eating or drug/alcohol use to control or get rid of anxiety or depression. Flashbacks or triggers might be present, even if the abuse or assault occurred years ago. None of these symptoms alone, however, should lead us to assume a counselee has been abused. For instance, sexual promiscuity—which can also be a red flag—might simply be a teen's sin pattern. Nevertheless, changes in behavior or sudden onset of these things should precipitate further thought and potentially more data gathering. A counselor should remain aware that abuse or assault *might* have happened and should wisely seek to determine if that is the case and whether it is connected to current presenting problems. Often due to shame, counselees might not share details of past events. So, if a counselor suspects sexual abuse, they should build trust, exercise patience, and pray that the Lord will help the counselee bring up the information when they are ready.

Given a person's wholistic nature, the impact of sexual abuse or assault might show up in a victim in many facets of life (recall chapter 5). The following are some common effects on a person:

- feelings such as sadness, anger, or fear
- a sense of guilt or shame
- blaming oneself for the abuse or assault
- anxiety, depression, post-trauma symptoms, substance abuse, eating disorders, and suicide attempts[6]

---

[6] The National Institute of Health reports statistically significant correlations between sexual abuse/assault and the development of these problems. See Laura P. Chen et al., "Sexual Abuse and Lifetime Diagnosis of Psychiatric Disorders: Systematic Review and Meta-analysis," National Institute of Health, July 2010, https://www.ncbi.nlm.nih.gov/pmc/articles/PMC2894717/.

- confusion
- relational struggles with others, including a loss of trust in people, isolation, or intimacy issues
- increased promiscuity
- becoming overly concerned about danger or increasing in fearfulness
- eating or sleeping disturbances, including nightmares or fear of vulnerability while sleeping
- physical illnesses such as STDs, STIs, pregnancy, or wounds from the event(s)
- an overactivated fight-or-flight response or feeling constantly on alert
- higher stress levels
- questioning God's goodness and sovereignty
- difficulties in understanding God as a good Father (particularly if the abuser is one's own father)[7]
- struggles with relationships within the church (whether the local church knew about the abuse or not)

Each of these effects is something that a biblical counselor should both explore and be ready to lovingly address using appropriate scriptures.

Finally, we should remember that it is developmentally appropriate and common for a victimized child to struggle with the abuse regularly as they get older and can comprehend more. They will likely revisit the abuse mentally several times throughout adolescence and adulthood. This does not indicate a lack of forgiveness or that a victimized counselee isn't over the abuse. Rather, it is natural to wrestle again with what happened in light of growing understanding. This, in fact, is why counselees sometimes wait until adulthood to seek counseling.

---

[7] See David Powlison, *Life beyond Your Parents' Mistakes: The Transforming Power of God's Love* (Greensboro, NC: New Growth Press, 2010).

The Bible's Perspective

The Bible includes several instances of sexual abuse, namely rape (Genesis 34; Judges 19; 2 Samuel 13[8]). In Genesis 34, Jacob's daughter, Dinah, was violated by Shechem, the son of a neighboring ruler. Her brothers murdered him, his father, and all of the men of his city in revenge. This story is but one reminder that Scripture takes sexual violations seriously, in part because all people—including women and children—are worthy of dignity, honor, and respect as image bearers of God. Because people are image bearers, in fact, the whole person is sacred, including the body. God condemns all sexual immorality (1 Thess 4:3–5; 1 Cor 6:18–20; Rom 1:24–27), no doubt in part because the body—once one trusts in Christ—becomes the temple of the Holy Spirit (1 Cor 6:19). Ultimately, violations against people are violations against the Creator.

The Bible also reminds us that the victim of sexual abuse or assault is not responsible for the perpetrator's actions. For example, Deut 22:25–27 says:

> [If a] man encounters an engaged woman in the open country, and he seizes and rapes her, only the man who raped her must die. Do nothing to the young woman, because she is not guilty of an offense deserving death. This case is just like one in which a man attacks his neighbor and murders him. When he found her in the field, the engaged woman cried out, but there was no one to rescue her.

Note that last sentence, which speaks of a situation quite common in cases of abuse or assault. For most abused men, women, and children, violations happen in secret; there is no rescuer or helper within earshot. Like the woman in the field, each is essentially helpless against attack. This should grieve us; we know with certainty it grieves God. Note also the severe punishment—death—for the man who violates a woman in this way. While today we tend to think about all sinful subjects in light of the

[8] Scholars differ on whether King David's first sexual encounter with Bathsheba, his married royal subject, qualifies as rape (see 2 Samuel 11).

grace Christ offers sinners, God's law takes these sexual sins very seriously and places full responsibility on the offender rather than the offended. Scripture calls us to "provide justice for the needy and . . . uphold the rights of the oppressed" (Ps 82:3).

Moreover, counselors and victims might need to wrestle with how God can be sovereign over all things—which he is—yet allow sin. In his infinite wisdom, God does allow sin in this world. And we cannot understand fully why he does not intervene against it more often, particularly in situations of sexual abuse and assault. It helps to recall that God grieves over sin, so much so that he sent his Son to redeem us from our own sin and to promise us a glorious, sin-free tomorrow.

The Helpful Example of Tamar in 2 Samuel 13

Let's consider a more extensive passage on sexual assault and draw some counseling implications. In 2 Samuel 13, King David's daughter Tamar is raped by her half-brother Amnon sometime after the Bathsheba incident. Because Tamar is a beautiful virgin and Amnon is so infatuated with her (v. 1–4), he agrees to a plan to deceive her into caring for him (vv. 5–10). Once the trap is laid, he overpowers her (vv. 11–14). Afterward, he sends her away because he hates her (v. 15). The aftermath of these events involves a brother killing a brother and years of family upheaval (vv. 21–38), as the rest of 2 Samuel shows.

We can offer six principles from this account to a counselee who has been sexually abused. First, every person is a precious image bearer of God. And like Tamar, all people should be highly valued and protected, especially those who are vulnerable and weak. Second, perpetrators are deceitful and often keep bad company that influences them in sinful directions (vv. 3–5). Amnon's sin was premeditated and involved lies, quite common of perpetrators. This, however, in no way reflects on Tamar the innocent victim. Third, this particular sin often affects more than just the initial victim. The whole royal family had to deal with the results of the rape and responses to it (vv. 20–38). The sin of abuse/assault can affect family members, friends, any future spouses, and others.

Fourth, as our definition of assault says, victims are powerless to stop it. Tamar pleaded with Amnon, even offering him a proper way to pursue her, yet he selfishly overpowered her (vv. 12–13). Victims are powerless and bear no blame for the abuse or assault. Fifth, sin often brings devastating results. Many relationships were severed, and Amnon died as a result of his actions. Even if there is repentance and forgiveness and no one but the victim and abuser know about what happened, the relationship between perpetrator and victim will likely permanently change. Finally, being victimized can bring long-lasting shame, despair, and hopelessness. Tamar "lived as a desolate woman" for the rest of her life (v. 20). Shame, despair, and hopelessness are common responses to sexual violations. They might be long-lasting.

The whole tragic event points to the world's great need for a Redeemer to come, as the larger narrative of 2 Samuel pictures.

Counseling Steps and Practical Procedures

The first component of counseling in the wake of sexual abuse or assault, regardless of when the events occurred, is to be present. Counselors should affirm their presence, and the Lord's, continually throughout the counseling process. This brings comfort, calm, and consistency at a time when a counselee might feel violated, hurt, and fearful. As a part of this step, we should encourage counselees to connect with their local churches to establish a support system or support group to walk with them through the healing process. We also might need to help educate a counselee's friends, family, and church members about how to love them well.

We should ensure counselees' safety, involving proper authorities should situations require it. If the abuse/assault was recently committed against an adult, or against an adult when they were a child, we can even help the counselee consider legal options (e.g., reporting to law enforcement) and help them make wise decisions based on what happened. While the potential scenarios vary, both counselor and counselee should understand the value of bringing sin into the light, to protect other potential victims and to ensure consequences for the perpetrator's actions and perhaps prompt that person to repent. A Bible study of God's responses to mistreatment and of the role of governing authorities might help in gauging the wisdom of proper reporting. At the same time, we must be ready to help counselees handle the possible repercussions of reporting.

Once our presence and their safety are established, a key part of initial and ongoing counseling is listening and gathering information wisely. We should focus on the key issues, exercising patience and discerning carefully when the counselee might be getting overwhelmed. Key factors to explore include the basic details of the event(s) (what happened, when, and by whom), the frequency and duration of the incident(s), the length of time since the incident(s) occurred, the counselee's relationship to the perpetrator and whether or not there is continued interaction with them, the involvement of others (who were complicit or ignored the event, or tried to help your counselee), and the resulting emotions both then and now. Many counselees benefit from having someone truly hear and affirm the reality of their suffering, while exercising patience in allowing them to work through the details of their stories. The counselor might only get portions of the story a little at a time. We should not assume the counselee is withholding information or lying; this may just reflect the rate at which they are understanding and piecing together what happened.

As counseling moves forward, we must be sensitive to any ongoing effects of the abuse or assault. We should continually affirm the counselee's dignity, that the violation against them was sinful and in no way their fault. We should address any sense of guilt, embarrassment, or shame, knowing that healing from such issues will likely be a long process. Similarly, we should deal with the resulting thoughts and emotions of the counselee. This might include working through any self-blame, hard feelings toward God, flashbacks of the event(s), replaying the event with different outcomes or things the counselee could have done differently, holding on to bitterness or anger, or the fear of the abuse/assault happening again. We might ask counselees to journal their thoughts or emotions in these areas (prayer journaling if possible) and should encourage them to focus on God's Word rather than feelings, fears, or faulty beliefs (Deut 31:6; Lam 3:24; Isa 41:10; Pss 56:3–4; 62; Rom 12:12; Phil 4:8; Titus 2:11–14; 2 Tim 1:7).

Next, we should grieve with our counselees (Rom 12:15). Counselors and those they help can grieve the reality of the sin and its personal impact, acknowledging both its depth and duration. We should seek to frame the event(s) in light of Scripture, recalling where applicable the implications from 2 Samuel 13 mentioned above.

Further, we should remember that ultimate hope does not come from a counselee's ability to help themselves or from our abilities as counselors. Since hope is only found in Christ, we should work with each counselee to explore the hope believers have through his work on the cross, his work in our lives, and the power of his Spirit living within us. We must give counselees this true hope, even while still lamenting the impact of sin. It may prove helpful to look in depth at the stories of Joseph (Genesis 37–50; see below) or Job, or passages like Heb 4:14–16; 1 Pet 1:3–9; or Rom 5:1–5 to aid counselees in realizing how God wants them to handle suffering and grow in his grace.

Further, we can give counselees growth assignments to explore areas where their perceived identity does not align with God's Word. Or we might prompt them to think through any ways they are not living in light of his truth. Remember that when it comes to formal counseling, Spirit-guided self-confrontation is usually more effective than direct confrontation. Our goal should be to help enable each counselee to come to their own conclusions about personal misbeliefs or wrong responses. This does not mean we should not directly point out sin if a counselee is blind to it. Rather, given the sensitivity of the struggle discussed in this chapter, we should help them look into the mirror of God's Word to see with their own eyes what God says to them (Jas 1:22–25).

At some point, typically late in the process, the counselor should gently and tactfully help the adult counselee acknowledge and take personal responsibility for any ways she might have contributed to the abuse (e.g., through enabling behavior or sinful speech) or for sinful ways she might have responded to the abuse (e.g., bitterness, revenge, unrighteous anger, or faulty beliefs). Despite a violation done against her, a counselee is still responsible for her thoughts, emotions, and behaviors before, during, or after the event(s) (Rom 12:19). While the counselee likely had no control over or culpability for the abuse itself, she can control her response to it. We can help counselees live in such a way that what happened to them no longer controls them.

Eventually, a counselor and counselee should consider what good might come out of the evil that was experienced and how the counselee might be able to minister to others on this side of it (2 Cor 1:3–6). We should discuss what it might look like to move toward forgiveness and reconciliation (Eph 4:31–32). Reconciliation does not necessitate that the offender face no legal ramifications for their actions (see chapter 20); yet, it is good to point out to Christian counselees that restoration between two parties reflects the restoration we have with the Father because of Christ.[9]

Conclusion: Inspiration from Joseph

Taking a long look at Joseph's story alongside your counselee can provide them with a powerful example of the surprising good that God can bring out of the ashes of abuse. Genesis 37–50 tells how Joseph was sinned against severely as a teenager: his brothers mocked him, threw him in a pit, and then sold him into slavery. Not long after, his master's wife repeatedly tried to seduce him, and when he wouldn't comply with her demands, she accused *him* of violating *her*. That injustice went unpunished when innocent Joseph was subsequently jailed. Yet at every point in his story, Joseph trusted that the Lord was with him. Joseph chose to see his goodness, to cling to his promises, and to trust in his provisions.

When the time was right, God lifted Joseph to a position of incredible authority. So great was his power, in fact, that he could've used it to execute

[9] Ideally, restoration results from the offending party's true repentance for their actions and the offended party granting forgiveness. However, when this two-way reconciliation is not possible, either due to a lack of repentance by the offender or because there's no ability to communicate with them, the counselor should still walk the counselee through the process of one-way attitudinal forgiveness. The inability to reconcile does not relieve the victim from the responsibility to forgive. For help in these complex matters, see Ken Sande, *The Peacemaker: A Biblical Guide to Resolving Personal Conflict*, 3rd ed. (Ada, MI: Baker, 2004); and Robert D. Jones, *Pursuing Peace* (see chap. 7, n. 2).

the woman whose lust and lies imprisoned him and to take revenge on his brothers. Yet Joseph chose to extend forgiveness, grace, and kindness (see esp. Gen 49:22–26; 50:19–20). In the end, Joseph realized that God had turned around all his suffering so that it accomplished his divine purposes. In fact, thousands of years later, Christians are inspired by his words to his brothers: "You intended to harm me, but God intended it all for good" (Gen 50:20 NLT). No doubt Joseph lacked understanding at points along the way, but his faith remained in his sovereign, good God. As counselors, we can invite our counselees to follow his example.

34

Guidance and Decision-Making

Justin wants to obey God. He likes his girlfriend, Amanda, but isn't sure she is "the one" for him. He definitely wants to avoid the kind of unhappy marriage his own parents experienced, so he really wants to know if the Lord wants him to marry her or not.

Jana loves children and admires several teachers she has had. Now a high school senior, Jana is thinking about going to college to study elementary education. But because she also enjoys science, she is considering possibly training for a career in the medical field instead. She wonders what God wants her to pursue.

Todd and Amy vacillate about schooling choices for their children. They are godly parents with godly friends who variously advocate homeschooling, public schooling, and private schooling. The pair doesn't know which decision is best, though they both want their choice to have God's blessing.

Everyone faces decisions like these—some are major, some minor; some impact the long term, some only the short term. How can we as biblical counselors help people make decisions? Let's consider some vital theological perspectives, followed by six practical steps.[1]

---

[1] For further resources along the same lines, see Garry Friesen and J. Robin Maxson, *Decision Making and the Will of God: A Biblical Alternative to the Traditional View,* rev.

Distinguishing God's Sovereign Will and God's Revealed Will

Understanding the Biblical Distinction

The Bible distinguishes between God's sovereign will and his revealed will. Deuteronomy 29:29 presents the distinction: "The hidden things belong to the LORD our God, but the revealed things belong to us and our children forever, so that we may follow all the words of this law." Two kinds of knowledge exist: secret things hidden from us and revealed things given to us. Or consider Joseph's words in Gen 50:20: "You planned evil against me; God planned it for good to bring about the present result—the survival of many." Note two distinct intentions wrapped up in one series of events. God's sovereign will in Joseph's life coexists with and yet mysteriously overrides his brothers' disobedience to God's revealed will.

God's *sovereign* will (also called his decretive, secret, or providential will) entails all God plans and eventually brings to pass as he sovereignly guides and uses every part of his universe—even evil—to accomplish his eternal purpose. God's *revealed* will (also called his directive, moral, preceptive, or desired will) involves all God requires us to do—what he has revealed in Scripture as his directive will for us to obey as we properly observe, interpret, and apply his Word. The table following summarizes these distinctions:

---

ed. (Colorado Springs: Multnomah, 2004). See also Kevin DeYoung, *Just Do Something: A Liberating Approach to Finding God's Will* (Chicago: Moody Press, 2009); Sinclair B. Ferguson, *Discovering God's Will* (Carlisle, PA: Banner of Truth, 1982); John MacArthur, *Found: God's Will: Find the Direction and Purpose God Wants for Your Life*, rev. ed. (Elgin, IL: David C. Cook, 2012); and James C. Petty, *Step by Step: Divine Guidance for Ordinary Christians* (Phillipsburg, NJ: P&R, 1999). See also the detailed Bible study on guidance in Wayne A. Mack, *Homework Manual for Biblical Living: Family and Marital Problems*, vol. 1 (Phillipsburg, NJ: P&R, 1979), 86–92.

God's Sovereign Will	God's Revealed Will
Key Passages Deut 29:29a; Gen 50:20b; Job 1–2, 42; Prov 16:9, 33; 20:24; Jer 10:23; Daniel 4; Rom 8:28; 11:33–36; Eph 1:10–11; Jas 4:13–18; Revelation 5	Key Passages Deut 29:29b; Gen 50:20a; Ps 19:7–11; Prov 2:1–6; John 17:17; Col 1:9–12; 2 Tim 3:14–17
1) Determined from eternity past	1) Written in Scripture, in time-space history
2) Seen in what happens in specific events	2) Seen in Scripture's general directives/ commands
3) Includes evil	3) Never includes evil
4) Unknowable in advance (beyond what the Bible promises will happen)	4) Knowable in advance and at all times

Pursuing God's Knowable, Revealed Will

What is God's revealed will for an individual you counsel? The Bible directs every person to love God and neighbors (Matt 22:36–40), to obey Jesus (Matt 28:20), to worship God (John 4:23–24), to glorify God (1 Cor 10:31), to fear God (Eccl 12:13), to please God (2 Cor 5:9), to live for Christ (2 Cor 5:15), and to walk in God's love, light, and wisdom (Eph 5:1–2, 8, 15–18).

How does someone know how to love God, obey Jesus, and please the Lord? Paul tells us, "Brothers and sisters, we ask and encourage you in the Lord Jesus, that as you have received instruction from us on how you should live and please God—as you are doing—do this even more. For you know what commands we gave you through the Lord Jesus" (1 Thess 4:1–2). Paul's readers knew how to please God based on Paul's apostolic instructions. Indeed, God commands us to know and to do his revealed will, found in his Word.

What does this involve? Based on a word study of God's revealed will, John MacArthur offers a helpful summary. It is God's will that every counselee, for instance, be saved (2 Pet 3:9), Spirit-filled (Eph 5:17–18), progressively sanctified (1 Thess 4:3–8), submissive (1 Pet 2:13–18), live in service to God (Acts 16:6–10), and give thanks (1 Thess 5:18). If these descriptors truly mark your walk with the Lord, MacArthur would say, then do whatever you want (Ps 37:4).[2]

What role does God's Spirit play in guidance and decision-making? Some believers teach that God's Spirit gives his people direct decision-making guidance apart from the Bible. After all, the Spirit "led" (Matt 4:1; Luke 4:1) and "drove" (Mark 1:12) Jesus into the wilderness to be tempted by Satan. Yet Jesus had a uniquely intimate relationship with the Spirit (Luke 3:22), and this temptation event seems to be an explicit, exclusive component of his redemptive mission. While Rom 8:14 and Gal 5:18 describe believers being "led by the Spirit," both passages pertain to Christian growth, not decision-making.[3]

How, then, does the Holy Spirit guide his people? We can identify three indispensable ways, all related to God's Word: (1) *inspiration*—in one sense, the Spirit wrote the Bible (2 Tim 3:16; 2 Pet 1:19–21), (2) *illumination*—the Spirit opens our eyes to understand the Bible (1 Cor 2:6–16; Ps 119:18), and (3) *progressive sanctification*—the Spirit gives us the desire and power to believe and obey the Bible (Phil 2:12–13; Eph 5:18; Zech 4:6), including serving others with our Spirit-given ministry gifts (1 Cor 12:1–11). We must never reduce biblical guidance to bare rationalism or cold formalism. It involves a Person, the Holy Spirit; he works actively in us, in and through his Word.[4]

---

[2] MacArthur, *Found: God's Will.*

[3] In Rom 8:14 the Spirit helps us put to death our remaining sin, confirming our identity as God's children. In Gal 5:18 the Spirit enables us to produce the Spirit's fruit and serve others.

[4] We recognize there are evangelical scholars who hold our same high view of Scripture and would agree essentially with this chapter, but whose view of spiritual gifts

Resisting a Popular Alternative Approach

Several components typically mark the most common alternative approach to our own. First, God has a specific, individual will for each person beyond the written Word. Second, we are responsible to discern that will. Third, God will reveal to us that specific, individual will. Fourth, he will do so through various means, such as prayer, the counsel of others, circumstances, open and closed doors, signs, or fleeces.

As much as those supporting this approach seek to honor God and to help people follow him, it falls short of biblical teaching in numerous ways.[5]

First, it doesn't distinguish between God's sovereign will and his revealed will. It assumes the existence of a third sense of God's will, an individual, revealed will.

Second, it doesn't provide biblical criteria to distinguish major decisions like marriage partner selection from minor decisions like which socks to wear. It assumes God has a directive will for us in every specific area of life.

Third, it minimizes God's agenda to make us wise, mature sons and daughters and to sanctify our beliefs and desires. It assumes Bible-believing, Spirit-filled believers need something besides God's Spirit working through his Word. God has given us his Word and by his Spirit he is training us to apply that Word in our daily lives, as we seek his help. That process requires more faith from us than expecting God to message us a detailed blueprint of what to do in every situation. Just as mature adults no longer need their parents to tell them what decisions to make, God's sons and daughters trained by his Word can discern what paths please him.

(e.g., prophecy) involves a broader understanding of the Spirit's guidance. For example, see Wayne A. Grudem et al., *Are Miraculous Gifts for Today? Four Views* (Grand Rapids: Zondervan, 1996).

[5] For a summary and critique, see Friesen and Maxson, *Decision Making*; Bruce K. Waltke, *Finding the Will of God: A Pagan Notion?* (Grand Rapids: Eerdmans, 2002).

Fourth, it undermines the believer's confidence in God's future, sovereign purposes in their life. It assumes wrong choices might make us miss God's "plan A" and doom us to "plan B."

Fifth, it insulates us from legitimate questions wise friends might raise about our decisions. Afterall, how can anyone dare question us if we declare, "The Lord led me to do X?" (A humbler approach calls for tentativeness and invites fellow believers to probe our thinking.)

Sixth, it denies the sole authority and sufficiency of Scripture. It assumes we need revelation apart from his Word, often through the following activities or experiences:

- Prayer. The Bible presents prayer as the way for us to talk to God, not for God to talk to us. We speak to God in prayer; God speaks to us in his Word. For that reason, we should ask God to illumine to us the meaning and application of his Word (Ps 119:18; Prov 2:1–6), and we should understand the plea for wisdom in Jas 1:5 in light of its immediate context (concerning trials) and of God's revealed Word in Jas 1:18–25 and 3:13–18. Of course, as we pray, God's Spirit might guide us to think more clearly about biblical truth.
- The counsel of others. While God certainly uses wise counselors, he uses them not to reveal a decision but to help us think more accurately, in light of his Word, about God, ourselves, and our situations.
- Circumstances and open or closed doors. The major problem with letting these determine a decision is that circumstances are not self-interpreting; they require our fallible interpretation. Paul, for example, bypassed an open door for ministry due to a wiser priority (2 Cor 2:12–13). As others have noted, open doors might lead into elevator shafts.
- Signs and fleeces. Using this approach is a specific form of the circumstantial approach above which bargains with God to reveal something to us through some upcoming event. In Judges 6 Gideon laid out a fleece to gain assurance from God that God would help him in battle. Yet this was not an instance of God revealing his will by the fleece. Gideon already knew what God

wanted; God had told him directly. Gideon's fleece expressed his weak faith. God graciously accommodated this doubting man.

Helping Counselees Make God-Pleasing Decisions

How can biblical counselors guide people in decision-making? Let's walk through a practical step-by-step process, stated below in terms of the actual counsel we would give someone.

1. Commit Yourself to God and Pray

Godly decision-making starts with a proper personal heart condition and right posture before God. Ask yourself heart-searching questions like these:

- Am I committed to pleasing God (2 Cor 5:9)? Do I want to do X (or not do X) for godly reasons or for self-centered ones?
- Is God's Word my final authority in every aspect of life (1 Thess 4:1–2)?
- Am I crying out to God for wisdom (Jas 1:5), humbling myself before God, knowing he "resists the proud, but gives grace to the humble" (Jas 4:6)?
- In decision-necessary areas about which Christians differ, am I seeking to love, serve, and prefer my believing brothers and sisters by willingly limiting my own freedom so as to pursue unity and not injure those with weaker consciences (Phil 2:1–4; Rom 14:1–15:7; 1 Cor 8:1–13; 10:23–11:1)?[6]
- Will I submit whatever decision I make to the Lord?

Instead of us making choices apart from the Lord, James warns, "Say, 'If the Lord wills, we will live and do this or that'" (Jas 4:15). So,

[6] See Friesen and Maxson, 374–419; Ferguson, *Discovering God's Will*, 66–70; Andrew David Naselli and J. D. Crowley, *Conscience: What It Is, How to Train It, and Loving Those Who Differ* (Wheaton, IL: Crossway, 2016); Joe Aldrich, *Lifestyle Evangelism: Crossing Traditional Boundaries to Reach the Unbelieving World* (Portland: Multnomah, 1981).

recommit yourself to God as needed and ask him to guide you in your decision-making.

2. Study Scripture

Study carefully and prayerfully the relevant Bible passages addressing your specific decision area. Search and scour God's Word. Don't just assume the Bible has nothing to say on the matter: be sure. Consult your pastor and use Bible study tools and trusted reference works to yield maximum light.

(Counselor, because the following four bullets address common guidance topics counselors are asked to weigh in on, we have included footnoted references to helpful resources giving biblical insight:

- Single versus marriage: "Is God calling me to stay single or get married?"[7]
- Marriage partner: "Whom should I marry?"[8]
- Educational and vocational choices: "Should I find a job after high school, pursue a vocational-technical field, or go to college? If the latter, where? What career should I pursue?"[9]
- Vocational Christian ministry or missions: "Am I called?")[10]

---

[7] See Friesen and Maxson, 289–99; Ferguson, 90–101; Ernie Baker, *Marry Wisely, Marry Well: A Blueprint for Personal Preparation* (Wapwallopen, PA: Shepherd Press, 2016).

[8] See Friesen and Maxson, 300–16; Ferguson, 90–101.

[9] See Friesen and Maxson, 342–54; Ferguson, 75–89; Os Guinness, *The Call: Finding and Fulfilling the Central Purpose of Your Life* (Nashville: Thomas Nelson, 2003); Ralph T. Mattson and Arthur F. Miller, *Finding a Job You Can Love* (Phillipsburg, NJ: P&R, 1999).

[10] See Friesen, 317–30; Dave Harvey, *Am I Called? The Summons to Pastoral Ministry* (Wheaton, IL: Crossway, 2012); Robert D. Jones, "Avoiding Infinite Mischief: Assessing Your Calling to Pastoral Ministry," *Journal of Modern Ministry* 6, no. 3 (Fall 2009): 9–23; Sebastian Traeger and Greg D. Gilbert, *The Gospel at Work: How Working for King Jesus Gives Purpose and Meaning to Our Jobs*, rev. ed. (Grand Rapids: Zondervan, 2018).

3. Gather Needed Information, Explore the Options, and Examine Your Heart

What are the relevant facts about yourself and the situation that apply to this decision? Do you have enough information? Do you need to research something? Who should you talk to? Have you explored the different options? What unanswered questions remain? After addressing all that, consider this suggested method that includes wisely searching your heart:

1. Brainstorm and draft a two-column list of pro and con factors related to each option you are considering.
2. Reorder each factor within each column in the order of its importance to you.
3. Assign a percentage weight to each item so the total pro list and the total con list each equal 100 percent. Force yourself to honestly ask which pro and con factors you most value.
4. Honestly and prayerfully consider your godly, ungodly, or mixed motives for including each pro and con item. (Counselor, know your biblical counseling training in addressing heart motives can bring an assessment focus often absent from other approaches.)
5. In joint decisions involving another person (e.g., your spouse or coleader), encourage that other person(s) to take the same steps outlined above, separately from you. Then discuss together your respective lists and the analyses you each made about the ranking, percentage weights, and motives for each factor. Be sure you and the other person listen so well to each other that you each can accurately summarize one another's perspectives and can work toward loving unity in your decision (Rom 12:10; Phil 2:2–4).

4. Seek Counsel from Others

The book of Proverbs repeatedly exalts the value of seeking godly counsel:

- Proverbs 11:14, "Without guidance, a people will fall, but with many counselors there is deliverance."
- Proverbs 12:15, "A fool's way is right in his own eyes, but whoever listens to counsel is wise."

- Proverbs 13:10, "Arrogance leads to nothing but strife, but wisdom is gained by those who take advice."
- Proverbs 15:22, "Plans fail when there is no counsel, but with many advisers they succeed."
- Proverbs 27:17, "Iron sharpens iron, and one person sharpens another."
- Proverbs 24:6, "You should wage war with sound guidance—victory comes with many counselors."

Consider seeking advice from those who care about you, who are spiritually mature and biblically wise, and who are available to help—especially those who have knowledge specific to your decision area. Start with your church elders and fellow church members. Know that in major decisions (e.g., job changes, career decisions, engagement, marriage), inviting key people for a group advisory meeting can give you access to collective wisdom. If the decision requires agreement from someone in authority over you, discuss your conclusions and intended decision with that person in a respectful way.

If doubts continue, if a choice involves a gray area, or if a decision remains unclear, practice what Jay Adams calls the "holding principle": if it's possible to delay the decision, don't act until you are sure in your conscience it's right to move forward.[11] As Rom 14:22–23 teaches, "Whatever you believe about these things, keep between yourself and God. Blessed is the one who does not condemn himself by what he approves. But whoever doubts stands condemned if he eats, because his eating is not from faith, and everything that is not from faith is sin." Put simply, in matters that can wait, don't move. In matters that can't, make the best decision possible per the steps below.

5. Decide and Act

Having prayerfully done the above and based on the information you have, decide. Make what you believe to be the wisest and most spiritually expedient choice. Within the Bible's boundaries, God gives you freedom. If you

[11] Jay E. Adams, "Counseling and Special Revelation," in *More than Redemption: A Theology of Christian Counseling* (Baker, 1979), 31–34.

are seeking to please God by obeying his Word, do what you think is best and trust God for the results. Don't let fear keep you from acting.

6. Entrust Your Wise Decisions into God's Hands and Live for Him

Once you make the decision, don't look back. Entrust your choice to God. If things don't turn out the way you hoped, you will be tempted to regret or second-guess your decision. Despite the care you took above, an undesired result will tempt you to become disappointed or angry with God or with those who advised you. Don't yield to that temptation.

Instead, trust your sovereign, wise, and good Father with whatever consequences flow from your decision. After all, "A person's heart plans his way, but the Lord determines his steps" (Prov 16:9). God's purposes for his people are always ultimately positive. As Paul reminds us, "We know that all things work together for the good of those who love God, who are called according to his purpose" (Rom 8:28); one "good" verse 29 describes is making us more like Christ, even amid hardships. As the Old and New Testaments repeatedly remind us, making wise choices doesn't guarantee our desired results; nevertheless, it does bring pleasure to God, inward peace, and the prospect of heavenly treasures to come. So, trust the Lord to be with you and to help you handle any adverse outcomes. And remember that part of trusting the Lord is learning from your decisions and growing in maturity. He is with you and for you, even if your hoped-for results never come.

Conclusion

For biblical counselors, the bottom-line goal is to help counselees walk in the way of godly wisdom and make decisions that best please the Lord. Recalling the biblical-theological truths above, along with our emphasis on heart motives throughout the book (e.g., chapters 1 and 10), will allow you to offer counselees a more Christ-centered approach to guidance and decision-making than most of them would practice without your help.

35

Physical Diseases, Injuries, and Disabilities

The bulk of this book has addressed problems that are primarily spiritual, directly related to the heart. But what about those related to the body? In this chapter we will focus on medically diagnosed body problems. As we saw in chapter 5, people consist of an inner (heart, soul, or spirit) and outer person (body) existing together as an embodied soul/spirit unity. We cited Ed Welch's fourfold summary of how the two parts might influence each other: (1) Heart problems can affect the body with psychosomatic consequences. (2) Body problems can affect the heart by limiting its expression. (3) Heart problems do not necessarily affect the body (i.e., ungodly people can enjoy good health, and godly people can suffer poor health). (4), body problems do not necessarily affect the heart.[1]

How can biblical counselors, keeping these dynamics in mind, help people facing a physical problem like disease, injury, or disability?[2] Let's consider nine strategies to weave into our ministry.[3]

[1] Welch, *Counselor's Guide to the Brain*, 29–36 (see chap. 5, n. 7).

[2] By *disabilities*, we refer to permanent, limiting, atypical physical conditions that result from disease, injury, or genetic abnormality. For help in counseling those with a disability, see Paul Tautges and Joni Eareckson Tada, *When Disability Hits Home* (Wapwallopen, PA: Shepherd Press, 2020). On the relationship between disease, disability, and various disorders, see John C. Kwasny, *Suffering in 3-D: Connecting the Church to Disease, Disability, and Disorder* (Wapwallopen, PA: Shepherd Press, 2019).

[3] Along with our appendix of recommended resources on suffering, see Kelly M.

1. Understand the Nature and Impact of the Person's Physical Problem

The place to start is the counselee's self-description of their symptoms and any diagnoses they have received. You should listen not only for the details of the problem but also how that problem is affecting them. A reputable medical website can give you general information about the disease, suggest clarifying questions to ask, and alert you to effects your counselee might face. Yet no website can tell you any particular person's specific symptoms, diagnosis, treatment, or about the conversations shared with their doctor.

Seek to find out what your counselee is experiencing. What consequences do they face? For example, those suffering from a chronic illness are typically more prone to sadness and depression for several reasons. (1) The disease itself can affect the brain's cognitive and mood functions. (2) The disease's symptoms might alter the person's lifestyle. Lethargy and dyskinesia (that is, involuntary movement) affect one's gait, energy levels, social involvement, and productivity. Add to that the financial costs, inconvenience, and physical discomfort associated with multiple doctor/hospital visits and repeated treatments. Spiritually mishandling these pressures invites depression. (3) If the disease is progressive and incurable, this added dimension of hopelessness further invites depression. Chronic, degenerative conditions with no medical remedy can tempt even the godliest heart to despair. We should encourage counselees to live by faith in the objective truths of God's Word while learning to address those feelings that arise from the body-heart dynamics related to their diseases.

Given the correlation between chronic illness and suicide, biblical counselors also should assess for suicidality. We should also explore the impact of the person's physical problem on their marriage and other relationships. Inviting a counselee's spouse to a session shows care for both people.

Lastly, inquire about any side effects or adverse reactions the person might be experiencing from any prescribed medications. This is especially important if the counselee is taking multiple medications since there might

---

Kapic, *Embodied Hope: A Theological Meditation on Pain and Suffering* (Downers Grove, IL: InterVarsity Press, 2017).

be unknown or harmful drug interactions. Encourage the counselee to inform their prescribing physician of these added symptoms.

2. Show Compassion to the Person in Their Suffering and Grieve with Them over Any Limitations or Losses Resulting from Their Physical Problems

Diseases, injuries, and disabilities—especially those that are long-term—often bring the loss of expectations and dreams. Unpack such losses and grieve with counselees when you hear about them. The woman with a chronic back injury might have lost a job she loved. The man with multiple sclerosis may never walk his daughter down the aisle or hold his first grandchild.

You can help in at least two ways. First, elevate your compassion. In chapter 13 we described compassion as that inward, deeply felt emotional response of pity for the plight of a suffering person, coupled with a desire to alleviate it. Spending time listening to your counselee will allow their adversities to grip you emotionally. So, review our Lord's compassion toward those dealing with disease (Mark 1:41), disability (Matt 20:34), or injury (Luke 10:33) and ask his Spirit to stir up within your soul the same attitude.

Second, teach the person to lament. Point them to lament psalms (e.g., Psalms 3–5; 9–10; 13; 77; 88), the book of Lamentations, or other passages (e.g., Job) that describe those who suffered and voiced their chronic pain. Helping counselees see in God's Word that God knows them, hears them, and feels their plight can help steer them to him, invite them to talk to him, and allow him to reframe their hardship from his hope-giving perspective.

3. Assure the Person That Godly People Suffer, and They Should Not Assume Their Physical Problems Are a Direct Divine Judgment

The Bible records instances of God's direct judgment that brought physical pain or death upon individuals, groups, and nations who disobeyed him. We see this even in the New Testament with Ananias and Sapphira (Acts 5:1–11), King Herod (Acts 12:22–24), and some believers in Corinth who abused the Lord's Supper and suffered sickness or death (1 Cor 11:28–30).

Yet, none of these events gives counselees warrant to view their personal physical problems as God's direct judgment on them. After all, disease and disability and every other hardship entered our world as a result of the fall outlined in Genesis 3; indeed, all creation groans under sin's effects (Rom 8:20–22). So, if a counselee voices the idea that their physical condition is a result of God's wrath on them, we should ask why. And then we should point them to our Lord's words in John 9:3 concerning the man born blind or the sickness of Lazarus in 11:4. Rather than presuming to know God's unrevealed mind, counselees should be encouraged to find hope and mercy in God's Word. Since physical suffering can add mental fog, patiently help your counselees sort out their clear and their confused guilt (recall chapter 7) and turn to Christ for forgiveness and freedom from any crippling assumptions or lies.

At the same time, remind your believing counselees of the many Bible examples of righteous people who suffered physical illness, injuries, and disabilities. Job, Asaph (Psalm 73), Paul, Timothy, and others, including our Lord Jesus, are among them.

4. Encourage the Person to Pray for Physical Healing and for God's Grace to Handle the Physical Problem if God Doesn't Heal at This Time

Thankfully, God can and sometimes does heal on this side of heaven in miraculous ways, often in conjunction with prayer. James 5:14–15 says, "Is anyone among you sick? He should call for the elders of the church, and they are to pray over him, anointing him with oil in the name of the Lord. The prayer of faith will save the sick person, and the Lord will raise him up; if he has committed sins, he will be forgiven." The scene speaks of seriously ill believers seeking the prayers of the elders and God honoring their requests. Contrast that with King Asa who "was afflicted with a disease in his feet. Though his disease was severe, even in his illness he did not seek help from the LORD, but only from the physicians" (2 Chr 16:12 NIV). While God uses physicians and medications, we must not put our hope in them.

Yet God doesn't promise to miraculously heal everyone who prays, not even the godliest people. While we don't know if Paul's thorn in the flesh was physical, we know he prayed three times—presumably intensely, and perhaps even over three seasons of prayer—but the Lord chose not to heal him (2 Cor 12:7–10; cf. 2 Tim 4:20). For his glory and our good, God might choose not to intervene. How, then, should we pray for an ailing counselee? Consider this sample prayer for a Christian woman with terminal cancer:

> Heavenly Father, I pray for my sister Tanya, your daughter, who loves you and seeks to trust and follow you. She and I know you are more than able to heal her, and so we humbly ask you to remove the cancer or make effective the medical means she is already pursuing. Please restore her body to health.
>
> Yet, Father, we don't presume to know your will. So, we submit our desire to yours. Should you choose not to heal her yet, help Tanya and all of us who care about her to rest in that. Give skill to her medical team as they treat her and grant her physical comfort during this difficult season.
>
> More than anything, help her to trust and love you. Give her endurance to fight the good fight of faith, to see that her greatest remaining enemy is not cancer but unbelief and fear. Help her to love [names of husband and children, if applicable] and to show them what it looks like to trust God in tough times. And Lord Jesus, help her to long for the glories of heaven, including the perfect, cancer-free body she will receive, and to see your face, the face of her Redeemer.

Praying over your counselee like this serves as a model from which she and others can learn to pray more effectively.

But what about cases involving chronic pain where there is no cure and no imminent expectation of death? One such sufferer observed:

> Chronic pain is different from many illnesses or disabilities. It is normally invisible. Treatment won't make the issue go away. Many types come and go at different times in life but are completely

> unpredictable, so you can't say "you will have this all your life" or "you will almost certainly be over it in a few years." The uncertainty, and the failure of people in your society to give it credence, add up to a condition that is difficult to deal with.

In such cases, pray for the sufferer to experience pain relief, to know God's special presence when an episode flares up, to persevere in faith, and to grow in Christlikeness.

5. Encourage the Person to Seek Skilled Medical Care to Wisely Steward Their God-Given Body

While God can heal people miraculously, he usually uses medical means. The existence of medical care displays God's grace to us amid physical suffering, and we should help counselees see and thank God for it—especially when it brings some relief or answers. Early on, we counselors should ascertain whether a person is receiving proper medical care. If not, we can point them to a general practitioner who can provide needed care or refer them to a specialist. At no time, of course, should biblical counselors dispense medical advice.

Moreover, we should help counselees pursue medical care for the right reasons—not just to feel better, perform more effectively, live longer, reduce long-term medical costs, or look fit, but because our bodies belong to God. He is the Creator, owner, and sustainer of every human; and for the Christian, he is also the Redeemer. By right of both creation and redemption, God owns our bodies and expects us to care for them. Each is a member of Christ and a temple of the Holy Spirit (1 Cor 6:15, 19). This also means seeking medical care to serve the Lord most effectively. Our bodies, after all, are the means by which we obey, worship, serve, and glorify him (Rom 6:11–14; 12:1; 1 Cor 10:31; Phil 1:20). We serve God as embodied persons. Medical doctor and biblical counselor Robert Smith summarizes these themes:

> Taking good care of the body . . . is proper STEWARDSHIP of the temple of the Holy Spirit. A Christian should go to the doctor not primarily to get well, but to be a good steward. . . . If

> getting well is the goal and he is told he cannot get well, the visit to the doctor is considered unsuccessful. However, a biblical view of illness will keep the visit from being unsuccessful. If a person is told he cannot get well and his goal is to serve and glorify God, even through an incurable illness, he will not be devastated by the information. In fact, the visit can be viewed as very successful, as it gave him information that can be used for his spiritual benefit. Motive makes the difference.[4]

Indeed, even why we seek medical care is a matter of the heart.

6. Give the Person Christ-Centered Hope, Not Temporal or Worldly Hope

While caring physicians offer their own form of hope to patients, biblical counselors supply much deeper hope that doesn't depend on temporal medical improvement.

In 2 Cor 4:7–18, the apostle Paul reflects on his own mortality and physical decline. His body—his outer person—is a jar of clay (v. 7), signifying its earthiness, frailty, and fragility. It carries the marks of death and mortality (vv. 8–12). Verse 16 says it is "being destroyed" ("wasting away," NIV), referring to the increasing toll his afflictions have exacted upon his body. Paul was far from healthy.[5] Yet amid his physical suffering, Paul did not despair or give up (vv. 7–9, 16). Why not? What hope did he hold on to and, by extension, can we offer our counselees? God gives believers three assurances amid physical suffering.

First, Christ can display his life in us and through us to others. God's power radiates from Paul's weak, fragile body (v. 7). The life of the crucified, risen Jesus can "be displayed in [his] mortal flesh," bringing life

---

[4] Robert D. Smith, *The Christian Counselor's Medical Desk Reference* (Stanley, NC: Timeless Texts, 2000), 5.

[5] See also 2 Cor 11:23–27; Acts 14:19; Gal 4:13–14; and possibly 2 Cor 12:7–10. (Scholars debate whether Paul's "thorn in the flesh" was an illness, an injury, or intense persecution itself).

to those Paul serves (vv. 9–12 NIV). Bodily weakness affords believers fresh opportunities for Christ's power to arise and be perfected in them (2 Cor 12:9–10). Moreover, God's comforting grace allows a counselee to offer that same grace to others who suffer (2 Cor 1:3–11).

Second, God will raise our earthly, mortal bodies and transform them into glorious, immortal bodies, which is the ultimate, final, and irreversible healing that no medication, surgery, or therapy can produce. Paul assures us, "For we know that the one who raised the Lord Jesus will also raise us with Jesus and present us with you" (2 Cor 4:14). He expands this promise a few verses later, referring to our bodies: "For we know that if our earthly tent we live in is destroyed, we have a building from God, an eternal dwelling in the heavens, not made with hands" (2 Cor 5:1; cf. 1 Cor 15:50–55; Phil 3:20–21). For this reason, Paul calls affliction "momentary" and "light" (2 Cor 4:17). He is confident, and your counselees can share that confidence, that one day God *will* heal forever each believer's broken body.

Third, God can renew and strengthen our hearts. Paul testifies in 2 Cor 4:16: "Therefore we do not give up. Even though our outer person is being destroyed, our inner person is being renewed day by day." One's outer person—their deteriorating body—might be sick, but their inner person can grow nevertheless. While physical trials tempt us, they cannot cause us to sin. Sickness can be the soil for significant spiritual growth as we commune with Christ and choose to grasp the "height and depth" of his love for us (Eph 3:16–19).[6]

Biblical counselors need not settle for offering paltry hope or wishful optimism. We can give granite-like guarantees to every afflicted counselee.

---

[6] For a version of these guarantees written to a sufferer, see Robert D. Jones, "Three Hope-Giving Guarantees When You Face Illness, Injury, or Disability," Biblical Counseling Coalition, August 21, 2020, https://www.biblicalcounselingcoalition.org/2020/08/21/three-hope-giving-guarantees-when-you-face-illness-injury-or-disability/.

7. Help the Person Embrace God's Sovereign, Wise, and Loving Purposes in Using Their Physical Problem to Make Them More Like Christ

In Rom 8:17–39, the apostle describes God's saving purposes for his people amid the groaning, fallen creation, which includes our physical decay (vv. 21–23). Verses 28–29 assure us such sufferings have purpose; God is using them to conform us believers into Christ's image. How does this happen? In what specific ways does God use trials to accomplish that? Encourage your counselees to consider and pray about these seven ways (see chapter 16) God uses hardships, including physical suffering, to make us like Christ: to enhance and deepen our relationship with God; experience a measure of Christ's sufferings; expose our remaining sin; engage us more actively in the body of Christ; exhibit to others Christ's work in us; equip us for wiser, more compassionate personal ministry; and elevate our longing for Christ's return.[7]

Consider two examples of this mindset. First, Jay Adams offers helpful counsel on preparing for a hospital stay. He writes, "One reason for the failure of believers to manifest a Christian attitude in given life situations is the lack of prior preparation." He then reminds us how the hospital is a place for (1) recovery (avoiding the hospital for a needed procedure is a worse decision than going), (2) meditation, (3) prayer, and (4) witnessing. Adams concludes, "You may look forward to hospitalization with joyous anticipation. You may know beforehand that this will be a blessed experience. It need not be feared as a grievous intrusion into your life, but received as a very special God-given opportunity for personal spiritual benefit and evangelism."[8] I (Bob) often think of various hospital visits to my members when I served as a vocational pastor. I sometimes visited older, seasoned Christians to minister to them, only to find them showing love, care, and encouragement to me as their young pastor. In such cases, I left their

[7] See chapter 16 for more details, along with Jones, *When Trouble Shows Up* (see chap. 16, n. 3).

[8] Jay E. Adams, "The Christian and the Hospital," *Journal of Biblical Counseling* 8, no. 1 (1985): 11–15.

hospital rooms wondering, *Who just ministered to whom?* Caring counselors give people a God-sized vision, even of an impending hospitalization.

In their article "Don't Waste Your Cancer," John Piper and David Powlison, both cancer survivors, present ten bold yet life-changing perspectives for viewing such a terminal disease. Here is their outline: "You will waste your cancer . . .

- if you do not believe it is designed for you by God.
- if you believe it is a curse and not a gift.
- if you seek comfort from your odds rather than from God.
- if you refuse to think about death.
- if you think that "beating" cancer means staying alive rather than cherishing Christ.
- if you spend too much time reading about cancer and not enough time reading about God.
- if you let it drive you into solitude instead of deepening your relationships with manifest affection.
- if you grieve as those who have no hope.
- if you treat sin as casually as before.
- if you fail to use it as a means of witness to the truth and glory of Christ."[9]

Of course, Piper and Powlison don't deny the disastrous impact of the fall or the terrible suffering cancer brings. But they embed those realities into the larger narrative of God's redemptive purposes. They show how our sovereign, wise, and loving God enables believers to redeem their cancer and daily live out the abundant life Christ has given them. While we must be sensitive to each counselee's ability to handle such daring perspectives, these truths carry life-transforming potential when timely introduced. They reinforce the other Christ-centered perspectives in this chapter.

---

[9] John Piper, with David Powlison. "Don't Waste Your Cancer," *Journal of Biblical Counseling* 24, no. 2 (Spring 2006): 2–8. A friend insightfully suggested an eleventh bullet: "You will waste your cancer if you think your suffering is only yours and not part of God's plan for his church." Sufferers have much to teach the body of Christ.

8. Help the Person Walk with Christ and Handle Life God's Way, without Letting Physical Problems become Unduly Central or Distracting

Counselees suffering with physical problems face the temptation to let their physical adversity consume and define them. As one person observed, "When your physical pain screams at you constantly, it's hard for it not to be central to your thinking." Someone else compared her chronic pain to slow-dripping water torture hitting the same spot each time.[10] Even offering counselees the massive amount of biblical truth in the preceding points—though designed to help people—can inadvertently lead them to fixate on their physical problem, to think too often and too much about it. Even well-meaning friends who caringly ask for an update ("How's your back pain today?") can unwittingly contribute to this by focusing solely on that one aspect of the person's life. Biblical counselors should help counselees embrace the bigger agenda: each is to love God and their neighbors and seek God's kingdom today.

9. Help the Person Love Their Friends, Family Members, and Caregivers and Demonstrate the Spirit's Fruit in Every Relationship

While dealing with physical problems can't make your counselees sin, it can tempt them. Galatians 5:13–21 warns of several fleshly relational responses that can be exacerbated when one is facing physical distress. Your counselees can become self-focused, irritable, or impatient. They can become relationally lazy or isolated and excuse their failures to actively love others "because" of their struggles. They might feel entitled to receive care and become unappreciative, critical, or demanding toward caregivers.[11] They might grow jealous of healthy, able-bodied people or show various strains of discontentment, sadness/depression, isolation, loneliness, and anger. They

[10] On chronic pain, see Michael R. Emlet, *Chronic Pain: Living by Faith When Your Body Hurts* (Greensboro, NC: New Growth Press, 2010).

[11] For help for caregivers, see Michael R. Emlet, *Help for the Caregiver: Facing the Challenges with Understanding and Strength* (Greensboro, NC: New Growth Press, 2008).

might even direct that anger at friends who have not been compassionate, a doctor who missed a serious diagnosis, or a surgeon whose mistake meant a lifetime in a wheelchair. Worse, they might be angry at God or pull away from him, especially if they understand the doctrine of God's sovereignty over every movement, moment, and molecule.

So, what is God's answer? To "walk by the Spirit," be "led by the Spirit," "live by the Spirit," and "keep in step with the Spirit" (Gal 5:16, 18, 25). How will such a Spirit-filled life counter the sinful tendencies above? "[T] he fruit of the Spirit is love, joy, peace, patience, kindness, goodness, faithfulness, gentleness, and self-control" (Gal 5:22–23). We should help counselees draw near to the Lord in prayer, meditate on his Word, actively participate with other believers as much as possible, and consciously seek his Spirit's help to replace their fleshly responses with the Spirit's relational fruit.

Conclusion

In counseling people with diseases, injuries, or disabilities, biblical counselors bring hope, meaning, and direction that no medical professional can provide. Through our personal care, the truth of God's Word, and the ministry of the church, we can help physical sufferers follow Christ in this life, experience his inward renewing grace, and prepare for the life to come.

36

Medical Care, Medical Referrals, and Psychotropic Medications

In our previous chapter we addressed counseling people with diagnosed and demonstrable physical diseases, injuries, or disabilities. This chapter discusses the role of medical care in counseling situations involving no known medical problem, though a physician's evaluation seems wise. We will consider when to encourage counselees to see a doctor and how to think about subsequent medical treatment, including cases where psychotropic medications might be prescribed. While we don't want counselors to act like medical professionals, we want them to care well for the whole person, since people are a complex unity of heart and body (per chapter 5). Doing so involves identifying when medical assistance may help as part of the counselee's care plan. The counselor can help the counselee understand the place of medical treatment in their care.

Sin versus Sickness

While ultimately all struggles result from our fallen condition, it is helpful to discern as far as possible whether a particular life struggle results from bodily problems, "heart" problems, or some combination of both. This task is not easy; the cause(s) of some struggles might not be clear. For instance, some who struggle with depression may find a strong physiological factor at play (e.g., postpartum depression), while some depression stems from unmet expectations and problematic thought patterns.

Counselors should remember that while there *might* be a biological factor at play in any counselee's situation, there is *always* a spiritual component. Each person has the choice of how to interpret and respond to an event. On one hand, counselees are responsible before God to love and obey him even when facing physical illnesses and disabilities. Scripture calls us to honor the Lord in all things, including in our beliefs, motives, thought patterns, and behavior. On the other hand, God's Spirit makes Christians response-able to do so. In Christ, God's grace motivates and empowers us to handle hardships (Heb 4:16; Phil 4:11–13). While the believing woman suffering from severe postpartum depression might be heavily influenced by her hormones, she is responsible and response-able for how she responds to those physical changes.

The counselor, then, should wisely seek to discern what aspects of a counselee's struggle are spiritual, but what also might be partially due to a fallen, broken body. Resources such as Ed Welch's *Blame it on the Brain*[1] and his *Counselor's Guide to the Brain and Its Disorders*[2] can aid us. In the first text, Welch gives examples like Alzheimer's disease and traumatic brain injury as clear "sickness" matters, but acknowledges that struggles such as anxiety, depression, and ADHD may also have underlying physiological components.

Regarding more severe symptoms such as auditory or visual hallucinations, manic episodes, severe eating disorders, and the like, the counselor should be aware of current, valid research on biological factors that may be involved. Much research has been done in the last decade on these disorders and their connection with brain anatomy and neurophysiology; some research also focuses on the connections between the above disorders and things like trauma or abuse. In these severe cases, counselors should consider possible biological factors and properly refer counselees to medical providers as part of overall care.

---

[1] Welch, *Blame It on the Brain* (see chap. 5, n. 7).

[2] Welch, *Counselor's Guide to the Brain* (see chap. 5, n. 7).

What happens if we come to the wrong conclusion here? If we assume that a sickness is a behavioral, volitional sin issue, we place an undue burden of responsibility and possible guilt on counselees beyond what might be present already. They may wrongly believe that if they simply pray more, read Scripture more, confess enough, or act better, they can overcome a struggle. They might lack a legitimate treatment for a bodily issue. However, if we assume that a sin struggle is a sickness, we might relieve appropriate responsibility and risk the counselee adopting an inappropriate view of their role in the struggle. Physical treatment might alleviate some symptoms, but the underlying heart issues might not be addressed. Wrongful assumptions either way can harm a counselee.

Given these risks, the counselor should lead each counselee toward Christ and matters of faith, repentance, and obedience, yet recommend supplemental medical assessment where possible biological factors might exist.

Medical Care, Including Medication, to Treat Physical Illness

Medical Treatment and Healing in Our Culture

In many places around the world, particularly in the United States, people are inundated with the message that medicine will fix any sort of life problem. This arises from the medical model: the philosophical theory that all life struggles, including counseling problems, are biological in nature, caused by some illness. Since we are viewed as only physical bodies, the "fix" is usually some pill to treat that problem. Most medical professionals hold this view and treat patients in light of these beliefs.

Pair this reality with the "quick-fix" or victim mentality also rampant in our culture, and it is easy to understand why medication becomes the go-to answer even for counseling problems. Our culture values productivity and high functioning, so anything that blocks those aims is a deficit to be treated, as quickly as possible. Rather than work on underlying issues, one takes a pill.

Despite biblical teaching that opposes these false beliefs, our counselees live in this context and largely operate within the same belief system. Even Christ followers tend to view suffering as unnecessary rather than redemptive and brokenness as something to be pitied rather than as something urging us to anticipate a future reality of restoration. As counselors, we must recognize these potential belief distortions within our counselees and even within ourselves. The media and the medical world send such messages day in and day out. Therefore, we must explore a proper, biblical understanding of medical treatment and physical healing.

Medicine and Physical Healing in Scripture

While the Bible doesn't provide an explicit theology of medical treatment or a list of medications and their uses, it does speak of physical healing. Since healing is the aim of medicine, the concept of physical healing in Scripture is pertinent. In the beginning, God created bodies as good; sin and sickness deviate from that goodness. Therefore, healing in this life directs men and women back to that original state of goodness and demonstrates God's grace until he finally restores believers' bodies.

However, while medicine may *assist* with healing, healing ultimately comes from God. He might heal supernaturally and directly, as Jesus demonstrated often in the Gospels; but he might also heal through physical means such as medication, surgery, or the body's naturally-created ability to recover. All avenues involve God, though his method of intervention differs. The Lord has established human bodies to function in particular ways, so any sort of medical intervention simply assists in that process. It is never the physician who heals; it is the Lord. Just like Jesus brought both physical and spiritual healing, as a picture of the restoration to come, so too might we pursue healing through these various avenues, including medication. While no clear Bible passage advocates or prohibits the use of medicinal treatment for physical ailments, we see examples of medicinal methods in the Bible, such as in the use of a cake of figs for King Hezekiah in Isa 38:21, wine for Timothy's stomach in 1 Tim 5:23, and both oil and wine for healing the man who was beaten in Jesus's story of the good Samaritan in Luke 10:30–36.

Limitations

Despite Scripture's mention of medical interventions, there are significant limitations to treatment. First, the finitude, fallibility, and fallenness of human persons as interpreters is present in both science in general and medicine in particular. This adds more room for misunderstanding and error. Second, creation is corrupted; therefore, the subject of medicine is distorted too. Third, the study of medicine has been divorced from the soul and matters of God and religion, a movement that has significant implications for its practice. People now generally think of counseling problems as physical, and physical ailments are things to be completely eradicated, rather than opportunities to develop Christian character.

Fourth, in contemporary American culture, people view medicine as a panacea for most of life's problems, even those not historically viewed as physical. While science can make significant advancements, many medications remain a result of observation, trial, and error. Medical science often can only demonstrate correlation, not causality. Finally, apart from Christ's return, death remains the ultimate reality for each person. While significant advancements have been made in the field of medicine, they have not removed this eventuality. Nor will they.

Grace despite Limitations

Despite the limitations, God's common grace flows through the field of medicine. First, human bodies still largely function the way God intended. While death and disease continue, the body still heals scratches, responds to bacteria, and mends bones. Medicine thus remains useful. Healing foreshadows the future God will bring when there will be no more pain and no more death. There is grace in God's demonstration of that future reality and in the use of medicine as part of that demonstration.

Since medicine emerges from scientific study—the discovery of empirical facts through observation—it demonstrates a consistency and order inherent in even God's fallen creation. God is not a God of chaos but of order, and medicine reflects this reality. Like science, medicine relies on the rationality God has established and makes use of it to aid healing.

Further, Christians have mandates to exercise dominion over creation (Gen 1:28), including over diseases, which are a result of the fall, and to love and care for one another (John 13:34–35; Phil 2:4). This includes wise efforts to relieve suffering, as Jesus often did.[3] Medicine is part of that healing supported in Scripture and reflects God's future restoration. At the same time, we must keep medicine in its rightful place, not making it a panacea, not giving it more authority than is due, and not forgetting God's sovereignty over people's health. We must view medicine appropriately, within its bounds, as a means to honor the Lord.

What Does This Mean for Psychotropic Medications?

We noted above that Scripture is not explicit about whether or not it is appropriate to take medication. It certainly doesn't mention using medications to treat heart (spiritual) struggles, however severe. However, we propose these perspectives:

1. Since Scripture does not explicitly address psychotropic medications, their careful use seems to be a wisdom issue in which Christians have liberty. Taking an antidepressant is not always sinful and not always right.
2. Science in this area is both useful and not. For many years, for instance, chemical imbalances were assumed to be significant contributing factors in struggles such as depression or anxiety. Recently, that theory has largely been dismissed. Evidence demonstrates that chemical-based antidepressant and antianxiety medications can in some cases alleviate symptoms, but we don't always know why.[4] While brain and body research advances and

---

[3] In Mark 1, for example, Jesus drove out demons, healed physical ailments, and preached the good news, all of which picture the relief from suffering that his kingdom ushers in.

[4] Joseph J. Schildkraut, "The Catecholamine Hypothesis of Affective Disorders: a Review of Supporting Evidence," *American Journal of Psychiatry,* April 1, 2006, https://ajp.psychiatryonline.org/doi/abs/10.1176/ajp.122.5.509.

we learn more about these struggles, theories and treatments change. We must humbly acknowledge our incomplete understanding of the brain.

3. We must exercise caution concerning psychotropic medications, but we also have some freedom in their use. As counselors, we must become better students of the body and not just students of the soul. Part of this is learning more, but part is recognizing our own areas of deficiency and humbly directing counselees toward those with more experience and expertise.

Evaluation of "Success" of Medication

How likely are psychotropic medications to produce results, and what can counselees expect? Consistently, evidence demonstrates that psychotropic medications have significant response rates, mostly in the 40 to 60 percent range, particularly for issues like depression, anxiety, and mood stabilization.[5] These efficacy rates are in about the same range as most general medications. However, the high rate of response to a placebo suggests that the effects of the medication are not simply in the medication itself. Instead, the *expectation* of results often lends itself to the *perception* of a decrease in symptoms. This does not undermine the results, but should set proper expectations for help.

Further, it can be very difficult to determine the actual success of psychotropic medicines because their success cannot be divorced from all other factors, such as one's environment and other forms of care. Research studies don't measure the impact of Christ, his Word, his church, and biblical counseling. We ultimately do not know the cause of many mental disorders. As we seek to assess people's struggles biblically, Michael Emlet reminds us, "We want biblical categories and themes to make sense of what we observe in others. Even then we need to remain humble, realizing that a

[5] See in particular Stefan Leucht et al., "Putting the Efficacy of Psychiatric and General Medicine Medication into Perspective," *British Journal of Psychiatry* 200 (2012); as well as Arif Khan and Walter A. Brown, "Antidepressants versus Placebo in Major Depression: An Overview," *World Psychiatry*, September 25, 2015, https://www.ncbi.nlm.nih.gov/pmc/articles/PMC4592645/.

complex array of factors that we many not fully understand could contribute to the person's struggle. The diagnostic task, whether using biblical categories or secular ones, is never like following a simple recipe. Wisdom is key."[6] In aiming to better understand people through the lens of Scripture, counselors should fully recognize people are complex; this includes the ways that the brain and the mind work. Counselors should also understand the multitude of contributing factors to the struggles of any given counselee and move to care for them accordingly.

Criteria

How should a biblical counselor determine when to recommend a counselee see a physician for a medical evaluation? Moreover, if a counselee sees a physician and receives a psychiatric diagnosis and is prescribed a psychotropic medication, how should that counselor advise them to think about the diagnosis and about taking the medication? The criteria below, while not exhaustive, can guide in these decisions. (Some of these criteria might apply more explicitly to one of these questions than the other.)

When Biblical Teaching Has Been Thoroughly Addressed

Biblical counselors are generally good at using Scripture to speak truth into the lives of counselees. In considering a medical referral or the use of psychotropic medication, we must not neglect doing what we do well. In *Blame It on the Brain*, Ed Welch observes that most psychiatric problems are both spiritual and physical. He notes, "You will never find a psychiatric problem where biblical counsel—counsel directed to the heart—is anything less than essential."[7] We cannot divorce ourselves from ongoing counsel from God's Word, even when there is evidence of a physical cause. Every counseling problem we encounter will have at least some spiritual component we should address.

---

[6] Michael R. Emlet, *Descriptions and Prescriptions: A Biblical Perspective on Psychiatric Diagnoses and Medications* (Greensboro, NC: New Growth Press, 2017), 42.

[7] Welch, *Blame it on the Brain*, 106.

Counselee's Goal for Medical Treatment Is Appropriate and Heart Matters Have Been Addressed

The counselor should also address heart issues and motivation, specifically as they relate to medical treatment. What is the counselee looking for—a "quick-fix" or assistance in holistically addressing their presenting problems? Also, the counselor should determine if the counselee's motivation to work on heart issues will continue should the medical treatment prove helpful. Will they assume their problem was purely biological, thus feeling no more reason to continue addressing spiritual matters? Are they looking for an easy way to deal with their struggles? The counselor should evaluate these points and communicate with the counselee the need to continue addressing core issues, despite any relief provided by medical treatment.

It Is Reasonable to Conclude There May Be a Biological Component

Since determining the possibility of a biological component lies outside the biblical counselor's training and expertise, it's essential to work with a physician to determine what contribution, if any, the body might be making. Indicators of a biological concern can include delusions, personality changes, confusion, or changes in eating or sleeping patterns.[8] These may be indications that there is a bodily factor contributing to a counselee's struggles. We can recommend a general medical evaluation to rule out or point to a biological concern, such as side effects from medications, metabolic disorders, infections, endocrine disorders, or vitamin deficiencies.

When Suicidal Thoughts Are Present

In cases of suicidal thoughts, active or passive, medications should be considered to stabilize thoughts or behaviors for the counselee's safety. In such

---

[8] For a list of potential biological indicators, see Smith, *Counselor's Medical Desk Reference*, 376–77 (see chap. 35, n. 4).

cases, the medication might calm a counselee, bring clarity and stability to their thinking, or reduce anxiety more quickly, thus potentially reducing harmful behaviors. The use of medication does not guarantee struggles will lessen; rather, suicidality simply leads us to expedite our consideration of a medical referral in the event it might prove helpful.

Any Prior Experience with Medical Treatment or Medication Has Been Positive

At the start of a counseling case, counselors should explore a person's medical condition and history, including past and present medications. If they used medication in the past, was it helpful? If so, there is a significant chance it might be helpful again.

Further, what were the counselee's reasons for pursuing medical treatment in the past? Was the counselee resistant to medical care, including medication? If so, why? The counselor can use information gleaned to determine any impact past treatment might have had and any possible areas that need to be addressed before a referral is made.

A Significant Decline in the Level of Functioning Is Present

Some counselees will experience a change in functioning as a result of their counseling struggles. This may present itself as difficulty in performing daily tasks like showering or cooking, but it may be more severe: like an inability to keep a steady job. In those instances, it may be helpful to consider medical treatment, including medication, to restore functionality. The *DSM-5* and other guides often use a change in functionality to trigger concern about or determine the presence of a disorder.

A helpful comparison here is standard treatment for the common headache. For some, a headache does not lead to any change in functionality. Others, namely those who experience migraines, may be debilitated by pain. They are unable to get out of bed or carry on normal conversation. In those cases, treatment of the source of pain allows a sufferer to function more normally.

Suffering May Be Reduced or Eliminated

Many times in counseling, we see people who are suffering tremendously from their struggles. Speaking to this, Michael Emlet writes, "[It] is God's design to relieve the suffering that arose as a result of the fall," and he points to numerous passages about Jesus's healing works as examples.[9] At the same time, Emlet observes, "While relieving suffering is a kingdom priority, seeking mere relief without a vision for God's transforming agenda in the midst of suffering may short-circuit all that God wants to do in the person's life."[10] Additionally, there are instances when God chooses not to heal to accomplish a greater purpose (2 Cor 12:8–9; Ps 119:67, 71). The counselor should evaluate the suffering experienced by a counselee to advise them concerning seeing a physician. In some cases, a reduction of suffering may allow room for further efforts to identify and address a counselee's core issues. In other cases, the Lord is using suffering to accomplish his purposes in a counselee.

Upon Prayer and Consideration, It Appears a Wise Choice under the Direction of the Holy Spirit

We need the Spirit to help us think biblically to discern when a referral for a medical evaluation is appropriate. He graciously gives wisdom. The counselor considering issuing such a referral should pray over the decision and actively seek the Holy Spirit's guidance throughout the decision-making process and as an overarching part of the conversation.[11]

---

[9] Emlet, *Descriptions and Prescriptions*, 73.

[10] Emlet, 76.

[11] For more about medical referrals, see Welch, *Counselor's Guide to the Brain;* and Charles Hodges, "When Medication Is Helpful in the Life of a Counselee," Biblical Counseling Coalition, August 14, 2019, https://www.biblicalcounselingcoalition.org/2019/08/14/when-medication-is-helpful-in-the-life-of-a-counselee.

Conclusion

While the above criteria are not exhaustive and might not apply to every scenario, they will help the counselor guide counselees in decision-making. Ultimately, the counselor's job is simply to recommend a medical assessment when it seems wise. We cannot act as medical professionals; our counsel can only go so far. However, the biblical counselor can feel confident considering a referral for medical evaluation, knowing we seek to care for the whole person.

PART FIVE

COUNSELING SPECIFIC AGE GROUPS

37

Counseling Children

This section contains several chapters designed to help counselors understand particular nuances in counseling approaches or typical life struggles for various age groups. The current chapter discusses counseling children ages three through twelve, which is commonly considered early and middle childhood.

While God intends parents to counsel their children and for the church to assist those parents and minister in other ways to children, various factors might necessitate that counselors step in to help children directly. Many parents, even some Christians, lack the skills or commitment to counsel their struggling children. In some cases, the parents are part of the problem and need parenting advice or counseling too. Sometimes children present with unusual problems that go beyond an average parent's knowledge or experience. Single parents, foster parents, and adoptive parents sometimes need special help. Moreover, children in group homes often need counseling.

Since more and more children are being brought to counseling, counselors must understand their unique presenting problems and be able to address them appropriately. Secular and Christian counselors understand we must not treat any counselee in isolation from the world in which they live. While we will not duplicate the discussion in chapter 5 about who we are as persons bearing God's image, counselors must keep in mind the complexity of each child. Like adults, children have bodies and souls; each has a personality, emotions, and a sinful heart; each lives in a particular relational context.

Despite this, a child is not simply a small adult. That means that if counseling is to be effective, we must consider developmental factors. Not only must we seek to understand these counselees but learn to communicate clearly in understandable ways that express love for these young neighbors. Understanding the complexities in context, development, and communication serves the counselor well in leading those in this age group.

A Brief Theology of the Family

To counsel children, the counselor must understand the normal and primary context in which children typically live, the family. While it's helpful to understand family relationships and dynamics, the family goes further than simple titles like father, mother, daughter, or son. Counselors must understand the purposes of the family as both representative of Christ's spiritual family and the context for learning, correction, and disciple-making.

Many of the struggles counselors encounter with young counselees and their families relate to a failure to either acknowledge or live out these theological principles. For instance, when parents fail to discipline and teach the ways of the Lord, (sinful) children more likely will be disobedient and defiant since godly parenting is a means of grace for the child. This does not remove the child's responsibility but recognizes the added hardship ("heat") involved. When a parent is overly harsh, children might withdraw and isolate themselves emotionally from their family. Parents must not only understand the importance of the context they provide for their children, but they must labor as the Lord directs them.

The following section deals with living within proper roles as well as guidelines for members of the family.

Roles and Responsibilities within the Family

God has established particular roles for both parents and children within the family,[1] all of which are designed to mirror the relationship with our heavenly Father. These responsibilities, then, are not optional; they are part of his good design for parents and their children.

God assigns parents these primary responsibilities:[2]

1. Teach their children (Deut 6:4–25; Eph 6:4)
2. Discipline their children (Prov 13:24; 19:18; 22:6, 15; 23:13–14; 29:15; Eph 6:4)
3. Act as a delegated authority (Eph 6:1)
4. Treat children lovingly and honorably as their neighbor (Eph 6:4)
5. Provide for their family (1 Tim 5:8)

Along with these clear directives for parents, God calls children to honor (Exod 20:12), obey (Eph 6:1; Col 3:20; 2 Tim 3:2), and listen to and learn from their parents (Prov 1:8), bringing their parents joy and not heartache and disgrace (Prov 10:1; 28:7; 29:15).

Family struggles often arise when parents or children fail to fulfill their role within the family, or when one or both have expectations of the other that go beyond these responsibilities. Often multiple parties within the family are failing simultaneously. Counselors must understand Scripture's teachings on the responsibilities of both parents and children to offer sound biblical counsel on a given familial struggle.

---

[1] See Andreas J. Köstenberger and David W. Jones, *Marriage and the Family: Biblical Essentials* (Wheaton, IL: Crossway, 2012).

[2] See Paul David Tripp, *Parenting: 14 Gospel Principles that Can Radically Change Your Family* (Wheaton, IL: Crossway, 2016); Tedd Tripp, *Shepherding a Child's Heart* (Wapwallopen, PA: Shepherd Press, 2005).

Noteworthy Considerations

Developmental Stages

There are significant aspects of child development that directly affect counseling.[3] Understanding child development gives practitioners a basic awareness of abilities and limitations within those age groups and helps determine age-appropriate counseling strategies.

Early Childhood (3–6 years old)

Early childhood is a stage of significant growth and change. A tremendous amount of learning happens in it, but there are clear physical, mental, emotional, and moral limitations at work too. Every child is different, but the following general considerations can help us understand children from three to six years of age.

Middle Childhood (6–12 years old)

The time of middle childhood is marked by continued yet slower growth. Children continue to develop in all of the aspects listed above. Some of these are particularly significant for counselors.

The Importance of Relationship—Entering and Understanding the Child's World

In chapters 13–15, we laid out the Enter-Understand-Bring model for counseling. The model is no different when we counsel children, though the process might look different. Before discussing specific methods of

---

[3] See Julie Lowe, "Counseling Children of Different Age Groups: Ages and Stages of Development," in *Caring for the Souls of Children: A Biblical Counselor's Manual*, ed. Amy Baker (Greensboro, NC: New Growth Press, 2020), 33–52; James R. Estep and Jonathan H. Kim, *Christian Formation: Integrating Theology and Human Development* (Nashville: B&H, 2010); and Robert S. Feldman, *Child Development* (London: Pearson, 2018).

entering, understanding, and bringing God's truth to bear, let's briefly explore the role of the counselor. Consider these key points:

Authority Structure

When counseling children, the built-in authority structure present in all counseling gets amplified in part because it is an adult-child relationship. The counselor must be mindful of this structure while seeking to enter and understand the child's world. A simple way the counselor can connect with the child is to consistently get down on their eye level, perhaps even sitting on the floor with them. This helps the child see the counselor as someone who pays attention and takes the time to connect.

Establishing Trust and Comfort

Many children are naturally shy, and it may take more time for those to open up about presenting struggles. Techniques given below can help overcome that. In addition, the counselor can express interest in the things the child is interested in: their friends, favorite activities, pets, or school subjects. Also, if the counselor is relaxed, the child will more likely be relaxed.

Entering the Child's World Rather than Demanding They Enter Ours

In Phil 2:5–8, Paul reminds us that Jesus condescended to us, entering our world to save us. Similarly, Paul notes in 1 Cor 9:22, "I have become all things to all people, so that I may by every possible means save some." This follows his statements that he became like the Greeks to minister to the Greeks, and like the Jews to minister to the Jews. The point is, Jesus and Paul knew their audiences and what they needed to respond to the gospel. As counselors, particularly when dealing with children, we must enter their world, understand their development, speak in their terms, and adjust to their level. We cannot require them to conform to an adult's method of counseling.

	Noteworthy Developments	Impact on Counseling
Physical	• Increase in motor skills, yet still have some difficulty with fine motor skills like drawing or writing • Typically have lots of energy • Advancements in language, logic, social cognition, and awareness of others • Prefrontal cortex is still developing; difficulty planning, prioritizing, and reflecting	• Minimize activities that require fine motor skills, as these take a lot of mental energy. • Use activities that allow space to move around. • Teach directly rather than asking the child to self-reflect.
Cognitive	• Most still using mainly concrete thought • Language skills still developing (vocabulary increasing quickly) • Lack of prefrontal cortex development leads to impulsivity • May struggle to focus on tasks for long periods of time	• Avoid stories that include analogies or symbolism. • Use words that are easy to understand; minimize questions. • Plan activities with shorter time limits.

	Noteworthy Developments	Impact on Counseling
Emotional	• Express and understand a broad range of emotions, but are just beginning to learn proper emotional responses (observation is significant); temper tantrums might arise from an inability to express or understand themselves • Begin to experience stress • Begin to develop empathy	• Can discuss emotions and emotional responses, but the counselor should also help parents model proper emotional expression. • Look for stress responses and teach basic stress-reduction techniques like deep breathing. • Identify and affirm empathy.
Moral	• Deciding right and wrong tends to stem from something/someone external to the child, based primarily on consequences for behavior • Children are sinful (Gen 8:21; Prov 22:15) and enslaved to their sin apart from Christ.	• Counselors can help parents model right behavior and encourage talking about it often (Deut 6:6–10), as well as helping them navigate age-appropriate discipline. • Counselors can help parents have proper expectations that their child will sin, yet retains personal responsibility.

	Noteworthy Developments	Impact on Counseling
Physical	• Continued improvement in gross and fine motor skills • Puberty typically begins from 8-14 years of age, causing an increase in hormone production which affects hunger, sleep, mood, stress, and the development of sex characteristics. • Increase in brain capacity, leading to cognitive developments below	• Activities that require more fine motor skills, like drawing, writing, or more complex games. • Puberty brings more comparisons with peers and a recognition of their own bodies; counselors should recognize these changes and their potential impact on the counselee's struggles. • Counselors should keep in mind advancements but still continued cognitive limitations.
Cognitive	• Better able to make decisions, plan ahead, and analyze consequences • Language ability increases • Able to concentrate easier and for • longer periods of time • More teachable as they understand more • Memory capacity increases	• Counselors can work through self-reflection exercises and use more symbolic stories. • Can use more advanced verbiage in conversations. • Activities can be longer lasting. • Interventions can be more creative and extensive, or build on previous activities. • Struggles may be more complex, with more influencing factors to consider.

	Noteworthy Developments	Impact on Counseling
Emotional	• Increased ability to empathize • Better emotional regulation, though it's still a struggle at times • Able to evaluate how others receive their emotional expressions and can adjust in response • For some, identity begins to stem from peers more than family • Begin social comparisons	• Can affirm and discuss empathy. • Counselors can help parents understand struggles with self-control and self-expression, modeling proper behavior. • Need to understand sources of identity and help the counselee work through this properly.
Moral	• Begin to make moral judgments and evaluations based on fairness and personal experiences • Move from punishment-based system to emphasis on social rules and moral principles • Begin to understand their own moral brokenness and judgment before God • Feel guilt for breaking moral law rather than because of impending punishment	• Can have more conversations about truths of Scripture, using logic and reason. • Greater understanding of the gospel and their need for a Savior; counselors can discuss the gospel directly and challenge appropriately for a response.

Confidentiality Versus Privacy

Confidentiality in counseling is a basic ethical requirement. Trust is an essential part of counseling, even between a counselor and a child. Little ones are more likely to openly share their struggles and respond to instruction if they feel they can trust their counselors. At the same time, minors need to know that their counselor and their parent or guardian reserve the right to speak privately to one another about the minor, per the counseling informed consent agreement.

Because of this, *privacy* is an important concept. Counselors should have some privilege to keep conversations with children private rather than sharing every detail with the parents. As we saw in chapter 20, there are clear limits to our confidentiality (e.g., if the child is hurting himself or planning to), and the need for privacy decreases for younger children, but it is helpful to provide a space where a child can express themselves without fear of a parent knowing everything they said. This requires a level of maturity, wisdom, and discernment on the part of the counselor. Matters pertinent to parents must be shared, and the parents should be able to trust the counselor to make these decisions. A pre-counseling conversation between the counselor and the parent can help. At any point, apart from an advance agreement between the counselor and parent, the parent can ask for specific details and they must be given. Confidentiality belongs to the parent.

Common Struggles for Children

While we could address many issues, let's consider several frequent problems (see also the next chapter on Counseling Adolescents) and how we might bring truth from Scripture to bear on these struggles.[4]

[4] For more on these topics, see the appropriate chapters in Part Four of our book, particularly for applicable biblical instruction and counseling techniques beyond those given below.

Family Conflict and Disobedience

Quite often, parents bring their children for counseling because of family conflict.[5] This might include fights with siblings or parents, consistent disobedience, or pushback on a particular topic related to the rules of the home. While the counselor should explore the specifics of each situation, let's remember these key points.

First, parents are responsible to model proper behavior and conflict resolution and to speak clearly in understandable ways, setting consequences for actions, and modeling self-control. (Deut 6:7; Eph 6:4; Prov 22:6). Second, children are responsible to honor and obey their parents. Despite the developmental limits noted above, children can make choices; apart from Christ, though, they are still enslaved to their sin and will continue to choose sin, even after coming to saving faith (Exod 20:12; Eph 6:1).

Problematic Emotions, Such as Anxiety or Depression

Children certainly experience emotions, and at times, disordered ones. While fluctuations of mood are natural, a persistently depressed or anxious mood lasting several weeks, alongside other symptoms like irritability, mood swings, withdrawal/isolation, changes in eating or sleeping patterns, or school difficulties can indicate a deeper issue. Children most often experience more somatic symptoms (e.g., upset stomach, sleeping/eating changes) than adults, so the counselor should dig deeper if these are presenting. They should also help parents identify and alleviate potential contributing factors on and within the child, such as conflict, bullying, false beliefs, or academic or social pressures.

Adjustment to Transitions

Childhood, especially ages three through twelve, may include many transitions; these might lead to feelings of confusion, fear, or a host of other

---

[5] A good resource on family conflict and disobedience is Corlette Sande, *The Young Peacemaker: Teaching Students to Respond to Conflict God's Way* (Wapwallopen, PA: Shepherd Press, 2010).

emotions. While transitions are a normal part of growing up, stability and predictability are important for a child. Transitions can disrupt that. When counseling children facing transitions, we should demonstrate increased patience, normalizing without diminishing the changes, listening well, and addressing any concerns.

Crisis Situations or Traumatic Events

Unfortunately, it is not uncommon for children to be subject to some kind of crisis or traumatic situation, including abuse or the death of a loved one. While chapters 29 and 30 on grief and trauma will help, there are specific things to remember when counseling a child through such events. Before anything else, safety must be established. Moreover, the counselor should remember that a child cannot understand on the same level as adults, which makes their understanding more difficult to counsel. A child who is repeatedly abused, for instance, will typically come to think this is simply how relationships work. Abuse can overwhelm, confuse, and distort what is good and can affect every area of life down the road. This is one reason victims of childhood violence or abuse are more likely to be in violent or abusive relationships as adults if they do not receive Christ-centered help.

Secure attachment to a safe caregiver is important. Secular research suggests that children who do not develop such because of neglect, abuse, or traumatic events often struggle with controlling their emotions and developing secure relationships later in life. For example, the Adverse Childhood Experiences (ACE) study,[6] along with resulting research, has demonstrated a high correlation between experiences of trauma in childhood and increases in mental illness, rates of suicide and self-harm, drug and alcohol use, and various physical health problems. Apart from God's grace, including biblical counseling intervention, childhood trauma might impact the long-term health of the individual in various ways. Such research, however, does not necessarily factor in the positive impact of genuine Christian

[6] "Preventing Adverse Childhood Experiences," Centers for Disease Control and Prevention, updated April 3, 2020, https://www.cdc.gov/violenceprevention/acestudy/index.html.

conversion, Christ-centered biblical counseling, and active membership in a healthy church as such children grow up. Nevertheless, a lack of biblically aligned relationships might create added heat in the child's life that influences him as he ages.

Finally, the counselor should remember that children rely on consistency and predictability. Crisis events and traumatic experiences upend that, which might have implications for the child's expectations moving forward. The counselor and parents should exercise patience (while still upholding discipline and instruction) as a child works through these sorts of events. Children are much more likely to experience somatic symptoms like difficulty sleeping, an upset stomach, or other bodily discomfort, as well as clinginess or withdrawal. A child might also give clues such as creating drawings that represent sexual behavior, or hiding information. A child might express new fears of people or places, particular people or places related to the event(s). These are difficult but typical; the counselor can help parents adjust and support their child(ren) in a way that affirms the hardship they are experiencing while also bringing comfort through biblical teaching.

Unique Approaches and Practical Exercises in Counseling Children[7]

A counselor must keep in mind that traditional talk therapy has some significant limitations with many children, particularly those below ten years old. Imagine trying to dialogue with an eight-year-old for thirty minutes or more; the child's attention span alone will create barriers. Further, developmentally, the child's vocabulary as well as their ability to articulate details about a situation or their emotions comes with age. The emotional vocabulary of an eight-year-old remains limited.

Yet we must not conclude children don't need counseling simply because it looks different than traditional talk therapy. Certainly counseling children should regularly incorporate counsel with the parents, as well as

[7] See also Julie Lowe, *Building Bridges: Biblical Counseling Activities for Children and Teens* (Greensboro, NC: New Growth Press, 2020).

getting their feedback on what's going on in the child's life, but we cannot assume all counseling issues with children will be "fixed" with better parenting. Children are sinners in need of salvation as surely as they are image bearers worthy of respect. They can communicate and receive counsel.

The primary way to offer that is to contextualize the message and its delivery in an appropriate way for each child, as Paul contextualized the gospel for different audiences. As discussed previously, Paul became like others to clearly communicate the gospel to them. Certainly, part of the message of the biblical counselor is the gospel, in some form or fashion. We should apply this concept to helping various age groups, including children.

Finally, parents should regularly be part of meeting with their child. I (Kristin) have the policy that I must meet with a parent or guardian in each session either before or after I meet with the child individually; the child cannot simply be dropped off for our session. Quite often, counseling children is just as much counseling their parents alongside them. We cannot do this if the parents are not present.

Age-Appropriate Intervention Strategies

What does this contextualization look like in practice? Specifically, this would mean employing activity-oriented approaches. Some may call this play therapy; essentially, it is using creative (often nonverbal) techniques to both understand the child and communicate with them in a developmentally appropriate way.[8] Below are a few examples:

- Role playing/modeling (using puppets or dolls): This allows the child to demonstrate or act things out in a way they can communicate.
- Creating stories together: The counselor participates but lets the child lead. The counselor observes what themes arise.
- Drawing/coloring/creating art: The child can express emotions without words for the counselor to observe.

[8] See Daniel S. Sweeney, *Counseling Children through the World of Play* (Carol Stream, IL: Tyndale House, 1997).

- Games or worksheets: The use of established worksheets brings structure but also helps draw out specific information when needed.

In all these examples, the dynamic is not the typical talk therapy dynamic. Instead, the counselor engages the child in an activity the child enjoys and that provides opportunities for the counselor to observe and ask some questions. Still, fewer words are used. Instead, the child can express their feelings and describe their situation in a way that is comfortable and familiar. This requires much wisdom and patience from the counselor, but it pays great dividends when done well.

Bringing parents into these times of expressive therapy can help them incorporate such activities into their own parenting. Demonstrating age-appropriate ways to understand and communicate with a child can help parents carry out their parental responsibility, foster their relationship, and help them lead in their home. This might mean doing a family role-play scenario or doing art together so the parents can see firsthand how their son expresses himself and what he is sharing.

Conclusion

Biblical counseling for children is an expanding and much-needed area of ministry, one we should not shy away from. Children experience struggles that are often like those experienced by adults, but counselors must shift in approach to effectively enter their world, understand them well, and bring appropriate truth to bear on their level.

Counseling Teenagers

Notable change marks the season of adolescence (ages thirteen to nineteen), as the young person transitions from being a child to becoming an adult. Experiences and decisions in these years can be life-altering. Counselors must not overlook the significant struggles those in this age group might face. This chapter, with its special focus on developmental considerations, provides an introductory foundation for counseling young people. Like adults, they need counsel, direction, and at times confrontation and correction.

Thinking Biblically about Teenagers

Since the Scriptures assign parents the privilege and duty of teaching their children (Deut 6:6–7; Eph 6:4),[1] a church actively equipping parents to better shepherd and counsel their kids and teens remains the biblical ideal. Yet Scripture also pictures the church having a broader role in teaching, instructing, and correcting everyone who is part of the church. Paul encourages mature, older adults to teach and train those who are younger or less

[1] For a basic biblical theology of the family, see Andreas Köstenberger and David Jones, *Marriage and the Family: Biblical Essentials* (Wheaton, IL: Crossway, 2012); or their larger work, *God, Marriage, and Family: Rebuilding the Biblical Foundation*, 2nd ed. (Wheaton, IL: Crossway, 2010).

mature (Titus 2:1–6; 2 Tim 2:1–2). Moreover, as we saw in chapter 37, there are many reasons we need trained biblical counselors to work with children and adolescents. And since parents play such a pivotal God-given role in the home, those who counsel adolescents should also aim to involve the parents and to help better equip them in their parenting.[2]

When counseling teens, counselors should keep in mind some foundational human commonalities. God created teens, and they bear his image. Yet, apart from Christ, they are sinful (Gen 8:21; Prov 22:15; Ps 58:3), enslaved to their sin. Unsaved teens not only will sin, but they do not have the capacity to choose what pleases the Lord. Second, it is ultimately the work of the Holy Spirit to draw them to salvation. The biblical counselor's role includes sharing the gospel message with an unbelieving counselee, but none can force a young person to accept it. Counselees will encounter significant struggles if they fail to acknowledge their need for the Lord or that ultimate power belongs to him. Given that many children and adolescents are unbelievers, we must not neglect this important reality.

God's Word provides counselors with timely truths to minister to teenagers. In it, we see hope-giving snapshots of teens who lived righteously amid various pressures: Joseph (in Genesis), Samuel, David, Daniel, Jesus's mother Mary, and Timothy are among them. The Psalms span the spectrum of emotions that make up a teenager's varied and changing feelings. The book of Proverbs can especially help teens and their counselors. It addresses "my son" twenty-three times and speaks to dozens of issues often relevant to all adolescents: money, sex, work, dealing with authority, anger, listening, godly speech, self-control, social skills, relationship with parents, friends, peer pressure, temptation, greed, laziness, the heart, gluttony, envy, discipline, lying, gossip, cheating, bragging, prayer, priorities, drunkenness, conflict, patience, and more. Proverbs also speaks of the joy and delight godly children bring their parents and the hurt, disgrace, and shame ungodly ones bring on their families (Prov 10:1; 15:20; 17:21, 25;

[2] For general resources on parenting teens, see Paul David Tripp, *Age of Opportunity: A Biblical Guide to Parenting Teens*, 2nd ed. (Phillipsburg, NJ: P&R, 2001), and Tripp, *Parenting: 14 Gospel Principles* (see chap. 37, n.2); and Tedd Tripp, *Shepherding a Child's Heart* (Wapwallopen, PA: Shepherd Press, 2005).

19:13, 26; 23:24–25; 28:7; 29:3, 15). And, of course, accepting and applying all the godly wisdom from Proverbs flows from a proper relationship with God ("the fear of the Lord," 1:7; 9:10) and centers in our hearts (4:23). As we saw in chapter 5, all divine image bearers are inescapably related to God.

Developmental Considerations

Adolescence is marked by physical, cognitive, emotional, and moral change and growth. Teens know they are no longer children, yet not adults. This age group is characterized by increased independence though those in it are still growing in physical and cognitive capacity.[3]

A few key ideas for relating to this age group stand out:

- As children become teenagers, they increasingly desire independence and individuality; this sometimes contributes to their sinful disobedience, to increased conflict and arguing. God repeatedly commands children and teens to obey their parents, and he frequently warns them about the dangers of disobeying and rebelling against their parents (Exod 20:12; Deut 21:18–21; Prov 20:20; 30:17; Ezek 18:1–20; Eph 6:1–3; Col 3:20). At the end of the day, teenage rebellion is simply rebellion that's done by teenagers—it's rebellion against God, parents, and sometimes other God-given authorities.[4]

---

[3] As in chapter 37 about counseling children, this chapter gives only an initial understanding of adolescent development. We strongly recommend practitioners consult more detailed texts like Lowe, "Counseling Children," 33–52 (see chap. 37, n. 3); Estep and Kim, *Christian Formation* (see chap. 37, n. 3); and Feldman, *Child Development* (London: Pearson, 2018). The following information draws from these sources as well as personal and professional observation.

[4] See also Rick Horne, *Get Outta My Face! How to Reach Angry, Unmotivated Teens with Biblical Counsel* (Wapwallopen, PA: Shepherd Press, 2009), and his *Get Offa My Case: Godly Parenting of an Angry Teen* (Wapwallopen, PA: Shepherd Press, 2012); Barbara Miller Juliani, *Dealing with Your Rebellious Teenager: Help for Worried Parents* (Greensboro, NC: New Growth, 2018); and Elyse Fitzpatrick, Jim Newheiser, and Laura Hendrickson, *When Good Kids Make Bad Choices: Help and Hope for Hurting Parents* (Eugene, OR: Harvest House, 2005).

	Noteworthy Developments	Impact on Counseling
Physical	• Puberty continues but eventually ends • Increase in sex characteristics and sexual interest/activity	• Counselee may wrestle with changing body and image • Counselee may consider their own sexual identity and behavior; counselor must be prepared to engage in such conversations
Cognitive	• Greater use of logic and abstract thought • Still often guided by impulses more than logical thought • More aware of and concerned with the evaluations of others • Remain self-focused, often with a grander view of self than others hold	• Better able to think through analogies or be self-reflective/problem-solving • Counselee may act out of impulse rather than considering consequences of behavior/choices • More value may be placed on peer opinion or perception than those of parents/counselor. • Might translate into self-centeredness or beliefs that their actions matter more than they actually do

	Noteworthy Developments	Impact on Counseling
Emotional	• Limbic system (emotions) develop before pre-frontal cortex (regulation and impulse control), so sometimes logic is secondary to feelings or impulses. • Reward parts of the brain are stronger than inhibition centers, so balancing risk versus reward is more difficult.	• Behaviors seem (and are) impulsive rather than logical and appropriate; counselor may have to help the adolescent work through this distinction and exercise self-control. • Emotions are at times overwhelming because they are new and intense; counselor might have to help the counselee navigate these feelings.
Moral	• Faith is ego-centric and self-serving early on, such as a set of moral codes or a way to gain acceptance. • As the adolescent gets older, faith transitions to a personal choice as well as the ability to wrestle with tougher concepts like the problem of evil or injustice.	• Spiritual conversations tend to operate within this system rather than being something personal beyond how it serves them. • Faith in many ways becomes their own, more than something passed down from their parents; counselors can stress personal choice and ownership of their faith.

- Parents retain the responsibility to teach and lead their children in the Lord, which includes helping teenagers think with more complexity about spiritual concepts.
- Adolescents are becoming more capable of intentionally acting with either good or bad motives, but they still lack a good bit of self-regulation. We should address one's heart of disobedience or disrespect, not just their actions.
- This stage is a prime time for continued teaching about self-control and emotional regulation. Youth are learning to connect spiritual teachings to life experiences and the place of discipline and instruction.
- Young people in this stage are much more aware of the treatment of others, and they continue to evaluate things like justice and fairness. This awareness, at times, might contribute to conflict, as teenagers might be more apt than children to see preferential treatment, rejection, or hypocrisy.

Common Struggles

General Pointers for Working with Adolescents

The counselor should keep in mind the following guidelines:

1. Trust might be harder to develop with a teen, but it is just as important. Establishing it might be more time-consuming, but it should be pursued.
2. Motivation to attend counseling might be lower for teens, particularly if attendance is required by their parents. The counselor might have to be extra diligent to engage the teenager.
3. The younger the person, the more difficult it is for them to think abstractly, so the counselor might need to get creative.
4. Each teenager is an individual, so counseling should be modified accordingly, reflecting the individual counselee and both their felt and real needs.

5. Counseling often is needed due to conflict within the home that stems from poor choices the teenager makes. In such cases, counselors should aim to care for both the parents and the teen; this includes offering sessions with individuals and with the whole family.[5]

Following are helpful insights related to common topics that arise when counseling teens.

Depression

Depression in adolescents often looks similar to adult depression in terms of emotional components and sleeping/eating changes. However, we typically see in it more thought and behavioral alterations when compared to adults. Thoughts and emotions might fluctuate higher and lower than normal and at a quicker pace. Teens might lack motivation or interest in once-held interests, withdraw from friends and family, or decrease in academic performance and increasingly struggle to maintain academic success. Depression isn't simply sadness; it presents itself in a variety of debilitating ways. This spectrum of symptoms is as broad for teenagers as it is for adults.

Another distinctive of adolescent depression is that it is often easier to connect it with situational stressors. These emotions might be influenced by (not caused by[6]) things like the rejection of their peers, poor performance in school or sports, parental failures, or a traumatic event. The counselor should seek to understand any connections between these life circumstances and the resulting responses, including thoughts, behaviors,

[5] See Fitzpatrick, Newheiser, and Hendrickson, *Good Kids Make Bad Choices*, and C. John Miller and Barbara Miller Juliani, *Come Back, Barbara: A Father's Pursuit of a Prodigal Daughter* (Phillipsburg, NJ: P&R, 1997).

[6] Recall the distinction in chapter 10 between contributing factors (box 1 heat) and heart causes (box 3). While many factors might contribute to teen behavior, ultimately their wrong responses come from their hearts, not situational heat.

and emotions, since many cases of teenage depression directly involve life circumstances. (For more on depression, see chapter 24.)

Anxiety and Stress

While emotional struggles can occur in childhood, adolescents often experience heightened levels of various emotions—including anxiety and stress—for the first time. While these emotions are common and our bodies are designed to handle them in small doses, their regulation is also partially influenced by emotional regulation centers in the brain (which are still developing in teenagers). As a result, anxiety and stress might feel either more overwhelming or last longer in a young person than in an adult. Box 1 heat might feel more impactful to a teenager than to the adult who can more easily sort through boxes 1–3.

Anxieties in adolescence are normally appropriately focused, involving school performance, situations with friends, and concerns about parents and siblings. In assessing a teenager's anxiety, the counselor should determine if the teen's level of concern is inappropriate for their circumstances or if they simply need to learn proper responses. We should help teenagers respond properly to feelings, much as we would guide adults. We should evaluate and approach feelings of anxiety and their resulting responses in all aspects of living: their hearts, thoughts, and behaviors. (For more on worry, anxiety, and fear, see chapter 22.)

Identity Issues

Adolescence brings a shift in identity away from parents and toward peers, as well as an increase in independence and abstract thought. Teens might experience struggles with their own identity: who they are, what they believe, who they want to be versus who others see them as. While teens don't typically verbalize these struggles explicitly, they might play out externally in many forms. Teenagers might experiment with friend groups, clothing choices, or even sexuality. When rejected by one group of friends, they might quickly move to another group, even altering their behavior or appearance to fit in. They might experiment with sexual expression, especially if their peers perceive it positively. Sometimes, particular behaviors are even a reaction against parental teaching and values to express independence. Lastly, many teens—consciously or not—pick someone to be like or to imitate; this might be anyone from a friend to a celebrity. Their perception of that person becomes their idealized identity.

As counselors, we must convey to counselees a biblical source of identity. True identity lies not in what one looks like or does (per se), but in who they are as God's image bearer (see chapter 5). Therefore, one's identity is either in Christ or not in Christ; each is either a child of God or a wayward orphan. This reality points toward identity permanence versus one that is fleeting and transient. The counselor should communicate these truths in a way each teenage counselee understands. Conversations might include evaluating their values and thinking through implications of their identity, drawing truths from God's Word about who they are and what Christ provides them.

Suicide and Self-Harm

The rates of suicide and self-harm are increasing among young people. Films, television shows, and other media have brought significant attention to suicide, making it unsurprising that more young people are choosing to attempt it or employ self-harm behaviors. Teens often lack emotional regulation yet experience higher levels of stress, anxiety, and depression than ever. Additionally, they may struggle with situations that adults might not—like bullying or overwhelming emotions they simply don't have the experience to deal with. (For more on suicide and self-harm, see chapter 26.)

Anger and Aggression

Unfortunately, anger and aggression in teenagers is common. While this is usually manageable without outside counsel, parents sometimes recognize that these matters are getting out of control and seek a counselor to provide additional support to them or guidance for their teenager. Emotional regulation might be a factor in some of these cases, but anger and aggression ultimately emerge from box 3 heart issues. For instance, the teen might feel a sense of entitlement, that they "deserve" something like independence, the ability to make their own choices without consequences, or to possess a tangible item like a cell phone. Or the teenager might have an elevated sense of self. When challenged, they might feel violated and subsequently respond with anger or aggression. In every case, biblical counselors should focus on personal responsibility and self-control. While recognizing possible developmental challenges teenagers may be facing, we must nevertheless help them address their sinful anger and stress what the Bible stresses. The human heart is intrinsically sinful; the gospel provides the remedy.

Additionally, sometimes parents fail to model self-control to a particular teenager, which influences the teen's responses. Regardless, anger and aggression issues cause struggles for both parents and teenagers. As counselors, we should acknowledge that and seek to understand both teens and their parents, counseling both as they work to resolve anger issues. With the parents, the counselor should focus on consistent, predictable parenting so they continually model controlled behavior and responses even when tested by the child (Eph 6:4; Col 3:21). This seeks to mirror the Lord's response to our own sin, a reminder that can help parents. With the teen, the counselor should address the source of anger, targeting heart beliefs and motives rather than simply the behavioral expressions. For all involved, the counselor can work on attitudes and thought patterns like bitterness, frustration, lack of self-control, self-elevation, and entitlement. (For more on anger and aggression, see chapter 21.)

Trauma

Like counselees of all ages, adolescents can experience trauma or abuse. They are not immune to sexual abuse, bullying, the death of a loved one, or the suicide of a friend. While a teen's response to a traumatic event is often similar to that of an adult, and reactive to a particular situation, older children or adolescents might also display self-harm behaviors, sexual promiscuity, fear of intimacy or closeness, drug use, or compulsive eating. While a lack of life experience and a still-developing brain might influence such extreme responses, they remain sinful reactions to situations that feel out of control or overwhelming.

In such cases, the counselor does well to explore the suffering while wisely working through the teenager's beliefs, attitudes, or behaviors (boxes 2 and 3), always bringing biblical truth (box 4) to bear on the situation and the counselee's responses. Given the nature of trauma, counseling this type of case might take time and require you to revisit these issues several times as the young person continues to grow and understand their trauma more and how to think biblically about it. (For more on trauma and abuse, see chapter 30.) Through Christ's Spirit, Word, and church, biblical counselors can help teenagers handle suffering in life-transforming ways.

Additional Considerations

Resistance

It's common for teenagers to resist counseling, especially when they don't understand the need for it or when their parents make them come against their will. Teenagers might refuse to engage in the counseling process for assorted reasons, such as these:

- They don't see any value to the counseling.
- They don't connect with you as counselor.
- They don't want to be there.
- They simply don't feel good that day.

When counseling resistant teens, we must patiently develop the relationship and build relational capital. This often takes much longer than it does with an adult. Once relationship is built, the resistance usually begins to lessen and the counseling can move forward. Trust and confidentiality are important for a young counselee. While confidentiality for someone under eighteen ultimately belongs to the parent or guardian (see chapter 37), a teenage counselee will be much less likely to share personal information about their struggles if they believe privacy has been violated. Having an initial, clear conversation with both parties, teenagers and parents, is essential; we must articulate how confidentiality will be handled. We recommend teenagers sign the same informed consent agreements parents do. (For more on confidentiality, see chapter 20).

A Desire for Independence

It is widely known that adolescents seek independence. Humanity as a whole shares this desire; Adam and Eve sought independence from God when they took the fruit in the garden. Yet not all independence is bad; after all, we want teens to mature and to eventually launch. Counselors might need to help families determine the role of proper independence from parents, for each individual teenager. Accomplishing this might look different for each teen in each family, but a counselor can help parents work through ways to build trust safely and appropriately. Sometimes parents just need help remembering that God is sovereign, and they are not.

Inclusion of Medical Treatment

As discussed in the last chapter, some parents might mention the use of medical (including medicinal) treatment for teenagers as it relates to a variety of struggles. Again, this requires wisdom. As with counseling children, the counselor will do well to discuss with the parent the wisdom of consulting a family physician or pediatrician with experience treating teenagers to determine if there is a physiological contributor such as hormone levels at work in a specific problem faced. But specific to medication, some additional concerns arise; they can bring significant side effects that should be carefully monitored. Children and teens are still developing physically and cognitively, so counselors should encourage parents to have clear conversations with their physicians regarding long-term effects of prescription use.

Use of Creative Interventions

While many young people are capable of engaging in typical talk-therapy conversations, the counselor might find it helpful to use nontraditional techniques or interventions with some teenagers. This approach might stem from resistance from the counselee, a lack of understanding, or simply their attention span. A counselor might consider using the following:

- modified creative methods, like using games, worksheets, or a white board
- art or other visually creative methods
- relationship-building activities, such as playing a game or going for a walk

These aim to create a genuine relationship between counselor and adolescent counselee. They can help you enter a teen's world, understand their real and felt needs, and bring them Christ and his answers.

Conclusion

The adolescent years are among the most formative years in a person's life. During this period teens can establish godly peer relationships, learn and practice conflict resolution, and grow significantly in their walks with the Lord. This chapter serves as a foundation for *how* to work with teens. As is the case with any other counselees, we must aim to lead them into a new or deeper walk with the Lord and to grow in Christlikeness. Understanding them better is a key factor in doing so.

39

Counseling Middle-Aged Adults

Younger counselors can understandably feel intimidated when God opens the door for them to counsel people older than they are. Understanding some of the common challenges in the next age demographic can help lower that experiential gap and increase confidence.

This chapter summarizes many of the pressures faced by people in the middle years of their lives, those in the forty to sixty-five-year-old range. Sometimes these challenges become the presenting problem in a session; as we will see, they all have the potential to rise to that level. At other times they remain background realities that simply add pressure to the middle-aged counselee, whatever the presenting issue might be. Either way, knowing these categories can help us more wisely enter the world of these men and women and better understand their daily experiences.

After looking at common challenges, we will focus on two major counseling problems that middle-agers might present. We will give you help in dealing with those issues and will also model ways to think biblically about other middle-age presenting problems so you can minister wisely to these individuals.

Common Challenges Middle-Aged Adults Face

We can cluster many of the concerns of middle-age men and women around four categories:

Physical Health

Middle-aged counselees are people beginning to experience signs of physical deterioration. This might include a general decline in strength and energy and the gradual or sudden appearance of new illnesses or disabilities. Moreover, their injuries and diseases might heal more slowly, adding the prospect of impatience to health concerns. Also, middle-aged women will experience menopause, and that might bring hot flashes (along with fears of public embarrassment), sadness over the end of their childbearing years, and impact their sexual relationships. Middle-aged men might experience erectile dysfunction and decreased sexual desire, possibly threatening their culturally derived definitions of manhood.

All these changes call middle-aged people to recognize their own mortality and we who counsel them to help them face the future realities of death. After all, because of the fall, life is "like vapor that appears for a little while, then vanishes" (Jas 4:14). This exhortation from Ecclesiastes 12 speaks loudly: "Remember your Creator in the days of your youth. . . . Here is the conclusion of the matter: Fear God and keep his commandments, for this is the duty of all mankind" (Eccl 12:1, 13 NIV).

Single, Marriage, or Remarriage

Whether never married or previously married, middle-aged single adults can sometimes despair of ever marrying or remarrying, since with age the likelihood of marriage statistically declines, the number of eligible singles decreases, and entering the dating world becomes more awkward.

Married couples facing an empty nest encounter new marriage dynamics, for better or for worse. Middle-aged counselees who have let their lives revolve around their children, for instance, might suddenly experience loneliness and purposelessness—especially stay-at-home or homeschooling moms who can feel a loss of life purpose or the challenge of reentering the workforce. Couples with poor communication patterns might begin to suffer previously unknown conflicts.

Counselors can help middle-aged couples establish or repair marital intimacy, pursue new and deepening peer friendships, and give themselves to ministry opportunities—even new ventures they could not pursue while the children were home.

Children and Grandchildren

Middle-aged parents carry legitimate concerns about the spiritual conditions, social relationships, and vocational directions of their teenagers and young adult children. Sadly, as their direct control lessens, these concerns can easily become inordinate, especially should sons or daughters not seem to be turning out the way their parents hoped. Maybe parents question their child's relationship with God and commitments to pursuing Christ and prioritizing church. Maybe they feel uncomfortable with their child's choice of friends, particularly their choice of a marriage partner. Maybe they even feel anxious about their child's college choices or career direction, or lack thereof.

Biblical counselors can help these Christian parents in two ways. First, we can help them trust God for what God has promised *them*. God has not promised parents the positive outcomes they envisioned for their children; outcomes depend on God's providence and the relationship each child has with him. Second, in light of this, we can help them entrust their children into God's hands, especially should those children turn away from the Lord and live in displeasing ways.[1] Parents must not take responsibility for choices that belong to their grown children.

The same dynamics extend to the concerns middle-aged parents have for their grandchildren. Their legitimate desire for their adult children to marry well might become a ruling heart demand for grandchildren after

---

[1] For resources on this problem, see Fitzpatrick, Newheiser, and Hendrickson, *Good Kids Make Bad Choices* (see chap. 38, n. 4); Jim Newheiser and Elyse Fitzpatrick, *You Never Stop Being a Parent: Thriving in Relationship with Your Adult Children* (Phillipsburg, NJ: P&R Publishing, 2010); Miller and Juliani, *Come Back, Barbara* (see chap. 38, n. 5); and Robert D. Jones, *Prodigal Children: Hope and Help for Parents* (Phillipsburg, NJ: P&R, 2018).

they do. That demand can lead them to pry and pressure their children to produce offspring. Once that want is met, their concerns about how their grandchildren are being raised and how they will turn out can become all-consuming. In this case too we must help counselees trust God for what God promises them and help them entrust their grandchildren to God. While they can offer advice to their adult children, they must allow them to parent the next generation without unsolicited interference.

Vocation, Finances, and Retirement

For most people in most vocations, the middle-age years are the most productive and enjoyable work years. A person has gained valuable experience, honed their skills, achieved at least some success, and increased their income. At the same time, those who have not experienced such satisfaction can prematurely long for retirement. Instead of working hard to use their accumulated skills and experience to advance their productivity and finish strong—doing their work heartily as unto the Lord (Col 3:17, 22–25)—they can become complacent and coast mindlessly toward retirement.

Still worse, in a youth-oriented employment culture, those who lose their job at middle-age will often find it harder to land a new one, at least one in the same field or on the same pay level. The onset of a disability within their household can make a similar impact. Couples might need to downgrade their lifestyles, downsize their homes, reduce their giving to their church or their children, and make other unwelcomed adjustments as a result.

All these circumstances can bring mounting financial pressures as people think about the future, especially if they have little savings and debilitating debt. Some counselees will face fears concerning if, when, and how they will be able to afford retirement and medical care in their final years. They might feel discouraged or guilty about not being able to help their adult children with college expenses, car payments, wedding expenses, or house down-payments.[2]

---

[2] For a biblically-based, practical guide on these and other financial matters, see Jim Newheiser, *Money, Debt, and Finances: Critical Questions and Answers* (Phillipsburg, NJ: P&R Publishing, 2021).

Helping Counselees Manage Midlife Crisis

Having considered some common challenges that middle-aged people experience, let's consider two specific major problems that might lead them to seek counseling. The first of these is the *midlife crisis*.

Coined in 1965, this term refers to that midlife period "when adults reckon with their mortality and their sense of a dwindling number of remaining years of productive life. While most people do not experience a severe crisis during middle age, some individuals do develop conditions such as depression and anxiety."[3] It's marked by a strong or crippling discontentment or self-doubt arising from a person's conclusion that they have failed to achieve their cherished life goals and find their present life unfulfilling. It tends to happen when many of the above common challenges converge and escalate beyond the person's ability to manage them.

So, how do we think biblically about this phenomenon?[4]

Defining the Problem

A person's self-evaluation involves two key components. First, they evaluate their life goals. This typically involves looking at career goals but can also include family, financial, fitness, ministry, leisure, or travel goals. These goals reflect what a person values. They might be godly or ungodly goals. Scripture, of course, defines what one's life goal should be—to please God (2 Cor 5:9), love God and others (Matt 22:36–40), seek his kingdom (Matt 6:33), live for Christ (2 Cor 5:15), and the like. Second, they evaluate their performance in achieving those goals. For believers, the performance might be deemed godly or ungodly, successful or failing, obedient or disobedient to God, and is frequently viewed as a mixture of both. A disappointing

[3] "Midlife," *Psychology Today*, last updated February 22, 2019, https://www.psychologytoday.com/ca/conditions/midlife.

[4] For additional biblical perspectives, see Elyse Fitzpatrick, *The Afternoon of Life: Finding Purpose and Joy in Midlife* (Phillipsburg, NJ: 2004); and Paul David Tripp, *Lost in the Middle: Midlife and the Grace of God* (Wapwallopen, PA: Shepherd Press, 2004).

assessment of one's performance can result in these symptoms, commonly referred to as midlife crisis:

- Guilt or self-recrimination ("I've blown it. I've failed. I've wasted my life.")
- Anger toward anyone who has thwarted the goals—self, others, or even God ("I can't believe he did that. If only she hadn't . . . If the Lord didn't . . .")
- Grief, despair, hopelessness, depression, suicidal thinking ("Life didn't turn out the way I wanted.")
- Uncertainty about the future ("So, now what? Where do I go from here?")
- Decreased energy or productivity ("What's the use of working hard?")
- Recklessness or irresponsibility resulting in high-risk behavior, such as a sexual affair. ("I deserve a fling.")

Symptoms can vary from person to person, but they stem from unbiblical goals or unbiblical performance.

Consider the four midlife case scenarios below that illustrate four possible combinations of goals and performance assessments. Note that while we use four men to save space and make the contrasting categories as clear as possible, women can express and experience similar dynamics.

		GOALS	
		Unbiblical	**Biblical**
Performance	Fail	1 Alex (midlife crisis) Bad Goal (unbiblical) Bad Performance (failed)	3 Connor (midlife crisis) Good Goal (biblical) Bad Performance (failed)
	Success	2 Ben (midlife crisis) Bad Goal (unbiblical) Good Performance (achieved)	4 Drake (biblical ideal midlife) Good Goal (biblical) Good Performance (achieved)

As the chart indicates, Alex set high goals for himself: to climb the company ladder to become a vice president, retire early, and move to Florida to enjoy his well-earned life of golfing. To his dismay, his boss bypassed him a third time for promotion. He gave the desired position, the one that could've made all Alex's dreams come true, to Alex's younger colleague.

Ben's is the classic rags-to-riches story. Unlike Alex, he achieved his goals. But he found them unsatisfying. Not long after high school, his summer job led to a restaurant manager position. Through hard work and some providential circumstances, he now owns three successful restaurants. But deep down, Ben knows there is something lacking. "I'm miserable inside," he confesses. "Every night I ask, 'is this all there is? Why does my amazing success not make me happy?"

Connor has a happy marriage, a well-paying job he enjoys, and good health. "But when I look around at the other men in my church," he says, "I feel like a total failure. I've been a Christian for forty years and have wasted my Christian life. My wife has been the spiritual leader in our home."

Unlike Alex and Ben, Connor began with Christ-centered goals. Sadly, he has failed to live up to them.

Contrast the experiences of these three men with Drake, who became a Christian in high school and was discipled during college through a healthy local church. He studied hard, graduated, took a state government job, and married a woman committed to Jesus. This is how he assesses his midlife:

> I have stayed in my same job for nearly thirty years. The pay is okay but not great, and the job has some thorns like every job in this life. But it's where the Lord has placed me, I'm able to serve people, and I've learned to be content. Karen and I have formed some deepening friendships in our small group, and we enjoy teaching a kids' Sunday School class. We've faced the usual challenges of midlife in a fallen world; my mom recently died unexpectedly. But life is good for us and I thank God for his faithful provisions.

Drake's self-evaluation expresses well-rounded godly goals. They included not just his work life but his family and church life. Today he feels gratitude toward God and maintains an active commitment to serve him. While his midlife pressures are real, they have not led to any crisis. Instead, he demonstrates the Spirit's fruit as he copes with them. There is nothing inevitable about a midlife crisis for those who follow Jesus.

Helping Those in Midlife Crisis

How might we help those in midlife crisis? First, help a counselee identify and reject the frequent lies embedded in the world's analysis of this problem. There are four.

Lie 1: "Midlife crisis is inevitable." While every middle-aged person will experience some of the challenges above, a crisis response is not inescapable.

Lie 2: "Midlife crisis is caused by physiological changes." While various physical changes will occur, they are opportunities to draw near to or away from the Lord, to make wise or unwise assessments, and to respond with faith and obedience or with hopelessness and ungodly action. Hormonal changes don't cause or justify ungodly emotions, thoughts, or behaviors.[5] Responses always come from a counselee's heart.

Lie 3: "Midlife crisis is caused by circumstantial changes." While people in their middle years might experience the challenges above, and they should elicit our compassion, such changes can't create wrong responses. As we saw in chapter 10, behavioral responses (box 2) come from the heart (box 3), not from the heat (box 1).

Lie 4: "The good life consists of personal happiness, high self-esteem, and taking pride in one's dreams and accomplishments." A midlife crisis arises when a person realizes they have not or will not experience their self-centered goals. Such goals tend to justify in their minds whatever it takes to find happiness, including irresponsible or reckless behavior (e.g., "I can drain my savings and travel the world.").

Second, help your counselee identify and repent of any unbiblical performance goals or any failures to live up to God's goals. Whether they are believers or not, encourage them to receive God's forgiveness in Jesus Christ. Reviewing the four case scenarios above can guide you in discerning their goals and their performance. From that assessment you can help them approach God's throne of grace to confess their sins and find forgiveness and grace to help them move forward (Heb 4:16; 1 John 1:9).

Third, help your counselee identify and pursue God's goals for their life based on God's Word, along with practical steps reflecting those goals. What will it look like for a particular counselee, in their specific situation, to please God, walk wisely, and seek his kingdom and his righteousness from this point forward (Eph 5:8–20; 1 Thess 4:1–2; Matt 6:33–34)? You might assign the person to meditate on such passages, to journal prayers and applications, and to frame a plan of new responses to their situation. Connecting a counselee to their church can help, since God uses his corporate means of grace—worship, teaching, and one-another encouragement, support, and exhortation—to help believers pursue godly goals. If possible, pair your counselee with a person or two who have navigated similar midlife challenges in God-pleasing ways.

---

[5] Welch, *Counselor's Guide to the Brain*, 151 (see chap. 5, n. 7).

Assure counselees that Christ through his Spirit, his Word, and his church can help them manage well whatever midlife stresses they encounter.

Helping Counselees Care for Aging or Dying Parents

The second specific major problem we will address involves helping counselees care for their parents as they age, experience declining health, or approach death. Along with our normal components of wise, compassionate biblical counseling, consider two categories to help these middle-aged people.

Expect Various Forms of Conflict

In these cases, counselees will sometimes experience some form of family conflict since each family member's individual desires might spike and become demands. Each person might have strong preferences for how the aging parent should be cared for, especially when it comes to the difficult decision about home care versus facility care. Consider the range of possible conflicts:

- Your counselee versus the parent needing care. The counselee's aging parent might or might not want your counselee to provide the primary care, for various reasons.
- Your counselee versus the parent's spouse (i.e., your counselee's other biological parent or stepparent). Assuming the spouse is able to provide care and to make competent decisions, that spouse might assert their will against your counselee. Moreover, the aging parent and spouse might disagree with each other.
- Your counselee versus your counselee's spouse, especially if the decision involves moving the needy parent into their home.
- Your counselee versus your counselee's children who might disagree with the decision to bring the grandparent(s) into their home, especially if a child must give up a bedroom.
- Your counselee versus your counselee's siblings. Depending on your counselee's relationships with their parents and siblings, they

might be more or less involved with the decision-making pertaining to a needy parent's care. Past sibling rivalry and jealousy can re-erupt when parental care decisions arise.

As with any counseling case, your initial tasks as counselor involve entering a counselee's world and understanding their felt and real needs related to the above relational problems. This includes understanding the respective positions and interests of each party in the conflict, while remembering you are only hearing one side of things (Prov 18:17).

Bringing Christ to your counselee involves helping them navigate these awkward, tense, or even hostile relationships in gracious, wise, God-pleasing ways through biblical peacemaking steps.[6] This starts with them grasping God's grace—his love and his promised presence and power for them in the conflicts—and seeking to please him in response to it. They then need to identify, repent of, and confess any ways they contributed to the relational breach. After that they must seek to love, forgive, and serve the needy parent and others involved.

Coaching Counselees in the Care Decisions

Having helped your counselee deal with any aforementioned conflicts, you should be ready to help them guide their aging parent and any others involved in the decision-making process to assess and determine the best way to care for that parent. The guidance process in chapter 34 outlines a step-by-step way.[7]

At the same time, know that either choice can become the occasion for further counseling oversight. If your counselee opts for a care facility for their aging parent(s), be prepared to help them deal with the confused guilt they might feel when doubts arise about whether they have done the right

---

[6] See Jones, *Pursuing Peace* (see chap. 7, n. 2); and Ken Sande and Tom Raabe, *Peacemaking for Families: A Biblical Guide to Handling Conflict in Your Home* (Carol Stream, IL: Tyndale House, 2002).

[7] For a helpful guide to assess home care versus nursing home care options, see Howard A. Eyrich, *The Art of Aging: Preparing and Caring* (Birmingham: Growth Advantage Communications, 2018).

thing—especially if some family members accuse them of being unloving. On the other hand, if the counselees opt for home care, help them find ways to get respite, support, Christian fellowship, and other forms of care for themselves or the other caregivers since this arrangement can place high stress on a caregiver's marriage and family life.[8] Discuss questions like these: Will they get days off or take vacations? If yes, how? Caring for parents can be a frequent occasion for marital conflict, even separation. Take note if caregivers cut back on church attendance, small group life, or ministry involvement.

Besides the home versus facility care issue, your counselees and their families might face other decisions concerning their aging parents:

- Should we still leave our children in our aging parents' care for an evening or weekend?
- When should they discontinue driving? Will they do so willingly, or must we take away their car keys?
- What specific role will each sibling play in the ongoing care plan?
- Who will oversee legal matters for the aging parents concerning their power of attorney, last will and testament, naming an executor, distribution of heirlooms, and a living will?
- Who is responsible for end-of-life care decisions?[9]

Conclusion: A Lesson from Timothy

We close with an encouragement to younger counselors who counsel people older, and sometimes significantly older, than themselves (see our next chapter). Remember Paul's words to his younger son in the faith, Timothy, who was likely in his early to mid-thirties at the time: "Don't let anyone despise your youth, but set an example for the believers in speech, in conduct, in love, in faith, and in purity" (1 Tim 4:12; cf. 5:1–2). While Timothy couldn't control how others perceived him, he could live such an exemplary

[8] See Michael Emlet, *Help for the Caregiver: Facing the Challenges with Understanding and Strength* (Greensboro, NC: New Growth Press, 2008).

[9] See Bill David, *Departing in Peace: Biblical Decision-Making at the End of Life* (Phillipsburg, NJ: P&R, 2017).

life that older people might overlook his age and accept his godly ministry in their lives. Thankfully, the categories of speech, conduct, love, faith, and purity are not age dependent. In fact, in counseling people older than us, we can draw confidence from the testimony of the psalmist in Ps 119:99–100, "I have more insight than all my teachers because your decrees are my meditation. I understand more than the elders because I obey your precepts." God's Word gives us the wisdom we need to help anyone.

So, as you pursue practical holiness and grow in your biblical counseling wisdom through Scripture, further training, and by engaging with this book, we believe you can provide fruitful biblical counseling to those older than you.

40

Counseling Older Adults

Those in the sixty-five and up age demographic represent an ever-growing percentage of the US population.[1] As the sizable baby boom generation (those born between 1946 and 1964) ages and life spans increase, what is called "the graying of America" becomes an increasingly relevant matter not only for social policymakers but also for counselors.

Perhaps the most acceptable term for those in the age group discussed herein is "older adults," followed by "senior adults," although no term avoids our American antipathy to aging.[2] Whatever term we use, our culture tends to associate it with varied disabilities, declining health, fading physical appearance, dependency on others, and growing irrelevance. As we noted in chapter 39 on middle age, this life phase often exerts pressure on adult children caregivers, especially when the older person faces severe disabilities or infirmities.

---

[1] "Stats for Stories: National Senior Citizens Day: August 21, 2021," United States Census Bureau, August 1, 2020, https://www.census.gov/newsroom/stories/senior-citizens-day.html.

[2] Ina Jaffe, "Times Have Changed; What Should We Call 'Old People'?," interview by Scott Simon, *Weekend Edition Saturday*, NPR, February 6, 2016, https://www.npr.org/2016/02/06/465819152/times-have-changed-what-should-we-call-old-people. Descriptors like "the elderly" are not preferred.

Rightly Viewing and Ministering to Older Adults

Let's explore several biblical ways to consider and minister to aging men and women.[3]

View Old Age as God's Blessing

The Bible speaks of aging as a divine gift, a sign of God's favor showing his faithful provision and preservation of aging believers in both their soul and body. Proverbs even reminds us, "Gray hair is a glorious crown; it is found in the ways of righteousness" (Prov 16:31; cf. 20:29; Dan 7:9). In Isa 46:3–4, God assures aging believers, "Listen to me, . . . all the remnant of the house of Israel, who have been sustained from the womb, carried along since birth. I will be the same until your old age, and I will bear you up when you turn gray. I have made you, and I will carry you; I will bear and rescue you." The psalmist's testimony echoes this: "I have been young and now I am old, yet I have not seen the righteous abandoned" (Ps 37:25).

Old age in Christians displays God's sustaining grace to onlookers, encouraging younger believers of God's faithfulness and their own ability to persevere. We most poignantly see this blessed status when the Bible describes the death of godly old men. Abraham "took his last breath and died at a good old age, old and contented" (Gen 25:8). Isaac "took his last breath and died, and was gathered to his people, old and full of days" (Gen 35:29). And after God humbled and then restored Job, "[he] died, old and full of days" (Job 42:17).

John Piper superbly summarizes this blessed state: "To resist [aging] seems to me a kind of unbelief that heaven is really good, and living a long time with God is good, and having the experience and the age to care in deeper ways for the young and share life-wisdom with them is good. . . . It

[3] See also Jay E. Adams, *Wrinkled But Not Ruined: Counsel for the Elderly* (Stanley, NC: Timeless Texts, 1999); *Shepherding God's Flock: A Handbook on Pastoral Ministry* (Grand Rapids: Zondervan, 1975), 262–71; Tim Challies, *Aging Gracefully* (Minneapolis, MN: Cruciform Press, 2018); Eyrich and Dabler, *The Art of Aging* (see chap. 39, n. 6); J. I. Packer, *Finishing Our Course with Joy: Guidance from God for Engaging with Our Aging* (Wheaton, IL: Crossway, 2014); and John Piper, *Rethinking Retirement: Finishing Life for the Glory of Christ* (Wheaton, IL: Crossway, 2009).

is good to grow old with God."[4] Aging under God's care is both a gift and something to long for.

Honor and Respect Older Adults

The twin verbs honor and respect summarize how people should treat older adults. We think immediately of the fifth commandment in the Decalogue: "Honor your father and your mother" (Exod 20:12; cf. Eph 6:1). But a close read of Scripture reveals that the call transcends the child-parent relationship, extending to the proper treatment of all older adults. Moses instructs Israel, "You are to rise in the presence of the elderly and honor the old" (Lev 19:32).

At the same time, respecting and honoring parents or older adults must not rise to veneration, worship, or blind obedience. At the wedding celebration described in John 2:1–11, for instance, Jesus's mother notified him that the wine had run out, suggesting he do something to address that. While Jesus accedes to her request and performs a miracle, he also voices a gentle rebuke: "What has this concern of yours to do with me, woman?" . . . "My hour has not yet come" (v. 4). The term "woman" suggests respect yet maintains some distance and independency, certainly not veneration. As John reveals in verse 11, our Lord's motive in the situation was not to blindly obey his mother but to reveal his glory and invite his disciples to believe in him. Moreover, Jesus taught that following him might require the opposite of obeying our parents (Matt 10:34–39; Mark 10:28–31; Luke 14:25–27).

Care for and Provide for Older Adults

Within God's economy, the responsibility for care and provision of senior adults belongs first to their adult children. In Matt 15:3–6 Jesus rebukes some Pharisees and teachers of the law for breaking God's commands by

---

[4] John Piper, "Is It Okay for a Christian to Have Cosmetic Surgery to Counteract Some Aspects of Aging?" YouTube, August 26, 2009, https://www.desiringgod.org/interviews/is-it-okay-for-a-christian-to-have-cosmetic-surgery-to-counteract-some-aspects-of-aging.

justifying—on hypocritical, pseudo-religious grounds—their withholding of financial help for their parents.

In 1 Timothy 5, the apostle Paul gave specific instructions about the physical and financial care of widows within the church: "If a widow has children or grandchildren, these should learn first of all to put their religion into practice by caring for their own family and so repaying their parents and grandparents, for this is pleasing to God." (v. 4 NIV). A few verses later he reinforces this principle by sternly warning adult children: "If anyone does not provide for his own family, especially for his own household, he has denied the faith and is worse than an unbeliever" (v. 8). Women too should provide for their widowed relatives (v. 16). However, if the widow is godly and has no biological family to care for her, then the church family should provide for her (vv. 8–16). Jesus's act of entrusting his mother into the care of his beloved disciple John reflects this same pattern (John 19:26–27).

Minister God's Word to Older Adults

In what ways do older adults need God's Word? First, if they are not believers already, they need to be evangelized and brought to faith in Christ. The Great Commission in Matt 28:19–20 makes no age exceptions. Unfortunately, some evangelical churches emphasize reaching children and teens for Christ to the seeming neglect of older adults. However, as aging non-Christians approach death and the prospect of an uncertain eternity, they sometimes carry intensified religious concerns that make them ripe for responding to the gospel. Their greatest need, after all, is Christ. Ultimately, there are only two ways to die: in the Lord (Rev 14:13) or in one's sins (John 8:21–24). This life is not the end of anyone's existence, nor are these present bodies in their final form (Matt 10:28; 25:46; Heb 9:27).

Second, once they believe, older adults need to be taught how to follow Christ daily. We must disarm the myth that old age and life experience automatically bring godly wisdom. In fact, the opposite is often true. As some people grow older, they become more hardened against the gospel. Their spiritual receptivity fossilizes. Consider these biblical examples:

- Ecclesiastes 4:13 observes, "Better is a poor but wise youth than an old but foolish king who no longer pays attention to warnings."
- First Kings 11:4 reports that when Solomon was old, his heart turned away to follow other gods. Only faithful devotion to the Lord can safeguard someone's heart—even if they were once counted among the wisest people who ever lived.
- In Job 32:4–9 the younger man Elihu comes closer to the truth than Job's three counselors. Out of respect for their age, Elihu waits to speak, and then replies, "I am young in years, while you are old; therefore I was timid and afraid to tell you what I know. I thought that age should speak and maturity should teach wisdom. But it is the spirit in a person—the breath from the Almighty—that gives anyone understanding. It is not only the old who are wise or the elderly who understand how to judge." Wisdom comes from God, not age.[5]

The problem with basing wisdom on experience is that experience must always be interpreted. In the Bible, fools repeat their patterns because they view life through their unbiblical lenses. Unbiblical presuppositions yield unbiblical interpretations that people reinforce each year of their lives. As Aslan declared about the evil Queen Jadis in C.S. Lewis's *The Magician's Nephew*, "Length of days with an evil heart is only length of misery."[6] Said differently, there is no fool like an old fool. Godly wisdom does not come from old age and life experience; it comes from knowing and living out God Word (Ps 19:7–11; Prov 1:1–7; 9:10; 2 Tim 3:14–17).

In 1 Tim 5:1–2 Paul strikes a helpful balance that can guide biblical counselors. Having encouraged Timothy in the previous verses (4:12–16) not to allow his relative youthfulness to keep him from ministering God's Word, he advises him, "Don't rebuke an older man, but exhort him as a father, younger men as brothers, older women as mothers, and the younger women as sisters." On the one hand, we must not "rebuke" an

[5] We consider 1 Kgs 13:11–32 and Ezra 3:12 (with Hag 2:1–5) further examples.

[6] C. S. Lewis, *The Magician's Nephew* (Harper Collins, 1955), 174.

older man—here this verb implies censure or harshness (e.g., NIV "rebuke . . . harshly"). As we counsel older adults, we must show them respect and honor. On the other hand, we need to exhort older men and women, as we would someone of any age. Older adults need God's counsel to deal with the problems and temptations noted below. God doesn't withhold his life-giving Word that will help them or give them a free pass to live in ungodly ways just because they are old.

While we must make proper adaptations and applications for the church and the societal culture in which God has placed us, here are some suggestions for counseling senior adults: (1) Rise when they enter the room (Lev 19:32).[7] (2) Address them respectfully in the session; for instance, use "Sir" or "Ma'am" or "Mr.," "Mrs.," or "Ms.," unless they prefer otherwise. (3) Humbly acknowledge your relative youthfulness where appropriate, without compromising God's truth or belaboring your age. (4) Be extra careful to base your counsel squarely on Scripture. (5) Give directives and growth assignments with a tone of recommendation ("May I suggest something that would help you?") rather than as commands ("Here's what you need to do . . ."), even if you are a pastor who carries God-given pastoral authority.

Encourage Older Adults to Minister to Others

Counseling older believers to continue serving the Lord actively means challenging the "I'm too old to serve" myth. Although their ministry methods and pace might need to shift a bit, believers are never too old to serve Christ. This also means confronting the "let the younger generation move in" mentality; we must remind older believers they are still part of the church body, gifted to serve, and able to provide the younger generations with insights from valuable life experience and accumulated expertise. In fact, the most effective ministry comes from seasoned men and women who have walked with God and followed his Word for many decades, people like the psalmist who share this ministry vision: "God, you have taught

[7] David W. Baker, "Leviticus," in *Cornerstone Biblical Commentary*, ed. Philip W. Comfort, vol. 2, *Leviticus, Numbers, Deuteronomy* (Carol Stream, IL: Tyndale House Publishers, 1996), 149.

me from my youth, and I still proclaim your wondrous works. Even while I am old and gray, God, do not abandon me, while I proclaim your power to another generation, your strength to all who are to come (Ps 71:17–18).

Paul certainly understood the importance of older adults within the body of Christ. In Titus 2:2–4, he told Titus that older men must be "self-controlled, worthy of respect, sensible, and sound in faith, love, and endurance" and older women must be "reverent in behavior, not slanderers, not slaves to excessive drinking." Pastors and counselors should teach older people how to apply the gospel in daily life. Moreover, older women should "teach what is good, so that they may encourage the young women to love their husbands and to love their children." Presumably, Paul would encourage older men to have similar mentoring relationships with younger men.

Two particular Bible characters can provide examples of different forms of active service. The account of eighty-five-year-old Caleb in Josh 14:6–15 shows us a man who followed the Lord "completely" (NIV "wholeheartedly"), even when it was unpopular (vv. 6–8, 14), believed in and pursued the Lord's promises energetically (vv. 9–12), and depended on the Lord's strength for success (vv. 12b). Joshua was in his eighties when he fought to gain the land promised to him! Consider also the moving description of the prophetess Anna in Luke 2:36–37: "She was well along in years, having lived with her husband seven years after her marriage; and was a widow for eighty-four years. She did not leave the temple, serving God night and day with fasting and prayers." Serving the Lord in one's later years does not require high-profile positions but steadfast, faithful ministries like fasting and praying.[8]

Scripture recognizes no form of retirement from serving the Lord, even if a person must discontinue some specific form of ministry. Biblical counselors should encourage older counselees to actively serve Christ. Sidelined seniors—sidelined by themselves or by leaders—deprive the

[8] Consider also Abraham's seventy-five years of age when he set out from Haran and that he was eighty-six when Ishmael was born and a hundred when Isaac was. (Sarah was ninety.) Moreover, Moses was eighty and Aaron was eighty-three when they confronted Pharaoh.

church of prized spiritual grandmothers and grandfathers.[9] As J. I. Packer pointedly puts it, spiritual gifts and ministry skills don't wither with age; they atrophy with disuse.[10]

Common Problems Aging Adults Face

Believers in every age group often face the same challenges. Young and old alike deal with sadness, anger, anxiety, conflict, and even addictions. In fact, counselors should not automatically assume that counseling problems older adults face are necessarily age related. The preceding chapters in this book apply also to aging men and women.

At the same time, certain types of problems are more common for older adults or are at least exacerbated by aging. Biblical counselors should be aware of seven categories:

Accelerated Physical Decline

While physical decline starts in middle age, the process continues at a greater pace among older adults. Aside from their greater likelihood of developing severe illnesses like cancer, strokes, or heart disease, even those with healthy bodies notice deterioration. Neurological decline means memory loss and sometimes dementia. Skeletal decline means bones break and tissue tears more frequently and mends more slowly. Cuts, abrasions, and strained tendons don't heal as fast. Muscular strength weakens, metabolism slows, and hearing and vision fade. Ecclesiastes 12:1–7 summarizes this decline with striking figurative imagery[11] that might help older adults see how the Bible speaks to their struggles. It concludes with a nod to the

---

[9] For a helpful challenge on this point, see James M. Houston and Michael Parker, *A Vision for the Aging Church: Renewing Ministry for and by Seniors* (Downers Grove, IL: IVP Academic, 2011).

[10] Packer, *Finishing Our Course with Joy*, 64.

[11] Scholars differ over which lines to understand literally versus figuratively, symbolically, metaphorically, or allegorically. See Tremper Longman III, *The Book of Ecclesiastes*, New International Commentary on the Old Testament (Grand Rapids: Eerdmans, 1998), 262–73.

writer's sense of the ongoing futility of doing life in this fallen world (v. 8). Verse 13, however, underscores the centrality of fearing God and keeping his commands from life's start until its finish; doing so is the very thing that brings purpose to life.

Counselors can point aging Christians to the kind of dependence on God seen in Ps 71:8–9: "My mouth is full of praise and honor to you all day long. Don't discard me in my old age. As my strength fails, do not abandon me." Recognizing this physical decline, J. I. Packer writes,

> Maintaining zeal Godward as our bodies wear out is the special discipline to which we aging Christians are called. Realism requires us to remember that memory, particularly short-term memory, will weaken; logical tightness of speech will loosen; powers of concentration will diminish; physical exhaustion will overtake us sooner or later, and energy levels will keep going lower. Zeal, however, should be unflagging every day, all day, and all the way.[12]

Amid bodily deterioration—the perishing of one's outward body—God can energize the inner being (2 Cor 4:7–16).

Grieving the Deaths of a Spouse, Close Friends, and Family Members

In some cases, aging believers, if married, might suffer watching the physical decline and death of their spouse and all the grief and loneliness associated with widowhood.[13] But whether single, married, or widowed, older adults will face the loss of friends and family members. Obituary notices about loved ones can become frequent and distressing. Unpacking passages like 1 Thess 4:13–18 with believers during a session can bring counselees comfort concerning the destination of their deceased spouses, friends, and family members who belong to Jesus and the hope of future reunion with

---

[12] Packer, *Finishing Our Course with Joy*, 76–77.

[13] See Carol W. Cornish, *The Undistracted Widow: Living for God After Losing Your Husband* (Wheaton, IL: Crossway, 2010).

them. We can also help counselees navigate their deeper grief concerning the deaths of unbelieving loved ones.[14]

Handling Changes Related to Retirement

Individuals approaching and entering retirement face many changes. Retirement planning involves financial decisions about retirement accounts and Social Security, decisions about where the person or couple will live, lifestyle changes, and marital adjustments—including the relational conflicts that come from being together 24/7. Regarding financial and legal matters, biblical counselors should recommend retiring counselees seek professional advice as needed. For relational conflicts and lifestyle shifts (e.g., ending a work career or relocating), we should help them pursue relational peace with their family members (Rom 12:18) and live contentedly whatever their circumstances (Phil 4:10–13).

Facing a Perceived Loss of Purpose, Control, and Usefulness

Retirement without significant activity, combined with physical decline, signals a loss of meaning and purpose in life. The ruling dominion granted by God to Adam and Eve (Gen 1:28), now much harder due to sin and the curse of a thorny ground, becomes even less easy due to aging. Various cultural pressures contribute to the feeling of a lack of purpose. Older adults can feel increasingly obsolete and functionally diminished in the fast-changing world of computer technology, digital electronics, and rapid social, political, and cultural shifts.

Another significant control factor arises when an older adult or couple can no longer live alone. Whether the family opts for relocating the aging person(s) to the home of an adult child or to a retirement home or care facility, the older adult(s) understandably feel a loss of independence.[15] And with housing relocation comes the loss of social connec-

[14] See chapter 29 on Grief.

[15] For helpful perspectives on housing options, see Eyrich, *The Art of Aging: Preparing and Caring*.

tion. Other forms of unwelcomed dependency include the loss of driving privileges, financial decision-making, power of attorney, and personal self-care and hygiene.

It's no wonder that suicide rates among older adults are higher than among middle-aged adults and increase with years lived.[16] Counselors have opportunities to enter a senior's world in sensitive ways to understand their real and felt needs, and bring them Christ amid their losses.

One pair of authors helpfully refers to the retirement stage as the believer's "third calling." They speak of it as a new stage of life in which Christians must consider what God calls them to do.[17] While believers who reach retirement age might discontinue their usual remunerative employment, they must not cease working for the Lord. Whether paid or unpaid, we retire to do new work.[18]

Guilt or Regrets over the Past

The struggles of midlife noted in our previous chapter, if unresolved, only intensify in old age. Midlife issues become old-age crises. Unresolved guilt about past sins, regrets about unwise choices, and unreconciled relationships with children, grandchildren, and friends continue to haunt an aging believer—especially when hopes of reconciliation diminish. The old adage "time heals all wounds" is a lie. Biblical counselors should help older counselees deal with past issues hindering their present joy and fruitfulness.

Burdens for the Welfare of One's Children and Grandchildren

Older adults can carry deep concerns and sometimes sinful fear about their children and grandchildren—regarding everything from their spiritual conditions, careers, finances, marital health, and parenting practices

---

[16] Ismael Conejero et al., "Suicide in Older Adults; Clinical Perspectives," Clinical Interventions in Aging, April 20, 2018, https://www.ncbi.nlm.nih.gov/pmc/articles/PMC5916258/.

[17] Richard Bergstrom and Leona Bergstrom, *Third Calling: What Are You Doing the Rest of Your Life?* (Edmonds, WA: ChurchHealth, 2016).

[18] Adams, *Wrinkled but Not Ruined*, 269.

to many more.[19] As we saw in chapter 39, the counselor's task is to affirm a counselees' concerns, bear their burdens with them, and help them deal with worry even as they encourage them to entrust their kids and grandkids to the care of our sovereign, wise, good God.

Financial Pressures

If not properly anticipated and planned for, the discontinuation of regular income combined with additional expenses can make the retirement years fiscally challenging. Physical decline might also incur additional medical expenses for both spouses to bear. Running into unexpected house repairs and maintenance needs—and having less energy to address them personally—might add further expenses. Counselors can help people facing these pressures gain a biblical view of money and possessions, seek financial planning or budgeting help as needed, and trust God without fear.

Fears of Death and of Dying

Death itself came as part of God's curse on the world after Adam's sin. God had issued a clear prohibition and warning to Adam in Gen 2:17: "You must not eat from the tree of the knowledge of good and evil, for on the day you eat from it, you will certainly die." Evangelical theologians rightly understand that death to include not just physical mortality (Gen 3:19, "you are dust, and you will return to dust") but spiritual death (separation from God) and eternal death (final condemnation). While Christ's atoning death and resurrection immediately solved the problem of spiritual and eternal death for believers, we must await its future application to the problem of physical death. One day God will raise our own remains from the dead, giving us incorruptible, immortal bodies like Christ's instead (Phil 3:21; 1 Cor 15:50–53). Until then, we each must face physical death and the decay and corruption that accompany it (2 Cor 4:7–18).

---

[19] For a helpful resource, see Larry E. McCall, *Grandparenting with Grace: Living the Gospel with the Next Generation* (Greensboro, NC: New Growth Press, 2019).

While the above gospel truths settle the issue of the fear of condemnation (Rom 8:1; Heb 2:14–15) for the aging believer, they don't prevent moments or seasons of doubt. Moreover, even if the believer clings strongly to the promise of heaven, that doesn't remove the fear of the physical dying process. Counselors must help Christians deal with fears and doubts about both death and dying. Passages like Luke 23:43; 1 Cor 15:20–58; 2 Cor 5:1–8; Phil 1:23; 3:20–21; 1 Thess 4:13–18; and Heb 2:14–15 can bring counselees solid comfort, assurance, and hope in this life and the life to come.

Conclusion

The suffering of older adults is often heightened in type and degree. So, along with a sound biblical theology of aging, biblical counselors need a sound biblical theology of suffering. (See the appendix.) We must be prepared to help senior adults learn to lament—to voice their struggles about aging to God—instead of grumbling to themselves and to others.

This hope-giving, captivating vision from Ps 92:12–15 is one to study with and to assign to aging believers so they will learn to cling to it:

> The righteous thrive like a palm tree and grow like a cedar tree in Lebanon.
> Planted in the house of the Lord, they thrive in the courts of our God.
> They will still bear fruit in old age, healthy and green, to declare,
> "The Lord is just; he is my rock, and there is no unrighteousness in him."

CONCLUSION

Enter their world. Understand their need. Bring them Christ. This simple three-step process summarizes the ministry vision imparted in this book. Christ-centered biblical counseling means bringing Jesus and his Word—the gospel and all its implications—into the disordered lives of sinning, suffering people. Each chapter has called us as counselors to prioritize our Savior's passion to help hurting people.

This book represents the collective wisdom of three evangelical seminary professors committed to teaching and practicing Christ-centered biblical counseling. Yet it also represents another piece of fruit from the modern biblical counseling movement.

The Growth in Biblical Counseling

Over the past fifty years, we have seen massive growth in our movement; this is measurable in myriad ways. Today we are witnessing a growing library of books, articles, and website media reflecting the theory and practice of biblical counseling. In fact, we have more than a thousand dedicated books and minibooks available to us in the field,[1] and an increasing num-

---

[1] See Bob Kellemen, *The Annual Guide to Biblical Counseling Resources: 2021 Edition* (Auburn, WA: RPM Ministries, 2021). To purchase a PDF download of this collated, linked, and annotated guide, see http://bit.ly/1AnnualGuideBC1.

ber of publishers are producing more. To that list of references we can add journals such as the *Journal of Biblical Counseling* and the *Journal of Biblical Soul Care*, and countless blog articles that reflect biblical counseling.

We also see growth in the number of Bible colleges and seminaries committed to training new generations of pastors and other vocational Christian workers in biblical counseling at the bachelor's, master's, and doctoral levels. These students go on to minister in North American and international churches, in church plants, and in mission work. As a result, an increasing number of churches that previously outsourced their counseling needs to community professionals are developing church-based biblical counseling ministries led by trained leaders and members. Moreover, parachurch organizations have developed, such as the Biblical Counseling Coalition (BCC),[2] the Christian Counseling and Educational Foundation (CCEF),[3] the Association of Certified Biblical Counselors (ACBC),[4] the International Association of Biblical Counselors (IABC),[5] and the Association of Biblical Counselors (ABC).[6] Many of these groups provide training, networking, online resources, and certification. Similar groups have formed internationally.

Where to Go from Here: Growing as a Biblical Counselor

We trust this volume becomes a lifelong resource for your ministry, that you will return to it as a reference for helping people. But we also urge you to grow in your knowledge and skill in bringing Christ and his Word to others. We recommend six ways to do so.

First, constantly apply God's Word to your own soul. Counsel yourself. In your personal Bible reading and private prayer, ask God to make his Word effective in your heart—especially when you struggle with various

[2] See www.biblicalcounselingcoalition.org.
[3] See www.ccef.org.
[4] See www.biblicalcounseling.com.
[5] See www.iabc.net.
[6] See www.christiancounseling.com.

versions of the same problems we've discussed. Ask Christ to forgive you, empower you, and help you follow him. With God's help, we will continue to do the same.

Second, learn from your completed cases. At the conclusion of each case, note takeaway lessons for next time. Learn from your successes and especially from your failures. Asking questions like these can help you:

- What have I learned about God, myself, people, and my ministry through this case?
- How has God providentially used my counselee and our interactions to make me more like Jesus?
- What did I do well that I need to continue to do in my next case?
- How should I improve to minister better next time?

Third, participate actively in the life and ministry of your local church. Whatever your specific biblical counseling setting, the local church remains "the pillar and foundation of the truth" (1 Tim 3:15). Through the corporate disciplines of worship, preaching, teaching, fellowship, small group life, and service, Christ will feed you, strengthen you, and equip you to grow. Moreover, seeking opportunities to regularly help lead people in God's Word, whether through assisting in Sunday school, discipleship classes, or teaching men's/women's Bible studies, will push you both to study Scripture in a disciplined way and to learn how to better apply it to real people. Counseling individuals with the Bible makes a person a better Bible teacher, and teaching people the Bible well cannot help but make someone a better biblical counselor: the two activities feed each other exquisitely.

Fourth, read widely. Acquainting yourself with general biblical-theological resources that help you better read your Bible and understand its redemptive flow, central themes, and doctrines is wise. Immersing yourself in biblical counseling resources, whether they be books, minibooks, journal articles, blog articles, or podcasts will arm you with tools you can use in your sessions. Reading topical resources—secular or Christian—can also help you address counseling issues you will encounter. Just make sure to read them through the lens of a biblical counseling model.

Fifth, pursue biblical counseling certification. Aside from the blessing of the credential itself, the certification process of groups like Association of Certified Biblical Counselors or the Association of Biblical Counselors provides individual, private, session-by-session supervision and feedback from an experienced biblical counseling supervisor.

Sixth, consider attaining further education. A masters or doctoral degree in biblical counseling brings several benefits. First, gaining increased skill in interpreting and applying the Bible helps you bring God's specific counsel to a specific counselee more effectively. Second, it helps you detect the lies of unbiblical counseling. Third, the academic setting involves immersion into a unique learning community of men and women from all over the world who are studying under seasoned biblical counseling professors. Finally, such a degree gives you added credibility in a counselee's eyes and might open doors for new vocational, writing, and speaking opportunities. Thankfully, in our day you can choose residential, online, or hybrid/modular options.

A Final Word

Thank you for taking this journey with us. We pray God will grant you the joy we have experienced in seeing disordered lives changed and changing through the gospel of our Lord Jesus Christ and the truth of his Word. We leave you with the apostle Paul's prayer-wish for the Ephesian elders in Acts 20:32. These words were designed to encourage them in their personal shepherding ministries:

And now I commit you to God and to the word of his grace,
which is able to build you up and
to give you an inheritance among all who are sanctified.

APPENDIX: RECOMMENDED RESOURCES ON SUFFERING

Many of the topics addressed in part 4 involve suffering. We recommend you as a counselor read several of the following resources on the subject to become more skilled in thinking biblically about the many different forms trials and hardship take. Not only can these serve as helpful reference works, but they might also make helpful reading assignments for some counselees. Each resource recognizes God's sovereignty, wisdom, and love amid suffering, displays compassion, and supplies the sufferer with hope and purpose. They are listed alphabetically by author.

Adams, Jay E. *How to Handle Trouble*. Phillipsburg, NJ: P&R, 1982.

———. *How to Overcome Evil: A Practical Exposition of Romans 12:14–21*. Phillipsburg, NJ: P&R, 1977.

Bridges, Jerry. *Trusting God: Even When Life Hurts*. Colorado Springs: NavPress, 1988. (See also his briefer version, *Is God Really in Control: Trusting God in a World of Hurt*. Colorado Springs: NavPress, 2006.)

Carson, D. A. *How Long, O Lord? Reflections on Suffering and Evil*. Rev. ed. Grand Rapids: Baker, 2006.

Clarkson, Margaret. *Destined for Glory: The Meaning of Suffering*. Grand Rapids: Eerdmans, 1983.

Eareckson Tada, Joni and Steven Estes. *When God Weeps: Why Our Sufferings Matter to the Almighty.* Grand Rapids: Zondervan, 1997.

Elliot, Elizabeth. *Suffering Is Never for Nothing*. Nashville: B&H, 2019.

Keller, Timothy. *Walking with God through Pain and Suffering*. New York: Penguin Random House, 2013.

McCartney, Dan G. *Why Does It Have to Hurt? The Meaning of Christian Suffering*. Phillipsburg, NJ: P&R, 1998.

Morgan, Christopher W. and Robert A. Peterson, eds. *Suffering and the Goodness of God*. Wheaton: Crossway, 2008.

Piper, John and Justin Taylor, eds. *Suffering and the Sovereignty of God.* Wheaton: Crossway, 2006.

Powlison, David. *God's Grace in Your Suffering*. Wheaton: Crossway, 2018.

Tripp, Paul David. *Suffering: Gospel Hope When Life Doesn't Make Sense.* Wheaton: Crossway, 2018.

Viars, Stephen. *Putting Your Past in Its Place: Moving Forward in Freedom and Forgiveness.* Eugene, OR: Harvest House, 2011.

Vroegop, Mark. *Dark Clouds, Deep Mercy: Discovering the Grace of Lament.* Wheaton: Crossway, 2019.

NAME/SUBJECT INDEX

D

E

F

G

H

W

Z

SCRIPTURE INDEX

Proverbs

Galatians

Ephesians

Philippians

Colossians